Tolley's
VAT Planning

2009–10

by
Neil Warren

Tax Writer of the Year
Taxation Awards 2008

LexisNexis®
Tolley

Members of the LexisNexis Group worldwide

United Kingdom	LexisNexis, a Division of Reed Elsevier (UK) Ltd, Halsbury House, 35 Chancery Lane, London, WC2A 1EL, and London House, 20–22 East London Street, Edinburgh EH7 4BQ
Australia	LexisNexis Butterworths, Chatswood, New South Wales
Austria	LexisNexis Verlag ARD Orac GmbH & Co KG, Vienna
Benelux	LexisNexis Benelux, Amsterdam
Canada	LexisNexis Canada, Markham, Ontario
China	LexisNexis China, Beijing and Shanghai
France	LexisNexis SA, Paris
Germany	LexisNexis Deutschland GmbH, Munster
Hong Kong	LexisNexis Hong Kong, Hong Kong
India	LexisNexis India, New Delhi
Italy	Giuffrè Editore, Milan
Japan	LexisNexis Japan, Tokyo
Malaysia	Malayan Law Journal Sdn Bhd, Kuala Lumpur
New Zealand	LexisNexis NZ Ltd, Wellington
Poland	Wydawnictwo Prawnicze LexisNexis Sp, Warsaw
Singapore	LexisNexis Singapore, Singapore
South Africa	LexisNexis Butterworths, Durban
USA	LexisNexis, Dayton, Ohio

© Reed Elsevier (UK) Ltd 2009
Published by LexisNexis

ISBN 978 0 7545 3728 1

Typeset by Columns Design Ltd, Caversham, Berkshire
Printed and bound in Great Britain by Hobbs the Printers Ltd, Totton, Hampshire

Visit LexisNexis at www.lexisnexis.co.uk

About this Book

This book addresses the many VAT issues that practitioners encounter on a regular basis. It aims to provide workable solutions to practical VAT problems, rather than to offer a lengthy discourse on VAT legislation. Each chapter analyses the advantages and disadvantages of various VAT positions, includes worked examples of key topics, and is concluded with practical planning points that could help save money for clients. The book has been updated to not only include a new chapter about VAT issues during the recession but also a revised chapter about how a business should deal with HMRC, taking into account issues such as online filing of returns, fewer routine VAT visits and a new penalty regime from April 2009.

Neil Warren had worked for Customs and Excise for 13 years before setting up his own tax and accountancy practice 12 years ago. He offers VAT consultancy services to a range of small and medium sized account-ants in the south-east, and is a regular contributor on VAT for leading Tolley's publications such as 'Taxation' and 'Practical VAT Newsletter'. He also lectures on VAT for a number of clients and institutes throughout the UK. In 2008, Neil was honoured as the Tax Writer of the Year at the prestigious Taxation Awards, having also been a shortlisted nominee in 2007.

Whilst care has been taken to ensure the accuracy of the contents of this book, no responsibility for loss occasioned to any person acting or refraining from action as a result of any statement in it can be accepted by the author or the publisher. Readers should take specialist professional advice before entering into any specific transaction.

Abbreviations and references

ABBREVIATIONS

CIS	=	Construction Industry Scheme
DAN	=	Deferment Approval Number
DGT	=	Daily Gross Takings
ECJ	=	European Court of Justice
ESL	=	EC Sales List
HMRC	=	Her Majesty's Revenue and Customs
MTIC VAT Fraud	=	Missing Trader Intra-Community VAT Fraud
SAD	=	Single Administrative Document
SD	=	Supplementary Declaration
SIVA	=	Simplified Import VAT Accounting
TURN	=	Trader's Unique Reference Number
VAT	=	Value Added Tax
VTD	=	VAT Tribunal Decision
s	=	Section
SA	=	Stamp Act 1891
Sch	=	Schedule

REFERENCES (*denotes current series)

AC	=	*Law Reports, Appeal Cases, (Incorporated Council of Law Reporting for England and Wales, 3 Stone Buildings, Lincoln's Inn, London WC2A 3XN)
Ad & E	=	Adolphus & Ellis's Reports
All ER	=	*All England Law Reports, LexisNexis Butterworths, 35 Chancery Lane, London WC2A 1EL)
App Cas	=	Law Reports, Appeal Cases
ATC	=	Annotated Tax Cases, (Gee & Co (Publishers) Ltd, 7 Swallow Place, London W1R 8AB)
B & Ad	=	Barnewall & Adolphus's Reports
B & Ald	=	Barnewall & Alderson's Reports
B & C	=	Barnewall & Cresswall's Reports
B & S	=	Best & Smith's Reports
BCLC	=	*British Company Law Cases

BTC	=	*British Tax Cases
CB	=	Common Bench Reports
Ch	=	*Law Reports, Chancery Division
Ch App	=	Law Reports, Chancery Appeals
CM & R	=	Crompton, Meeson & Roscoe's Reports
E & B	=	Ellis & Blackburn's Reports
East	=	East's Reports
Ex D	=	Law Reports, Exchequer Division
Exch	=	Exchequer Reports
F(Ct of Sess)	=	Fraser, Court of Session Cases, 5th Series
HL Cas	=	Clark's House of Lords Cases
IR	=	*Irish Reports, (Law Reporting Council, Law Library, Four Courts, Dublin)
Ir LR	=	Irish Law Reports
KB	=	Law Reports, King's Bench Division
LR	=	Law Reports (followed by Court abbreviation)
LT	=	Law Times Reports
M & W	=	Meeson & Welsby's Reports
P	=	Law Reports, Probate, Divorce & Admiralty Division
QB/QBD	=	*Law Reports, Queen's Bench Division
QBR	=	Queen's Bench Reports
R (Ct of Sess)	=	Rettie, Court of Session Cases, 4th Series
SC	=	*Court of Session Cases (Scotland)
Sc LR	=	Scottish Law Reporter
SLT	=	Scots Law Times Reports
Sol Jo	=	Solicitors' Journal, Oyez Publishing Ltd, Norwich House, 11/13 Norwich St, London EC4A 1AB
STC	=	*Simon's Tax Cases, (LexisNexis Butterworths, as above)
Taunt	=	Taunton's Reports
TC	=	*Official Tax Cases, (The Stationery Office, 123 Kingsway, London WC2B 6PQ)
TLR	=	Times Law Reports
WLR	=	*Weekly Law Reports, (Incorporated Council of Law Reporting, as above)
WN	=	Weekly Notes, (Incorporated Council of Law Reporting, as above)

The first number in the citation refers to the volume, and the second to the page, so that [1978] 2 WLR 10 means that the report is to be found on page ten of the second volume of the Weekly Law Reports for 1978. Where no volume number is given, only one volume was produced in that year. Some series, such as the ATC, have continuous volume numbers.

Where legal decisions are very recent and in the lower Courts, it must be remembered that they may be reversed on appeal. But references to the official Tax Cases ('TC') may be taken as final.

In English cases, Scottish and N. Irish decisions (unless there is a difference of law between the countries) are generally followed but are not binding, and Republic of Ireland decisions are considered (and vice versa). Privy Council decisions are of persuasive, but not binding, authority.

Acts of Parliament and Statutory Instruments (SI) (formerly Statutory Rules and Orders) (SR & O) are obtainable from:

The Stationery Office
123 Kingsway
London
WC2B 6PQ
Tel: 020 7242 6393/6410;
Fax 020 7242 6394;
Internet: www.the-stationery-office.co.uk.
Email: london.bookshop@theso.co.uk

Contents

Contents

Contents

Contents

Contents

Chapter 1

Registration

Key topics in this chapter:

- Turnover limits for compulsory registration.

- Rules for VAT registration when buying a business.

- Applying for a VAT number.

- Registering for VAT on either a voluntary or intending trader basis.

- Input tax recovery on goods or services acquired before the date of registration (and before the date of incorporation for limited companies).

- Situations when a business can apply for exemption from being registered even when it has exceeded the compulsory turnover limits.

- Notifying HM Revenue and Customs (HMRC) of changes to business details.

- Backdating the date of VAT registration and penalties for belated notification.

Introduction

1.1   A taxable person needs to be registered for VAT in the UK if the value of his taxable supplies in the last 12 months has exceeded the VAT registration limits – or he expects the value of his supplies to exceed the limit in the next 30 days.

The registration limits for the last 3 years are as follows:

1 May 2009 to current	£68,000
1 April 2008 to 30 April 2009	£67,000
1 April 2007 to 31 March 2008	£64,000
1 April 2006 to 31 March 2007	£61,000

A 'taxable person' is defined in the legislation as being someone who is either registered for VAT or should have been registered for VAT. This is an important point and means that anyone who is not yet registered but should be (on the basis that the value of their taxable sales has exceeded the registration limit at some point in the past) is still classed as a taxable person.

There are occasions when a business can be registered for VAT even if the limits above have not been exceeded (voluntary registration) and there are also instances when a business can register without ever having made any taxable supplies (intending trader).

If a business fails to register for VAT, then it will face penalties based on the length of time it was late with its notification.

The key point to remember is that it is only the value of **taxable** supplies that counts towards the registration limits quoted above. If a business has exempt or non-business income, these amounts are excluded from the calculation. This is a technical issue that can cause confusion with many clients and advisers – see Example 1

Example 1

John trades as an estate agent and in the 12-month period ending 30 June 2009, his total income is as follows:

- commission earned from selling houses (taxable) £50,000

- commission earned from selling mortgages (exempt) £20,000

Does John need to register for VAT?

Solution – although John's total income of £70,000 is above the VAT registration limit of £68,000, the key figure is the value of his taxable income ie £50,000. As this is less than £68,000, he has no obligation to register for VAT.

Note – 'taxable' income is any income where the goods or services supplied by the business would be charged at a VAT rate of either 0% (zero-rated), 5% (reduced rate) or 15% (17.5%) (standard rated). Don't forget that any zero-rated supply is still classed as taxable – but at a rate of 0%.

Compulsory registration

Turnover limits, EU acquisitions, services received from abroad

1.2   As explained above, there are two main situations when a business needs to be VAT registered on a compulsory basis – if the annual turnover limits have been exceeded or if it is expected that the annual limit will be exceeded in the next 30 days. In effect, the latter rule means that any large business that has significant trading levels will need to be VAT registered from its first day of trading.

However, there are two other situations when a business will also have to register:

(a)   if the value of its 'acquisitions' (ie value of goods bought from other EU countries) exceeds certain limits. The rules on this subject state that if the value of acquisitions made by a business at the end of any month, in the period beginning with 1 January in that year, have exceeded the annual VAT registration limit (ie £68,000 per annum with effect from 1 May 2009) or are expected to exceed the limit in the next thirty days, then the business must be VAT registered. See **11.11** for an example of how this rule works in practice;

(b)   if an unregistered business or person receives certain services from abroad, then it may need to register if the value of these supplies (and any other taxable supplies it makes) exceed the registration limits. See **14.3** for practical examples of how this rule works in practice.

In the case of the annual turnover limit being exceeded, then notification of the need to be registered must be made within 30 days of the end of the month in which the limit has been exceeded. The registration date will then be the first date of the following month.

The effect of the annual registration test is that an unregistered business needs to review the value of its annual taxable supplies at the end of each calendar month. See Example 2.

Example 2

Steve is a self-employed plumber (making wholly taxable supplies), and the value of work carried out in recent months has been as follows:

12 months to 31 March 2009	£63,000
12 months to 30 April 2009	£62,000
12 months to 31 May 2009	£69,000
12 months to 30 June 2009	£66,000

When should he become VAT registered?

Solution – until 30 April 2009, the annual VAT registration limit was £67,000 – this figure was increased to £68,000 from 1 May 2009. The point at which Steve has exceeded the limit is 31 May 2009 – which means he must notify HMRC of his liability to be VAT registered within 30 days of this date, and be registered with effect from 1 July 2009.

As illustrated by Example 1, it is important to remember that only the value of taxable supplies is taken into account for the registration limits – any exempt or non-business supplies are ignored. As a separate point, a new business will need to monitor its turnover from its first day of trading because it is possible that it might exceed the £68,000 limit after, for example, the fifth month of trading. It is not acceptable practice to wait until after the first year of trading has been completed and then identify whether registration is needed.

If a business trades as a second-hand car dealer or any other trader dealing in second-hand goods that uses a margin scheme, the taxable turnover is the full value of the sale, not the margin being achieved.

However, in the case of a tour operator using the tour operators' margin scheme, the taxable supplies represent the full margin (ie difference between buying prices and selling prices).

Transfer of a going concern

1.3   If a person takes over a business as a going concern, then it is necessary to take into account the taxable sales of the previous owner to determine if VAT registration is required. If these sales exceeded the limits, then the new owner must register for VAT from the first day he takes ownership of the business. See Example 3.

Example 3

Jean took over a florist shop as a going concern on 1 June 2009. The sales of the previous owner (all taxable) were £75,000 per year. Jean has decided to gain a temporary profit advantage by not registering for VAT until her own sales have exceeded £68,000 – all her sales are to the general public who are not able to recover input tax.

Solution – Jean's approach is incorrect – as the new owner, she needs to take into account the turnover of the previous owners and because this was in excess of the registration limit, she needs to register from her first day of trading.

Applying for VAT registration

1.4   When a business applies for VAT registration, the majority of applications will be made to register a business as a sole trader, partnership or limited company. In all three cases an application must be made on Form VAT 1; Form VAT 2 also needs to be completed in the case of a partnership.

The application needs to be sent to the regional registration unit appropriate to the post code of the business and the business must be registered from its principal place of business (it is not acceptable to register the address from an accountant's office or postal address).

As a useful tip, it is always of benefit if a taxpayer's VAT quarters coincide with its financial year. In many cases, a new business will have a year-end of 31 March to coincide with the tax year, so a request for this date (or any other date for different year-ends) can be made at the time of registering for VAT.

HMRC attempts to process all applications within 3 weeks, and a business can help in achieving this target by giving full and complete information at the time an application is submitted. It may be useful to provide supporting evidence to prove an application is genuine – HMRC looks very closely at applications where it suspects a possible link to what is known as 'carousel fraud' (see Chapter 19). In cases where it needs further information, HMRC will write to the business requesting more details to verify the application.

If HMRC is satisfied with the application, the following course of events will take place:

- HMRC will send a certificate of registration to the principal place of business, confirming the effective date of registration, the registration number, the date on which the first period ends and the length of future VAT periods (ie quarterly, monthly, annual);

- a business must start keeping records and charging VAT to its customers from the date it knows it has to be registered;

- HMRC will automatically send VAT returns to the business about a month before the end of each period – these need to be completed and submitted (and all tax paid) within one month of the due date to avoid a default situation. However, the benefits of filing VAT returns online are considerable and it will be compulsory for many businesses to file online after 1 April 2010 – see Chapter 18 for further details.

Supplies made before a VAT registration number has been allocated

1.5 What happens if a business needs to start charging VAT from, say, 1 June 2009, but that date arrives and it has still not received details of its VAT registration number from HMRC?

The rules state that a business must start charging VAT from the date it knows it has to be registered. This means that it can charge VAT before it is actually registered but, until it has received a VAT registration number, it must not show VAT as a separate item on any invoice raised. This can be achieved by changing its prices to include VAT and explaining to any VAT registered customers (who will want to be able to reclaim input tax) that it will send them VAT invoices at a later date. When the business has received confirmation of its VAT number, it must send the necessary invoices showing VAT within 30 days.

The positive point about these procedures is that the business will still be collecting VAT from its customers at the time an invoice is raised.

Input tax on goods and services obtained before VAT registration

1.6 When a business first registers for VAT, it is possible that it may have incurred VAT on expenditure before its date of registration. The positive point is that there is some scope to reclaim this VAT on the first return submitted by the business. The rules for making such a claim depend on whether the expenditure in question is related to goods or services:

(1) Goods – the following conditions must be satisfied:

  (a) the goods are still held at the time when the business became VAT registered;

  (b) they must have been supplied to the registered business within the 3-year period before the date of VAT registration (rising to 4 years with effect from 1 April 2010);
    Example – if the date of registration is 1 October 2009, the goods must have been purchased after 1 April 2006. If the date of registration is 1 May 2010, the goods must have been purchased after 1 May 2006. The 4-year limit is fully effective in this situation because the date of registration is after 1 April 2010.

  (c) the goods are to be used by the business that is now registered for VAT, and in connection with its taxable supplies (ie, no partial exemption issues);

  (d) all the normal rules allow the input tax to be reclaimed, ie holding proper tax invoice etc.

  In effect, the goods in question will either relate to capital items being used by the business, eg computers, fixtures and fittings etc, or stock bought before the date of registration that will be sold after the business becomes VAT registered.

(2) Services – the following conditions must be satisfied:

  (a) the services are for the purpose of the business that is now VAT registered;

  (b) the services were acquired within the 6-month period before the date of registration;

  (c) the services have not been supplied by the taxable person before he became registered, ie they have not been recharged to a customer.

There is no scope to extend either the 3 or 4-year time period in relation to goods or the 6-month period in relation to services. The only possible way around this issue would be to backdate the registration.

An interesting tribunal case was *Chilli Club Restaurant Ltd v Revenue and Customs Comrs* [2007] SWTI 1378 (EDN/06/65 20043) where the company paid VAT on the installation of mezzanine flooring in its restaurant before it became VAT registered. The flooring supply was classed as 'goods' by the directors, who therefore reclaimed input tax on the basis that it was incurred within the 3-year period before the date of registration. However, HMRC ruled that the supply was for 'services' and not eligible for a claim because it was incurred more than 6 months before the business registered for VAT.

The tribunal agreed with HMRC, but felt that HMRC should then have shown some flexibility in allowing the business to backdate its date of registration in order to be within the 6-month claim period.

Input tax on goods or services before incorporation

1.7 It is very common for a private individual to purchase an asset before he starts his business, and then trade as a limited company when the commencement takes place.

Again, there are rules that allow input tax to be reclaimed on pre-incorporation expenditure:

(1) the person to whom the supply was made became a member, officer or employee of the company and was reimbursed (or has received an under-taking to be reimbursed) by the company for the whole amount of the price paid for the goods or services;

(2) the person to whom the supply was made was not a taxable person at the time the expenditure was incurred, ie no input tax has been reclaimed already through another business;

(3) the other rules mentioned above concerning input tax on goods and services have been fully met, eg 3-year time limit in relation to purchase of goods and 6-month period for services.

Voluntary registration

1.8 The analysis at **1.2** explains the various procedures that apply when a business has to be VAT registered on a compulsory basis. In these situations, the business has no choice but to be registered and join the 'VAT club'.

However, there are various situations when it is in the interests of the business to be VAT registered, even when its turnover has not exceeded the annual limits. There are three main situations when a business would want to register for VAT on a voluntary basis as follows.

● *Most or all business income is zero-rated* – this means that the business would be able to avoid charging VAT on all or most of its income, but would benefit from input tax recovery on its costs and overheads. The net result would be that the business would be a repayment trader as far as VAT is concerned.

- *The majority of sales are to other VAT registered businesses* – if a business makes sales wholly or mainly to other VAT registered businesses, then the VAT it charges to its customers is not a problem because they can claim it back as input tax. This assumes that the customer in question does not suffer an input tax restriction through being partly exempt. By being VAT registered in this situation, a business can then benefit from input tax recovery on its costs without suffering a competitive disadvantage on the output tax charged to its customers.

- *A business is incurring major amounts of VAT on capital expenditure* – a new business that is investing major sums of money on capital expenditure may decide that it wants to register for VAT as soon as possible in order to reclaim input tax at the earliest opportunity. The thinking may be that if the business develops as intended with future growth, then it will need to be VAT registered anyway. It would therefore be sensible to register from day one, and boost cash flow when it is needed most, ie by recovering input tax on relevant costs.

See Example 4 to identify when a business could benefit from being VAT registered on a voluntary basis.

Example 4

Geoff is a self-employed carpenter, who makes wooden tables for a wide range of businesses that are registered for VAT. He spends a lot of money on raw materials and tools, and has also bought a new van for £10,000 plus VAT. His annual sales are £45,000.

Gordon is a self-employed tax adviser, who does a lot of work advising insurance companies on tax issues. His annual income is £45,000.

What is the best VAT route for these two businesses?

Solution – it is definitely in the interests of Geoff to become VAT registered as soon as possible. He will be able to reclaim input tax on all of his raw materials and tools, and on the purchase of his van. The VAT he charges to his customers will not be a problem because they are registered for VAT themselves, and can therefore reclaim input tax.

However, it is best for Gordon to remain as an unregistered business. The nature of his business means he is unlikely to have any significant input tax to reclaim, and the additional VAT charged on his fees will be a problem for his clients because insurance companies are mainly exempt from VAT.

In reality, HMRC is very fair when it comes to approving registrations on a voluntary basis. As long as it is satisfied that the business has a genuine need for registration and is carrying on a legitimate activity, it tends to approve applications without any problem.

An intention to trade in the future

1.9 It is common practice for certain types of business to incur large amounts of expenditure before they actually make a taxable supply. Examples could include a business that builds new houses, or a new business that needs to carry out major property alterations before it can start trading.

In such cases, a business can register for VAT as an intending trader – however, it is important to remember the following points:

* HMRC will obviously look very closely at intending trader applications. It will need to be convinced that the business has a genuine intention to make taxable supplies and that the application is not just an attempt to obtain large amounts of VAT repayments on a non-business project;

* it is important that traders provide HMRC with as much evidence of their intention to trade as possible. This evidence could be in the form of planning permission from a local authority to trade as a certain business, correspondence with potential customers or suppliers;

* HMRC will want to know the likely date when taxable supplies will commence – this could be evidenced by, for example, a cash flow forecast or business plan.

Exemption from registration

1.10 In most cases, a business that exceeds the VAT registration limits must register for VAT in accordance with the rules mentioned earlier in this chapter.

However, there is scope for a business to request exemption from registration if it can convince HMRC that:

* the business is wholly making zero-rated supplies and would therefore always be a repayment trader if registered for VAT; or

* the business mainly makes zero-rated supplies and even though some supplies are standard rated, the business would still be in a net repayment position for VAT, ie input tax exceeds output tax on a regular basis; or

* although the business has exceeded the compulsory registration limits, this situation was caused by a one-off sale (or unusual trading circumstances). A letter should be sent to HMRC advising of this situation but with a

request for the registration to not be processed on the basis that future trading by the business will again be below the registration limits.

The reason that HMRC will allow a business to receive exemption from registration in the first two situations is because it will save the cost of administering a registration for which it receives no revenue.

If a business feels it can qualify for exemption under the above rules, it will need to write to HMRC giving full details of its trading circumstances at the time when it has exceeded the registration limits.

The two main advantages for a business requesting exemption from registration are as follows:

● it avoids the need to complete regular VAT returns and keep records to comply with the requirements of being VAT registered;

● if there are some standard rated supplies made by the business, then the exemption avoids making an output tax charge to these customers.

The main disadvantage of being exempt from registration is that a business is sacrificing the opportunity to reclaim input tax on goods or services purchased for the business. In reality, the key point will be for a business to carry out an analysis of the costs and benefits of being VAT registered. See Example 5 below.

Example 5

Jean rents a small unit in a shopping centre selling fruit (zero-rated). Her sales for the 12 months ending 31 March 2009 were £70,000, exceeding the VAT limit for the first time. Her main costs in the business are rent (exempt from VAT), the wages of two employees (outside the scope) and the fruit she buys for resale (zero-rated). Her accountant is not VAT registered and has offered to complete VAT returns for her at a cost of £300 per year.

Solution – the main overheads and costs of the business do not attract any VAT, so Jean will have negligible input tax to reclaim if she became VAT registered. It would be very unlikely if the total amount of input tax she could reclaim exceeded the accountancy fee of £300 to complete her returns. Her best option is to apply to HMRC to receive exemption from registration on the basis that she makes zero-rated sales and would therefore always be a repayment trader.

An important point to remember as far as VAT exemption is concerned is that the taxpayer still has a responsibility to notify HMRC of any material change in the business that could affect the decision of HMRC to grant exemption from VAT registration. Any such change needs to be notified to HMRC within 30 days of the day on which the material change took place – see Example 6.

Example 6

ABC Ltd trades from a small shop in the High Street, selling take-away sandwiches that are zero-rated for VAT purposes. The company received exemption from VAT registration because it managed to convince HMRC that it would always be in a net repayment situation.

On 3 May 2009, the business diversified its activities by opening a café on its premises to sell sandwiches and light meals to customers – it will also continue to do take-away sales.

Solution – the new café represents a material change to the business of ABC Ltd. The company has 30 days from 3 May to notify HMRC of the change, and will probably need to be VAT registered due to the fact that the catering sales made on the premises will be standard rated for VAT.

Changes of business details

1.11 It is important that a business ensures that its VAT registration details with HMRC are accurate. This means that changes in any of the following details must be notified when they take place:

● names of the proprietors or partners in the business;

● trading name, trading activity or address of principal place of business;

● any additional partners taken on by the business and the relevant date when this happened;

● any change in legal entity (the same VAT number can be retained in most cases by completing Form VAT 68), e g transfer from a sole trader to a limited company.

Note – it is now possible to apply for VAT registration and notify changes by using HMRC's eVAT service. The business must first be authorised to use the eVAT service, which can be done via VAT Online Services on the HMRC website (at www.hmrc.gov.uk).

The 'VAT trap'

1.12 Many businesses that have traded below the VAT registration limit will be faced with a dilemma when they increase their sales to the point when they may need to be VAT registered. In basic terms, the question that all businesses will need to consider is: should I expand my business and register for VAT, even though my profits could reduce by being VAT registered? Or should I restrict my level of activity by trading just below the VAT registration limits?

See Example 7 for an example of how being VAT registered can adversely affect the trading of a business. This particular business has been caught by what is sometimes known as the 'VAT trap'.

Example 7

Alan is a mobile caterer selling hot food from a small unit. His prices are determined by the prices charged by similar outlets in the same area. His sales have always been just below the VAT registration limit, but he has now been approached by a potential new customer who wants to buy £2,000 of beef burgers from him each year. This extra business will take him above the VAT registration limit. Should Alan accept the business offered by the new client?

Solution – most of Alan's purchases are zero-rated so he would have very little scope to reclaim input tax if he became VAT registered. It would also be difficult for him to increase prices charged to his customers because this would make him less competitive in the market place – he would probably have to absorb the VAT charge within his existing prices.

If Alan's sales increased from £67,000 to £69,000 as a result of the extra work (ie above the registration limit of £68,000, effective from 1 May 2009), the likely impact on his business could be as follows:

● the new work will create additional profit of perhaps £1,000 (assuming 50% gross profit);

● by being VAT registered and not able to increase selling prices, the business will pay £10,276 in output tax (£69,000 × 7/47 with a VAT rate of 17.5%) with very little input tax to reclaim on its expenses;

● the business has been caught by the 'VAT trap' and is worse off financially than if it had continued to trade below the VAT registration limit.

Consequences of late registration – backdated registration date and possible penalties

Identifying correct date of registration

1.13   An unregistered business has a duty to monitor its activity levels on a monthly basis, and then register for VAT when it has exceeded certain limits as specified at **1.2**.

If a business fails to register for VAT at the correct time, there are two main outcomes:

● the correct date of registration will be worked out and the business will become VAT registered and liable to VAT on its taxable supplies from that date;

- the business could also be faced with a penalty for belated notification of its liability to be VAT registered.

If an adviser is acting for a client where HMRC has attempted to backdate the registration, there are a number of measures to take to ensure the revised date is correct:

- the calculation of supplies should only take taxable supplies into account. If a business makes some sales that are exempt, then the value of these sales should not be included in the calculation, as illustrated in Example 1;

- the calculations should also exclude the sale of any capital assets made by the business;

- if a business has exceeded the registration limit because of a one-off large sale which is unlikely to be repeated, then it can escape the need to be VAT registered if its future taxable sales will be £66,000 per annum or less (based on current deregistration limit effective from 1 May 2009);

- remember that the registration limit changes each year. It is important to ensure that the officer has used the limits in force at the correct period of time, e g if checking the level of sales for 2001, then the relevant limit in that year was £52,000 up to 31 March and £54,000 from 1 April;

- if an officer has used annual accounts to arrive at an effective date of registration, then check that the accounts do not include adjustments that would not have created a tax point for VAT purposes, e g if the accounts to 31 December 2002 include closing work in progress of £10,000 within the sales figure, then the relevant date for VAT registration purposes is when this work was invoiced (obviously at a later date);

- ensure that the officer's arithmetic is correct and that he has extracted his figures from the correct accounting records relevant to sales.

Arrears of tax through late registration

1.14   If a business was registered for VAT from an incorrect date, then it will be required to complete a single VAT return to cover the period from when it should have been registered to the date when it actually became registered. In some cases, this period can be for many years.

The ideal situation for a business will be to recharge its customers for any unpaid VAT – this situation is most likely to be practical if the customer is VAT registered and able to recover input tax. The VAT charge should be 17.5% of the original value of the services performed (or 15% if the sale was made between 1 December 2008 and 31 December 2009) and should be made by issuing a VAT-only invoice. However, no output tax needs to be declared on zero-rated or exempt sales made by the business. It is also important to remember that some sales could only be subject to the reduced rate of VAT (5%) – see Chapter 22 for further details.

If a business is unable to recharge VAT to its customers, then the sales made in the period under review will be deemed by HMRC to have been made on a VAT inclusive basis. The business will then need to declare output tax based on 7/47 of the sales value for any standard rated sales that it has made (or 3/23 of the sales value between 1 December 2008 and 31 December 2009 when the standard rate of VAT was temporarily reduced to 15%).

The positive point is that the business will be able to reclaim input tax (subject to normal rules) for the period covered by the return.

An important point to remember is that the backdating of VAT registration will affect the profits made by a business – an income tax and Class 4 National Insurance saving could therefore be made to help alleviate the impact of the large VAT bill.

Penalty calculation and possible mitigation

1.15 The calculation of a belated notification penalty under current and future legislation is based on the net amount of tax payable for the period from when the business should have registered for VAT to the time when it actually became registered. The amount of the penalty then varies according to the total length of this period.

If the date of registration should have been before 1 April 2010:

• where the period is less than 9 months a penalty of 5% (or £50 if greater) will be applied;

• for a period of between 9 and 18 months, a penalty of 10% (or £50 if greater) will be applied;

• for a period exceeding 18 months, a penalty of 15% (or £50 if greater) will be applied.

If the date of registration should have been any date on or after 1 April 2010:

• a penalty of between 10% and 30% of the tax outstanding can be charged, ie based on the rates that apply for showing a lack of reasonable care. However, HMRC has confirmed that most penalties will be in the lower range, taking into account the quality of disclosure made by the taxpayer in informing HMRC about the VAT owed;

• there is no penalty if the late registration has not produced a tax loss – this is good news for any business that wholly or mainly sells zero-rated items and would be in a VAT repayment position;

• if a person makes a full and unprompted disclosure within 12 months of first becoming liable for a failure to notify penalty, the penalty can be reduced to zero.

There are two main ways of reducing the penalty or seeking its total withdrawal:

(a) reasonable excuse provisions – if it can be shown that the business had a reasonable excuse for belated notification, then a penalty will not be charged by HMRC;

(b) HMRC has the power to mitigate the penalty.

In terms of the reasonable excuse situation, HMRC has indicated that the following reasons for late registration may be acceptable as possible explanations.

● *Compassionate circumstances* – where an individual is totally responsible for running a small business and he, or a member of his immediate family, was seriously ill or recovering from such an illness at the time notification was required.

● *Transfer of a business as a going concern* – where such a business is taken over with little or no break in the trading and returns have been submitted and VAT paid on time under the registration number of the previous owner.

● *Doubt about liabilities of supplies* – where there is written evidence of an enquiry to HMRC about the liability of supplies and the liability has remained in doubt.

● *Uncertainty about employment status* – where there are genuine doubts as to whether a person is employed or self-employed or where correspondence with HMRC can be produced about these doubts.

If a taxpayer cannot convince HMRC (or an independent VAT tribunal) that he had a reasonable excuse for registering late, his priority should then be to ensure the penalty is as low as possible through mitigation.

The officer will take a number of factors into account when reviewing a penalty charge – including the following general headings:

(i) how the infringement occurred;

(ii) the degree of co-operation received from the taxpayer in quantifying the arrears;

(iii) any other relevant factors that may be put forward by the taxpayer or an adviser acting on his behalf.

See Example 8 for an illustration of how mitigation might work in the case of a penalty for belated notification (based on current penalty system).

Example 8

DEF Ltd should have been registered for VAT on 1 March 2008 – it did not actually register until 1 October 2008. The company acknowledged the late registration by notifying HMRC of the problem itself, and calculated the arrears of tax due for the extra period to be £15,000. It explained to HMRC that the reason it was late registering for VAT was because the directors were too busy to remember to review their turnover limits at the end of each month.

Solution – the reason for DEF Ltd being late registering for VAT will not gain any reasonable excuse concession, or any mitigation of the penalty. However, the disclosure of the lateness itself and the full quantification of the arrears will probably earn a 50% reduction in the penalty by mitigation.

The actual penalty will be calculated as follows:

Tax due £15,000 × 5% penalty (as period of lateness was less than 9 months) =	£750
Mitigation of 50% for disclosure and calculation of arrears	(£375)
Penalty due to HMRC	£375

Planning points to consider

1.16   The following planning points should be given consideration.

- A new or existing business will need to monitor the level of its taxable sales at the end of each calendar month to identify if it has exceeded the £68,000 limit. It is not acceptable to wait until the end of the first 12 months of trading and then apply the relevant test. Remember, however, that it is only taxable sales that count, not exempt or non-business sales.

- A transferee taking over a business as a going concern must take the turnover of the previous owners into account when deciding if it needs to be VAT registered from its first day of trading.

- A business trading in second-hand goods must base the value of its taxable turnover on the full value of the sale, not just the margin that would be used under a second-hand VAT scheme.

- To make accounting simpler, it is worthwhile for a business to seek VAT periods at the time of registration that coincide with its financial year, e g a business with 31 March year end should request calendar VAT periods.

- Ensure that a newly registered business has identified opportunities to reclaim input tax on any relevant expenditure incurred before its date of registration. However, expenditure on goods must have been incurred within the 3 or 4-year period before the registration date; a 6-month time limit is imposed for services.

- It may be in the best interest of many businesses to register for VAT on a voluntary basis – particularly if they are making mainly zero-rated supplies or mainly working for other VAT registered businesses. Advisers should regularly review the activities of all non-registered clients to see if they could benefit from voluntary registration.

- If HMRC backdates a registration, make sure the officer's calculations and procedures for calculating the actual date are correct. Remember that if any arrears of VAT are established through the backdating of the registration, there is likely to be scope to reduce self-assessment tax liabilities because of reduced profits.

- A new penalty system takes effect for all late registrations where the correct date of registration falls on or after 1 April 2010. However, the reality of the situation is that most cases in the next couple of years will still be based on the existing penalty system.

Chapter 2

Deregistration

Key topics in this chapter:

● Opportunities for a business to deregister from VAT and occasions when this would be beneficial.

● Situations when deregistration is compulsory – e g sale of a business, ceasing to trade.

● Procedures for reclaiming input tax on post deregistration expenses using Form VAT 427.

● Sale of a business – either cancelling an existing VAT registration or new owners retaining the same VAT number.

● Dealing with a change in legal entity – VAT 68 procedures.

● Output tax liability on stock and assets owned by a business at the time it deregisters from VAT.

● Output tax issues on land and property owned at time of deregistration.

● Administration procedures for deregistration.

Introduction

2.1   It is often assumed that once a business becomes VAT registered and joins the 'VAT club', it will remain registered until it is either sold or ceases to trade. In reality, this is not necessarily true. There are a number of situations where a tax adviser can be proactive as far as VAT deregistration is concerned, often to the clear benefit of the client.

Going back to basics, the main rule as far as VAT registration is concerned is that a business must register for VAT when it has made taxable supplies in the previous 12 months exceeding £68,000 – or expects to make taxable supplies of £68,000 or more in the next 30 days. The latter clause in the legislation effectively means that all large businesses have to register for VAT as soon as they start to trade.

Once registered, a business will charge VAT on its standard rated and reduced-rate supplies, and as long as it is not making exempt or non-business supplies, will recover all input tax on relevant expenditure.

Deregistration must be requested if a business has ceased to make taxable supplies, ie the business has closed down or has been sold – but there are two other main situations where a business can request deregistration:

- if HMRC is satisfied that the value of taxable supplies in the next 12 months will not exceed £66,000. This figure is known as the deregistration limit and usually increases in the Budget each year in the same way as the registration limit. The limit of £66,000 was effective from 1 May 2009 – a rate of £65,000 applied for the period from 1 April 2008 to 30 April 2009;

- most or all sales are zero-rated and the business submits repayment VAT returns (needless to say, not many businesses seek to deregister under this clause).

Reasons for requesting deregistration on a voluntary basis

2.2   The main reasons why some businesses would be keen to request deregistration at the earliest opportunity are as follows:

(a)   the majority of sales are standard rated and made to members of the public or to other businesses who are not VAT registered – in other words, VAT is an extra charge to these customers because they do not have the opportunity to reclaim input tax. In the case of sales to non-registered businesses, VAT would become an extra cost that they would treat as a business overhead. Remember, it is not just small businesses that may not be VAT registered but also large companies who cannot register because they only make exempt supplies – eg insurance companies, banks, most financial institutions;

(b)   the nature of the business means there is very little input tax to reclaim – this is particularly the case for many service-based businesses. This situation could mean that even though output tax charged to customers is not an issue (if supplies are made to other businesses able to reclaim input tax), the negligible input tax to reclaim could mean it is not productive to spend unnecessary time on the administration of VAT, ie completing returns, keeping certain records etc.

The above situations therefore mean that it is important for advisers to review the trading levels of certain clients – to see if a request for deregistration could be worthwhile. This is particularly relevant in the current economic climate where many businesses have suffered reduced sales in the last couple of years.

See Example 1 which illustrates the impact of VAT on different types of business.

Example 1

John provides accountancy services and tax advice to funeral directors. He is VAT registered and his normal charge out rate is £100 per hour plus VAT.

Jill provides accountancy services and tax advice to funeral directors. She only works on a part-time basis so has always traded below the VAT registration limits. Her charge out rate is £100 per hour – no VAT.

Jack provides accountancy services and tax advice to butchers' shops. All of his customers are VAT registered and he charges £100 per hour plus VAT.

Which of the three businesses above is suffering a loss of competitiveness because of VAT?

Solution – in this example, only one business is suffering a commercial disadvantage by being VAT registered, namely John. This is because funeral directors are partially exempt, and are unable to reclaim all of their input tax. In effect, VAT becomes part of their overhead cost – in contrast to a butcher's shop, which is able to reclaim all of the VAT charged by Jack as input tax. In reality, the funeral directors would save money by using the services of Jill – who does not have to charge VAT.

Reductions in future turnover

2.3 At 2.1 above, it was explained that one of the reasons why a business could request deregistration from VAT is if it can satisfy HMRC that its taxable turnover in the next 12 months will be less than £66,000.

The main reasons why this situation could emerge are as follows:

● the business has lost a key customer(s) that has not been replaced by new customers. In such cases, the value of future sales will obviously decrease.

● the business owner may decide to simplify his operation, the result of which could be a decrease in income and expenditure – for example, a carpet fitter employing ten people and renting premises may decide to make all staff redundant, close the premises and just trade on his own fitting carpets;

● the business owner may decide to reduce his working hours – to a level where he expects to trade below the VAT deregistration limits – for example, an architect working 5 days a week making a lifestyle decision to only work 4 days a week will (all things being equal) encounter a 20% reduction in his turnover.

Example 2 illustrates a typical situation (extending Example 1) where a business could encounter a trading problem that produces a VAT benefit.

Example 2

John, from Example 1 above (who provides accountancy and tax services to funeral directors), has relied on one particular funeral director for nearly 25% of his £72,000 per annum turnover. The funeral director in question has now closed his business, and will no longer require the services of an accountant. John has therefore decided that this is a good opportunity for him to work less hours – he therefore does not intend to replace the lost business with any new clients.

Solution – in this example, it is clear that John's taxable turnover in the future will be about £54,000 per year (ie £72,000 × 75%) – well below the deregistration threshold of £66,000. He is entitled to deregister from VAT.

The dilemma now faced by John is whether he can increase his charge-out rate to remaining customers, who will be financially better off anyway because of the VAT saving on his fees. An increase from £100 per hour to £105 per hour would probably compensate John for the loss of input tax he will suffer as a result of not being VAT registered – but his clients (all partly exempt businesses) are still better off by the new arrangement.

Anti-avoidance measure

2.4 As with many aspects of VAT, HMRC has anti-avoidance measures in place to stay one step ahead of the game. One important measure as far as deregistration is concerned is that the fall in turnover must not be because a business intends to suspend trading for 30 days or more. See Example 3.

Example 3

Bill trades as a fish and chip shop, and his taxable sales are £5,750 per month (£69,000 per annum). He is VAT registered. Next year, he is planning to close his shop for 6 weeks to go on a long holiday to Australia – he sees an opportunity to deregister for VAT as his taxable turnover will be less than £66,000 in the next 12 months.

Solution – it is clear that the reason for the decrease in turnover is because of the suspension of trading for more than 30 days. In reality, the business is still trading above the VAT threshold in normal circumstances. Any request for deregistration would be refused.

Exclusion of capital assets

2.5 One point to remember is that the sale of capital assets is excluded from any calculation to see if taxable turnover in the next year will be less than £66,000.

For example, if a business expects sales to be £70,000 in the next 12 months but this includes the sale of a machine for £10,000, then the relevant figure for VAT deregistration is £60,000. An application to deregister could therefore be made.

Administrative savings by not being VAT registered

2.6   Having identified situations where a business may request deregistration on the basis of past or future turnover, there is another way of escaping the system on a voluntary basis. Basically, this occurs when a business can convince HMRC that all, or most, of its sales are, or will be, zero-rated, and therefore any VAT return submitted would always be a repayment claim.

In most cases, a business making zero-rated supplies will be reluctant to deregister from VAT because of the loss of input tax recovery. However, certain businesses have negligible input tax to claim, and therefore gain little advantage in being registered. See Example 4.

Example 4

Mrs E runs a business that buys eggs (zero-rated) from a local farm and sells them to surrounding shops. Her turnover from this activity is £70,000 per annum. She makes all of the collections and deliveries on her bicycle and therefore incurs no motoring expenses. She works from home and therefore suffers no premises costs. The accountant she uses is not registered for VAT, but charges her £500 per year to complete four VAT returns, which have no output tax and only about £10 per quarter input tax on a small amount of telephone and stationery expenditure.

Solution – it is clearly a 'win:win' situation for Mrs E to deregister for VAT – she will save £460 per year (£500 accountancy fees less the £40 loss of input tax) and HMRC will not have to administer a registration that does not produce any revenue for the exchequer.

As an extra point, the circumstances in the case of Mrs E above are very clear because she is only making zero-rated supplies. However, HMRC will also allow a business to deregister or not register in the first place if there are some standard rated supplies being made as well. The key test it will consider is whether input tax is likely to exceed output tax on a regular basis. Once it has established this is the case, the taxpayer's request for deregistration is likely to be granted.

Compulsory deregistration

Ceasing to trade

2.7   The examples illustrated at **2.2–2.6** above considered situations where a taxable person 'may' request deregistration – in other words, he or his adviser has identified that he is entitled to exit the VAT system, and it is in his best interests to do so.

There are other circumstances where deregistration is compulsory, ie the business 'must' cancel its VAT number.

The obvious situation is where a business has ceased to trade. The effective date of deregistration is the date when the final taxable supply was made, and deregistration is requested by completing Form VAT 7, and returning it to the National Registration Service. The legislation requires that the form must be completed within 30 days of cessation. HMRC has the power to charge a penalty if this deadline is not met (for any business involved in deregistering a business, HMRC has a very well written leaflet that covers most aspects – Notice 700/11 May 2002).

In reality, it is unlikely that HMRC will charge a penalty if the 30-day notification is not made. This is because many businesses delay cancelling their registration as a matter of course because they want to recover input tax on all outstanding expenses – and think this can only be done by retaining their VAT registration number. The correct approach is to notify HMRC immediately that cessation has taken place – and then make post deregistration claims of input tax on Form VAT 427. See Example 5.

Example 5

Mrs Smith ceased to trade as a computer consultant on 31 March 2009. Her accountant will not be doing her final self-employment accounts until September – and will raise his invoice for this work (£800 + VAT) in October. Mrs Smith is VAT registered and her VAT periods end in March, June, September and December.

Solution – the incorrect approach (but adopted by many people in practice) would be for Mrs Smith to retain her VAT number until the end of December 2009 – so that she can recover input tax on her accountancy fees on the December 2009 return.

The correct approach would be for her to notify HMRC of the cessation of trading within 30 days and then submit Form VAT 427 at a later date to recover the input tax on her accountancy fees.

With regard to VAT 427 claims, there are some important points to remember:

- a claim cannot be made for any goods purchased after the registration has been cancelled – this is a reasonable rule because HMRC will not be receiving any output tax on these goods, so they are reluctant to allow any input tax claim;

● a claim for services can only be made if the services were received for the purposes of the taxable business activities of the registration;

● any claim must be submitted with original invoices (copies are not accepted).

Sale of a business

2.8 The next situation to consider as far as compulsory deregistration is concerned is when a business is sold. In reality, the end result is likely to be the same (ie cancellation of VAT number) but it is possible that the new owner may want to retain the VAT registration number of the previous owner.

The main disadvantage with new owners taking over an existing VAT registration is that they are also agreeing to take over any potential VAT debts of the previous business. This could cause problems if, for example, a VAT inspection going back 3 or 4 years found a number of underpayments that were relevant to the period when the previous owner was running the business. The new owner would then be liable to pay this debt to HMRC. The arrangement could work in favour of the new owner if the errors detected had produced a VAT overpayment – he would then benefit from an unexpected VAT windfall. However, most VAT inspections produce assessments of tax rather than rebates, so the latter situation is less common in practice.

One positive concession granted by HMRC is that it will not apply any penalty against the new owner of the business for any period before he took ownership.

The procedure for retaining a VAT number is that the new and former owners of the business must complete and sign Form VAT 68 – which must be approved by HMRC who will carry out various checks.

Change of legal entity

2.9 The other main situation where a registration must be cancelled is if a business changes its legal entity. For example, a common situation in recent years (due to favourable rates of corporation tax) has been for a sole trader or partnership to incorporate its business.

In such situations, there are again two options:

● the parties involved can sign Form VAT 68 so that the new entity retains the same VAT registration number. This arrangement would be sensible in the case of incorporation mentioned above – as the same persons are involved in both businesses;

- to apply for a new VAT registration number – this might be the best approach when, for example, a sole trader takes on a partner, ie there are different people involved in the old and new business.

Note – the situation when an existing partnership takes on an extra partner is not a change in legal entity. In such cases, the only information needed by HMRC is a new VAT 2 (list of partners) to reflect the addition of the new partner.

Note – where a new entity retains the VAT registration number of the previous business, the requirement from 1 September 2007 is that the new owner (or buyer) must retain the business records of the previous owner. This will enable the buyer to comply with his obligations to HMRC, eg being able to produce records in the event of a VAT visit.

Consequences of deregistration

Output tax on stock and assets held at time of deregistration

2.10   When a business deregisters from VAT, it must account for output tax on any stocks and assets held at the time of deregistration. There is a concession from HMRC that this output tax can be ignored if the total VAT declared would be less than £1,000 (ie gross value of less than £6,714).

With regard to these rules, there are a number of important points to take into account, all of which help to reduce the output tax liability, in many cases to zero:

- output tax is not due on any stocks or assets where input tax has not been claimed on the original purchase. In effect, HMRC is acknowledging that because no input tax credit has been given on the goods in question, it is not seeking an output tax payment. However, this concession does not apply if the goods in question were not subject to a VAT charge because they were taken over as part of a transfer of a going concern deal;

- no output tax is due on goods that are zero-rated or exempt;

- no output tax is due on intangible assets such as copyrights and goodwill – these assets are ignored and the rules only apply to tangible assets;

- in many situations, assets or stock held will be taken into the private ownership of the business owners or used to carry on trading in the future (if the business is deregistering due to the turnover rules rather than because it is closing down). In such cases, output tax will be due at cost price on the stock items, ie there is no requirement to include a profit element on the goods. In the case of assets and stock, the value can be based on the 'price one would expect to pay for them in their present condition'. This enables the calculation to take into account the impact of any out-of-date or damaged goods and, in the case of assets, any depreciation or wear and tear allowances;

- in all cases of estimates, HMRC would expect calculations to be based on a fair and sensible approach – for example, it would not be reasonable to declare that a van was worth £3,000, if the van in question was bought for £10,000 only 3 months before the business deregistered.

The rules become slightly more complicated if land and property assets are involved in the equation – for further details, see **2.12** below.

For an illustration of the above issues, see Example 6.

Example 6

Mike runs a shop that sells confectionery, tobacco and newspapers. His taxable turnover for the 12 months to 31 March 2009 was £53,000 and his expected taxable sales for the next 12 months are expected to be £55,000. He has decided to deregister from VAT.

The cost value of Mike's stock at 31 March 2009 was £20,000 (cost price excluding VAT) – of which newspapers were £4,000. He also has a car that he bought 12 months ago for £10,000 plus VAT and a computer that he bought from a friend (not VAT registered) for £1,000.

Solution – it is clear that the value of stock and assets on hand exceeds £6,714 – so Mike has an output tax liability to declare on his final VAT return. However, the first concession is that he can ignore the computer because it was bought from an unregistered person. In the case of the car, Mike would not have reclaimed input tax on the initial purchase (non-deductible input tax) so the onward supply is exempt under *VAT Act 1994, Sch 9, Group 14*. The newspapers are zero-rated so they can also be excluded. Output tax is therefore due on the remaining stock (£16,000 × 17.5% = £2,800).

It is important that the impact of any output tax liability is discussed at the planning stage of any discussions about deregistering for VAT. It can be a shock to many business owners if they suddenly have a large output tax liability on stock and assets – in many cases, the impact of this bill could make the option of deregistration much less attractive.

Transfer of a going concern

2.11   Another important consideration is to assess whether deregistration is taking place because a business is being sold or transferred as a going concern. In such cases, the transfer of stock and assets is outside the scope of VAT, with no output tax payment needed by the seller.

One requirement for a transfer of a going concern situation is for the new owner to be VAT registered, but there are other important rules to follow as well. See Chapter 4 for a detailed analysis of the issues involving the transfer of a going concern.

Land and property issues

2.12 As explained at 2.10 above, output tax is due on the value of any stock and assets owned by the business at the time of deregistration.

In the case of land and property, a number of different situations apply as far as output tax is concerned at the time of deregistration.

Note – in the examples that follow, it is being assumed that a business is deregistering on the basis of reduced turnover but is retaining land or buildings within the business.

- **The land or buildings were bought as an exempt supply but the option to tax has been exercised since that date.**

  In this situation, the business would have charged output tax on any supplies connected with the property since it made the option to tax election on the property, e g rent charged to a tenant. It would have also reclaimed input tax on any related costs, e g refurbishment. The positive point, however, is that there is no output tax liability to declare on the final VAT return at the time of deregistration on the value of the opted land or buildings. This is because no input tax claim was made when the land or buildings were first purchased.

  However, it needs to be recognised that an option to tax election is effective for 20 years once it has been made. So, if the business sells the property at a future date, then it will need to reregister for VAT and account for tax on the selling proceeds, assuming the sale takes place within the 20-year life of the option.

- **The land or buildings were purchased with VAT and input tax reclaimed – but the supply would now be classed as exempt from VAT if sold to a third party.**

  The above situation could apply if a business purchased a brand new commercial property but never opted to tax the property (it would still be able to recover input tax on the initial purchase as long as the building was used for its own trading purposes, making taxable supplies). Once the property was then 3 years old, the onward sale of the property would be exempt. The output tax liability at the time of deregistration would not apply because it excludes all zero-rated or exempt goods – so as long as a property would be an exempt supply if sold at the date of deregistration, then no output tax liability would be evident.

However, there may be a problem for the business in this situation with the capital goods scheme – if the property in question cost more than £250,000 plus VAT when it was first purchased and deregistration is taking place within 10 years of this date. See Chapter 9 for details about the capital goods scheme.

- **The land or buildings were purchased with VAT and input tax reclaimed – the buyer made the election to opt to tax the property.**

In this situation, an output tax liability exists at the time of deregistration because input tax was claimed on the initial purchase of the land or buildings and the option to tax election makes this a taxable supply.

Note – the reality of this situation is that the business would be unlikely to deregister because of the high output tax payment that would be due on the market value of the land or buildings on its final VAT return. The sensible and possibly only option would be for the business to defer the cancellation of its VAT registration until the property is sold.

Administration issues

2.13 When the date of cancellation of registration has been arranged, either a formal notice of cancellation will be sent (Form VAT 35) or a formal notice of exemption from registration is sent (Form VAT 8). Assuming that the VAT registration number has not been reallocated to a new owner, the final VAT return (VAT 193) must be completed in the normal way and sent to HMRC with full payment due.

Once the VAT registration is cancelled, it is important that the business does not issue any more VAT invoices (showing its VAT registration number) or charge VAT to any customers. HMRC should be consulted about the situation where a business uses an existing stock of business stationery, but crosses out the VAT registration number.

Planning points to consider

2.14 The following points should be given consideration.

- Review the VAT registration position of all businesses on an annual basis to see if a client could be eligible for deregistration and, if he is, whether it would be commercially beneficial for him to do so. This is particularly relevant in the current economic climate where a fall in sales volume has been suffered by many businesses in the UK.

- Any request for deregistration based on future turnover cannot be made because of a decision to suspend trading for 30 days or more.

- A business that is in a repayment situation but has taxable supplies exceeding the VAT limits can still apply for deregistration. This decision would be made if the business is unlikely to lose much input tax by deregistering, and wants to save the administrative burden of being registered.

- Remember that a deregistered business can claim input tax on certain relevant expenses after it has been deregistered. This can be done by using Form VAT 427 – but any claim must be supported by original tax invoices.

- Be aware of the opportunity for the same VAT number to be retained by the new owners in situations where the business has been transferred as a going concern. However, there are potential risks for the new owner of the business, who is effectively taking over the possible VAT debts of the previous owner.

- There is no output tax liability on the value of stocks and assets held at the time of deregistration if the amount of VAT involved is less than £1,000. There are also other concessions to reduce the potential output tax charge, e g no output tax due on zero-rated or exempt goods; output tax calculations are based on the present condition of the goods, i e taking damage and depreciation into account.

- If a business owns land and property at the time of deregistration, then it is important to be clear about the output tax rules that apply in relation to the option to tax and potential problems with the capital goods scheme.

Chapter 3

Group Registration and Divisional Registration

Key topics in this chapter:

- Main rules for group registration – the 'control' test.

- Forms to complete and procedures to follow if applying for a group registration.

- Benefits and consequences of a group registration.

- Being aware of strict anti-avoidance powers that are available to HMRC if it considers that group registration structures are being abused.

- The need for holding companies to make genuine taxable supplies if they are to be registered for VAT in their own right.

- Group registrations where the only taxable supplies are between group members.

- Key rules and procedures for divisional registration.

Introduction

3.1 The basic principle of group registration is that a number of different legal entities (usually limited companies under common control) can be registered for VAT as a single taxable person, ie instead of each entity submitting its own VAT return, there is only one return submitted for the entire 'group'.

There are a number of important rules to be met before a group registration can be established, the main rule being that the companies within the group must all be under the control of one individual or one entity.

The two main advantages of being registered for VAT on a group basis are as follows:

(a) there is no VAT charged on supplies made between group members;

(b) from an administrative point of view, there is only one quarterly (or monthly) VAT return to submit for the entire group.

In recent years, there has been a tendency for some group registrations to be used as a tax avoidance strategy to create a good input tax result for companies who have exempt income. HMRC has been very active in closing down the opportunities for such manipulation to take place. See 3.5 below.

Divisional registration exists when one corporate body is split into a number of self-accounting units (divisions) and the company wishes to register each unit separately for VAT. Each unit will submit its own VAT return. However, the corporate body still remains liable for all of the debts and VAT responsibilities of each division.

Rules for group registration

3.2   The key rule for group registration is that the group of companies seeking to be registered must meet the 'control test'. If the control rule is not met, then the application for group registration will be refused.

The control test can be met if any of the following situations apply:

- the controlling company or individual has a majority of the voting rights in the other companies – this is usually achieved by owning at least 51% of the ordinary share capital of the subsidiary company;

- the controlling company is a member of the subsidiary company and has the right to appoint or remove a majority of its board of directors;

- the subsidiary company is a subsidiary company of another company which is also owned by the controlling company.

See Example 1 for an illustration of a practical example of how the control test would be applied.

Example 1

ABC Holding Co Ltd owns 75% of the shares in DEF Ltd. The latter company owns 100% of the shares in GHI Ltd. ABC Holding Co Ltd also has a joint venture arrangement whereby it owns 50% of the shares in JKL Ltd.

To date, each of the companies has been registered for VAT in its own right – but the group finance director now wishes to apply for a group registration to bring all four companies under one VAT umbrella.

Solution – there is no problem with DEF Ltd being part of the group registration as it is controlled by ABC Holding Co Ltd because of share capital ownership. Equally, GHI Ltd is effectively owned by ABC Holding Co Ltd as well through its relationship with DEF Ltd. However, JKL Ltd cannot be part of the group because it is not controlled by ABC Holding Co Ltd. A separate company has the same level of control over the company (the joint owner) so the control test is not met.

Note – it is possible that the control objective can be met by one private individual owning the majority of shares in a number of different companies. Equally, two or more individuals as a partnership can control all of the other entities. However, the most common arrangement is where a master company owns shares in a series of trading companies eg as a holding company structure.

Other rules that need to be met in order to satisfy the group registration requirements are as follows:

- each of the bodies within the group must be established in the UK or have a fixed establishment in the UK;

- where applicable, the group structure must satisfy the anti-avoidance rules specified by HMRC to avoid the rules being exploited for an unfair tax gain (these rules are mainly designed to counter specific planning measures carried out by larger organisations so are outside the scope of this book – see **3.5** below for a brief summary of the key points).

A company is established in the UK if its principal place of business is in the UK, and the management and control of the company is UK based. A company is classed as having a fixed establishment in the UK if it has a real and permanent trading presence in the UK.

For VAT purposes, a company is not classed as being established in the UK or having a fixed establishment in the UK just by being incorporated in the UK and having its registered office in the UK – or if it is a UK branch of an overseas company.

Applying for a group registration

3.3   The basic outcome of applying for a new group registration is that the existing VAT registration numbers of the separate entities will be cancelled, and a new registration formed for the group.

Once a group registration has been created, it is fairly simple to add new entities to the group or, where appropriate, remove individual members from the group.

There are three main forms to complete when applying for a group registration:

- VAT 1 – main registration form signed by the representative member;

- VAT 50 – signed by either the applicant company or the person controlling the group;

- VAT 51 – relevant to each company applying to join the group (signed by the same person as the Form VAT 50).

Note – there is also Form VAT 56 that is used if there is a change in the representative member of the group.

Once a group registration has been established, Forms VAT 50 and VAT 51 will also need to be completed for each company that joins or leaves the group.

HMRC aims to approve an application for group registration within 15 days (and allocate a new registration number) but it has 90 days to make enquiries about the application and confirm its validity. The main aims of its checking procedures are as follows:

- to confirm the control test for the group is properly achieved;

- to ensure there are no revenue risks as far as the application is concerned.

In reality, the main reasons why an application would be refused to protect the revenue are as follows:

- the group's members have a poor history of complying with VAT requirements, which might pose a threat to HMRC's ability to collect VAT;

- HMRC suspects that the applicants intend to manipulate the group registration process through the use of tax avoidance schemes;

- group registration would create a distortion in the VAT liability of the group's supplies eg through partial exemption calculations.

Note – HMRC has confirmed that it will not refuse an application where the revenue loss follows from the normal operations of the group, eg because of the elimination of the VAT charge on supplies between group members. See Example 2.

Example 2

Jones Ltd is the holding company of two companies: Jones Estate Agency Services Ltd and Jones Surveyors Ltd. Jones Ltd employs 50 staff carrying out head office functions such as central finance, purchasing and marketing. It makes a quarterly management charge of £50,000 plus VAT to each of the two trading companies. Each of the three trading companies is registered for VAT on an individual basis – Jones Surveyors Ltd is fully taxable but Jones Estate Agency Services Ltd has some exempt income relevant to fees for arranging mortgages. What are the benefits in forming a group registration?

Solution – one of the main benefits of group registration is that charges between group members ignore VAT. Jones Ltd can continue to charge its subsidiary companies £50,000 per quarter for its management services but the group registration arrangement means it must not add VAT to this fee. This does not produce any tax saving to Jones Surveyors Ltd because this company is fully taxable and able to recover any VAT it is charged as input tax. However, Jones Estate Agency Services Ltd has some exempt income, so would suffer a restriction on the input tax charged by its parent company.

In the situation above, there is a tax saving as a result of group registration but this is a normal benefit of the group structure, so would not be blocked by HMRC.

If HMRC is not satisfied with the validity or fairness of an application, it will seek further information to establish the motives for requesting group registration. In reality, the motives should be mainly linked to the administrative benefits of the arrangement, namely the need to avoid charging VAT on inter-company supplies and the benefits of only completing one VAT return each period.

HMRC will make a judgment based on the information it has received and any refusal of the taxpayer to co-operate in providing the requested information will be taken into account when it makes its decision.

Benefits and implications of group registration

3.4 Once a group registration has been established, the following key features will be evident.

- *Only one return needs to be completed for each VAT period* – however, there could still be considerable work involved in collating the figures submitted by each individual member of the group so it is important that the person completing the VAT return has good communication in place to ensure that all relevant figures are included on the consolidated return.

- *No VAT needs to be accounted for on supplies between group members* – as a consequence of this concession, there is also no need for VAT invoices to be issued for supplies between group members – charges could, for example, be dealt with by raising journals through inter-company accounts in the nominal ledger.

- *All members of the group are jointly and severally liable for any VAT due from the representative member* – this means that if the representative member cannot pay the debt owing to HMRC on, for example, the group VAT return, then each individual member is held liable for the amount of the debt until it is discharged.

- *The cash accounting limits, partial exemption de minimis limits, payment on account limits – all apply on a group basis rather than on an individual member basis* – this situation means, for example, that if company A has taxable turnover of £700,000 per year and company B has taxable turnover of £800,000 per year, then both companies would each be able to use cash accounting if they were registered for VAT on an individual basis. However, if the two companies were registered as part of a

VAT group, then the combined taxable turnover of £1,500,000 becomes relevant – and this exceeds the cash accounting limit of £1,350,000 per year.

- *Input tax recovery is based on how the VAT group as a whole uses the goods and services received by each individual member* – this is a very important point and is illustrated in Example 3 below.

- *Voluntary disclosure limits are based on the group as a whole* – if company A identifies an underpayment of £100,000, this would normally need to be corrected by making a voluntary disclosure to HMRC because the amount of tax clearly exceeds the voluntary disclosure limits (a disclosure must be made if the net error is more than £2,000 until 30 June 2008, this figure being increased to £10,000 or 1% of turnover up to £50,000 for errors discovered after 1 July 2008). However, if company B is in the same VAT group and has identified an error of £99,000 overpaid VAT, then the net group error is now less than the disclosure limits. The net underpayment of £1,000 can be corrected on the next VAT return submitted by the group.

Example 3

Following on from Example 2, Jones Ltd purchases new computer equipment that it leases to Jones Estate Agency Services Ltd for £2,000 per quarter. Jones Estate Agency Services Ltd uses the equipment to store all details of its mortgage customers and mortgage lenders with whom it deals.

Solution – although the supply from Jones Ltd to Jones Estate Agency Services Ltd is taxable (lease of computer equipment), the key point is that the VAT group is using the equipment in connection with its exempt supplies, ie arranging mortgages. The VAT group treatment is what counts and, therefore, Jones Ltd cannot reclaim the input tax on the initial purchase of the equipment.

Anti-avoidance measures

3.5 As explained at **3.1** above, HMRC has been very active in recent years to try and close loopholes in the legislation that have allowed certain group structures to produce an unfair result in terms of input tax recovery. For example, certain groups have benefited from an unfair recovery by introducing or taking a partly exempt company out of the group at a critical stage.

HMRC has extensive powers to deal with the manipulation of VAT groups – but these powers will mainly be applied to larger company structures where the amount of tax at stake is considerable.

The best advice to any adviser is to be very wary about implementing any scheme or structure for a client that appears too good to be true. One of the key principles of VAT is that input tax can be recovered to the extent that it relates to taxable supplies. If an arrangement appears to give high input tax recovery on an expense or asset that appears mainly relevant to exempt supplies, then there will almost certainly be a problem with the validity of the scheme.

Holding companies

3.6   The main function of many holding companies is to own shares and receive dividends in subsidiary companies – but they will sometimes make management charges to these subsidiary companies, and employ staff in support functions such as finance and administration.

As long as the management services are genuine supplies, then the holding company will be able to register for VAT in its own right, as these supplies are taxable. However, it is more common for the company to be a member of a VAT group.

When reviewing the validity of management services, HMRC takes the following points into account.

● Does the holding company employ any staff – ie who could be producing work or providing services that could be recharged to a subsidiary company as a genuine management charge?

● Are the directors the only people employed by the holding company – and are they also directors of the subsidiary companies as well? In such cases, there is unlikely to be a management charge arrangement.

● What supplies are covered by the charge? Is there evidence of purchase invoices being processed through the accounts of the holding company (for example, a group purchasing arrangement may be in place for certain overheads)? This type of arrangement would then add credibility to a recharge arrangement for services provided to subsidiary companies.

● Does the management charge have a proper basis of calculation – for example, cost basis plus percentage mark-up or recharge based on number of labour hours provided by the holding company to its subsidiaries?

No taxable supplies other than management services to a group member

3.7   There is no problem forming a group registration if the only taxable supplies relate to management services supplied by one group member to another. The initial thinking might be that this measure would be blocked because it will, in reality, generate nil VAT returns in most cases. See Example 4 to illustrate this point.

Example 4

Good Causes Ltd is a registered charity that owns a trading subsidiary called Good Causes Trading Ltd. Neither company is registered for VAT because their supplies are either outside the scope of VAT or exempt from VAT. However, Good Causes Ltd incurs costs on behalf of Good Causes Trading Ltd, and wants to make a management charge of £100,000 per annum for these services.

Solution – The problem with the above situation is that Good Causes Ltd will need to charge output tax on the management services once it has exceeded the VAT registration limit (£68,000 per annum with effect from 1 May 2009) but Good Causes Trading Ltd will not be able to reclaim this VAT as input tax because it is not making any taxable supplies.

However, the two companies could register for VAT as a group registration (the control conditions are met without any problem), which means that supplies of goods and services between group members are made without charging VAT.

The end result is that the VAT returns will always be nil because there is no taxable income being generated by either company outside of the VAT group. This is not a problem. The reality is that Good Causes Ltd is making supplies that would require it to register for VAT in its own right – but these supplies escape a VAT charge because they are being made to another entity in the same VAT group.

Property transactions

3.8 An option to tax election made on land or buildings by a member of a VAT group will apply to all other members of the same VAT group (see Chapter 28 for a detailed analysis of the option to tax regulations). The election will also apply to future group members, ie those that join the group after the election has been made. The election will also remain valid for those companies that may leave the VAT group in the future.

The capital goods scheme is a complex part of the VAT legislation (see Chapter 9) and a scheme adjustment may be needed when a company leaves or joins a VAT group.

Divisional registration

3.9 As explained at **3.1** above, divisional registration allows a company that is divided into self-accounting units to submit divisional VAT returns

– rather than one overall return for the company. Each division will have its own VAT registration number – however, the corporate body is still treated as a single taxable person and is responsible for the VAT debts and responsibilities of all the divisions.

The main reason why a company could request divisional registration is because it would anticipate genuine difficulties in getting all of its VAT figures together within the 30-day deadline to submit one corporate return.

HMRC rules for divisional registration to be granted are as follows:

● all divisions must be independent accounting units with their own account-ing system – and must either be operating from different geographical locations, supplying different commodities or carrying out different func-tions, e g manufacture, wholesale, retail, export etc;

● all the divisions must be registered, even those whose turnover is below the compulsory registration limits;

● the corporate body as a whole must be, or be treated as being, fully taxable, i e if there is any partial exemption implications, then the corporate body must be de minimis;

● all divisions must complete VAT returns for the same periods – i e it is not allowed for some divisions to complete their returns under calendar quarters and others to complete their returns in months ending April, July, October and January.

An important point to remember is that charges between different divisions of the same company do not qualify as supplies for VAT purposes – and no VAT should be charged (or VAT invoices issued) for these transactions.

A company applying for divisional registration must make its application by letter and send it to the National Registration Service, along with Form VAT 1 for each division of the company. The letter must state why the company has a need for divisional registration.

Note – a corporate body constituted outside the UK may apply for divisional registration as long as it has at least two self-accounting units in the UK and it can also comply with the above conditions.

The need to avoid an overlap between group registration and divisional registration

3.10   If a company that belongs to a VAT group wishes to benefit from divisional registration, it will firstly have to leave the VAT group and then make an application for divisional registration. This is because group registration is only available to corporate bodies under common control, not divisions of those corporate bodies. Equally, an existing divisional registration must be cancelled if the corporate body wishes to join a VAT group.

Overall, therefore, group registration and divisional registration operate totally independently – there is no scope for any overlap of the two arrangements.

Planning points to consider

3.11 The following points should be given consideration.

- For a group registration to be accepted by HMRC, the control test needs to be fully met. This means that joint venture arrangements (50:50 control between separate parties) will not be eligible for group registration.

- A holding company making management charges to its trading subsidiaries will have to charge VAT on these supplies if it is registered for VAT. This could lead to a source of non-claimable VAT if the recipient makes some exempt supplies. A group registration avoids this problem because no VAT is charged on supplies between entities within the same group.

- However, be aware of the need to consider input tax for the group as a whole and its relationship to supplies made to external customers. If input tax incurred by one group company relates to exempt supplies made by another group company, then the input tax will be classed as relevant to an exempt supply, ie partial exemption implications.

- Ensure that a holding company registered for VAT is making genuine taxable supplies to its trading subsidiaries, eg for management services, consultancy fees, etc.

- There is scope for a group registration to be formed even if the only taxable supplies relate to management services between group members. This strategy will avoid output tax being charged on such supplies and therefore prevent non-reclaimable input tax being incurred by the recipient.

- A request for divisional registration must clearly explain why the business feels it needs this facility – usually this is because of difficulties collating all figures together within one VAT return for a company based on different regions, products, etc.

Chapter 4

Transfer of a Going Concern

Key topics in this chapter:

- What constitutes the transfer of a going concern (sale of a business).

- Key rules that need to be in place for an arrangement to qualify as the transfer of a going concern.

- Important points to consider for a property rental business or for a sale that involves a property where the option to tax has been made.

- Input tax deduction on the costs of selling a business.

- Approach adopted by HMRC when reviewing transfer of a going concern situation.

- VAT liability of goodwill payments.

- Record-keeping rules following the sale of a business.

- The option to retain the seller's VAT number.

Identifying transfer of a going concern situation

Introduction

4.1 There is a widely used phrase in accounting circles: 'If in doubt, charge VAT'.

In most cases, this is probably sound advice, especially if the person being charged VAT is able to fully reclaim it as input tax. However, there is one situation where this phrase should not be used – that is, concerning the transfer of a business (for a consideration) as a going concern. Basically, this is because HMRC has the power in certain circumstances to disallow any input tax claimed by the buyer, even if he holds a proper tax invoice and the seller has accounted for output tax on the amount charged.

The transfer of a going concern rules basically state that if certain important conditions are met, then the sale proceeds of the transfer (including all assets sold) will not constitute a taxable supply – in other words, the proceeds will be outside the scope of VAT.

In reality, charging or not charging VAT on the transfer of a business as a going concern is a very important topic – simply because the amounts of money involved can be so large.

What is the transfer of a going concern?

4.2 The key point to remember is that for the transfer of a going concern situation to apply, there must be the sale of the whole business, or part of a business. It is not acceptable to asset strip a business (selling different assets to different people) and claim this is the transfer of a going concern. If the business is not being transferred as a going concern, then normal VAT rules apply, ie output tax must be charged on the supply, unless it is specifically zero-rated, exempt or outside the scope of VAT. See Examples 1 and 2 below.

Example 1

Mr Jones owns a jeweller's shop in a local town centre, and has decided he wants to retire and live in Spain. He holds a big closing down sale to sell his stock; he then sells the fixtures and fittings to another jeweller's shop in the next street; a property developer buys the freehold of the shop because he wants to convert the property into luxury flats.

Solution – in this particular case, there is no transfer of a going concern situation, and the VAT liability of each separate sale must be considered. The sale of stock, fixtures and fittings will be standard rated, and the sale of the freehold property will be exempt unless the seller has opted to tax the property at any time or if it is less than 3 years old.

However, if Mr Jones had sold the business as a whole and the buyer was continuing to trade as a jeweller's shop, then this would have been the sale of a going concern, and no VAT would have been charged if the relevant rules had been met.

Example 2

Mrs Smith runs a bakery shop in the local town centre. She does not own the property from which she trades – this is rented on a 5-year negotiable lease. However, she owns the fixtures and fittings and other plant and equipment, and the business name of 'Smiths Bakeries' has established a good reputation during the last 20 years.

Mrs Smith has decided to retire and sells the business to one of her staff, Miss Baker, who will continue trading as a baker, but changes the name of the business to 'Eat Well'.

Solution – although Mrs Smith does not own the property from where the business trades, she is still selling a business to Miss Baker, and therefore the transfer of a going concern rules will apply. Miss Baker will benefit from the use of all assets bought from her employer, as well as the business location, good trading name, supplier accounts and experience of the staff in the business.

The key point is that Miss Baker is continuing the same type of business as Mrs Smith (we develop the theme of what constitutes the same business in the next section). It is irrelevant that Miss Baker intends to change the trading name of the business – it is what the business is doing that counts (ie continuing to trade as a baker), not what it is called.

Key rules for transfer of a going concern situation to be met

4.3   The two examples illustrated at **4.2** were both very clear-cut. In the first example, there was no business sale, and the assets of the business were being sold off on an individual basis. In the second example, an actual business was being sold – in effect, all that was changing was the ownership of the business from one person to another.

There are other situations where the rules may not be so simple, for example, in the following scenarios.

- What would happen if the person buying the business wanted to change the activity slightly – for example, buying an Indian restaurant but changing it into a Chinese restaurant?

- What if the new owner wanted to close the business down for 6 months and go on a world cruise before he started trading? Does the break in trading jeopardise the transfer of a going concern rules?

- What if the new owner had no intention of running the business himself – but wanted to sell it straight away for a profit to a third party?

There are five main conditions (discussed below) that need to be met to satisfy the transfer of a going concern rules – as long as these are all satisfied, then the supply from the vendor to the buyer can be made without charging VAT.

(A) Same type of business must be operated by new owner

4.4   The person buying the business must use the assets to carry on the same type of business as the seller. If this is not the case, then the transfer is not as a going concern, and VAT must be charged.

In effect, HMRC is quite flexible on this rule – partly because it accepts that there can be grey areas as to whether exactly the same type of business is being operated.

To quote two tribunal cases, the going concern rules applied in the case of *Tahmassebi t/a Sale Pepe v Customs and Excise Comrs* (2 March 1995, unreported) (MAN/94/197 13177). In this case, an Indian restaurant became an Italian restaurant, and the decision confirmed that the same type of business was being operated, ie a restaurant, even though the menu was different.

In the case of *G Draper (Marlow) Ltd v Comrs of Customs and Excise* (28 April 1986, unreported) (LON/85/439 2079), the ownership of a public house was transferred, but the new owners radically changed the business to appeal to a totally different client base (eg a local beer drinking pub was turned into a trendy wine bar). In this case, the decision was that the new business was carrying on the same business as its predecessor, ie the sale of alcohol to the general public, even though its customer base was different.

However, the rules do need to be carefully considered to avoid potential pitfalls – see Example 3.

Example 3

ABC Ltd owns a pub which it rents out to tenants – the tenants are effectively in business on their own account, selling beers wines and spirits to the general public. ABC Ltd exercised the option to tax on the pub when it first acquired the freehold interest.

The pub performs so well that another company, DEF Ltd, agrees to buy the pub from ABC Ltd – which it will operate as a pub on its own account.

Solution – the initial conclusion might be to say that the business has been sold as a going concern and therefore no VAT is due on the consideration paid by DEF Ltd.

However, ABC Ltd is in the business of property rental, and the new owner is in the business of running a pub. So there is a change in activity – which means the going concern rules have not been met. As ABC Ltd has opted to tax the property, it must charge output tax on the proceeds. However, DEF Ltd should be able to recover input tax on this amount, so its only problem is the initial cash flow outlay.

(B) Any part transfer must be capable of separate operation

4.5   It is possible that a vendor may decide to sell part of his business and retain ownership of another part. For example, a publican operating a catering function within his pub may decide to sell the catering arm of his business, but retain the wet sales.

However, the key point is that the person selling the business must be able to continue running the remaining part of the business without the part that has been sold. In most cases, this should not prove a problem.

(C) The new owner must be VAT registered

4.6   This is an important point for all tax advisers acting for a vendor. If the vendor is VAT registered, then the buyer must also be VAT registered in order for the VAT charge to be outside the scope of VAT.

In effect, the new owners are likely to be VAT registered as a matter of course, but there are some situations that could avoid a need for registering:

- If, at the date the transfer takes place, the buyer does not anticipate that his sales in the next 12 months will exceed the deregistration limits (£65,000 of annual taxable sales with effect from 1 April 2008), then he has no obligation to register for VAT. This could apply, for example, if he decides to work shorter hours.

- If the seller was registered for VAT on a voluntary basis, then the buyer will not have an obligation to register because the turnover in the previous 12 months was below the compulsory registration limit (which is relevant for the new owner – if the compulsory VAT registration limit was exceeded by the previous owner in his last 12 months, then he has an obligation to register himself as well from the first day he takes ownership of the business).

In theory, it is possible for a buyer to not have a VAT number at the time of the transfer. This is because the strict wording of the law (*SI 1995/1268, reg 5*) states the condition as being that the buyer 'immediately becomes as a result of the transfer a taxable person'. A 'taxable person' is defined as someone who is registered or should be registered for VAT. However, it is recommended that any element of doubt be avoided by ensuring the buyer is VAT registered at the time of the transfer.

Consider the circumstances illustrated at Example 4.

Example 4

Mr Giles trades as a surveyor and is selling his practice as a going concern to Mr Hardwick on 1 October 2008. The taxable turnover of the business in the 12 months to 30 September 2008 was £70,000 – ie above the compulsory VAT registration limit. However, Mr Hardwick enjoys fishing and has decided to reduce the activity of the practice and only work 4 days a week instead of the 5 worked by Mr Giles.

Solution – in effect, Mr Hardwick's expected turnover in the next 12 months will be £56,000 (all other things being equal) which is below the deregistration limit of £65,000 that applied at this date. He does not need to register for VAT.

If Mr Hardwick does not register for VAT, then the transfer of a going concern conditions are not met and Mr Giles must charge VAT on the sale proceeds.

Note – remember, however, that the option of voluntary registration is always open to a business, even if it trades below the compulsory registration limits.

(D) The transfer must put the new owner in possession of a business which can be operated as such and the business must be a going concern at the time of the transfer

4.7 In this situation there should be no break in trading immediately before or after the transfer.

There will inevitably be situations where a business has ceased to trade because of lack of profits and commercial viability. In such cases, employees will be laid off, stock will have been sold, and advertising to generate new business will have been cancelled.

If the business is then sold, possibly to a company that thinks it can recreate a profitable operation, then it has to be carefully considered whether the business is now a 'going concern' at the time of transfer. If not, then the transfer conditions have not been met, and VAT must be charged on the supply.

In effect, the key question to consider is whether the new owner is placed in a position after the transfer where he is in possession of a business, or whether he has effectively bought an empty shell that he needs to build up from scratch.

As a separate point, a break in trading does not necessarily mean that a business is not a going concern. For example, if a seaside guest house only trades from May to September when the weather is good, then it will still be a going concern if it is sold the following March, even though it would not have traded for 6 months. This is because the break in trading is due to the seasonal nature of its trade, not the fact that it has been permanently closed down.

Again, the new owner should not have a long break in trading after he has bought the business. For example, a 3-month closure for redecoration works would not be a problem – but closure for 12 months while the new owner went on a round the world cruise is not likely to be acceptable.

(E) There should not be consecutive transfers of the same business

4.8   There are some situations where company A will sell its assets to company B, which immediately sells them to company C. This arrangement can sometimes apply to property rental businesses, where lease issues are quite complex.

In such cases, company B is not eligible to benefit from the special transfer provisions – because it is not carrying on the same business as company A.

Option to tax

4.9   With most complex subjects on VAT, issues concerning property and the option to tax are never too far away.

The key point as far as land and buildings are concerned is to remember that there is an extra stage to the rules.

Basically, if the seller has opted to tax the property that is now being sold, then the buyer must also make an election to tax the property in question before the supply is made and confirm in writing to the seller that this option will not be disapplied. If this condition is not met, then the seller must charge VAT on the property part of the deal, even if the transfer of a going concern rules are fully met. See Example 5.

Example 5

Mr Smith is selling his restaurant business as a going concern to Mr Jones, and the sale proceeds of £2m can be split as follows: £400,000 fixtures and fittings; £600,000 goodwill; freehold property on which an option to tax election has been made is £1m. What is the position as far as the option to tax is concerned?

Solution – before the deal is completed, Mr Jones must opt to tax the property with HMRC and provide evidence of this action to Mr Smith. The whole deal will then qualify as outside the scope of VAT.

However, if Mr Jones fails to make the election, or decides it is not in his best interests to make the election (eg he expects to make a big profit on selling the property in a few years time to a buyer that may not be able to recover VAT), then the deal will have to charge £175,000 VAT on the property only. The fixtures, fittings and goodwill will still be outside the scope of the tax.

Property rental business

4.10   A situation that has become quite common in recent years has been where a property has been sold to a third party – but with an existing lease in place with a tenant. In these situations, the sale can qualify as a transfer of a going concern (sale of a property rental business).

However, if the seller has opted to tax the property in question, then the buyer must also elect to tax the property himself before the deal is completed. If this election is made without any problem, the VAT charge can be avoided.

Input tax

4.11   Although the sale of a business as a going concern is not classed as a taxable supply, input tax can still be recovered on the related costs of the sale (eg solicitors' fees) as long as the business in question was only making taxable supplies, ie able to fully recover its input tax. If the business was partly exempt, then the costs would be classed as a general overhead item and input tax apportioned according to its partial exemption method.

See Example 6.

Example 6

Mike owns an estate agency business, which has two main sources of income: sale of houses on a commission-only basis (taxable activity); fees earned on arranging insurance products and mortgages for customers (exempt activity).

The business has always adopted the standard method of calculation as far as partial exemption is concerned (non-attributable input tax apportioned according to income percentages) and the taxable sales have always been 60% of total sales.

Mike is now selling the business to John for £1.3m and the sale qualifies as a going concern because all of the relevant conditions are met – no output tax is therefore charged on the proceeds. Mike's legal and other costs related to the sale are £65,000 plus VAT of £11,375.

Solution – as part of Mike's activities are exempt, he cannot recover all of the input tax incurred on the costs of selling his business to John. The VAT charge of £11,375 is classed as non-attributable input tax within his partial exemption calculation, so he can recover 60% of this amount on his return, ie £6,825. If Mike's activities were wholly taxable (ie commission from house sales only) then he would have been able to recover all of the VAT on his disposal costs.

HMRC approach to a transfer

4.12   Imagine the following situation: Mr Jones has traded as a limited company and now sells his jewellery business for £430,000 as a going concern, and charges output tax of £75,250 to the new owner (assuming

VAT rate of 17.5%). He then disappears to Spain, and liquidates the company without ever paying the final output tax liability to HMRC. This is bad news for HMRC because it has no way of recovering the VAT debt because the company no longer has any assets – and the chances are that Mr Jones will be out of sight, out of mind.

In this situation, HMRC will probably use its powers to confirm that the business was the transfer of a going concern, meeting the various rules, and that the supply was therefore outside the scope of VAT. The input tax then claimed by the buyer would be non-reclaimable on the basis that it does not relate to a taxable supply.

In effect, therefore, sound VAT advice on transfer of a going concern issues is probably quite unique in that it is probably more important for the buyer to get it right than the seller. The other relevant point is that even if the buyer is able to recover input tax on any charge, there is a significant cash flow disadvantage if he has to pay 17.5% of the buying price as VAT, and then wait 3 months to recover the money on his first VAT return.

As far as identifying a transfer of a going concern situation is concerned, HMRC will obviously analyse the key issues described at **4.3–4.8**.

However, it is also advised to take the following points into account when determining whether there has been the transfer of a going concern.

- *Goodwill* – a charge for goodwill (see **4.13**) normally indicates a transfer of a going concern because the buyer is making payment for an intangible asset.

- *Customer lists, knowledge of customers* – the sale or transfer of a list of potential or previous customers is normally a good indication of a transfer of a going concern. Equally, if a purchaser takes over existing contracts with suppliers or customers (and related obligations) then this also suggests that the buyer is carrying on the business of the seller.

- *Stock* – the transfer of stock to a single purchaser can indicate a transfer of a going concern. In contrast, the sale of stock to a number of different parties could indicate that assets are being divided rather than a business being sold.

- *Premises, plant and equipment* – many businesses are closely linked to their premises, and the transfer/sale of the premises clearly suggests a transfer of a going concern, as long as the buyer is not intending to totally change the nature of trading in the building. The sale of plant and equipment is also a good indicator, however, it is possible that the buyer may already have his own equipment, so there could still be a perfectly valid transfer of a going concern arrangement without plant and equipment being a part of the sale.

- *Staff* – if the new business takes over the contracts of existing staff, this will again suggest a transfer of a going concern

- *Advertisements* – the way in which a sale is publicised is also relevant. For example, a newspaper advertisement using the phrase: 'under new management' clearly indicates an existing business is being continued but by a new owner.

The key point to remember is that it is important to look at the bigger picture when making conclusions about whether an arrangement qualifies as the transfer of a going concern. It is not appropriate to make a conclusion based on one piece of information in isolation. For example, it would be wrong to conclude that a transfer of a going concern situation could not apply just because the new owners did not buy the fixtures and fittings from the previous owner (in this situation, the decision not to buy the fixtures and fittings is likely to be for commercial motives).

Goodwill

4.13 The key advantage for a person selling his business as a going concern, rather than the separate sale of assets, is that he should also be able to receive some payment for goodwill.

Goodwill is an intangible asset, and reflects the difference between the value of the assets a person is buying, and the actually payment made. For example, if a business comprises stock, fixtures and fittings and a freehold property with a combined value of £380,000, but the business is sold for £430,000, then the additional £50,000 relates to goodwill (the buyer is effectively paying for the benefit he will gain from the trading name, customer database, location of the shop and possibly staff that will continue to be employed by the new owners).

For VAT purposes, the money received for goodwill is standard rated – unless the transfer of a going concern rules are met.

Change in legal entity and sales of shares

Change in legal entity

4.14 A common situation that occurs in business is where a sole trader decides to expand his activities by taking on a partner. Equally, an existing partnership may be expanded to include an extra partner and, very common in recent times, a sole trader or partnership business may become a limited company. The benefits of becoming a limited company were particularly good in the early part of this century, due to generous corporation tax rules.

As far as VAT is concerned, a change in legal entity (ie sole trader business becoming a partnership) represents the transfer of a going concern. However, the addition of a new partner to an existing partnership does not produce a transfer of a going concern situation.

The VAT registration issues of a change in legal entity are considered at 2.9.

Sale of shares

4.15   When a business is transferred that trades as a limited company, there are two main ways of making the sale:

(a)   the existing owner could sell his shares to the new owner – in this situation, there is no transfer of a business as a going concern because one person is just taking over the existing business from another person through a share transfer; or

(b)   the company assets could be sold to the new owner (including goodwill) – in this situation, there could be a transfer of a going concern if the usual rules are met.

Record-keeping requirements

4.16   The seller of a business will retain the records of his business that are relevant to the period before the date of his sale. However, since 1 September 2007:

- The seller must give the buyer any information the latter needs to comply with his duties under the *VATA 1994*.

- If the buyer of the business decides to retain the VAT number of the seller (see **4.17**), then the seller is still required to transfer his records to the buyer. However, the seller has the right to approach HMRC for permission to retain his records if this is appropriate to his circumstances.

- HMRC can also disclose to the buyer any information it holds on the business that is needed for him to comply with his VAT obligations.

Note – the three main situations where the above conditions become relevant relate to partial exemption issues (agreed special methods in the past etc), option to tax elections (in relation to commercial property) and the capital goods scheme. The capital goods scheme requires adjustments for up to 10 years in the case of land and property transactions, and is often still relevant when a business is transferred.

Retaining the seller's VAT number

4.17   It is possible for the buyer of a business to retain the seller's VAT registration number by completing Form VAT 68. However, this is an unwise move in most cases because the new owner is also taking over the potential VAT debts of the previous business. It is suggested that a new VAT registration number be obtained to avoid this potential risk.

Planning points to consider

4.18   The following points should be given consideration.

- When acting for the buyer of a business, ensure that VAT is not incorrectly charged by the vendor – if a transfer of a going concern arrangement is evident, then HMRC has the power to disallow any input tax claimed by the buyer, even if he holds a proper tax invoice and has paid the VAT to the seller in good faith. Remember – the transfer of a going concern rules are compulsory – it is not possible to choose to 'opt out' by, for example, playing safe and charging VAT.

- It is also important for buyers to avoid paying VAT if possible because of the cash flow problems of paying the VAT to the seller and then waiting up to three months to reclaim it on a VAT return.

- If acting for the seller, remember that the buyer must be VAT registered or become VAT registered as a result of the sale – otherwise the transfer of a going concern rules are not met.

- In most cases, it will be clear if a business is being sold as a going concern, or whether individual assets are being sold. Advisers need to be aware of the key rules to consider in cases that are not as clear-cut – as explained at **4.3**.

- Be aware that even though the proceeds from a transfer of a going concern sale are outside the scope of VAT, the related input tax on selling costs can still be reclaimed as long as the business has activities that are wholly taxable. If part of the business income is exempt, then a restriction on the input tax claimed will be evident using the normal partial exemption method adopted by the business.

- There are important issues to consider if the sale of a going concern includes a property where the option to tax election has been made by the seller – as explained at **4.9**. The decision to opt to tax a property is very important for any business, because once made, it cannot be revoked for 20 years.

Chapter 5

Artificial Separation of Business Activities

Key topics in this chapter:

- What constitutes an artificial separation of business activities.

- Legislation and key rules to determine whether two or more businesses will be classed as one business.

- Financial, organisational and economic links between businesses.

- The importance of normal commercial arrangements between two separated businesses.

- The motive to avoid paying VAT.

- Arrangements for businesses involving members of the same family.

- Effect of an HMRC direction that only one business exists in practice.

- Case examples on artificial separation of business activities.

- Approach to be adopted when dealing with clients.

Separating business activities

Introduction

5.1 Many clients have an interest in more than one business – and from a VAT aspect, a challenge occurs when one of these businesses is VAT registered, and the other is trading below the VAT registration threshold. If the business trading below the VAT limits is mainly dealing with members of the public (ie who are unable to reclaim any of the VAT they pay as input tax) then it is in the interests of the owners to avoid VAT registration if possible.

However, HMRC has very extensive powers to rule that two or more businesses could be treated as a single business, effectively bringing all entities into the VAT system. It will take this course of action if it considers that the separation of business activities has been carried out in an 'artificial' manner, with the primary intention of the arrangement being to avoid paying VAT.

For tax advisers, there are many opportunities available to advise clients about the correct manner of properly setting up separate business activities – but it is important that clients follow through any advice given with proper action. A review of tribunal cases on this subject highlights that most arrangements that fail are due to the fact that the owner(s) did not create a clear division between their different business activities.

Definition of an 'artificial' scheme

5.2 The dictionary definition of 'artificial' is something that is not real. In effect, therefore, the key question an adviser should ask when discussing the separation of business activities with a client is:

> 'Is this a genuine business arrangement made for commercial reasons and with commercial motives – or is it an artificial measure designed to avoid paying VAT?'

Consider Example 1 below.

Example 1

Mr A owns 12 laundrettes, each with taxable turnover of about £60,000 per year. Each laundrette operates in a different town, under the trading name of 'Keep Clean'.

Mr A decides that in order to avoid becoming VAT registered, he will set up a separate limited company for each different outlet – each limited company will then be trading below the VAT registration limit and he will therefore avoid the need to register for VAT. This is important for him on a commercial basis, because all of his customers are members of the public, unable to recover any VAT charged as input tax.

Solution – this situation illustrates both the motives and benefits of separating business activities. It is clear that there is, in reality, only one business, but Mr A has devised a specific scheme to try and create twelve different businesses. In this situation, HMRC will issue a directive that there is only one actual business, with a combined turnover exceeding the VAT limits.

Note – it is important that HMRC has the power to take action in these situations, otherwise there would be a massive competitive disadvantage for other laundrettes who accept the requirement to be VAT registered.

Legislation and key rules

5.3 The power of HMRC to deal with artificial business separations was greatly strengthened after the 1997 Budget, when a new *para 1A* was inserted into the legislation as an amendment to *VAT Act 1994, Sch 1*. The new paragraph gave extra weight to *para 2* – with the following words:

'1A

(1) *Paragraph 2* below is for the purpose of preventing the maintenance or creation of any artificial separation of business activities carried on by two or more persons from resulting in an avoidance of VAT.

(2) In determining for the purpose of *sub-paragraph 1A* above whether any separation of business activities is artificial, regard shall be had to the extent to which the different persons carrying on those activities are closely bound to one another by financial, economic and organisational links'.

We will consider each of the points mentioned in the last sentence of *para 2* – and the key questions HMRC considers when looking at a particular arrangement.

(a) Financial links:

- Is financial support given by one part of the business to another?
- Would one part of the business not be financially viable without support from another part of the business?
- Is there a common financial interest in the proceeds of the business?

(b) Economic links:

- Are both businesses trying to realise the same economic objective?
- Do the activities of one part of the business benefit the other part?
- Are both businesses supplying the same circle of customers?

(c) Organisational links:

- Do both businesses have common management?
- Are there common employees?
- Are premises shared?
- Is there common use of the same equipment?

Normal commercial arrangements

5.4 One of the main changes in VAT thinking in recent years has been for tribunals and higher courts to consider an issue based on what the customer perceives to be happening – or what he perceives that he is buying with his money.

Consider the circumstances in Example 2

Example 2

Mr B provides accountancy services from his office in the High Street. Mr C trades from the same premises, offering a service to complete tax returns.

Neither of the two businesses is VAT registered, as they each have sales of £40,000 per annum. The following facts apply to their respective organisations:

- Mr B and Mr C use the same computers to carry out their work – they sit together in an open plan office in the same room;

- they have many common clients, with Mr B doing the accounts work and Mr C the tax returns for these clients;

- Mr B employs a receptionist who also spends a lot of her time working for Mr C;

- Mr C employs a secretary who also spends a lot of her time doing work for Mr B;

- they have a joint advert in the local newspaper – promoting a combined service of 'preparing accounts and completing tax returns'.

They receive a visit from HMRC, who decide that there is only one combined business, therefore trading above the VAT limits.

Solution – this particular arrangement has made it very easy for HMRC to rule that there is only one business evident in practice. As mentioned at 5.3, there are clearly financial, economic and organisational links between the two businesses. Equally important, any customer dealing with the business would only perceive that there was, in reality, one business.

At this stage, it is useful to consider three key words on this topic – 'normal commercial arrangements'.

The key question to consider when looking at an arrangement is to ask the question: Are the links between the two businesses based on standard commercial arrangements?

For example, in the case of Mr B and Mr C, there is a situation of staff being employed by one of the businesses but partly used by another business. In such situations, it would be expected that any time spent doing the work of the other party would be charged at an agreed rate on a time basis, with an invoice raised explaining the services carried out.

Equally, if one business benefits from using the assets of another business (and it should be noted that from an accounting aspect, an asset can only be owned by one business) then it would be expected that a charge arrangement would be evident for these supplies.

In reality, if a formal charging structure is not in place for two closely linked businesses, then it will be a clear indication to HMRC that it is dealing with a case of artificial separation.

Motive to avoid paying VAT

5.5 As discussed at 5.3, a key phrase in the legislation at *para 2* was 'resulting in an avoidance of VAT' (*VAT Act 1994, Sch 1 para 2*).

Consider the following examples.

Example 3

Mary and June share the premises of a unit in a local village, running a health food shop. They both trade as separate legal entities, and neither is VAT registered. Their combined turnover is £80,000 per year. Mary sells organic fruit and June sells organic vegetables (all take-away sales). They maintain that the reason for keeping their businesses separate is because Mary has a high level of expertise in issues concerning fruit, and June specialises in vegetables.

Solution – the key point with this situation is that the supplies made by Mary and June would all be zero-rated if they became VAT registered – so the arrangement between them regarding the structure of the business does not result 'in an avoidance of VAT'. It could be argued that there would be benefits in both of them registering for VAT on a voluntary basis, because they could then recover input tax on overheads they incur – producing a direct improvement to overall profits.

Example 4

Bill and Ben are sole traders, working from a small unit offering carpentry services to the general public. Bill makes and repairs tables – Ben makes and repairs chairs. Their turnover is £25,000 each – and they have very close organisational, financial and economic links, sharing the same equipment, premises and customer base.

Solution – the structure would be prone to challenge by HMRC – but the key point is that the combined turnover of Bill and Ben (£25,000 × 2 = £50,000) is still below the VAT registration threshold. The motive to avoid VAT cannot therefore be proved by HMRC.

However, if the businesses grow so that combined trading exceeds the VAT registration limit, then the operation will need to be reviewed to ensure there will be no problems with HMRC in the future.

In effect, therefore, the approach adopted by HMRC is to clearly identify situations where tax is being lost through artificial arrangements being created. In the case of a business making exclusively or mainly zero-rated supplies, or in cases where the combined taxable turnover of the different businesses is less than the VAT registration limit, this would not be appropriate.

Family business arrangements

5.6 As a general point, it is more difficult for HMRC to combine businesses where the individuals are not members of the same family. This is because one of the key arguments that could be put forward for individuals who are not related to each other is as follows:

'The main reason for having two separate businesses is not the avoidance of VAT but because we want to ensure that we are each rewarded with profits according to our own efforts'.

In other words, there are clear commercial reasons for separate trading, even though the arrangement may appear artificial.

However, the reasons why many family business arrangements fail to convince HMRC is due to the following reasons.

- Normal commercial arrangements do not tend to be followed in such a strict manner. For example, if the husband is running one business, and the wife running another business that is closely linked to the husband's business, then there should be market rate charges made for any shared overheads, equipment, staff etc.

  In reality, this principle of recharging for shared overheads tends to be forgotten where family members are involved.

- In many cases, the activities of one part of the business benefit the other part. For example, a common situation where many taxpayers have encountered problems is where the husband operates as a publican for the wet sales (and is VAT registered) and the wife operates as a sole trader running the catering part of the business (trading below the VAT limits).

- Problems in such cases tend to be that cash takings for the two parts of the business can be confused; staff on duty carry out work for both parts of the business (even though they are only on the payroll of the publican); there is no formal charge arrangement to cover the cost of equipment and overheads used by the wife in her catering activity. Again, the family issue in this arrangement makes it less important to ensure arm's length transactions are the norm.

- Common management – in reality, the husband and wife are likely to make joint decisions regarding the overall direction of the combined business – rather than each separate part. This makes it more difficult to convince HMRC that there are two distinct businesses in operation.

However, despite the list of potential problems above, it is by no means impossible for family members to have separate businesses which are acceptable to HMRC.

Effect of a direction issued by HMRC

5.7 A positive point is that HMRC cannot issue a direction on a retrospective basis. This is confirmed in *VATA 1994, Sch 1 para 2*:

> 'The persons named in the direction shall be treated as a single taxable person carrying on the activities of a business named in the direction and *that taxable person shall be liable to be registered under this Schedule with effect from the date of the direction or, if the direction so provides, such later date as may be specified therein.*' (emphasis added)

The above regulation means that separation could prove effective until it is discovered by HMRC, which could be many years. However, there is still a risk that HMRC could take a stronger view and rule that there never was a separation of activities. For example, a chaotic arrangement between a husband and wife (no written agreements, separate structures, etc) could be deemed to have been one business from the first day of trading. Furthermore, a backdated registration is not limited to a 3 or 4 year adjustment period as with VAT errors – in the worst case scenario, a registration could be backdated to 1973.

As explained above, HMRC will carry out a very detailed review of a commercial arrangement where it considers there has been an artificial separation of business activities. The officer will fully consider the motives of the separation – the avoidance of VAT obviously being the prime consideration.

If he is satisfied that an arrangement is artificial, then a direction will be issued which effectively treats the combined business entities as a single taxable person from the date of the direction. The taxable person is then liable to be registered from the date of the direction. The direction must be served on each person named in it.

The effects of a direction are as follows:

(a) in reality, if two or more persons are trading individually, then the combined business will be treated as a partnership;

(b) as far as VAT is concerned, each constituent member is jointly and severally liable for any VAT due from the taxable person;

(c) in effect, any failure to comply with VAT requirements is treated as a failure by each of the constituent members severally.

Tribunal cases and case law

5.8 It is always useful to consider the views of the higher courts on subjects where issues are not clear-cut, and for this particular subject, there has been a range of interesting and significant cases over the years.

To give a balanced view on this topic, we will first consider three cases won by HMRC, and then three cases won by the taxpayer.

Cases won by HMRC

5.9 HMRC was successful in the three cases summarised below.

(a) *Smith t/a Ty Gwyn Hotel v Customs and Excise Comrs* (3 September 2001, unreported) (MAN/01/0065 17406) – in this particular case, Mrs Smith ran the catering part of the business, but the only payment she made to her husband towards the facilities she enjoyed was to provide free sandwiches to pub customers on a Thursday night. It was argued by the Smiths that this was her way of paying for the kitchen and equipment facilities she enjoyed within the premises.

However, the reality of the situation is that no person in business would sublet such a large part of his premises and allow gas and electric supplies to be freely used in return for a weekly plate of sandwiches.

Comment – this case illustrates the importance of ensuring 'normal commercial arrangements' are in place for two businesses that are closely linked.

(b) *Ashcroft v Customs and Excise Comrs* (16 October 2001, unreported) (MAN/00/0055 17476) – Mrs Ashcroft ran the catering part of a pub activity, but she was so successful that the level of business soon exceeded the VAT registration limit. Once this happened, the Ashcrofts merged the two parts of the business into the partnership anyway. This proved that the reason for the initial separation was to avoid VAT – making it easy for Customs to prove it was not a genuine commercial arrangement.

The tribunal also noted that during the period of Mrs Ashcroft's independence, there was no effort made by her husband to charge her for the share of the overheads and assets she enjoyed.

Comment – again, as well as the absence of 'normal commercial arrangements', the VAT-avoidance motive in this case is very strong. Advisers need to ensure that clients who separate business activities have genuine commercial motives for their actions, eg to operate independently so that profits are rewarded according to the effort put in to the activity in question.

(c) *Williams v Customs and Excise Comrs* (7 July 1987, unreported) (LON/87/132 2445) – in this case, a married couple were carrying on business as a café and bread shop from the same premises. Customs ruled that there was only one business.

Comment – it would be very difficult in this particular case to prove there were separate businesses because it would be quite complicated to keep the purchases separate. For example, if the two businesses were using the same kitchen, then they would be presumably using the same bread, rolls and cakes served in each part. Again, overhead issues would need to be very clearly analysed and recharged at an appropriate market rate in order to highlight that normal commercial arrangements were in place.

Cases won by the taxpayer

5.10   In each of the cases summarised below, there are a number of key themes that recur, explaining why the taxpayers were successful in their appeal:

- motives for separation of the businesses other than the avoidance of paying VAT;

- normal commercial arrangements between the parties when it comes to issues such as dealing with shared overheads;

- separate accounting arrangements in place, separate purchasing, invoicing procedures, bank account, completion of tax returns, etc.

The following three cases were won by the taxpayer.

(a) *Skelton Waste Disposal v Customs and Excise Comrs* (6 July 2001, unreported) (MAN/00/866 17351) – in this case, Dean Langton (son of Maurice) was very ambitious and keen to branch off with a separate business of his own. He formed Skelton Mini Skips, which was not VAT registered, and claimed successfully that this was a different business from Skelton Waste Disposal (in which he was a partner with his father).

 Comment – the key point in this situation was that the motivation for the arrangement was not considered to be the avoidance of VAT – but the opportunity for Dean Langton to trade independently of his father and develop profits in his own right. All of the arrangements were based on normal commercial terms, and the fact that both businesses had 'Skelton' within the trading name was not considered the key issue overall. The case also highlights that members of the same family can operate separate business activities, as long as they are properly formulated.

(b) *Townsend v Customs and Excise Comrs* (9 October 2000, unreported) (LON/00/349, LON/00/350 17081) – the Townsends ran separate pottery businesses – Mrs Townsend painted and decorated pottery blanks, and Mr Townsend made studio pieces. The tribunal considered that the arrangements for the two businesses were made on normal commercial terms, and that they were operated at arm's length to each other. These factors were considered more important than the fact that the couple were married and involved in a similar trade.

 Comment – Customs must have been disappointed to lose this case, on the basis that they considered there to be close financial, economic and organisational links between the two businesses. However, the case emphasises the point that it is up to Customs to prove artificial separation of business activities, not the taxpayer to prove his innocence. In this situation, they failed to convince the tribunal that there was only one business in existence.

(c) *Wallace t/a Inn House v Customs and Excise Comrs* (30 January 2001, unreported) (LON/00/599 17109) – Mr Wallace owned the King's Head pub and was VAT registered. His partner, Mrs Greenland, who lived with him, carried on the catering side of the business at the pub. She was not VAT registered.

Mrs Greenland had exclusive use of the kitchen, hired and fired her own staff, and paid Mr Wallace for all of the gas she used. She also paid Mr Wallace a market rate for other costs she incurred, and produced her own accounts and paid her own self-assessment tax.

Comment – again, normal commercial terms were clearly in place for this arrangement. Even though there was a VAT advantage in the arrangement (no output tax liability on the catering sales), the avoidance of VAT motive could not be proved as the reason for the agreement being made.

Approach to be adopted by tax advisers acting for clients

5.11 A key tip for tax advisers is to stand back and ask the question: 'How would this arrangement look in the eyes of an HMRC officer?' Would the arrangement come across as being two or more distinct businesses, each aiming to make profits in their own right, or would it appear that an artificial situation has been created, with the aim of ensuring at least one of the businesses does not have to register and pay VAT.

To help with this assessment, there are five key questions that tax advisers need to ask.

(a) *What is the key motive for separating the business?* Just because two parties are married or living together does not mean they cannot run separate businesses. The human rights legislation has been well publicised in recent years, and one of these rights is the opportunity to trade in business for a profit.

The key point is to be satisfied that VAT avoidance is not the main motive for separating a business.

(b) *Do normal commercial relationships exist for all issues affecting the businesses?* As a matter of course, most businesses use assets and incur overheads. It is therefore important that if each of the two businesses are to be considered genuine trading entities, they must pay for any assets used or overheads incurred. Equally importantly, these overheads must be paid for at reasonable levels, ie open market rates.

(c) *What do the customers perceive to be happening?* A recent case the author was asked to advise on concerned two ladies trading from the same premises, one selling dietary supplements and vitamin pills, the other selling health foods. The accountant was worried that HMRC might see the entities as one concern.

The key point in this situation was that if a customer came into the shop to complain about the goods they had purchased, this complaint could only be dealt with by the lady running her own part of the business.

Neither of the ladies knew anything about the products sold by the other – there was total independence as far as trading names, invoicing, suppliers, bank accounts, profit margins and product range were concerned. In other words, from the customers' viewpoint, there is no overlap between the two ladies, they just happened to be sharing the same premises as an arrangement convenient to both parties.

(d) *Does one of the parties have a controlling influence over the other party?* Going back to the laundrette example at **5.2**, one of the main features of this situation was that one director and one shareholder had control of all twelve of the different limited companies. In effect, this is displaying common financial, organisational and economic links.

With regard to the pub examples considered in this chapter, a separation would fail if, for example, it was agreed that the husband retained all of the profit made by the wife's catering business in order to pay overhead costs. In this situation, the wife is no longer in business on her own account if the extraction of profit went to her husband.

(e) *How will the arrangement look in the eyes of an HMRC officer?* Although effective tax planning is the right of any taxpayer, there is sometimes a thin line between avoidance and evasion. It is important to assess whether there is any blatant limitation in the arrangement being reviewed, that would make it look like a VAT evasion scheme rather than a genuine business arrangement.

It is important to remember that just because the arrangement may pass the test on a number of issues (for example, separate invoicing and banking arrangements), it is the overall picture that is important.

Planning points to consider

5.12   The following points should be given consideration.

- If advising clients on the separation of business activities, it is important to ensure that avoidance of VAT is not the main motive for the arrangement.

- Remember, there will only be a potential problem with HMRC if the arrangement results in HMRC losing VAT – two businesses with a combined turnover of less than the registration limits, or businesses selling wholly or mainly zero-rated items (where a registration would produce VAT repayments) is not a problem.

- The emphasis on normal commercial arrangements between different entities is vital to the success of a separation. Any overheads, shared assets, staff costs etc must be properly charged at a fair market rate.

- History tends to show that there are more problems with the separation of business activities from a VAT point of view when members of the same family are involved. If possible, consider whether a third party could become involved with the ownership of one of the businesses, which gives increased independence to the situation.

- It is important to note that there are only VAT advantages to be gained if the non-registered business is trading with members of the public (or VAT-exempt businesses) who cannot reclaim any VAT charged. If the business which is not VAT registered is mainly working for other registered entities, then it is probably in its best interests to register for VAT on a voluntary basis, to benefit from the opportunity to recover input tax.

Chapter 6

Cash Accounting Scheme

Key topics in this chapter:

- Conditions for joining the cash accounting scheme, including turnover limits and record-keeping requirements.

- How the scheme operates in practice.

- Limitations of the scheme for certain businesses, e g businesses selling mainly zero-rated items.

- Potential problems with the scheme for advisers to be aware of, for example, dealing with part-payments, part exchange transactions, discounts etc.

- Completing VAT returns.

- Rules for leaving the cash accounting scheme.

Introduction

6.1 An intention of government policy has always been to try and simplify VAT procedures for a small business. The cash accounting scheme is one such measure, allowing certain businesses to pay output tax when they receive payment from customers, rather than the earlier date when a sales invoice is raised. In the current economic climate, when customers are taking longer to pay their bills, this is a very worthwhile benefit.

The scheme was extended on 1 April 2007, so that it can now be used by any business making annual taxable sales (excluding VAT) of £1,350,000 or less. The previous limit was £660,000.

In effect, the two main advantages of the scheme are automatic bad debt relief (output tax is never paid until payment has been received from a customer, so there is no need to worry about trying to recover VAT on unpaid sales invoices) and the deferral of the time for payment of VAT where extended credit is given. Retailers would never use the scheme because they already account for VAT at the time they receive payment from a customer.

The main disadvantage of the scheme is that input tax can only be reclaimed when payment is made to suppliers – not on the date of the purchase invoice. However, this negative point tends to be outweighed for most taxpayers by the advantages gained by the output tax benefits.

Conditions for joining the scheme

6.2 Unlike many special schemes, there is no requirement to notify HMRC in advance that a business intends to adopt cash accounting. If a business is eligible to use the scheme, then it can choose to do so at the beginning of any VAT period.

However, there are a number of important conditions that must be met before the decision to adopt the scheme can be made, as follows.

- *Turnover limit* – as mentioned at **6.1**, the cash accounting scheme can only be used by a small business with an annual taxable turnover (VAT exclusive) of £1,350,000 or less (£660,000 or less before 1 April 2007). This amount includes zero-rated, reduced-rated and standard rated supplies, but excludes any exempt sales. The value of any sales of capital assets (eg sale of plant, equipment or a van) is also excluded from the £1,350,000 calculation.

- *Returns and payments up to date* – a business should have submitted all of its returns for previous periods. With regard to payments, a business must also be up to date with its VAT payments to HMRC. However, it is also acceptable if they have an outstanding balance owed, but which has been agreed by a 'time to pay arrangement'. The basic thinking is that because the cash accounting scheme is a concession by HMRC, it only intends to give the benefits of the scheme to compliant traders.

- *No major VAT problems in the last 12 months* – the business must not have been convicted of any VAT offences during the previous 12 months. It must also be free from any penalty for VAT evasion involving dishonest conduct.

- *No retrospective use of the scheme* – any use of the cash accounting scheme can only be from a current VAT period. It is not acceptable to try and backdate the scheme and gain advantages in earlier periods.

How the cash accounting scheme works

Output tax is declared when payment is received from a customer

6.3 As explained at **6.1**, the main advantage of the cash accounting scheme is that a business has no output tax liability until the date when payment is received from a customer – in other words, no money received means no VAT bill due to HMRC. This is in contrast to the normal VAT accounting rules, where VAT is payable on the date of an invoice or receipt of payment, whichever happens sooner. See Example 1.

Example 1

Anita is a self-employed computer consultant and requires all of her customers to pay sales invoices within 60 days of the date of the invoice. She raises the following sales invoices during the VAT period ended 30 September 2008 (when the standard rated of VAT was still 17.5%):

31/7/08	£10,000 plus VAT	– invoice paid 2 October 2008
31/8/08	£5,000 plus VAT	– invoice paid 23 October 2008
30/9/08	£7,000 plus VAT	– invoice paid 30 November 2008

Solution – under normal VAT accounting rules, the date of the sales invoice would create a VAT liability for each of the above sales invoices. Anita would therefore pay output tax of £3,850 on her September 2008 VAT return (ie £22,000 × 17.5%).

However, if she had made a decision to adopt the cash accounting scheme from the beginning of this period (and remember, there is no requirement to advise HMRC of this decision), then her cash flow position would be improved because she would not need to pay the output tax of £3,850 until the December 2008 VAT return, ie to coincide with payment dates.

Note – the position above with normal VAT accounting does not produce a disastrous result for the business because two out of the three invoices raised will have been paid by customers before the VAT bill becomes due at the end of October. However, imagine the potential problems a business could face if it was paying VAT to HMRC on major sales invoices that were still unpaid at the time when the VAT bill is due for payment.

A frequently asked question concerns the treatment of bounced cheques. In reality, a bounced cheque means that a customer has not made payment, and therefore no output tax liability exists under the cash accounting scheme. However, if the cheque is automatically represented by the bank and then is successfully cleared, VAT will then become payable.

Input tax can only be reclaimed when payment is made to suppliers

6.4   The main principle of the cash accounting scheme is to base VAT payments on cash book accounting rather than a day book basis. This principle applies to input tax as well as output tax, meaning that input tax can only be reclaimed when a purchase invoice has been paid to a supplier.

In effect, the input tax rule means that the cash accounting scheme will be unsuitable for some businesses – or it may be suitable for some businesses in the future, but not at the current time. See Examples 2 and 3.

Example 2

John trades as an exporter of handbags to the USA. He buys the handbags from wholesalers in the UK – who give him 90 days credit. He also incurs input tax on a wide range of other expenses from UK suppliers for various services – who also give him good payment terms because they realise that it takes a long time for him to be paid by his American customers.

Solution – the cash accounting scheme is totally unsuitable for John. This is because he is gaining no output tax advantage because all of his sales are zero-rated as export of goods to a non-EU country.

In effect, his cash flow will be adversely affected by the scheme because it will delay the point when he can reclaim input tax on his supplier invoices by at least one VAT quarter.

Example 3

Jack has just started in business as a wholesaler of stationery, selling goods to retail stationers throughout the country. He is registered for VAT and trades from a small industrial unit. He has purchased goods costing £20,000 plus VAT as the initial stock in his unit, and also paid an additional £20,000 plus VAT for various items of equipment, fixtures and fittings.

He has managed to negotiate generous payment terms with both the stock and asset suppliers. He wants to know if the cash accounting scheme will be worthwhile for him.

Solution – in the longer term, the cash accounting scheme should be beneficial for Jack because the output tax gains will exceed the negative point about input tax claims being delayed until supplier invoices are paid.

However, in the first few months, it is clear that the initial outlay of expenditure on stock and capital equipment means that his input tax will almost certainly exceed his output tax, ie repayment position as far as VAT is concerned. It is therefore sensible to delay using the cash accounting scheme until the time when the business will be in a net VAT payment situation. This decision is particularly important because obviously a business needs every cash flow advantage it can obtain in the early period of trading.

Adjustments when a business first starts to use the scheme

6.5 If an existing business decides to use the scheme, a key issue will be to ensure that output tax is not paid twice on the same supplies, and that input tax claims are likewise not duplicated.

For example, if a sales invoice is raised on 31 March 2009, and paid in April 2009, then a business on calendar VAT quarters and normal VAT accounting will pay the output tax on the March 2009 return. If a decision is then made to adopt cash accounting with effect from 1 April 2009, then this particular invoice must be excluded from the cash accounting calculations for the June 2009 period – otherwise the output tax liability will be duplicated. The same principle must be applied with purchase invoices.

The other situation that could arise for a new business that adopts the scheme from the day it first becomes VAT registered is where it wants to reclaim input tax on the first return relevant to assets/stock purchased before it became registered for VAT. These expenses were obviously paid before the business became registered (ie payment date outside of the VAT period) but HMRC still allows the VAT on such purchases to be reclaimed on the first return.

Allocation of part payments on invoices with supplies at different rates of VAT

6.6 Where a part-payment is received from a customer, which is not directly linked to specific invoices, then the payment must be allocated to invoices in date order (earliest first). This situation is then likely to mean that one sales invoice is part paid – and if this invoice includes a standard rated and zero-rated element, then the VAT payment should be apportioned according to the percentage of standard rated sales on the invoice. See Example 4.

Example 4

Doreen uses the cash accounting scheme and has two sales invoices unpaid from her customer ABC Ltd:

- invoice no 234 (dated 1 August 2009) – £2,000 plus VAT (of 15%) of £300 – total £2,300; and

- invoice no 238 (dated 15 August 2009) – £5,000 plus VAT of £150 – because £4,000 of goods on this invoice were zero-rated.

She receives a lump-sum payment on account from ABC Ltd for £4,000.

Solution – the first £2,300 of the payment will be allocated to the earliest sales invoice no 234, creating an output tax liability of £300.

The balance of the payment (£1,700) will be allocated to sales invoice no 238. The output tax to declare on this part of the payment is: £1,700 divided by £5,150 × £150 = £49.51. The remaining output tax on this invoice (£100.49) will be declared on future receipts of money from the customer.

Payments in kind: part exchange transactions

6.7 It is possible that a business could receive part or full payment for its supplies as a non-monetary consideration, for example, a part exchange transaction. In such cases, output tax is due on the full value of the supply. For a business using the cash accounting scheme, this principle still applies, and the 'payment' date is deemed to be when the goods and payment are received. See Example 5.

Example 5

DEF Ltd sells tractors and is VAT registered using the cash accounting scheme. It sells a tractor to Mr Smith for £10,000 plus VAT and receives £6,000 cash plus Mr Smith's old tractor to settle the account. Mr Smith is not VAT registered.

Solution – the cash book entry for this transaction will be £6,000 for the payment by Mr Smith – but the output tax liability is £1,750 with a VAT rate of 17.5%, ie on the full value of the supply. Assuming that the business took ownership of Mr Smith's old tractor on the same date as Mr Smith made payment for the balance due, then this will be the date when output tax is payable under the cash accounting scheme.

Prompt payment discount

6.8 A basic rule of VAT is that when prompt payment discount is offered to a customer, VAT is only chargeable on the discounted amount, irrespective of whether the customer takes the discount or not.

A business using cash accounting should therefore account for output tax according to the amount of VAT shown on the sales invoice, not 7/47 of the gross payment received from the customer.

Equally, however, a business that receives prompt payment discount from a supplier should adopt the same principle as far as input tax is concerned.

Partial exemption

6.9 A business that makes both taxable and exempt supplies is classed as partially exempt as far as VAT is concerned (see Chapters 24 and 25). In most cases, this means there is a restriction on input tax recovery based on the standard method of calculation for partial exemption – whereby taxable outputs are calculated as a proportion of total outputs, ie including exempt supplies to give an input tax recovery rate on general overheads.

For a business on the cash accounting scheme, the same principle of input tax restriction applies, but the outputs calculation under the standard method is based on payments received for taxable and exempt supplies in a VAT period, not on invoices raised.

Input tax recovery for a partly exempt business using the cash accounting scheme will still be based on payments made.

Completing VAT returns

6.10   One of the main aims of the cash accounting scheme is to simplify the administrative burden of VAT for small businesses – as well as the other two main benefits of automatic bad debt relief and a delay in paying output tax until payment is received from a customer.

For a small business, the record keeping process is simplified by the cash accounting scheme because a cash book system can be used as the main record, avoiding the need for a sales day book and purchase day book to be maintained as well.

In terms of completing the VAT return, the points below are relevant.

Box 1 – output tax will be based on payments received from customers during the period covered by the VAT return. This will include payments by cash, cheque and other means, as well as the value of any non-monetary payments such as part-exchange transactions (see **6.7**).

Box 4 – input tax will be based on payments made to suppliers during the period covered by the VAT return. This will include payments by cash, cheque, standing orders, direct debit and credit card – for credit card transactions, the key date is when the supplier makes out the sales voucher, not the date when payment is made to the card company.

Box 6 – the value of outputs (VAT exclusive) will also be based on payments received from customers.

Box 7 – the value of inputs (VAT exclusive) should also be based on payments made to suppliers.

Box 8 – this box is the exception to the rule. In the case of supplies made to other EU countries, the Box 8 entry should be based on the value of goods and services supplied to customers, not on the total value of payments received.

Note – in effect, the consistency between Boxes 1, 4, 6 and 7 as far as the method of calculation is concerned (that is, based on payments made and received rather than invoices raised) should enable the usual ratio checks to apply between the boxes:

- Box 6 figure multiplied by 17.5% (or 15% until 31 December 2009) should be equal to Box 1 output tax figure if the business only makes standard rated supplies;

- Box 7 figure multiplied by 17.5% (or 15% until 31 December 2009) should be equal to or greater than Box 4 input tax figure.

Leaving the scheme

6.11   There are three situations that could arise which would result in a business withdrawing from the cash accounting scheme:

(a) voluntary withdrawal – a business may withdraw from the scheme at the end of any VAT period (see **6.12**);

(b) turnover above the limits of the scheme – if a business expands so that its taxable turnover exceeds £1.6m per annum, then it may need to withdraw from the scheme, however, HMRC has some generous concessions in place that could avoid the need for an exit to be made (see **6.13**);

(c) compulsory withdrawal – due to non-compliance with HMRC regulations (see **6.14**).

If a business leaves the scheme, there are various transitional rules in place regarding the payment of tax that need to be carefully considered (see 6.15).

Voluntary withdrawal

6.12 A business is entitled to withdraw from using the scheme at the end of any VAT period; there are a number of commercial reasons why it might make this decision, for example:

• *change in mixture of goods being sold* – if a business that previously sold all standard rated items suddenly changes its activity so that the majority of sales are zero-rated, then the benefits of using the cash accounting scheme could be eroded. This is because the benefits in delaying payment of output tax will not be relevant if sales are mainly zero-rated – the delay in reclaiming input tax until payment is made to suppliers may then be more of a problem;

• *customers make payment quicker than suppliers are paid* – this would be an enviable position for any business as far as cash flow is concerned, ie where customers make instant payment (or even payment in advance) but the business is able to enjoy extended payment terms with its suppliers. In such cases, the output tax benefits of the cash accounting scheme will be eroded but the delay in reclaiming input tax may be a problem.

Again, as with entry to the scheme, there is no requirement to notify HMRC of the decision to leave.

Withdrawal due to turnover limit being exceeded

6.13 Although the entry limit for a business is an annual taxable turnover of £1,350,000, a business does not have to withdraw from the scheme until the value of its taxable supplies in the year ended has exceeded £1,600,000. The only disadvantage is that the calculation must include the disposals of any stock or capital assets.

However, HMRC will exceptionally allow a business to remain in the scheme as long as it can prove the following:

- the limit was exceeded because of a large 'one-off' increase in sales which has not occurred before and is not expected to occur again (eg the sale of a capital asset or an exceptional sale outside of the normal activities of the business); and

- the sale arose from a genuine commercial activity; and

- there are reasonable grounds for believing that turnover in the next 12 months will be below £1,350,000.

For an extension to be granted, all three of the above conditions must be met – and applications must be made to (and granted by) HMRC for a business to remain in the scheme. See Example 6.

Example 6

JKL Ltd is a company that offers computer consultancy services and achieved taxable turnover of £1,700,000 in the year to 31 July 2008 (excluding VAT).

The reason for this exceptional year is because the company imported a special shipment of computers for a customer and sold them at a good profit. The sales value of these computers was £900,000. This is the first time the company has been involved in the sale of goods, and the situation is not expected to repeat itself.

The company has been using the cash accounting scheme for many years and has enjoyed the benefits of the scheme because many customers take a long time to settle their invoices.

Solution – if the above facts are correct, then HMRC will almost certainly allow the business to continue using the cash accounting scheme, even though its sales figure for the year to 31 July 2008 exceeded the £1,600,000 limit. The reason for the increase in turnover for the year is clearly due to a one-off sale that is unlikely to be repeated, and expected turnover for year ended 31 July 2009 is expected to revert to levels achieved in past years.

Compulsory withdrawal

6.14 As explained earlier in the chapter, the cash accounting scheme is a concession offered by HMRC to assist small businesses. If this concession is abused by non-compliant taxpayers, then HMRC is perfectly entitled to withdraw its use.

A business will be expelled from using the scheme in the following circumstances:

- if it fails to meet the record-keeping requirements to enable calculations to be properly made for VAT purposes;

- if it has been convicted of an offence in connection with VAT since using the scheme or accepted an offer to compound proceedings in connection with a VAT offence;

- if it has been assessed for a VAT penalty involving dishonest conduct.

In the above cases, HMRC will write to the taxpayer to withdraw the use of the scheme.

As a separate point, HMRC also has the power to withdraw the use of the scheme for any other reason where it feels it is necessary to safeguard the tax yield.

Rules to apply when a business withdraws from the cash accounting scheme

6.15 Unless special transitional rules can be applied (see **6.16**), a business must account for VAT as follows on the final return it submits when it is within the cash accounting scheme:

- all VAT that it would have been required to pay to HMRC during the time the scheme was operated if it had not been operating the scheme, *minus*

- all VAT accounted for and paid to HMRC in accordance with the scheme, subject to any adjustments for input tax credit.

In effect, the above conditions mean that at the point of leaving the scheme, the business will have accounted for, and declared, a total output tax figure (and reclaimed total input tax) the same as if it had never been in the scheme in the first place. In other words, output tax will be declared on unpaid sales invoices on this return (unless bad debt relief can be claimed) and input tax will be claimed on any unpaid purchase invoices.

Transitional rules

6.16 The rules discussed at **6.15** could create a large and unexpected VAT bill for a business on the final return it submits when it is within the cash accounting scheme.

In order to alleviate the effect of this large payment, special transitional rules are available for businesses that leave the scheme either because of the turnover limits or because they choose to withdraw on a voluntary basis. The transitional rules are not available to any business where use of the scheme has been withdrawn by HMRC because of non-compliance issues. There is also an exclusion from using the transitional rules for any business whose taxable turnover exceeded £1,350,000 in the 3-month period in which it ceases to operate the scheme.

The transitional rules can be summarised as follows:

- the business can continue to operate the scheme in respect of its 'scheme supplies' for 6 months after the end of the VAT period in which it ceased to operate the scheme;

- 'scheme supplies' means supplies made and received while the business operated the scheme;

- on the VAT return for the first period that ends 6 months or more after the end of the VAT period in which it ceased to operate the scheme, the business must then pay VAT under the rules at **6.15**, ie to bring its VAT accounting up to date again.

In effect, the transitional rules are extending the benefits of the scheme for 6 months after its official use has been withdrawn. There is no need to apply to HMRC to use the transitional arrangements.

Other matters concerning the cash accounting scheme

Transfer of a going concern

6.17   When a business is transferred as a going concern, then one of two situations will apply: either the new business retains the VAT registration number of the old business or the new business applies for its own VAT number. In the latter case, the transferor must, within 2 months or longer period as HMRC allows, account for and pay VAT due on all supplies made and received which have not otherwise been accounted for on any return (less input tax credit).

If the same VAT number is retained, the transferor must advise the new owner of the use of the scheme, and the new owner then takes over the accounting responsibilities in the normal way, ie as if there had been no change in ownership.

Cessation of business

6.18   The 2-month rule described above must also be applied if a business ceases to trade. However, HMRC will normally allow the business to continue to use the cash accounting scheme while stocks and assets are being sold – it is only when the final return is then submitted that all output tax on unpaid sales invoices needs to be accounted for (subject to bad debt relief being claimed and input tax credits also being adjusted).

Anti-avoidance measures

6.19   A risk to HMRC of a business using the cash accounting scheme is the situation when an advance tax invoice could be raised by a supplier, giving his customer the chance to reclaim input tax on the invoice, even though payment will not be made for many months. The delay in payment will then avoid an output tax declaration by the supplier if he is on the cash accounting scheme.

However, HMRC has rules in place to avoid this abuse – the scheme specifically excludes any supplies where a VAT invoice is issued and full payment of the amount shown on the invoice is not due within 6 months from the invoice date. Also, the scheme excludes any supplies where a VAT invoice is raised in advance of goods being delivered or services performed.

In reality, HMRC rightly wants to avoid the situation where it is allowing a business to reclaim input tax on supplies where the output tax payment on the same supply is being delayed on either a temporary or permanent basis.

Factored debts

6.20 Where debts are sold or transferred to become the debts of a factor company, output tax must be accounted for on their full value in the period in which they are sold or assigned. Obviously, this date will usually occur before payment is made by the final customer. Again, if the transfer occurs as soon as a sales invoice is raised, then the benefits of the cash accounting scheme may be negligible for the business in question.

An alternative scheme used in factoring arrangements is where the business retains ownership of the customer's debt, but receives advances of money from the factor company, usually based on a percentage of its turnover. The customer will then remit payment direct to the factor company to settle his account. In this situation, the business must declare output tax in the VAT period in which the customer pays the factor. The actual date of payment will be shown on statements issued by the factor company, and it is important to remember that output tax is due on the full value of the payment made by the customer – not net of any commission charged by the factor company.

Planning points to consider

6.21 The following points should be given consideration.

- Review client lists to identify those that could benefit from adopting the cash accounting scheme, ie those within the annual turnover limit of £1,350,000 per year (taxable sales excluding VAT) and whose trading circumstances could produce worthwhile benefits.

- The cash flow benefits and automatic bad debt relief given by the scheme could be particularly useful for many clients in the current economic climate.

- The cash accounting scheme is not suitable for taxpayers supplying mainly zero-rated items, or for a business where customers pay in advance or as soon as sales invoices are raised.

- The greatest benefits of the scheme will be enjoyed by businesses that mainly supply standard-rated items, and also give generous payment terms to their customers, ie where they have a delay before they receive money.

- Always review whether the cash accounting scheme continues to be of benefit to clients – a change in the mixture of standard/zero-rated goods could mean it is more beneficial for a business to account for VAT under normal accounting rules.

- A business that exceeds the exit level of £1.6m per annum in taxable supplies can still remain in the scheme if it can prove to HMRC that the increase in sales for the year in question was due to a one-off sale and that it expects taxable supplies in the next 12 months to be less than £1,350,000.

- Be aware of HMRC anti-avoidance rules that exclude transactions from the scheme that are invoiced in advance of goods being supplied to customers or services performed. It is not acceptable to HMRC for a business to claim input tax when another business is able to delay paying output tax on the same supply.

Chapter 7

Annual Accounting Scheme

Key topics in this chapter:

- The rules that apply for a business to be able to join the annual accounting scheme.

- How the scheme works in practice – one VAT return each year, regular payments on account and balancing payment due at the end of the accounting period.

- Withdrawal from the annual accounting scheme – turnover limits, compulsory withdrawal, voluntary withdrawal.

- Disadvantages and potential problems of using the scheme.

- Types of business that could benefit from using the scheme.

Introduction

7.1 The annual accounting scheme was introduced in 1990, and its aim is to save administration time for a small business by only requiring the submission of one annual VAT return instead of four quarterly returns.

For many years, the scheme was only available to a small business with taxable turnover of £600,000 or less but this level was increased to £660,000 with effect from 1 April 2004 and increased again to £1,350,000 from 1 April 2006. In reality, however, the number of businesses that have opted to use the scheme has not been as many as expected, mainly because there are a number of disadvantages that have tended to outweigh the positive points.

The basic rules of the scheme are as follows:

- a business submits one VAT return per year, usually coinciding with its financial year;

- the business gets an extra month to submit the annual return, ie it is due 2 months after the end of the period rather than one;

- VAT is usually paid on a monthly basis throughout the year – any remaining balance is then paid or repaid at the end of the year after the annual return has been submitted.

Eligibility to use the scheme

7.2   A business is able to apply for and adopt annual accounting if the following condition is met:

- *Taxable turnover in the next 12 months is expected to be £1,350,000 or less* – the turnover level excludes the sale of capital assets and also the value of any exempt supplies made by the business. Once a business has joined the scheme, it can remain in the scheme until the value of its annual taxable sales (VAT exclusive) exceeds £1,600,000.

A business can apply to join the annual accounting scheme as soon as it becomes VAT registered, as long as it expects its taxable sales in the 12-month period to be £1,350,000 or less.

The scheme is generally open to all businesses that meet the above criteria, however, there are a few exceptions when HMRC will refuse an application:

(a)   a business cannot join the scheme if it is part of a group or divisional registration;

(b)   once a business has left the scheme, it cannot rejoin for at least 12 months;

(c)   a business can be refused admission if its has a rising VAT debt. There should not be a problem if this rising debt is still a small amount, and if settlement has been negotiated through a time to pay agreement;

(d)   an insolvent business cannot join the scheme.

How the scheme works

Application process

7.3   An application to use the scheme must be made on form VAT 600(AA). There is another form that can be used if a business wishes to join the annual accounting and flat rate schemes at the same time (VAT 600(AA) and FRS). The form can be downloaded from the HMRC website (www.hmrc.gov.uk) or is produced at the back of VAT Notice 732.

Once HMRC approves a business to use the scheme, it will confirm the amount and timing of the interim payments made by electronic means and the due date for the annual return and balancing payment.

At this stage, it is important that a business reviews the level of payments being proposed to ensure they are reasonable:

- if the payments are too low, then the business will face a large balancing payment at the end of its accounting year;

- if the payments are too high, then working capital could be stretched for the business until the overpayment is corrected at the end of the year.

Note – if a business feels there are genuine grounds to increase or decrease the payments during the year (eg the business is trading significantly better or worse than expected) then the local VAT Business Advice Centre should be contacted.

First year of using the scheme

7.4   One of the rules of the scheme is that no annual accounting period can exceed 12 months (apart from a new business that is applying to use the scheme from the date it registered for VAT, in which case 12 months and 30 days is possible). In effect, a business applying to join the scheme midway through its chosen accounting year will have one return to complete of less than 12 months, followed by annual returns thereafter. See Example 1.

Example 1

John trades as a plumber and has decided he would like to save time on his VAT affairs by using the annual accounting scheme. He applies to join the scheme on 10 July 2008 and chooses an accounting year up to 31 March. He is currently using calendar VAT quarters.

Solution – the first period that John will need to submit a return for when he uses the scheme is the period from 1 July 2008 to 31 March 2009. He will then submit an annual return each year up to 31 March. It would not be acceptable for John's first period to cover 1 July 2008 to 31 March 2010 because the period would then exceed 12 months, contrary to the scheme rules.

As a separate point, if John had applied to join the scheme on 28 September 2008, then the first annual accounting return would have been effective from 1 October 2008 to 31 March 2009. This is because HMRC would already have issued his quarterly return for the September 2008 period before receiving his application to join the scheme.

Payments on account

7.5   A key condition of the annual accounting scheme is the requirement to make regular payments on account throughout the year. The rules for these payments are as follows.

(a) For the first accounting period of less than 12 months (as per Example 1 above), there are special transitional rules regarding payments on account. These rules depend on the number of months in the period, however, if the period is less than 4 months, no interim payments are required. There will also need to be agreed payments on account for a newly registered business that is joining the scheme from its date of registration – based on expected VAT payments in its first 12 months of trading.

(b) Normal accounting year – the procedures for payments on account in a full accounting year (ie a 12-month period) are as follows:

- the total VAT paid in the previous 12 months is calculated; 10% of this amount is then due for each payment in months 4 to 12 of the accounting year. However, a business can alternatively apply to make quarterly payments on account at the end of months 4, 7 and 10. In such cases, the payments made will be each based on 25% of the previous year's VAT liability;

- the monthly or quarterly payments in each of the above months will be made by electronic means on the last working day of the month;

- a business can make additional voluntary payments at any time, as long as the payments are in multiples of £5 and made by electronic means;

- the balance of tax is payable 2 months after the end of the accounting period when the annual return is submitted – this payment does not need to be made by electronic means;

- if a business expects its actual liability of VAT to increase or decrease compared to the previous year (eg because of a significant increase in trading levels), then it should contact its VAT Business Advice Centre with information on how it has calculated the revised interim payments.

For an illustration of the workings of the payment arrangement, see Example 2.

Example 2

ABC Ltd paid VAT of £22,000 in the year to 31 March 2008. It was approved to use the annual accounting scheme with effect from 1 April 2008. For year ended 31 March 2009, it paid instalments of £2,200 from July 2008 to March 2009, ie based on 10% of the previous year's liability for each period. When the company submitted its annual VAT return for year ended 31 March 2009, the actual amount due was £25,000.

Solution – a balancing payment of £5,200 is due by 31 May 2009, ie within 2 months of the end of the annual accounting period. This figure is the difference between the VAT liability for the year (£25,000) and the interim payments made from months 4 to 12 (£2,200 × 9 = £19,800).

Repayment traders

7.6   There is no problem with a repayment trader applying to join the annual accounting scheme. A repayment trader is defined as a trader whose VAT returns regularly show that input tax exceeds output tax. This situation would mainly apply to businesses where most or all of sales are zero-rated, eg newsagents, farmers, milkmen, builders working on new residential properties, export traders.

However, the problem for a repayment trader adopting the scheme is that any repayment due from HMRC would not be paid until the annual return has been submitted. This creates a negative result as far as cash flow is concerned – particularly if the business had a large amount of input tax to reclaim early in the accounting year, for example on capital equipment.

Leaving the annual accounting scheme

7.7   A business ceases to be authorised to use the scheme in the following circumstances.

- *Turnover exceeds £1.6m* – the key figure is the taxable sales for the 12-month period shown on the annual return.

- *Expulsion by HMRC* – as with all concessions, HMRC has the facility to withdraw the use of the scheme for any business that does not follow the rules. In reality, this means that if a business has a poor record as far as making payments are concerned, or has failed to submit two annual returns on time, then it can be removed from the scheme. HMRC also has the power to withdraw a business from the scheme if it considers it to be necessary 'for the protection of the revenue', ie to safeguard the tax yield.

- *Cessation of trading* – if a business ceases to trade or ceases to be VAT registered, then it will obviously withdraw from using the annual account-ing scheme.

Note – a business may elect to use the scheme but then decide it would prefer to again submit quarterly returns and adopt normal VAT account-ing. It can leave the scheme at any time by writing to HMRC – this means that a final return must be completed under the scheme, with the balance of any tax being paid within 2 months of the termination date. If a business has chosen to withdraw from the scheme, it cannot apply to rejoin again for at least 12 months.

Incorrect estimates of future taxable sales

7.8   One of the rules of admission is that a business can only join if it expects the value of its taxable turnover to be less than £1,350,000 in the next 12 months. However, even if it gets its estimate wrong and exceeds this limit, there is no problem as long as the actual taxable sales do not exceed £1.6m. See Example 3.

Example 3

ABC Ltd joined the annual accounting scheme on 1 April 2008 and expected its sales in the next 12 months to be £1,125,000. However, the trading year proved exceptionally strong and actual taxable sales were £1,500,000 for the accounting year ended 31 March 2009.

Solution – although ABC Ltd should not have joined the annual accounting scheme, it will not be penalised for getting its turnover estimate wrong, and can remain in the scheme as long as actual sales are always less than the exit level of £1.6m per year.

Potential problems of using the annual accounting scheme

7.9 The annual accounting scheme has not been as popular as originally anticipated by HMRC when it was first introduced. A series of amendments to the scheme have been made over a number of years to try and make it more attractive to users. However, the following are potential problems with the scheme of which advisers need to be aware.

- *Payments on account could be too high* – one main problem that could occur with the payment on account arrangement is that they could be too high. This could occur due to a number of reasons: purchase of major capital items with high input tax recovery; decrease in trading levels compared to previous year; change in emphasis from standard rated to zero-rated sales.

  The positive point is that if a business identifies at any time that its payments on account are too high, it can make an application to HMRC to reduce them. This request should be made to the local VAT Business Advice Centre. In reality, however, this effectively means that a business needs to calculate its VAT liability anyway (in order to confirm the payments on account are reasonable) and so it may as well complete the quarterly return in the normal way.

  As the scheme is mainly available to small businesses that are unlikely to have large accounts teams, there is a big risk that any large difference between the true tax liability and payments on account will be overlooked.

- *Payments on account could be too low* – the risk that payments on account could be too low and a business does not anticipate the high balancing payment is another limitation of the scheme.

This situation could be particularly relevant for an expanding business that has increased its activity levels, eg turnover doubled in the last 12 months. Imagine if a busy company was trading very heavily, and accepting low payments on account under the annual accounting scheme. The annual return is then submitted, producing an unexpected balancing payment that could cause immediate cash flow problems.

- *Electronic payments on account could cause cash flow problems* – it is inevitable that many small businesses have periods where cash flow is very tight. In the case of quarterly returns where payment is sent by cheque, it is possible for the business to delay payment if cash flow is very tight (although obviously any late payment will bring the business into the default surcharge system).

  However, a problem with the annual accounting scheme is that the monthly payments on account must all be made by electronic means. These payments could create potential cash flow pressure on a small business, which may not be in its best interests. The end result again tends to be a reluctance to join the annual accounting scheme.

- *The move away from quarterly VAT accounting may mean that the records of a business are not kept up to date* – for most small businesses, keeping records and accounts is an unwanted task that many would be happy to delay as long as possible. In reality, the discipline of completing a quarterly VAT return is a good method of ensuring records are kept reasonably up to date. If this discipline is removed by the annual accounting scheme, there is a risk that accounts will be completed at the end of the year on a last-minute basis. There could be a large number of anomalies where clients have forgotten the detail of many transactions that took place earlier in the year.

It is a proven fact that a large majority of self-assessment tax returns are filed in the deadline months of October and January each year, solely due to the natural tendency of many people to leave things to the last minute. The annual accounting scheme, by effectively extending deadlines, could contribute further to this approach.

Types of business that could benefit from using the annual accounting scheme

7.10   Although the annual accounting scheme has definite limitations (see **7.9**), there are many instances where the scheme could be appropriate. The following examples make it worthy of consideration.

- If a client has a persistent record of putting returns in late, and incurring default penalties, then the reduced number of VAT returns and discipline of monthly electronic payments may be beneficial. In reality, the client could save time on completing returns – and spend more time running his business rather than paying VAT penalties and receiving unwanted letters from HMRC.

- The scheme is quite attractive to businesses that are partly exempt because they only have to do one partial exemption calculation per year. The annual accounting period would coincide with the partial exemption year, ie ending on March, April or May, and there would effectively be no need for an annual adjustment in the scheme because this would be automatic with the 12-month return. Many small partly exempt businesses could be voluntary/non-profit making organisations (eg a members' golf club) so volunteer officers would welcome the reduced administration time.

- There could also be financial savings for any business that does not feel confident about completing its own VAT return and has to pay for external expertise. Although it would be fair to argue that there is more work involved in completing an annual return rather than quarterly return, there should still be a welcome saving of fees for the client.

- HMRC does not penalise a business that has low payments on account and a high balance of tax due after the year end, so there is scope for a growing (but well-managed) business to gain a cash flow advantage from the scheme. However, the directors will need to ensure that money is put aside for the balancing payment due after the end of the year. See Example 4.

Example 4

John uses the annual accounting scheme and paid VAT of £30,000 in the year to 31 March 2008. For year ended 31 March 2009, he has paid instalments of £3,000 per month from July 2008 to March 2009, ie based on a monthly payment of 10% of last year's liability.

However, John's business has enjoyed significant trading growth, and his actual VAT liability for the year ended 31 March 2009 is £60,000.

Solution – John will have a large balancing payment to make when he submits his annual VAT return by 31 May 2009. He will have to pay £33,000 (£60,000 less £27,000) by this date. However, the payment delay has given him a positive cash flow benefit compared to normal quarterly returns. The priority though, is to ensure he has funds available to pay the amount due and that it has not already been spent on other projects.

Planning points to consider

7.11 The following points should be given consideration.

- The annual accounting scheme was extended from 1 April 2006 so that all businesses with expected taxable turnover of £1,350,000 or less can join.

This is a significant increase compared to the previous limit of £660,000 per year. Many advisers have still not recognised the increased limits, so there may be clients who could benefit from using the scheme.

- It should be noted that payments on account that are either too high or too low can be adjusted during the year by writing to the local VAT Business Advice Centre and requesting revised payment terms. The payments on account are based on the previous year's VAT liabilities and many businesses will owe less tax in the current year because of the difficult economic climate.

- It is unlikely that the annual accounting scheme will benefit repayment traders because they have to wait until the end of the accounting year to receive any repayment due. Any scheme users that have recently become repayment traders (e g change in activity so that most sales are zero-rated rather than standard rated) would almost certainly benefit from applying to leave the scheme on a voluntary basis.

- Be aware of the potential advantages of the scheme that may appeal to certain traders – particularly the time-saving benefits of completing only one return each year. The scheme may also appeal to partly-exempt taxpayers who will only need to make one partial exemption calculation per year (the annual accounting period must coincide with the partial exemption tax year, i e 31 March, 30 April or 31 May).

Chapter 8

Flat Rate Scheme

Key topics in this chapter:

- Turnover limits for using the flat rate scheme.

- How the flat rate scheme works.

- Applying to use the scheme and potential problems for taxpayers using the scheme.

- Choosing the relevant flat rate percentage to apply for a particular business.

- Sources of business income that need to be included in the scheme in some cases, e g bank interest, buy-to-let income, sale of capital assets.

- Situations where the flat rate scheme could produce tax savings for a business.

- Completing VAT returns.

- The three alternative methods of calculating sales using the scheme – basic turnover method, cash-based method and retail method.

- Dealing with EU acquisitions and other international transactions using the scheme.

- Rules for leaving the scheme – voluntary and compulsory withdrawal.

Introduction

8.1   The flat rate scheme was first introduced in April 2002, with the aim of simplifying the record-keeping requirements of a small business in relation to VAT.

The basic principles of the flat rate scheme are as follows:

- It is only available to small businesses with VAT exclusive annual taxable turnover up to £150,000. A second test based on a total turnover figure of £187,500 (ie including exempt and non-business income) was abolished on 31 March 2009.

- A business still charges VAT on its sales invoices in the normal way, ie adding 17.5% VAT for standard rated sales (15% until 31 December 2009), 5% for reduced rate sales and 0% for zero-rated sales.

- Instead of paying VAT based on output tax less input tax, a business will apply a given flat-rate percentage to its gross (VAT inclusive) income – the percentage is based on the category of business to which it belongs.

A business using the flat rate scheme does not reclaim input tax, unless it relates to capital expenditure goods costing more than £2,000 including VAT. The definition of capital expenditure goods follows that of normal accounting principles, eg it includes money spent on vans, plant and machinery, fixtures and fittings.

The key point with the flat rate scheme is that HMRC publicises the scheme to promote the potential time saving and administrative benefits for a small business. VAT specialists and accountants generally publicise the scheme to promote tax savings for certain users whose specific circumstances produce a good result. The HMRC approach is understandable – the aim of the scheme is to be tax neutral rather than to create savings for certain types of business. However, the reality of the situation is that most clients are more interested in the tax savings rather than the time savings.

How the scheme works

8.2   The flat rate scheme is simple to operate and works on the following basis:

- under normal accounting, a business separately records the VAT on its sales (usually invoices) as output tax and the VAT on its purchase and expense invoices as input tax. Its VAT liability for a period equates to output tax less input tax. With the flat rate scheme, there is no need to record sales or purchase invoices in this manner;

- the flat rate scheme only requires a business to record its VAT inclusive sales or takings for a period – this sales figure also includes any zero-rated or exempt supplies made during the period – see **8.9**. However, any sales that are outside the scope of VAT are excluded from the calculation. This exclusion would include any services provided for overseas customers where the place of supply is established as being outside the UK;

- a specific percentage is applied to the VAT inclusive sales figure, and this becomes the VAT payable by the business in the relevant period. The percentage to apply depends on the trade sector of the business in question – see **8.8**;

- if a business buys capital expenditure goods exceeding £2,000 including VAT, it is entitled to reclaim input tax on these items subject to the normal rules. The items must be used in relation to taxable supplies and must be assets used in the business – not purchased for resale;

  Note – a recent tribunal case (*Sally March v HMRC* [2009] UKFTT 94 (TC)) confirmed that VAT paid by a business that was building a new riding arena for a riding school did not qualify for an input tax claim within the scheme. This is because the supplies in question were of 'building services' rather than 'capital goods.' The bricks and materials bought in relation to the project were also excluded from any input tax claim.

- there are special rules in place to deal with stock and assets held at the time of VAT registration – so that a claim for input tax can be made where appropriate on the first VAT return submitted by the business.

See Example 1 to illustrate the workings of the scheme in a practical situation.

Example 1

ABC Management Consultants are VAT registered and use the flat rate scheme. The value of sales invoices raised in the VAT quarter to 31 March 2009 was £20,000 plus VAT. However, they purchased a highly sophisticated piece of capital equipment for use in their business on 28 February 2009, at a cost of £1,900 plus VAT. How much VAT is due under the flat rate scheme?

Solution – the first relevant point is that because the equipment purchased is a capital item costing more than £2,000 including VAT (£1,900 plus VAT at 15% = £2,185) the input tax item on this purchase can be claimed separately, ie outside the flat rate scheme.

A management consultant currently has a flat rate of 11% (12.5% when the VAT rate returns to 17.5% again) under the scheme and must apply this percentage to its VAT inclusive sales figure of £23,000.

The amount of tax due is £2,245, ie £2,530 less £285.

Note – if the business sells the capital asset in the future, it must account for output tax on the proceeds of the sale, that is on the basis that it has obtained input tax recovery on the purchase of the asset. It is not acceptable to include the sale of the asset within the flat rate scheme calculation, ie output tax must be accounted for on the full selling price.

Applying to use the scheme

8.3   As explained above, any business can apply to use the flat rate scheme if it meets the relevant turnover limit given at **8.1**. The application can be made at any time (usually from the beginning of a VAT period) – either by post (Form VAT 600 (FRS)), e-mail or telephone (the National Advice Service can take application details over the phone on 0845 010 9000).

HMRC has the power to refuse use of the scheme if it considers it necessary to safeguard the tax yield. It will notify the business that its application has been accepted (or declined) and the date from which it can operate the scheme. If the application is denied, then the reasons for the refusal will be given.

An important benefit of adopting the scheme for a newly registered business is that the business will benefit from an extra 1% discount from its usual flat rate in its first year of registration. For a business with turnover at the maximum level allowed by the scheme (£150,000 plus VAT), this 1% discount could be worth up to £1,725.

Potential problems of using the scheme

8.4 As with many aspects of tax, a situation that may be suitable for one business may prove totally unsuitable for another. Example 2 illustrates one situation where the scheme produces a disastrous result for a taxpayer. Advisers should be aware of the important points in relation to the scheme that are mentioned in this section.

Example 2

John trades as an accountant and tax adviser but is not very good at producing accounts or completing tax returns. He therefore subcontracts all of his accounts and tax work to three local practitioners, all of whom are VAT registered.

John's annual sales figure is £150,000 (excluding VAT), most of which relates to accountancy work. His sole expense is the cost of the subcontractor fees of £110,000 (excluding VAT). This leaves John a nice profit of £40,000. Should he use the flat rate scheme?

Solution – John must avoid the flat rate scheme at all costs. Under normal accounting, with a VAT rate of 17.5%, his annual VAT bill would be £7,000 (output tax of £26,250 less input tax of £19,250). However, the flat rate scheme (13% flat rate for accountants when the VAT rate is 17.5%) gives him a tax bill of £22,912.50 (£150,000 x 1.175 x 13%). He is worse off by an incredible £15,912.50. This is because the nature of his trading produces exceptionally high input tax – far greater than is recognised by the 13% flat rate for accountants.

Appropriate scheme percentage needs to be applied to all sales

8.5   The appropriate scheme percentage needs to be applied to zero-rate, lower-rate and exempt sales (see **8.9**) – not just standard-rated sales.

This is possibly the point that causes most confusion among many clients, and some advisers. Basically, the flat rate percentage is applied to the gross receipts of a business, so effectively it means that some VAT is being paid on zero-rated or exempt supplies that are made. The flat-rate percentages are lower for trade sectors with a high prevalence of zero-rated or exempt sales (eg the flat-rate percentage for a business retailing food, confectionery, tobacco, newspapers or children's clothing is 2%) but the scheme may not be favourable for a business where the extent of zero-rated sales is unknown on a period-by-period basis. For an illustration of this point, see Example 3.

Example 3

DEF Builders Ltd is registered for VAT and uses the flat rate scheme. It has just completed a large job erecting a new roof for a builder on a new residential property (zero-rated supply). The value of the work carried out was £30,000 and it was the only job the company performed during the VAT quarter ended 31 March 2010 (VAT rate is 17.5% again). A sales invoice was raised for the completed work on 31 March 2010.

GHI Builders Ltd is registered for VAT and uses the flat rate scheme. It has just completed a large job erecting a new roof for a builder on an existing residential property (standard-rated supply). The value of the work carried out was £30,000 plus VAT and it was the only job GHI performed during the VAT quarter ended 31 March 2010. A sales invoice was raised for the completed work on 31 March 2010.

What is the VAT position of the two companies?

Solution – assuming that both companies supply labour and materials, the flat rate for general building or construction services is 8.5%. This will produce a VAT bill of £2,550 for DEF Builders Ltd (ie £30,000 x 8.5%), and leave them with net income on the job carried out of £27,450 (ie £30,000 less £2,550).

GHI Builders Ltd will have a VAT bill of £2,996.25 (ie £30,000 plus VAT × 8.5%), leaving them with net income on the job carried out of £32,253.75 (ie £35,250 less £2,996.25).

As can be seen, the flat rate scheme has produced a very bad result for DEF Builders Ltd because it has produced an output tax liability on a job where the company charged no VAT. However, for GHI Builders Ltd (and for any building company carrying out wholly or mainly standard-rated work), the 8.5% flat rate may prove very attractive.

Flat rate scheme not suitable for repayment traders

8.6 The lowest flat-rate percentage for any trade sector is 2%. Therefore, it is impractical for any repayment trader (eg a business with wholly or mainly zero-rated sales) to use the scheme because it is impossible to obtain repayments from HMRC. In reality, the scheme is only suitable for businesses that, over a period of time, are in a net payment position to HMRC.

Flat rate scheme may produce a high tax bill for a business with two different activities

8.7 A rule of the flat rate scheme is that if a business has two or more different activities, the flat rate to be chosen will be based on the activity that represents the greater or greatest proportion of its turnover. In some cases, this situation may produce a very favourable result for a taxpayer – for example, where the VAT bill on his secondary activity would be higher than on his main activity – but the opposite result can also occur.

Another important point is that if the mix of sales between the two different activities changes (ie creating the situation when the secondary activity becomes the main business) then the flat-rate percentage will need to reflect this change – but from the date that coincides with the anniversary of the business joining the scheme in the first place.

An interesting tribunal case on this point which involved a publican was *Morgan (t/a The Harrow Inn) v Revenue and Customs Comrs* (30 June 2006, unreported) (MAN/05/0726 19671). The case produced a bad result for the taxpayer, due to the fact that the catering part of the business became more significant in terms of turnover than the wet sales.

At the time of applying to join the flat rate scheme, the Morgans described their business as a pub and used the appropriate flat rate of 5.5% from 1 January 2004. However, the catering activity soon became the greater part of total sales, meaning that the flat rate percentage should have been increased to 12% (percentage for catering) on the anniversary date of when the scheme was first adopted, namely 1 January 2005. The Morgans failed to adjust the percentage, and the tribunal supported HMRC's assessment to the higher rate.

The essential learning point form the *Morgan* case is that the mix of sales for any business using the flat rate scheme should be reviewed on an annual basis. If a higher rate becomes appropriate, then the taxpayer must either pay an increased amount of tax or withdraw from the flat rate scheme and adopt normal VAT accounting methods.

Choosing a business category

8.8 The choice of the trade sector and the relevant flat-rate percentage to adopt is down to the individual business to choose from the table produced by HMRC. In making a choice, the everyday meaning of the words should be used.

To assist businesses in their choice of trade sector, HMRC has produced a ready reckoner (available at www.hmrc.gov.uk) that lists trades and trade sectors. This includes drop-down lists of trades that HMRC believes belong in each sector.

Once HMRC has approved a business to join the scheme, it will not change the category of business on a retrospective basis as long as the choice made by the business was reasonable and records have been kept as to why it was chosen. For example, there may be certain businesses that could overlap into two different categories, and the final choice will require a careful analysis of the business activity to decide the most appropriate category.

Many advisers and clients are concerned about the prospect of an HMRC officer making a routine visit then telling the taxpayer he has chosen the wrong flat rate percentage (too low), and that a retrospective assessment for the last three years would be issued.

However, reassurance is given by HMRC's VAT Notice 733 (para 4.3), which states:

> 'if we approve you to join the scheme, we will not change your choice of sector retrospectively as long as your choice was reasonable. It will be sensible to keep a record of why you chose your sector in case you need to show us that your choice was reasonable.'

To HMRC's credit, there have not been reports about visiting officers hunting for easy game by unfairly reclassifying flat rate categories and going against the spirit of para 4.3. There may have been a few cases where officers have 'tested the waters' with an alternative proposal – but nothing too heavy-handed.

A list of categories and the appropriate percentage rates can be found at Appendix 8A.

One case where HMRC did challenge the taxpayer's chosen category (incorrectly) at a VAT Tribunal was in the case of *Chilly Wizard Ice Cream Co Ltd v Revenue and Customs Comrs* [2007] STC 464 (LON/06/10 19977). Chilly Wizard operated an outdoor kiosk selling ice-cream and milkshakes, including two tables and six chairs for the use of customers. They had opted to use the favourable 2% flat rate that applied to 'retailers of food, confectionery, tobacco, newspapers or children's clothing'. However, HMRC ruled that the chosen rate should have been 12% for 'catering services, including restaurants and takeaways'.

The tribunal's reasoning confirmed that the there was no element of service (catering) in the supplies being made by the business – the supplies being of goods to meet the need of individuals for refreshment. The tribunal also hinted that 'takeaways' would generally involve hot food. On this basis, the tribunal supported the taxpayer's conclusion that his main activity was 'retailing food', ie the 2% flat rate was the correct option.

Consider all forms of business income

8.9   During the recent months, the author has been in close liaison with HMRC's policy team in Liverpool to discuss some of the finer points of the flat rate scheme, particularly concerning whether certain categories of business income should be included or excluded from the calculations.

It is crucial that all advisers are aware of the issues raised in this section because the income sources are very common for many individuals.

The starting point is to remember that a VAT registration includes all supplies made by a 'taxable person'. Hence, a sole trader who runs a restaurant and also repairs cars will need to account for VAT on both activities if he is registered. However, there would be no problem if the two activities were under different legal entities, eg if the sole trader was in a partnership in the car repair business with his friend.

Buy-to-let income – excluded or included?

Example 4

> Steve is an accountant who is registered for VAT as a sole trader. He uses the flat rate scheme (11.5% rate for accountants) and also owns a flat in Leicester that he rents out for £1,000 per month. Does he also apply the flat rate scheme percentage to his rental income?
>
> *Solution* – as explained in a previous section, a disadvantage of the scheme is that the relevant percentage is applied to exempt and zero-rated business income, and rental income is definitely exempt. However, is the income from a buy-to-let arrangement classed as business or private income? If it is private income, it can be excluded.

Unfortunately, the view of HMRC (with which the author agrees) is that rental income must be included because of the EU definition of 'economic activity' (Directive 2006/112/EC, Art 9(1)). To quote from the Directive:

> 'The exploitation of tangible or intangible property for the purposes of obtaining income therefrom on a continuing basis shall in particular be regarded as an economic activity.'

The VAT registration of a sole trader includes all of his activities – it is the person rather than the business that is registered. However, the good news is that many clients will avoid a problem where they have different legal entities for their business and property income.

So then, if this example does apply to your client, should you go back three years and calculate any underpaid VAT on the rental income and adjust your next VAT return (if it is below the error notification limit of £10,000 or 1% of Box 6 outputs to a ceiling of £50,000)? And moving forward, should you withdraw from the scheme if the inclusion of rental income means you are worse off with the scheme? Or should you consider a change in the legal entity of the business or property?

The answer is 'yes' with the first question and 'possibly' with the others.

Note – see **8.21** with regard to withdrawing from the scheme.

Sale of capital assets and bank interest received – included or excluded?

Example 5

Steve from the previous example has enjoyed a very profitable month. He has sold his buy-to-let flat in Leicester for £200,000 and his Mercedes business car for £20,000. He has invested the money from these asset sales in his business bank account and earned interest of £500. What are the flat rate scheme issues?

Solution – going back to the basic scheme rules, the relevant percentage is applied to exempt and zero-rated business income. This creates a VAT liability for a taxpayer on income where no VAT has been charged to a customer.

The two asset sales in this example are both sources of exempt income, and we have already confirmed that the property activity is classed as 'business' within EU law. In technical terms, the car sale is exempt under *VATA 1994, Sch 9, Group 14* ('Supplies of goods where input tax cannot be recovered', ie including motor cars available for private use).

The logical solution is for Steve to withdraw from the scheme before these two assets are sold – and revert to normal VAT accounting. The VAT bill of £25,300 (£200,000 + £20,000 x scheme percentage of 11.5%) would definitely outweigh any other gains!

However, supposing the horse has already bolted and you have a client who had a similar situation to Steve, and sold a property last year that they did not account for VAT on through the flat rate scheme?

The good news is that HMRC accepts that the issue of 'proportionality' would be relevant, and they would almost certainly allow the business to withdraw from the scheme on a retrospective basis. Proportionality is a rule of EU law that embodies a basic principle of fairness, ie it is relevant when the application of the law goes beyond its intended objectives.

However, placing reliance on proportionality for the car sale can be risky, as HMRC could potentially argue that the flat rate percentages already take into account the fact that many businesses have some exempt income.

Furthermore, HMRC also considers that the scheme percentage needs to be applied to income earned from business bank interest (but not dividend income that is outside the scope of VAT) – bad news for Steve and the £500 of interest earned on his account.

Is HMRC correct in its opinion? Should the bank interest be classed as exempt income under *VATA 1994, Sch 9, Group 5* or does it fall outside the scope of VAT as non-business investment income? The HMRC view could be challenged at a tribunal but the low amounts of tax that tend to be involved with the scheme (because it is only available to small businesses) make such a challenge unlikely. So the sensible outcome is to declare interest earned from a business bank account within the scheme calculations (as exempt income), especially as interest rates are currently quite low to further reduce the amount of tax at stake.

International trade – included or excluded?

Example 6

Steve has now produced accounts for a French business customer and charged a fee of £5,000. He has also sold the same customer a computer for £1,000. He has not charged VAT on either sale – what about the flat rate scheme?

Solution – Steve is correct to not charge VAT to his customer. The completion of the accounts represents a service within *VATA 1994, Sch 5 para 3*, and the place of supply for EU business customers is where the customer is based, ie France rather than the UK. So the French business customer will deal with VAT under the reverse charge procedures.

The sale of the computer is a sale of goods to another EU business, which is zero-rated as long as Steve shows the VAT number of the customer on his sales invoice and holds proof that the computer has left the UK. The French customer will again deal with the VAT on his own return by accounting for acquisition tax in Box 2.

With regard to the flat rate scheme, there is good and bad news. The good news is that the accountancy fee is excluded from the scheme calculation because the income is outside the scope of UK VAT. However, the sale of the goods is included because it is zero-rated.

The concern that has been raised with HMRC was that the latter situation produces double taxation because tax is being paid twice on the same supply, ie flat rate scheme tax in the UK and acquisition tax in France.

The author submitted the view that income from selling goods to VAT registered businesses in other EU countries should be excluded from the scheme.

HMRC disagreed.

Its view on this is the same as explained with the earlier example. HMRC considers that the flat rate percentages are adjusted to take into account the fact that many businesses have a proportion of zero-rated or exempt income – hence, in its opinion, there is no double taxation.

So then, what is the solution? Hopefully this situation will not be a new revelation to any reader as it has already been explained in HMRC's VAT Notice 733 (para 6.4). However, as with earlier examples, a big zero-rated sale may warrant a rapid exit from the scheme.

Potential savings to be made by using the flat rate scheme

8.10   As explained at **8.1**, HMRC is very keen to promote the time saving and administrative benefits of the flat rate scheme, rather than potential tax savings for certain categories of business. However, the fact remains that the nature of the scheme and its calculations produce some winners and some losers. It is important to identify those clients who will benefit from using the scheme, and those clients who should avoid it at all costs because of the higher VAT bill they could encounter.

In some cases (and this is the point that would be stressed by HMRC) it may be beneficial for a business to still use the scheme, even if it produces a slightly higher tax bill. For example, if a business finds the record-keeping requirements of normal VAT accounting very onerous, it may be prepared to enjoy the simplicity of the flat rate scheme even if there is a financial cost in terms of extra VAT to pay. If a business has been submitting late returns and incurring default surcharge penalties due to record-keeping problems, then the flat rate scheme will prove a winner if it avoids future penalties.

However, an adviser should be aware of the situations discussed at **8.11–8.15** when reviewing the VAT affairs of a client (and it is worthwhile to review the possible benefits of the scheme on an annual basis).

Making use of the 10% and 11% flat rates for activities not listed elsewhere

8.11   One of the aims of the flat rate scheme is to ease the administrative burden for small businesses. As a result of this aim, HMRC sensibly limited the total number of different categories within the scheme to 55. After all, it would be a minefield of bureaucracy if a small business owner had to go through a list of 500 different categories of business, all with different flat-rate percentages, to see where he belonged.

As a result of the limit in the number of categories, HMRC has included two categories that can benefit certain businesses:

- any other activity that is not listed elsewhere 10% (9% for the temporary period when the VAT rate is 15%); and

- business services that are not listed elsewhere 11% (9.5% whilst the VAT rate of 15% is in place).

The above percentages are very favourable for any qualifying small business that has negligible input tax – see Example 7.

Example 7

James is VAT registered and considering the use of the flat rate scheme. The nature of his business means that all of his outputs are standard rated and he has negligible input tax to reclaim on his costs (total of £500 per year). His taxable sales are expected to be £149,000 per year excluding VAT.

An examination of the various categories under the flat rate scheme shows there is no specific category for the type of business being carried out by James, so he would qualify for the 10% rate as an activity that is not listed elsewhere (assuming VAT rate of 17.5%). Is it worthwhile for James to adopt the flat rate scheme?

Solution – by adopting the flat rate scheme, James' annual VAT bill will be calculated as follows:

Gross turnover (£149,000 × 1.175) × 10% flat rate = £17,507.50

Under normal VAT accounting, his VAT bill would be:

Output tax (£149,000 × 17.5%) = £26,075

Input tax = £500

Payable = £25,575.

The net VAT saving to James is £8,067.50 per year.

Note – the two reasons why the flat rate scheme produces such a good deal in this particular example is because the nature of the business means that James has very little input tax and also the activity he carries out does not have its own flat rate category and therefore can benefit from the generous flat rate of 10%.

In reality, the nature of the global economy and the emphasis of the UK economy on service trades means that many business activities could fall into the 10% category (or at worst the 11% category for business services that are not listed elsewhere). Unless these businesses have a high amount of input tax, then the flat rate scheme should prove a winner.

Businesses with more than one activity

8.12   The rules of the flat rate scheme state that where a business has turnover generated from two or more activities, then the flat-rate percentage applied should be based on the activity with the greater or greatest percentage of turnover. This situation can also produce tax savings for certain categories of business – see Example 8.

Example 8

The Green Man is a small village pub with two main activities – the sale of drinks as a public house, and a thriving bed and breakfast activity using six letting rooms on the premises.

The accounting figures for the previous 12 months (VAT exclusive) were as follows:

Wet sales	£80,000
Bed and breakfast sales	£70,000
Input tax on wet sale activity	£9,000
Input tax on bed and breakfast activity	£1,000

The above figures take into account the key trends for this type of business. For example, the main expenses of the bed and breakfast activity (staff costs, food for breakfast, premises costs such as rates and water) will have very little input tax; the wet sales will have high input tax because all purchases of goods will be standard rated.

The above situation is acknowledged through the flat rate scheme percentages because a pub is given a flat rate of 5.5%, compared to a rate of 9.5% for hotels/accommodation (again based on a VAT rate of 17.5%).

However, in the case of the Green Man, the overall rate to be applied for the business will be the lower rate of 5.5% because the wet sales represent the greater percentage of sales (53% of total sales).

So what is the VAT saving using the flat rate scheme?

Solution – under normal VAT accounting, output tax of £26,250 (£150,000 × 17.5%) will be reduced by input tax of £10,000 (£9,000 plus £1,000), leaving a bill to pay of £16,250.

With the flat rate scheme, a 5.5% flat rate is applied to gross turnover of £176,250 (£150,000 × 1.175), leaving a liability of £9,693.75.

The net saving is £6,556.25.

The situation in Example 8 could apply to many other businesses that have a core activity with a lower flat-rate percentage, and a secondary activity that would be liable to a higher flat rate. For example, consider a health food shop that sells goods (2% flat rate) but where the sole proprietor also offers his services as a dietician, preparing menus for clients looking to lose weight. If his fee income as a dietician is £70,000 plus VAT and is the secondary part of the business, then he can charge £12,250 in output tax to his customers – but effectively only pays over £1,645 to HMRC under the flat rate scheme (although obviously he will lose some input tax by using the scheme).

Benefit from 1% extra saving in first year of trading

8.13   A new business needs to make the most of any bonus income that can be gained in its early years of trading, especially during difficult economic times.

When the flat rate scheme was first introduced in 2002, many of the rates were very unattractive and offered little financial incentive. For example, a computer consultant was faced with a flat-rate percentage of 14.5%, giving very little scope for potential benefit unless his total input tax was extremely low.

From 1 January 2004, revised flat rates were introduced and, equally importantly, a 1% reduction in the flat rate was also given to newly registered businesses in their first year. The combination of these two measures has made the scheme more attractive to many businesses – see Example 9.

Example 9

JKL Accounting Services Ltd is a new business that achieved turnover of £125,000 in its first year (VAT exclusive) – it became VAT registered from day one, and applied the flat-rate percentage for accountants of 13% (assuming VAT rate of 17.5%). The company estimated that the flat rate scheme would not save any money compared to normal VAT accounting but would save administration time in preparing the quarterly returns (as explained above, saving of time is the key benefit publicised by HMRC).

At the end of the year, the company discovers that it should only have accounted for VAT at 12% of its gross income, due to the 1% discount in its first year of registration. This results in a VAT rebate of £1,468.75 (£125,000 plus VAT × 1%) – the flat rate scheme has now proved a financial winner for the company.

As an interesting aside, there may be cases where a business uses the flat rate scheme in its first year of trading but then decides that the loss of the 1% first year discount will not make it worthwhile to continue with the scheme thereafter. A plus point is that there is no minimum period where a business must stay in the scheme – it can leave voluntarily at the end of any VAT period, as long as written notification is made to HMRC.

Flexible use of flat-rate percentages

8.14   As explained at 8.8, one of the conditions of the flat rate scheme is that it is up to the taxpayer to identify which category he belongs to – and HMRC has confirmed it will not challenge this decision as long as the choice made was reasonable and records are kept as to why it was chosen.

In choosing the category, the words should be given their ordinary meanings. However, be aware of the existence of a ready reckoner that is available on the HMRC website (www.hmrc.gov.uk) that lists trades and trade sectors and how HMRC feel they should be applied within the flat rate scheme.

In reality, any situation where decisions are based upon words and the interpretation of words means there will be different conclusions reached on the same situation by different people. In such situations, it is important that tax advisers look very carefully at the flat-rate percentages and make sure they choose the correct one for their clients, which could also be the most favourable. See Example 10.

Example 10

Jim Jones is a self-employed tax consultant, registered for VAT and wishing to use the flat rate scheme. He reviews the list of business categories and decides that the most appropriate rate to apply is the 13% rate for accountancy services. But is he correct?

Solution – in reality, the work of a tax adviser is very different to that of an accountant because a tax adviser can work very effectively without knowing a thing about balance sheets, debits and credits, journals and SSAPs.

A tax adviser could benefit from the 11% rate for professional or business services not listed elsewhere – although the HMRC website indicates he could be classed as a management consultant (see 8.23 about the tribunal case that clarified the definition of a management consultant). The rate for a management consultant is 12.5% – not as good as the 11% rate but still better than the 13% rate for accountants.

Construction industry concession

8.15   As a final example on the benefits of the flat rate scheme, consider the following annual VAT figures for two building companies and the difference between the two as far as the scheme is concerned:

- ABC Ltd is a decorating company with annual turnover of £150,000 (VAT exclusive). It employs direct labour of £94,500; purchases materials costing £16,500 (VAT exclusive); pays overheads of £4,000 (all subject to VAT) – these costs leave a profit of £35,000.

- DEF Ltd is a decorating company with annual turnover of £150,000 (VAT exclusive). It employs direct labour of £94,500; purchases materials costing £14,500 (VAT exclusive); pays overheads of £6,000 (all subject to VAT) – these costs leave a profit of £35,000.

Under normal VAT accounting and 17.5% rate of VAT, both of the above companies would pay VAT of £22,662 (output tax of £26,250 less input tax of £3,588) – but what about the flat rate scheme?

The dilemma is whether the companies would be classed as providing labour-only building services, which would qualify for an unattractive flat rate of 13.5% (and a VAT bill of £23,794 which produces a higher liability than normal accounting) or providing general building services. The latter attracts a favourable flat rate of 8.5% – the final VAT bill of £14,981 is a good result.

The decision as to which category to apply is helpfully clarified by HMRC in its flat rate scheme leaflet:

> 'Use "labour only" if the value of materials supplied is less than 10% of your total turnover. If the value of the materials is more than this, builders should use the "General building" flat rate.'

In the two examples above, ABC Ltd has a material cost equal to 11% of turnover and therefore can benefit from the 8.5% general building rate. However, the material costs for DEF Ltd are only 9.7% of turnover, ie they must apply the flat rate of 13.5%.

Completing VAT returns

8.16   The key point with completing VAT returns under the flat rate scheme is that most of the nine boxes will be zero – unless the business has dealings with other EU countries. The treatment of the nine boxes is as follows:

Box 1 – this will be the VAT payable by the business under the flat rate scheme. There may, on rare occasions, be an extra sum due to reflect output tax payable on the sale of any capital assets on which input tax was reclaimed when the asset was purchased.

Box 2 – complete in the normal way if the business has acquisitions from other EU countries. If a business does not have EU acquisitions, the box will be blank.

Box 3 – total of Box 1 and Box 2.

Box 4 – the input tax box will usually be zero because the flat rate scheme ignores input tax issues, including any acquisition VAT declared in Box 2 of the return. The only exceptions are to reclaim input tax on capital expenditure where the VAT inclusive value of the item is more than £2,000, or to claim input tax on stock/assets on hand at the time of registration.

Box 5 – Box 3 less Box 4 in the usual way.

Box 6 – enter the value of turnover to which the flat rate scheme percentage was applied.

Box 7 – usually nil, apart from the related cost of the capital expenditure and assets on hand issues explained in Box 4 above.

Boxes 8 and 9 – complete as normal. Again, these boxes will be zero for any business that does not deal with the EU.

Other matters

8.17 The points below should also be taken into account when dealing with the flat rate scheme.

Basis of calculating turnover

8.18 There are three methods that can be used to calculate turnover in a relevant period – the basic turnover method, the cash-based turnover method and the retailer's method. Once adopted, a method should normally be used for at least 12 months.

The *basic turnover* method will be based on sales made with a tax point in the relevant VAT period (ie date of invoice or receipt of payment, whichever happens sooner) and will usually be based on invoices raised.

The *cash-based turnover* method is based on supplies for which a business has been paid during a period and can benefit a business that gives extended credit terms to its customers. The basic rules of the cash-based turnover method are the same as for cash accounting.

The *retailer's turnover* method uses daily gross takings as the basis for calculating its sales value.

Dealing with acquisitions from EU countries

8.19 Under normal accounting arrangements, a taxable business will import goods from other EU countries without VAT being charged and will then apply the reverse charge calculation by accounting for output tax in Box 2 of the return, and claiming the same amount of input tax in Box 4.

For a business using the flat rate scheme, the Box 2 entry will still apply but there will be no opportunity to reclaim input tax in Box 4. The only exception to this rule is if the item being imported is a capital asset exceeding £2,000 including VAT – or relates to stock and assets on hand at the time of registering for VAT.

Disbursements

8.20   A business that makes genuine disbursements on behalf of a client can exclude the value of these disbursements from the turnover calculation it makes under the flat rate scheme. An example of a genuine disbursement relates to MoT test fees recharged by a car repair business to his customer or a solicitor who invoices his customer for, eg stamp duty or land registry fees paid on his behalf in relation to a property deal.

However, a recharge of expenses for providing a service is not classed as a disbursement. See Example 11.

Example 11

Jane is a tax lecturer and charges £1,000 for giving a lecture in Edinburgh. She also charges her client £100 for her return rail fare and £75 for her overnight accommodation. How does she deal with the VAT?

Solution – Jane will charge 17.5% VAT (15% until 31 December 2009) on her total fee of £1,175. The total amount charged (£1,175 plus VAT) is then the relevant figure for her flat rate scheme calculations. The rail fare and hotel expenses are not classed as disbursements.

Leaving the scheme

8.21   There are two main ways for a business to leave the scheme – either on a voluntary basis if it decides it no longer wishes to use the scheme or a compulsory basis if its turnover figure exceeds the specified limits. A business can withdraw voluntarily at any time, but must write to HMRC to confirm its withdrawal. In reality, the withdrawal date will normally coincide with the end of a VAT period.

A compulsory withdrawal would be necessary if the value of its total income (including VAT and exempt supplies) at the anniversary of its start date has exceeded £225,000. The only exception to this withdrawal is if HMRC is satisfied that total taxable income in the next 12 months will be less than £150,000, that is, again trading within the limits of the scheme. An example of when this situation might apply is if the turnover in the previous year was exceptionally high due to a one-off sale made by the business that is unlikely to be repeated.

If a business decides to leave the scheme on a voluntary basis, it cannot normally rejoin again for at least 12 months.

With effect from 1 April 2009, HMRC amended the legislation to clarify the basis of 'income' in relation to the leaving test for the flat rate scheme. There was previous confusion about whether the income test should be based on invoiced sales or payment dates if the taxpayer was using the cash based turnover method. The amendment to *VAT Regulations 1995*

(SI 1995/2518), *reg 55M* confirms that the relevant figure is determined by the method used by the taxpayer when he completes his VAT returns.

Backdated request to join the flat rate scheme

8.22   A common question that is often asked is whether it is acceptable to backdate an application to join the flat rate scheme, ie to recalculate previous VAT liabilities using the scheme rather than normal VAT accounting. This question is obviously raised in relation to circumstances where the scheme produces an exceptionally good result for a taxpayer and he would like to extend these benefits on a historic basis.

The answer to this question is essentially 'no', even though the regulations (*VAT Regulations 1995, reg 55B(1)(b)*) authorise HMRC to allow traders to join the scheme on any date it approves, ie past, present or future. However, its policy is to only allow backdated entry 'in exceptional circumstances'.

A recent tribunal case involving a journalist offered some hope (*David Burke* (unreported, 1 October 2008) (MAN/08/0523 20881)) but HMRC is to appeal the case. Mr Burke received a VAT visit in 2004 but the visiting officer had not told him he would be better off by joining the scheme. Mr. Burke put forward the view (successfully) that the failure of the officer to inform him about the scheme warranted an exceptional circumstance and that he should be allowed to join the scheme on a retrospective basis. The tribunal supported his view.

Note – as a point of interest, Mr Burke's VAT saving with the scheme was £20,000 over 5 years. This illustrates the importance of advisers considering the benefits of the scheme for all clients. There are many businesses who are still unaware of the scheme (or aware of it but not using it) who could save a lot of tax.

HMRC approach to the scheme

8.23   A major concern for any taxpayer using the scheme would be if an HMRC officer made a routine VAT visit and told the taxpayer he had chosen the wrong flat rate percentage (too low) and he wanted to issue a retrospective assessment for the last three years. As explained above, the policy of HMRC is to not challenge a taxpayer's chosen flat rate category as long as the choice was made on a sensible and reasonable basis. This is the correct approach because the aim should be to encourage more users – not less.

As a separate comment, do not assume that HMRC's decision regarding a taxpayer's flat rate category is always final and correct. A tribunal case to support this statement is *Calibre TAS Ltd* (27 September 2007, unreported) (LON/07/594 20508).

The taxpayer's activity was to produce reports in personal injury cases, assessing the injured party's earnings potential before and after the injury.

The appellant joined the flat rate scheme on 1 April 2004 under the category of 'Business services that are not listed elsewhere' at 11%. However, HMRC strangely challenged this conclusion, and initially deemed the taxpayer to be a 'Lawyer' at 13%. HMRC subsequently changed its thinking so that he was classed as a 'Management consultant' at 12.5%.

The tribunal considered the definition of 'management consultancy' to broadly mean 'advice as to how a business should be run or restructured' – and concluded that the appellant did not provide such services. It agreed with the taxpayer's view that the 11% rate was correct for 'Business services that are not listed elsewhere' – and allowed the taxpayer's appeal with costs.

Planning points to consider

8.24   The following planning points should be given consideration.

- Note that the flat rate scheme allows a business buying capital goods costing more than £2,000 including VAT to reclaim input tax on the purchase of the assets. There may be opportunities for a business to buy a slightly more expensive asset (e g upgraded computer) to exceed the £2,000 limit to benefit from the VAT saving. However, be aware that a claim does not apply in relation to building projects, e g an office extension, because the supplies in such cases are of 'building services' rather than 'capital goods'.

- Be aware of the main disadvantage of the flat rate scheme – namely that the flat-rate percentage needs to be applied to zero-rated and exempt sales. This could make the scheme very unattractive to taxpayers who have an unpredictable level of zero-rated sales, such as builders. Exempt income also includes buy-to-let income, the sale of certain property and other capital assets and, according to HMRC, interest received on a business bank account.

- The flat rate scheme offers potential savings of tax to certain users. As with any scheme based on averages, there will always be winners and losers – and the five examples given at **8.11–8.15** illustrate where a lot of money can be saved by using the scheme.

- Even if a business has exceeded the turnover limit where it must leave the scheme (£225,000 per year on the anniversary of when it joined the scheme), there may be scope to remain within the scheme if HMRC is satisfied that the total taxable income in the next 12 months will be less than £150,000 – again within the scheme limits.

- Review a client's chosen flat-rate category on an annual basis to ensure it is still valid. This is particularly important for a business with two or more activities because the flat rate is based on the activity with the greater (greatest) percentage of turnover. If the secondary activity overtakes the main activity in terms of turnover, then this will become the relevant activity as far as the flat-rate scheme is concerned.

- Remember that a business can benefit from an extra 1% discount on the relevant flat rate % in its first year of VAT registration. This could produce a considerable saving of tax in a 12-month period.

- Be aware that most of the flat rate percentages were reduced for the period 1 December 2008 to 31 December 2009 to coincide with the temporary reduction in the standard rated of VAT from 17.5% to 15%. See Appendix 8A.

Appendix 8A — Trade Sectors and Flat Rate Percentages for the Flat Rate Scheme

The table below shows the trade sectors and flat rate percentages in alphabetical order.

Trade sector (from 1 January 2004)	Flat rate percentage*
Accountancy or book-keeping	13 (11.5%)
Advertising	9.5 (8.5%)
Agricultural services	7.5 (7%)
Any other activity not listed elsewhere	10 (9%)
Architect, civil and structural engineer or surveyor	12.5 (11%)
Boarding or care of animals	10.5 (9.5%)
Business services that are not listed elsewhere	11 (9.5%)
Catering services, including restaurants and takeaways	12 (10.5%)
Computer and IT consultancy or data processing	13 (11.5%)
Computer repair services	11 (10%)
Dealing in waste or scrap	9.5 (8.5%)
Entertainment or journalism	11 (9.5%)
Estate agency or property management services	11 (9.5%)
Farming or agriculture that is not listed elsewhere	6 (5.5%)
Film, radio, television or video production	10.5 (9.5%)
Financial services	11.5 (10.5%)
Forestry or fishing	9 (8%)
General building or construction services	
Note – Use 'General building' if the value of materials supplied is more than 10% of your turnover. If the value of the materials is less than this, use the 'Labour only' flat rate.	8.5 (7.5%)

Trade sector (from 1 January 2004)	Flat rate percentage*
Hairdressing or other beauty treatment services	12 (10.5%)
Hiring or renting goods	8.5 (7.5%)
Hotel or accommodation	9.5 (8.5%)
Investigation or security	10 (9%)
Labour-only building or construction services	
Note – Use 'Labour-only' if the value of materials supplied is less than 10% of your turnover. If the value of the materials is more than this, use the 'General building' flat rate.	13.5 (11.5%)
Laundry or dry-cleaning services	11 (9.5%)
Lawyer or legal services	13 (12%)
Library, archive, museum or other cultural activity	7.5 (7.5%)
Management consultancy	12.5 (11%)
Manufacturing food	7.5 (7.5%)
Manufacturing that is not listed elsewhere	8.5 (7.5%)
Manufacturing yarn, textiles or clothing	8.5 (7.5%)
Manufacturing fabricated metal products	10 (8.5%)
Membership organisation	5.5 (5.5%)
Mining or quarrying	9 (8%)
Packaging	8.5 (7.5%)
Photography	9.5 (8.5%)
Post Offices	2 (2%)
Printing	7.5 (6.5%)
Pubs	5.5 (5.5%)
Publishing	9.5 (8.5%)
Real estate activity not listed elsewhere	12 (11%)
Repairing personal or household goods	8.5 (7.5%)
Repairing vehicles	7.5 (6.5%)
Retailing food, confectionery, tobacco, newspapers or children's clothing	2 (2%)
Retailing pharmaceuticals, medical goods, cosmetics or toiletries	7 (6%)
Retailing vehicles or fuel	7 (5.5%)
Retailing that is not listed elsewhere	6 (5.5%)
Secretarial services	11 (9.5%)
Social work	8.5 (8%)
Sport or recreation	7 (6%)
Transport or storage, including couriers, freight, removals and taxis	9 (8%)
Travel agency	9 (8%)
Veterinary medicine	9.5 (8%)
Wholesaling agricultural products	6 (5%)
Wholesaling food	5.5 (5%)
Wholesaling that is not listed elsewhere	7 (6%)

* Based on VAT rate of 17.5% (percentages based on 15% rate of VAT are shown in brackets).

Chapter 9

Capital Goods Scheme

Key topics in this chapter:

- Situations when the capital goods scheme will apply.

- Capital expenditure that is included (and excluded) within the scheme.

- How to calculate the annual adjustments required by the capital goods scheme.

- How to deal with assets purchased before a business was registered for VAT.

- Dealing with the sale of capital items before the end of the final adjustment period.

- The disposal test and rules for final adjustment periods after an asset has been sold.

- The requirement for the buyer of a business to take over the remaining intervals for capital items included within the scheme.

Introduction

9.1 The capital goods scheme was introduced in 1990, and was specifically intended to close a loophole in the legislation whereby certain businesses were able to gain an unfair rate of input tax recovery on their capital expenditure.

Basically, the capital goods scheme means that when considering input tax recovery on major capital expenditure, it is necessary to consider the use of the item over a 5 or 10-year period, not just at the time it is purchased. In effect, therefore, input tax claimed on the initial purchase is adjusted over a 5 or 10-year period, which means the capital goods scheme is mainly relevant to businesses making some exempt supplies.

Situations when the capital goods scheme is relevant

9.2 If a business only makes exempt supplies, then it will not be VAT registered because it is not making taxable supplies. In such cases, any VAT charged on the purchase of capital equipment becomes part of the cost of the equipment, ie the gross amount of the invoice is capitalised to the fixed asset account. A business only making exempt supplies has no opportunity to reclaim any input tax on its purchases.

If a business wholly makes taxable supplies, and no exempt supplies, then input tax can be fully reclaimed on the purchase of any capital equipment used for the business (with the exception of motor cars in most cases). If the business continues to make wholly taxable supplies over a 5 or 10-year period, then there will be no adjustment to make to the initial claim of input tax.

The situation where the capital goods scheme is relevant is where a business has some exempt supplies and some taxable supplies over a 5 or 10-year period – see Example 1.

Example 1

ABC Ltd bought a freehold unit on 1 October 1997 for £400,000 plus VAT. As its activity in 1997 was to provide accountancy and taxation services (taxable activity), it reclaimed all of the input tax (£70,000) on its November 1997 VAT return.

On 1 October 2002, the company decided to move its accountancy and tax practice to a new location, and use the freehold unit to develop a new activity acting as insurance brokers (an exempt activity).

Solution – the initial purchase of the freehold unit is within the capital goods scheme (to confirm which items are included and which are excluded, see 9.3) so input tax needs to be adjusted over a 10-year period as the expenditure relates to property (if the purchase had been for computer equipment, then the adjustment period is reduced to 5 years).

In effect, the end result is that the company will recover half of the input tax. This is because the building was used to make taxable supplies for 5 years and exempt supplies for 5 years. However, in terms of cash flow, the initial input tax would have been fully recovered, and then half of the input tax would have been paid back to HMRC in years 6 to 10 (see 9.6 on how calculations are made under the scheme).

Items within the capital goods scheme

9.3 The situation at Example 1 above illustrates why the capital goods scheme plays an important part in ensuring a 'fair' rate of input tax recovery on a major item of expenditure. Consider what would happen if, for example, there was no capital goods scheme, and that the change of use to the insurance brokers office took place after 5 months instead of 5 years.

In this situation, the initial input tax would be reclaimed in full (as relevant to taxable supplies at the time of purchase) and no clawback of tax would be evident after the change in activity. This would be commercially unfair to other insurance brokers not able to gain any input tax recovery.

So what items are included within the capital goods scheme?

Basically, the following main categories of expenditure need to be taken into consideration (all quoted figures exclude VAT):

● a computer, or an item of computer equipment, costing £50,000 or more;

● land, a building or part of a building or civil engineering work or part of a civil engineering work where the value of the interest supplied to the owner is £250,000 or more (excluding any zero-rated or exempt elements);

● a building which the owner alters, or an extension to an annexe which he constructs, where additional floor area is created in the altered building of 10% or more of the original floor area before the work was carried out. The value of the work in connection with the alteration must be £250,000 or more;

● a building which the owner refurbishes or fits out where the value of the expenditure on the taxable supplies of services and of 'goods affixed' to the building (excluding any zero-rated expenditure) is £250,000 or more. However, only capitalised expenditure is included – not repairs and maintenance costs charged to the profit and loss account.

Capital expenditure for property

9.4 In many cases, a property transaction will include the initial purchase of land, plus the construction of a building on the land in question. In such cases, the combination of the land and property costs form one capital project as far as the £250,000 limit is concerned. However, if the purchase price of the land was zero-rated or exempt (eg no option to tax election in place for the seller of the land), this cost would be excluded.

As far as the items classed as capital expenditure are concerned, this will include the following:

● taxable goods and services supplied in connection with the construction (but excluding zero-rated items);

● the interest in the land if the supply was taxable (other than zero-rated land);

- the costs of making the building ready for occupation including: professional and management services (e g architects, surveyors, site managers); demolition and site clearance costs; materials used in the course of construction; equipment hire; haulage; landscaping; services relevant to building and civil engineering work.

Tips to consider

9.5   The above categories usually make it easy to identify if a project falls within the capital goods scheme. However, a few points need to be remembered.

- The scheme requires expenditure on computer equipment to be considered over a 5-year period – all other expenditure over a 10-year period. This is known as the 'adjustment period'.

- With regard to computer equipment, the scheme only applies to individual computers, and items of computer equipment. It would not therefore include a computerised telephone exchange or any item of computer software.

- The purchase of 50 separate computers at £1,000 each would not be included within the scheme – even though the total value of the expenditure reaches the £50,000 limit. However, a new computer server costing £50,000 would be within the scheme.

- All values relevant to the capital goods scheme are VAT exclusive. So a new computer costing £52,000 including VAT would not be included.

- The capital goods scheme only applies to capital items purchased by the business – and not items that are purchased for resale. A business involved in selling computers would therefore exclude all goods bought for resale to customers.

- The work that is classed as 'civil engineering' relates to the everyday meaning of the term – including work on roads, bridges, golf courses, running tracks and installation of pipes for connection to main services.

- The phrase 'goods affixed' should also be given its everyday meaning – in general, they are items that would be sold with the property, e g windows, permanent flooring, air conditioning, permanent partitioning.

- Be aware of the impact of a phased refurbishment. If it is clear that there is only one overall refurbishment contract, then this would be included within the capital goods scheme if the value of the expenditure exceeded £250,000. But if the refurbishments were carried out in very distinct parts and with distinct contracts (e g first floor refurbished in 2005; ground floor in 2006; second floor in 2007) then the value of each project would be taken in isolation.

- There may be occasions during the life of an asset when it is not used by the business eg a computer that has broken down and needs major repair works. In such situations, calculations for the capital goods scheme are still made as if the asset is still being used by the business.

As a final point, it is important to be clear about what actually constitutes capital expenditure. In basic terms, the VAT definition follows normal accounting principles. If the expenditure is capitalised to the balance sheet as a fixed asset addition, then it needs to be taken into account. In the case of computer equipment, the amount capitalised includes any delivery or installation costs.

To highlight the principles explained above, see Example 2.

Example 2

Alan is VAT consultant for Kelly and Co accountants, and has four queries from clients as to whether their proposed projects fall within the capital goods scheme.

- Client A runs a large restaurant in a 10,000 square metre complex which he owns. He is planning to build a 1,500 square metre extension at a cost of £200,000 excluding VAT.

- Client B is to undertake a massive office refurbishment project costing £300,000 excluding VAT – analysed as follows: new windows and air conditioning system £170,000; new office furniture £130,000.

- Client C runs a carpet warehouse and intends to build a new car park on some land at the back of the building. The cost of the building works on the car park will be £260,000 including VAT.

- Client D has decided to install Sage Line 50 to all of its computers across the country – at a total cost of £60,000 excluding VAT.

The answer to the above queries is that none of them fall within the capital goods scheme!

Although Client A is building an extension that adds more than 10% floor space to his existing premises, the value of the project is less than £250,000. For Client B, the office furniture is not classed as 'goods affixed' to the building – so this expenditure of £130,000 is not taken into account for the capital goods scheme – the balance of the expenditure on the windows and air conditioning is then under the £250,000 limit. Client C escapes because the VAT exclusive value of the project is less than £250,000 and Client D has no worries because the expenditure is on computer software.

Calculation method for the capital goods scheme

9.6   Having fully analysed the scope of the capital goods scheme, the next stage is to look at the calculations of the scheme, and how these are carried out in practice.

There are three key principles to consider:

- if an item of qualifying expenditure is wholly used by a business in making taxable supplies throughout the 10-year period relevant to the scheme (5 years in the case of computer expenditure) then there will be no adjustments to make. This is because the 100% taxable use would have produced a full input tax recovery on the initial expenditure – and as the asset continues to be used wholly for the taxable part of the business, this 100% recovery continues to be correct;

- if an item of qualifying expenditure is wholly used by the business in making exempt supplies throughout the 10-year period relevant to the scheme (5 years in the case of computer expenditure) then there will again be no adjustments to make. This is because the initial purchase would not have recovered any input tax – and as the asset continues to be wholly used for the exempt part of the business, the 0% recovery rate continues to be correct;

- in effect, therefore, the only adjustment that needs to be made is if the item in question is used by both taxable and exempt parts of the business (where the % level of taxable and exempt business changes each year under its partial exemption method) or if there is a clear change of use at some time during the 10-year period – as in Example 1 at **9.2**.

Basically, the formula that needs to be used each year to make the necessary calculations is as follows:

$$\frac{\text{Total input tax on the capital item}}{A} \times \text{the adjustment \%}$$

Where 'A' = number of years relevant to the expenditure, ie 5 for computer expenditure and 10 for all other expenditure.

The adjustment % is the difference (if any) between the extent to which the item was used in making taxable supplies at the time of the initial purchase (ie in accordance with the partial exemption method adopted by the business) and the extent of the use in the period being adjusted.

A number of other key points need to be taken into account:

- the first interval under the 5 or 10-year interval period relates to the period from the date the item is bought up to the end of the partial exemption year of the business. In effect, this means up to 31 March, 30 April or 31 May – depending on when the VAT periods end;

- any adjustment of VAT payable or repayable under the scheme needs to be corrected on the second VAT return of the following tax year, ie the VAT return which incorporates 30 September. So a business on calendar VAT quarters would make the capital goods scheme adjustment for the year ended 31 March 2009 on its September 2009 return. Any adjustment should be added to or deducted from Box 4;

- the reason why the adjustment period is made in the September period is because it avoids a partially exempt business having to do two adjustment calculations on the same return. This is because the partial exemption annual adjustment is always made in the period covered by 30 June – HMRC is generously giving an extra 3 months for the capital goods scheme adjustment to be made. See Example 3 for a full calculation within the scheme.

Example 3

ABC Ltd (from Example 1) purchased a new computer server for its head office at a cost of £100,000 plus VAT on 1 October 2004.

The equipment will be used for the overall company business, ie relevant to both taxable supplies (accountancy and taxation services) and exempt supplies (insurance brokers).

The company is on the standard method for partial exemption purposes (input tax on residual expenditure apportioned according to ratio of taxable to taxable plus exempt income) and has the following recovery rates for each of the tax years ending 31 March 2005 to 31 March 2009: 32%, 40%, 26%, 38%, 39%.

Solution – the first interval covers the period October 2004 to 31 March 2005 – producing an initial input tax recovery of £5,600 (ie £17,500 × 32%).

The taxable use has increased in the second interval from 32% to 40% – an additional 8%. Using the standard formula for the capital goods scheme, the additional input tax recovery for year ended 31 March 2006 will be: £17,500 × 8% divided by 5 = £280. This amount will be reclaimed in box 4 of the September 2006 return.

The taxable use in the third interval has decreased to 26% – and this will now produce a repayment to Customs of £210 on the September 2007 return, ie £17,500 × 6% divided by 5. In the final two intervals, additional amounts reclaimed will be £210 and £245.

Looking at the overall picture, the total input tax recovery on this item is as follows:

Year ended 31 March 2005	£5,600
Year ended 31 March 2006	£280
Year ended 31 March 2007	(£210)
Year ended 31 March 2008	£210
Year ended 31 March 2009	£245
Total recovery of tax	£6,125

Taking the average (mean) recovery rate for the 5-year period, for example:

(32 + 40 + 26 + 38 + 39 divided by 5 = 35)

confirms the accuracy of our overall figure: £17,500 x 35% = £6,125.

This brings us back to the key overall principle of the capital goods scheme – which is fairness to both the taxpayer and HMRC.

Dealing with assets purchased before a business was VAT registered

9.7   One concession granted by HMRC is that a business can reclaim input tax on goods acquired for the business before it became VAT registered, as long as a number of conditions are met, eg the asset must have been bought within 3 years before VAT registration (rising to 4 years by 1 April 2010); it must still be owned by the business at the time it becomes VAT registered; it must be used for the purpose of the business that is now VAT registered.

As far as the capital goods scheme is concerned, items bought before the business is registered will be relevant to the scheme if the £50,000 limit for computer equipment and £250,000 limit for property expenditure is exceeded. In such cases, the first interval period under the capital goods scheme will be the period from the date of registration for VAT up to the end of the tax year that follows, ie 31 March, 30 April or 31 May, depending on the VAT return dates of the business.

Sale of capital items during the adjustment period

9.8   The circumstances at Example 3 above assume that the asset in question is owned for the full 5-year period relevant to the capital goods scheme for computer equipment costing more than £50,000. However, it is possible that the item could be sold before the 5-year period has expired (10 years for buildings).

The first point to remember is that when it comes to partially exempt businesses, HMRC is always suspicious that complex VAT avoidance schemes could result in an unfair recovery of input tax. Anti-avoidance legislation is therefore in place through what is known as a 'disposal test'.

The basic rules for dealing with the sale of an asset during the adjustment period are as follows:

- for the interval period when the asset is sold, a normal calculation under the scheme is carried out, ie as if the asset was owned for the full period

- for the remaining complete intervals in the adjustment period, the input tax recovery will by 100% if the sale of the asset was a taxable supply (subject to the disposal test) and 0% if the sale of the asset was an exempt supply (ie as in certain property transactions). However, as well as the 'disposal test' (see **9.9**) another condition is that the value of the input tax recovered in the remaining complete intervals cannot exceed the output tax chargeable on the supply of the capital item.

The disposal test

9.9 The disposal test is not applied to bona fide commercial transactions – and is only in place to prevent a partially exempt business such as a bank or insurance company trying to get an unfair rate of input tax recovery through the disposal of a capital asset. This could occur if, for example, they made a significant exempt supply of a long lease of a property, followed immediately by the taxable disposal of the freehold for low consideration.

The basic rule of the disposal test (if it applies) is that the total amount of input tax reclaimed on the item (including the initial deduction in the first interval, and subsequent adjustments under the scheme) cannot exceed the output tax charged on the supply of the capital item.

However, the key point is that the disposal test only applies when HMRC considers a business is trying to gain an unjustified tax advantage. It will not be applied in the following circumstances:

- sales of computer equipment;

- where the owner sells an item at a loss due to the market conditions, eg a downturn in property prices;

- where the value of the capital item has depreciated (as would normally be the case with computers);

- where the value of the capital item is reduced for other legitimate reasons (eg discounted price for a quick sale).

To follow through the principles of dealing with disposals under the capital goods scheme, see Example 4.

Example 4

Taking Example 3 above a stage further, assume that ABC Ltd actually sold the equipment in year 3 for £20,000 plus VAT.

In this case, the first three intervals remain unchanged, ie deductions of £5,600 plus £280 less £210. However, because the sale of the equipment is a taxable supply, the recovery rates for years 4 and 5 would be 100% – creating additional input tax to reclaim of £2,380 for each of the 2 years (ie £17,500 × 68% divided by 5). However, the maximum amount that can actually be claimed is £3,500 because the amount charged as output tax on the disposal cannot be exceeded.

Sale of a capital item when a business is sold

9.10 The proceeds from the sale of a business are usually outside the scope of VAT as long as certain important conditions are met (see Chapter 4 – Transfer of a Going Concern). However, the new owner must still take over the responsibility for dealing with any remaining adjustment periods for assets subject to the capital goods scheme. In effect, the capital goods scheme does not cease to be relevant just because an asset has been transferred to a new owner.

To give an example, if Bill bought a property on 1 June 2004 which was subject to the capital goods scheme, and sold it to Ben as part of a business sale on 1 August 2009, the following outcome would apply:

- Bill would have accounted for six annual adjustments within the capital goods scheme, ie the first interval period to 31 March 2005 (assuming he is on calendar VAT returns), followed by four annual adjustments to 31 March 2009, and a final adjustment from 1 April 2009 to 31 July 2009.

- Ben takes over the remaining four interval periods (to complete the ten that are required for property transactions within the capital goods scheme), which must be made on the anniversary of when he bought the business, ie 1 August 2010 to 2013. He will still include any under or overpayment of tax on the second tax return after the end of his partial exemption year, ie the VAT return that includes 30 September.

The outcome of the above arrangement is that Ben might need to pay additional tax to HMRC, or, if the calculations are favourable, claim some tax in the final four adjustment periods. He needs to be aware of this situation when he buys the business from Bill. The other priority is for Ben to ensure he acquires adequate records from Bill about the original transaction (date when asset was purchased, initial deduction of input tax, copy of purchase invoice etc) to support his calculations in the event of a VAT visit.

Planning points to consider

9.11   The following planning points should be given consideration.

- It is important that tax advisers do not see the capital goods scheme as a threat – by recommending to clients that they deliberately try to keep projected capital expenditure below the £50,000 and £250,000 limits. In the case of a partially exempt business that expects to increase its level of taxable activities in the future, any expenditure on assets relevant to taxable and exempt supplies will actually produce a tax advantage by being within the scheme.

- Remember, the key point of the capital goods scheme is 'fairness' – so if the final calculations indicate that a business with 90% exempt income has managed to reclaim 50% of the input tax on a capital item, then there is likely to be an error in the computations.

- Although a business is only obliged to keep records for 6 years, it is important to ensure that records relating to a capital goods scheme item are kept for the full 10-year period (if the item relates to property).

- Be aware of the 'disposal test' to ensure there is no unfair input tax recovery on assets that are sold by a partially exempt business before the end of the adjustment period.

- Remember, a business that wholly makes taxable supplies over a 5 or 10-year period (ie no exempt supplies) will not be affected by the capital goods scheme calculations. This is because it will reclaim 100% of the input tax on the initial purchase of the equipment (subject to normal rules) and will not have any need to amend this percentage because the exclusive taxable use continues over the 5 or 10-year period relevant to the scheme

- The capital goods scheme annual adjustment is always declared on the second VAT return following the end of the tax year (ie the return which includes 30 September). This is different to the annual adjustment for partial exemption purposes, which is always declared in the first VAT quarter after the end of the tax year (ie the return which includes 30 June).

- Individual computers purchased with a total value exceeding £50,000 are excluded from the capital goods scheme. It is only relevant if one item of equipment is being bought worth more than £50,000. Expenditure on computer software is also excluded from the scheme.

- Do not forget that the new owner must take over the responsibility for any remaining scheme calculations of the seller in the event of a business sale (transfer of a going concern). It is important that the buyer is given adequate records from the seller to ensure accurate calculations can be carried out.

Chapter 10

Other Special Schemes: Retail Schemes and Second-hand Margin Schemes

---

Key topics in this chapter:

- The five different retail schemes approved by HMRC which can be used by a retail business that is registered for VAT.

- The rules and potential problems of each of the five different retail schemes.

- A practical example of each of the five different schemes – looking at situations when a scheme can produce a higher/lower tax bill for certain types of business.

- Procedures concerning second-hand margin schemes – available to traders dealing in second-hand goods.

Introduction

10.1   There are certain businesses that are allowed to calculate their output tax using a special method approved by HMRC – the main example being retailers. It would be very difficult for a retailer dealing mainly in small cash transactions to issue a tax invoice for every sale – a retailer is therefore allowed to use one of five different retail schemes.

Equally, many businesses that deal in second-hand goods (eg car traders, antique dealers) would be at a disadvantage under normal VAT accounting rules (ie output tax due on full value of supply) because most of the goods they purchase are bought from the general public, that is, there is no source of input tax to reclaim. In such cases, VAT would cease to be a margin tax and become a sales tax – but this situation is assisted by second-hand schemes for these types of traders.

Retail schemes

Introduction

10.2   The aim of a retail scheme is to enable a retailer to calculate his output tax liability in a simple, cost effective manner. If the retailer only sells goods at one rate of tax, then his output tax position is very simple – it becomes more complicated if he sells goods at different rates of tax. See Example 1.

Example 1

Jones is a clothes retailer and has two shops in the local High Street. The first shop sells women's clothes; the second shop sells a mixture of women's and girls' clothing.

On 15 July 2008, the gross takings from the first shop were £2,500; the sales of the second shop were £3,250.

What is the position of the two shops as far as output tax is concerned?

Solution – there is no problem with the output tax position of the first shop because all goods are being sold at one rate of tax, ie standard rated for adult clothing. The output tax liability will be: £2,500 × 7/47 = £372.34.

Note – 7/47 is the fraction relevant to a VAT rate of 17.5%. The fraction is reduced to 3/23 when the rate of VAT is 15%.

However, there is a problem for the second shop because some of the sales are standard rated (adult clothing) and some sales will be zero-rated as children's clothing. A special method of calculation will be needed to establish how much of the £3,250 is zero-rated and how much is standard rated – this objective will be achieved by the business adopting one of the five retail schemes published by HMRC – see 10.3.

As far as HMRC is concerned, it is content for a retailer to choose his own preferred scheme (as long as he is eligible) – the choice will often depend on the extent of computer technology available to him and how comfortable he is using this technology. Equally, however, the retailer may prefer a particular scheme due to a potential tax saving with its operation.

As with many VAT issues, HMRC has the power to refuse the use of a particular retail scheme in the following circumstances:

- if the use of a particular scheme does not produce a fair and reasonable result;

- it is necessary to do so for the protection of the revenue, ie to safeguard the tax yield;

- the retailer could reasonably be expected to account for VAT in the normal way.

Note – the condition about a scheme producing a fair and reasonable result does not mean that HMRC will direct the trader to adopt the scheme that produces the largest output tax liability. It means the method chosen must give a sensible overall calculation as far as output tax is concerned.

When VAT was first introduced in 1973, most calculations were based on manual records and limited computer involvement – hence why retail schemes have been simplified over the years. In reality, many retailers now adopt a 'point of sale' scheme, which means they are able to identify the output tax liability at the time a supply is made and produce a report of total standard/zero-rated sales made on a daily basis. This means, in effect, that the output tax calculation is an exact science, avoiding the need for estimates to be made.

Five approved retail schemes

10.3 A business with annual VAT exclusive turnover exceeding £130 (£100m until 31 March 2009) is only eligible to use a retail scheme if it agrees a bespoke scheme with HMRC.

There are five different schemes that are available to a business with turnover less than £130m as follows:

- Point of Sale Scheme – see **10.4**;

- Apportionment Scheme 1 – see **10.6**;

- Apportionment Scheme 2 – see **10.9**;

- Direct Calculation Scheme 1 – see **10.12**;

- Direct Calculation Scheme 2 – see **10.15**;

To assist with the understanding of each scheme, we will consider three points in each case:

(a) the rules that apply;

(b) types of business that may wish to use the scheme and potential problems; and

(c) a working example of each scheme.

Point of Sale Scheme

Rules

10.4 The rules of the scheme are as follows:

- this is the only scheme that can be adopted if all sales are standard rated or all sales are only taxable at the reduced rate;

- the turnover limit is £130m (£100m until 31 March 2009) excluding VAT;

- it can be used for services as well as goods, e g catering activities;

- there is no need to work out stock values at the end of a period or expected selling prices;

- no annual adjustment is required;

- the VAT liability of supplies needs to be correctly identifiable at the point of sale – usually with a multi-button till, electronic till or bar-coding system. These supplies could be zero-rated, standard rated, exempt or subject to VAT at the reduced rate – the correct VAT liability needs to be declared when the sale is made. See Example 2 below.

Types of business

10.5 The types of business that could use the scheme and potential problems are as follows:

- the scheme is simple to use and would therefore benefit users who want to simplify their VAT affairs as much as possible;

- the scheme largely relies on electronic tills that could be expensive to purchase. It is also important that staff are able to correctly operate these tills;

- as long as the tills and staff operating them are effective, the scheme gives a very accurate declaration of output tax due on goods or services supplied by a business;

- for a multi-button till system, lack of experience or knowledge by a member(s) of staff could prove costly for the business if staff members incorrectly classify zero-rated items as standard rated;

- to counter the above problem, a simple system of having, for instance, a different coloured price sticker for zero-rated goods, could help reduce errors made by a cashier.

Example 2

Smith Chemists sell a range of goods that are subject to VAT at standard rate, zero-rate and the reduced rate of VAT. A multi-button till is used to identify the VAT liability at the point of sale. All staff using the till are well trained on the VAT treatment of specific products.

The daily gross takings for the business in the VAT quarter ended 31 August 2008 are as follows:

Standard rated sales	£32,385
Zero-rated sales	£14,265
Reduced rate sales	£2,485

What is the output tax liability for the business?

Solution – output tax for the period is:

$(£32,385 \times 7/47) + (£2,485 \times 1/21) = £4,823.29 + £118.33 = £4,941.62.$

Note – the main products sold by a chemist that are subject to the reduced rate of VAT are contraceptive products and smoking cessation products.

Apportionment Scheme 1

Rules

10.6   The rules of the scheme are as follows:

- an annual turnover limit (VAT exclusive) of £1m;

- the scheme requires a business to calculate the proportion of purchases in each VAT period that are bought at different rates of VAT – these different proportions are then applied to the sales made by the business in the same period to calculate output tax;

- an annual adjustment is required with the scheme – up to the end of March, April or May each year depending on the date that coincides with the end of the VAT period;

- the scheme cannot be used for services;

- the scheme does not require stock valuations or calculations of expected selling prices.

Types of business

10.7   The type of business that could use Apportionment Scheme 1 and potential problems are as follows:

- the scheme is suitable for a small business that does not have electronic equipment or suitable method of identifying VAT liability at point of sale;

- all sales made by a business can be entered at the point of sale without being concerned about the rate of VAT that applies on the goods in question;

- the main disadvantage of the scheme is that because it is based on purchases, it will produce a higher tax bill (compared to a point of sale scheme) for a business that achieves a higher mark-up on zero-rated goods.

This is an important point for a business such as a confectioner, tobacconist and newsagent where a higher mark-up is achieved on newspapers (zero-rated) compared to cigarettes (standard rated).

See Example 3 below.

Calculating output tax

10.8   The following is an illustration of how to calculate output tax with the scheme.

For each VAT period (quarterly or monthly):

Step 1	Add up daily gross takings =	A
Step 2	Add up the cost, including VAT, of all goods received for resale at the standard rate =	B
Step 3	Add up the cost, including VAT, of all goods received for resale at the reduced rate =	C
Step 4	Add up the cost, including VAT, of all goods received for resale at standard, reduced and zero-rates =	D
Step 5	Calculate the proportion of daily gross takings from sales at the standard rate by dividing the total at Step 2 by the total at Step 4 and multiplying by the total in Step 1	
Step 6	Calculate the proportion of daily gross takings from sales at the reduced rate by dividing the total at Step 3 by the total at Step 4 and multiplying by the total in Step 1	
Step 7	To calculate output tax, add the total at Step 5 multiplied by the VAT fraction for standard-rated goods to the total at Step 6 multiplied by the VAT fraction for reduced rate goods	

In algebraic form (based on standard rate of 17.5% and reduced rate of 5%):

Output tax = (B divided by D × A × 7/47) + (C divided by D × A × 1/21).

Example 3

Janet sells newspapers and cigarettes and has decided to use Apportionment Scheme 1 as far as calculating her output tax liability is concerned. For quarter ended 30 June 2008, the total purchases of newspapers were £8,000 and cigarettes £12,000 plus VAT.

The daily gross takings of the business for the period were £28,000 including VAT. What is Janet's output tax liability?

As a separate point, Janet estimates that her newspaper sales for the period were £12,000. Is Apportionment Scheme 1 the most appropriate retail scheme for her to use? Would she be better advised to invest in a multi-button till and adopt the Point of Sale Scheme?

Solution – the proportion of standard rated purchases is (£12,000 + VAT) divided by (£12,000 + VAT + £8,000). It is important to note that the standard rated proportions include VAT because the calculations are being applied to a daily gross takings figure that also includes VAT.

The proportion of standard rated goods (63.8%, ie £14,100 divided by £22,100) gives an output tax liability as follows:

£28,000 × 63.8% × 7/47 = £2,660.59.

The next question is to consider whether the Point of Sale Scheme would give a better result. In principle, the answer is likely to be yes, because the mark-up achieved on newspapers is always higher than that achieved on cigarettes – and Apportionment Scheme 1 does not favour the situation where a higher mark-up is achieved on zero-rated goods.

If Janet estimates that her newspaper sales in the period are £12,000, this means her cigarette sales would be £16,000 (£28,000 gross takings less £12,000 for newspaper sales), giving an output tax liability of £2,382.98 (£16,000 × 7/47). This is a saving of £277.61 compared to Apportionment Scheme 1.

Note – remember that Janet will need to do an annual adjustment with Apportionment Scheme 1.

Apportionment Scheme 2

Rules

10.9 The rules of the scheme are as follows:

- the taxable turnover is less than £130m excluding VAT (£100m until 31 March 2009);

- supplies must be made at two different rates of VAT;

- the scheme is based on calculating expected selling prices of goods either used from stock or purchased during a period;

- the supplies of services (eg catering) must be dealt with outside the scheme;

- no annual adjustment is required but a rolling calculation method is used

- a stocktake is required at the beginning of the scheme being used, but not thereafter.

Types of business

10.10   The types of business that could use Apportionment Scheme 2 and the potential problems are as follows:

- the scheme will provide a more accurate calculation of output tax compared to Apportionment Scheme 1 because it is based on selling rather than purchase prices – and output tax is a tax on sales;

- the scheme can be complex to operate – especially in the early stages when opening stock valuations need to be included;

- an example of a business that could benefit from using the scheme is the newspaper/cigarette sales business highlighted in Example 3, ie with a higher mark-up on zero-rated goods. A business with a higher mark-up on zero-rated goods will enjoy the benefits of the scheme because the expected selling prices form the basis of output tax payments.

See Example 4 below.

Calculating output tax

10.11   The following are illustrations of how to calculate output tax with the scheme.

(a) For the first three quarterly VAT periods or the first eleven monthly VAT periods:

Step 1	Calculate the expected selling price, including VAT, of standard-rated goods for retail sale in stock at the commencement of using the scheme =	A
Step 2	Calculate the expected selling price, including VAT, of reduced rate goods in stock for retail sale at the commencement of using the scheme =	B
Step 3	Calculate the expected selling price, including VAT, of all goods in stock for retail sale at the commencement of using the scheme (ie including zero-rated goods) =	C
Step 4	Add up daily gross takings for the VAT period =	D
Step 5	Add up expected selling prices, including VAT, of standard-rated goods:	
	(i) received, made or grown for retail sale since starting to use the scheme; and	
	(ii) acquired from other EC countries since starting to use the scheme =	E
Step 6	Add the total in Step 5 to the total in Step 1	
Step 7	Add up expected selling prices, including VAT, of reduced rate goods:	

(i) received, made or grown for retail sale since starting to use the scheme; and

(ii) acquired from other EC countries since starting to use the scheme = F

Step 8 Add the total in Step 7 to the total in Step 2

Step 9 Add up expected selling prices, including VAT, of all goods (standard rated, reduced rate and zero-rated):

(i) received, made or grown for retail sale since starting to use the scheme; and

(ii) acquired from other EC countries since starting to use the scheme = G

Step 10 Add the total in Step 9 to the total in Step 3

Step 11 Calculate the proportion of gross takings from sales at the standard rate by dividing the total at Step 6 by the total at Step 10 and multiplying by the total at Step 4

Step 12 Calculate the proportion of gross takings from sales at the reduced rate by dividing the total at Step 8 by the total at Step 10 and multiplying by the total at Step 4

Step 13 To calculate output tax, add the total at Step 11 multiplied by the VAT fraction for standard-rated goods to the total at Step 12 multiplied by the VAT fraction for reduced rate goods

In algebraic form, output tax (based on standard-rate of 17.5% and reduced rate of 5%) is:

$((A + E)$ divided by $(C + G)$ x D x 7/47$) + ((B + F)$ divided by $(C + G)$ × D x 1/21$)$.

(b) For the fourth and all later quarterly VAT periods or the twelfth and all later monthly VAT periods:

Step A Add up daily gross takings for the VAT period = H

Step B Add up expected selling prices, including VAT, of standard-rated goods:

(i) received, made or grown for retail sale ; and

(ii) acquired from other EC countries in the current VAT period and the previous three quarterly (or eleven monthly) VAT periods = J

Step C Add up expected selling prices, including VAT, of reduced rate goods

(i) received, made or grown for retail sale; and

(ii) acquired from other EC countries in the current VAT period and the previous three quarterly (or eleven monthly) VAT periods = K

Step D   Add up expected selling prices, including VAT, of all goods standard rated, reduced rate and zero-rated)

         (i)   received, made or grown for retail sale; and

         (ii)   acquired from other EC countries in the current VAT period and the previous three quarterly (or eleven monthly) VAT periods =   L

Step E   Calculate the proportion of gross takings from sales at the standard rate by dividing the total at Step B by the total at Step D and multiplying by the total in Step A

Step F   Calculate the proportion of gross takings from sales at the reduced rate by dividing the total at Step C by the total at Step D and multiplying by the total at Step A

Step G   To calculate output tax, add the total at Step E multiplied by the VAT fraction for standard-rated goods to the total at Step F multiplied by the VAT fraction for reduced rate goods

In algebraic form, output tax (based on standard-rate of 17.5% and reduced rate of 5%) is:

(J divided by L × H × 7/47) + (K divided by L × H × 1/21).

Example 4

John is a clothes retailer and has been using Apportionment Scheme 2 for many years.

He is about to complete his VAT return for period ended 30 September 2008, and has extracted the following key figures from his records:

- expected sales of standard rated goods purchased during last four quarters up to 30 September 2008 – £350,000 including VAT;

- expected sales of all goods purchased during last four quarters up to 30 September 2008 – £450,000;

- daily gross takings for period – £300,000.

What is John's output tax liability using Apportionment Scheme 2?

Solution – the proportion of expected standard rated sales (based on goods purchased for the last four quarters) is £350,000 divided by £450,000 (ie 77.78% to two decimal places).

If this proportion is applied to daily gross takings for the period, the output tax liability is as follows:

£350,000/£450,000 x £300,000 × 7/47 = £34,751.77.

Direct Calculation Scheme 1

Rules

10.12   The rules of the scheme are as follows:

- the annual VAT exclusive turnover must not exceed £1m;

- identify the rate of VAT which is in the minority for the business, e g if 70% of sales made by the business are standard-rated and 30% of sales are zero-rated, the minority rate of tax is zero-rated;

- calculate the expected selling price of minority rate goods bought during the VAT period in question;

- supplies of services with the same VAT liability as the minority goods must be dealt with outside the scheme;

- any supplies of catering must be dealt with outside the scheme;

- no annual adjustment or stocktaking is required.

Types of business

10.13   The types of business that could use the Direct Calculation Scheme 1 and the potential problems are as follows:

- the scheme is fairly simple to operate and could benefit a business that has, for example, a very small volume of sales at one particular rate of VAT (e g 99% of sales are standard-rated and 1% of sales are zero-rated). In such cases, it would not be worthwhile for the business to invest in electronic equipment to identify the VAT liability at the point of sale or to carry out some of the detailed computations involved with the other schemes;

- there is scope for the scheme to be based on the mark-up of the 'majority' goods rather than the minority goods if this is easier to calculate. For example, a business mainly selling newspapers may find it easier to mark-up these goods (because the paperwork may be easier to handle) than for tobacco/confectionery items which could have been bought on many different small purchase invoices;

- the main problem with the use of the scheme would be if expected selling prices are not calculated correctly. If the mark-up on zero-rated goods is inflated, then the output tax paid by the business will be too low.

Calculating output tax

10.14   If the minority goods are zero-rated, then output tax will be calculated by deducting the expected selling prices of zero-rated items from the daily gross takings figure. Output tax will then be due at 7/47 of the remaining figure (this assumes the business does not have any reduced rate or exempt supplies).

If the minority goods are standard rated, then the daily gross takings figure becomes irrelevant. This is because output tax will be due on 7/47 of the expected selling price of standard rated goods (this again assumes the business does not have any reduced rate supplies). See Example 5 below.

It is important to note that the scheme will also allow the majority item to be marked up where this is easier to calculate.

Example 5

Jill is VAT registered and trades as a sports retail shop. All sales are standard rated with the exception of books on fitness, which are zero-rated as printed matter.

Her gross takings for the VAT period ending 30 September 2008 were £23,000 including VAT. She bought 50 fitness books during the quarter for £5 each – she applies a 50% mark up to each book that is purchased.

What is Jill's output tax for this period using Direct Calculation Scheme 1?

Solution – the expected selling price of the books (minority goods) is £375, ie cost price of £250 plus mark up of 50%.

This gives an output tax liability of: £23,000 less £375 × 7/47 = £3,369.68.

Note – in effect, the tax saving for Jill is only £55.85 (£375 × 7/47) compared to the situation where she treated all sales as standard rated. In effect, there is little incentive for her to spend resources on electronic tills or point of sale training just for the VAT benefits.

Direct Calculation Scheme 2

Rules

10.15 Exactly the same rules as for Direct Calculation Scheme 1 (see 10.12), apart from the fact that it can be used by a business with annual sales of £130m or less rather than £1m. There is also a requirement to carry out an annual stock-take adjustment.

Types of business

10.16 The scheme could produce benefits compared to Direct Calculation Scheme 1 where the minority goods are standard rated, and these goods are slow moving as far as stock turnover is concerned. In these cases, the scheme delays paying output tax on these goods until they are sold – instead of the period when they were purchased.

Calculating output tax

10.17   How to calculate output tax with the Direct Calculation Scheme 2:

- for each VAT period, the same rules apply as for Direct Calculation Scheme 1;

- an annual adjustment is required after the fourth quarter in which the scheme is used (and annually thereafter) which takes into account the opening and closing stock values of the minority rate goods. The calculation made applies a mark-up to the cost of goods sold by the business (ie opening stock *plus* purchases *minus* closing stock) rather than the goods purchased by the business during the year;

- the difference in output tax identified in the fourth quarter (compared to the four quarterly calculations) will produce either an under or overpayment of tax. This difference should be adjusted on this return.

See Example 6.

Example 6

Jean sells children's clothes as a retailer (zero-rated). Her only standard rated supplies relate to the sale of wardrobes. Each wardrobe is purchased for £1,000 plus VAT and sells for £2,000 plus VAT. Jean has been using the Direct Calculation Scheme 2 for many years.

For year ended 31 August 2008 (the anniversary date of when she first used Direct Calculation Scheme 2), the quantity of wardrobes she purchased was as follows:

Opening stock 1 September 2008	15
Quarter ended 30 November 2008	12
Quarter ended 28 February 2009	30
Quarter ended 31 May 2009	10
Quarter ended 31 August 2009	18
Closing stock 31 August 2009	35

What is the output tax position for Jean using Direct Calculation Scheme 2 compared to Direct Calculation Scheme 1?

Solution – under Direct Calculation Scheme 1, Jean would account for output tax on the expected selling prices of goods purchased during the four periods in question: £2,000 × 70 wardrobes × 17.5% = £24,500

Under Direct Calculation Scheme 2, the output tax liability will be based on the actual quantity of wardrobes sold, ie adjusting for opening and closing stock. The annual adjustment calculation will be made on the August 2009 return.

The total output tax declared in the four quarters (including the annual adjustment) will be as follows:

£2,000 × 50 wardrobes sold x 17.5% = £17,500.

Note – 50 wardrobes sold equates to opening stock of 15 wardrobes plus 70 wardrobes bought during the year less 35 wardrobes held in stock at 31 August 2009. In reality, the output tax saving for Jean with Direct Calculation Scheme 2 is due to the fact that she has not yet accounted for tax on the stock increase of wardrobes that was evident during the year (ie 20 additional wardrobes in stock x £2,000 x 17.5% = £7,000).

Other issues concerning retailers

Tax invoices

10.18   A retailer makes most or all of his sales to the general public, and does not therefore have an obligation to issue a tax invoice for every sale that is made. However, he should issue an invoice if requested by a customer – it could be that the customer is buying, for example, stationery items from a retail outlet and wants to reclaim input tax on his own VAT return.

When a retailer is asked for an invoice, there are two options available to him.

Less detailed tax invoice

10.19   If the value of the sale is £250 or less, and provided the supply is not to a person in another EU country, a VAT invoice only needs to record the following details:

- the name, address and VAT registration number of the retailer;

- the date of the sale;

- a description to identify the goods or services sold;

- the gross amount of the sale (ie including VAT);

- for each rate of VAT chargeable, the gross amount payable including VAT, and the rate of VAT that applies.

Modified tax invoice

10.20   This invoice is very similar to a full tax invoice, but the main difference is that it only shows the VAT inclusive price of each standard rated or reduced rated supply rather than the VAT exclusive price, ie £117.50 including VAT rather than £100 + £17.50 VAT.

Note – there is no £250 limit for a modified tax invoice – but it can only be issued with the agreement of the customer.

Daily gross takings

10.21 The key challenge for any retailer is to be able to accurately record his daily gross takings. It is not acceptable for him to just record a weekly or monthly takings total – takings must be recorded on a daily basis.

HMRC considers retailers to be high risk in terms of a potential tax loss because of the emphasis on cash transactions. This brings to mind a trader the author encountered about twenty years ago as a visiting officer for Customs and Excise. The trader admitted that he did not find accounting for VAT a challenge but rather the process of entering sales in his business till rather than his back pocket! But there are other issues to consider as far as recording takings are concerned – see Example 7.

Example 7

Janet is the owner of the White Horse pub in Bournemouth. The cash in her till (adjusting for float) at the end of the day's trading is £350. However, she is unsure about how to deal with the following issues as far as VAT is concerned:

- A member of staff stole £50 of cash from the till – she has now been sacked.

- The window cleaner was paid £20 cash from the till for cleaning the pub windows.

- Janet enjoys a drink herself and consumed four glasses of wine without paying for them – the retail selling price of a glass of wine is £3 and the cost price is £1.50.

Solution – remember the basic definition of VAT, ie a tax on the 'supply of goods or services'. This means the £70 cash removed from the till (illegally in the case of the staff member) relates to sales that have already taken place. The amount of £70 should therefore be included in the takings figure.

Sales to the business owner also need to be included because a supply of goods has again taken place (even though no money has been exchanged). However, the good news for Janet is that she only needs to account for output tax on the cost price of the goods, ie £1.50 x 4 glasses = £6.

The total daily gross takings figure for VAT purposes is therefore £426 (£350+£50+£20+£6).

Flat rate scheme

10.22 The flat rate scheme (FRS) is available to a business with annual taxable sales of less than £150,000 and essentially means that output tax is calculated by applying a specific flat rate percentage to the gross sales made by a business. This is in contrast to the usual method of VAT accounting, ie VAT payable = output tax *minus* input tax. A full analysis of the scheme is given in Chapter 8.

Although the aim of the FRS is to simplify VAT accounting, it can save a lot of tax for certain types of business. Here is an example of a significant tax saving for a retailer.

Example 8

Steve sells ice-creams, chocolates and cans of drink from a small kiosk on Blackpool beach – all of his sales are standard rated. His only overheads are the rent of the kiosk and staff costs, ie no input tax to reclaim.

His figures for the year ended 31 December 2009 (all relevant to 15% VAT) are as follows:

● Sales including VAT – £138,000 (ie £120,000 plus VAT of £18,000);

● Cost of goods for resale – £60,000 plus VAT of £9,000 = £69,000 (ie 50% gross profit being achieved).

Should Steve use the FRS to calculate his VAT rather than a retail scheme?

Solution – Steve's business qualifies for a very generous flat rate percentage of 2% – 'Retailing food, confectionery, tobacco, newspapers or children's clothing'.

Under normal VAT accounting, his annual VAT bill will be £9,000 (£18,000 output tax less £9,000 input tax). With the flat rate scheme his bill will be £2,760 (£138,000 x 2%) – a big saving of £6,240 per year. In his first year of VAT registration, an extra 1% discount is given on the flat rate percentage – producing a further one-off saving of £1,380.

Final points

10.23 In concluding this section, a few other points should be noted as far as VAT and retail sales are concerned:

● VAT Notice 727 is the main source of information published by HMRC as far as retail schemes are concerned. The notice has the force of law and considers each of the five different retail schemes in detail;

● where a business has both retail and non-retail sales, a retail scheme can only be used for the retail sales. VAT on the non-retail sales must be accounted for outside the scheme in the normal way;

● there is no problem with a retailer using the annual accounting scheme if his yearly sales are less than £1.35m excluding VAT (see Chapter 7).

Margin schemes for second-hand goods

Introduction

10.24   The basic rule of VAT is that output tax is due on the full value of goods sold by a business (unless the goods are specifically zero-rated, exempt or subject to the reduced rate of VAT).

However, there are special schemes in place that reduce the output tax liability on goods sold by certain businesses – through what is known as a second-hand margin scheme.

The following traders can apply a margin scheme:

● motor vehicle dealers;

● businesses trading in works of art, antiques or collectors' items;

● second-hand goods dealers;

● traders who obtain goods in their own name, but are acting as an agent, in relation to a supply.

How a margin scheme works

10.25   Under a margin scheme, VAT is accounted for on the difference between the purchases and sales of eligible goods in each VAT period. In effect, output tax is being declared on the 'profit margin' – if no profit is made, then no VAT is payable. The seller's margin is not revealed to the buyer.

The VAT registration test for a trader dealing in margin goods is still based on the gross value of his sales, and the record keeping requirements for a business using a margin scheme are very strict. If these requirements cannot be met, then a business could be ineligible to use a second-hand scheme and would then have to account for output tax on the full value of a sale in the normal way.

As a separate point, the scheme cannot be used for any goods that have been purchased on a VAT invoice on which input tax is recoverable. However, input tax incurred on expenditure to improve the item can be reclaimed in the normal way, eg an antique dealer paying a fee to a restorer to renovate an item can reclaim input tax on the charges made by the restorer. However, the cost of the restoration cannot be added to the purchase price of the item under the margin scheme.

For an illustration of a typical margin scheme transaction for a car dealer, see Example 9 below.

Example 9

Local Motors purchases a second-hand car from a member of the public for £2,000. An amount of £500 plus VAT is paid to a local repair firm to re-spray the car, and then £100 plus VAT is paid to a valet company to clean the interior. The car is then sold to another member of the public for £3,000.

What is the VAT position?

Solution – Local Motors must ensure they keep proper records concerning the buying and selling of this vehicle, and record the car in a proper stock book giving full details of, eg registration number, date of purchase/sale etc.

The input tax on the repair/valeting charges can be reclaimed in Box 4 of the relevant return in the normal way.

The margin made by the business on the sale is £1,000 (ie £3,000 less £2,000) and this margin is treated as VAT inclusive. An output tax liability of £148.93 must be included in Box 1 of the relevant return, ie £1,000 × 7/47 (assuming a VAT rate of 17.5%).

Note – a good source of information concerning margin schemes (including the finer details concerning record-keeping requirements) is VAT Notice 718 – Margin scheme for second-hand goods, works of art, antiques and collectors' items.

Conditions of the scheme

10.26   The opportunity to account for VAT on the margin rather than the selling price is a very generous concession. As a consequence, HMRC has very strict rules in place to ensure the benefits of the scheme are not exploited:

- When buying goods from a private person or unregistered dealer, the buyer must make out a purchase invoice showing the seller's name and address, the date of the transaction, the total price for the goods, the invoice and stock book number and a description of the goods.

- A stock book with the full details of each item bought and sold by the business must be kept.

- When selling goods, a sales invoice should be raised for the customer. The invoice should record details of the stock book number, date of sale, description of the goods and total price including VAT. The invoice should also be noted along the lines of: 'this is a second-hand margin scheme supply'.

- The sales invoice should also include a declaration that:

  'Input tax deduction has not been and will not be claimed by me in respect of the goods sold on this invoice.'

  In effect, this is confirmation to the customer that the goods have been accounted for under the margin scheme.

- The customer must be given the invoice for his retention – the seller must retain a copy and also update his stock book so that the margin on the deal can be properly calculated.

The conditions of the margin scheme have the force of law. Therefore, if HMRC is not satisfied with the standard of record-keeping, it has the power to assess output tax on the full selling price of the goods. The exercise of this power would be disastrous for any business using the scheme, so the importance of accurate accounting should be stressed to all clients.

As a general point, the quality of accounting under the margin scheme is often dependent on the standard of the stock book maintained by each particular business. For example, in the case of an antique shop, it is important that items are fully described – the phrase 'antique table' is not particularly useful if the shop has 50 different tables in stock!

Goods sold at a loss or nil profit

10.27   A common mistake made by many businesses using the margin scheme is to add up all of the selling prices of goods sold in a VAT period to give a total selling price; they then enter the purchase prices against each item and add this list of figures up as well to give a total purchase price; they then account for output tax on the difference between the two figures.

The above approach sounds logical but the mistake being made is that the margin is effectively being reduced by any loss that is made on an item. The rule as far as the scheme is concerned is that no output tax is due on a loss – but the loss cannot be offset against profits made on other items. This principle is illustrated by Example 10.

Example 10

Daphne is registered for VAT selling antique furniture and accounts for output tax using the margin scheme. She has made only two sales for the VAT period ending 31 May 2008 – one at a loss of £2,000 and the other at a profit of £1,500.

Solution – although Daphne has made an overall loss of £500 (£2,000 less £1,500), she still has an output tax liability of £223.40 on the item sold at a profit (£1,500 x 7/47). There is no scope to reduce this liability against the second item. In effect, Daphne's trading loss for the period is now £723.40 (ie the loss of £500 plus the output tax of £223.40 she must now pay).

As a final point, if an item is sold at a nil profit (ie selling price equals purchase price) then no output tax liability exists on the sale if the margin scheme is being used.

Completing a VAT return

10.28 The completion of the VAT return for a business using the margin scheme follows similar principles as for any other trader:

Box 1 (output tax) – records the output tax payable on the margin.

Box 4 (input tax) – this figure will be nil as far as goods purchased under the scheme are concerned – but would include input tax incurred by the business on expenses and overheads.

Box 6 (outputs) – records the total selling price, less output tax accounted for on the margin.

Box 7 (inputs) – records the purchase price paid for the goods.

Sales to other EU businesses

10.29 VAT often becomes interesting when two different aspects of the system overlap into one transaction. Consider the following example.

Example 11

Jeff is registered for VAT in the UK and has bought an antique table for £2,000 from a private individual in Birmingham. The table is now being sold to an antique dealer who is registered for VAT in Holland. The selling price is £5,000. What is the best option as far as VAT is concerned?

Solution – the margin scheme is available throughout the EU, so the antique dealer in Holland will probably be keen to acquire the goods under the margin scheme himself. This means that he can resell the goods in Holland and only account for output tax on his own profit margin.

The alternative situation would be for the goods to be excluded from the margin scheme and be treated as a normal sale of goods. This means that Jeff will zero-rate the supply of goods to the Dutch customer (as long as he shows the customer's VAT number on his invoice and obtains proof that the goods left the UK) – the latter must then account for output tax using the reverse charge on his own VAT return in Holland.

The reverse charge means the Dutch dealer will include output tax in Box 2 of his return (based on purchase price multiplied by standard rate of VAT in Holland). He will then reclaim input tax in Box 4 of his return (same amount) but he will then have to account for output tax on the full selling price of the item when it is eventually sold.

The conclusion is that the margin scheme is a good result for the Dutch customer – but normal accounting outside of the margin scheme is a good result for Jeff because he has no output tax liability on his supply (through zero-rating the goods as a sale to a VAT registered business in another EU country).

Global Accounting

10.30   At this point, a few readers may be thinking of the administrative nightmare of the margin scheme for clients who sell a high volume of goods at very low selling prices. For example, think of a business that trades in second-hand thimbles, buying thimbles from car boot sales and then selling them on to members of the public. The paperwork involved in each transaction would be very cumbersome, for example, having to fill in a purchase and sales invoice every time a £1.50 thimble is sold!

In this situation, a business can adopt what is known as Global Accounting which allows accounting for output tax on the total margin made during a VAT period, ie not on an item by item basis.

Again, HMRC imposes very strict rules about which businesses are eligible to use Global Accounting – not least because any business adopting the scheme is gaining automatic VAT relief on items sold at a loss.

The principal rules for the scheme are as follows:

- every individual item for which the scheme is used must have been obtained for a price of £500 or less;

- the goods were not purchased on an invoice on which VAT was shown separately;

- the goods are not sold on a VAT invoice or similar document showing an amount as being VAT or as being attributable to VAT;

- records and accounts are kept as specified by HMRC;

- the scheme cannot be used for sales of motor vehicles; motor cycles; aircraft; boats and outboard motors; caravans and motor caravans; horses and ponies.

In the case of motor vehicles, there is scope to use Global Accounting if the vehicle is broken up and individual components are sold as scrap (as long as no individual component is valued at more than £500).

Note – when a business first starts to use Global Accounting, it must calculate an opening stock figure that will be counted as purchases in its first VAT period. The basis of the stock valuation should be as accurate as possible. A closing stock adjustment will be needed on the final VAT return if a business ceases to use the scheme.

Horses and ponies

10.31   As a final point, it is very common for the margin scheme to be used for trading in horses and ponies. The scheme will not apply to the sale of a horse that the trader has bred himself – simply because it is not classed as second-hand at this point in time.

The values of deals for horses and ponies can be significant – so the British Equestrian Trade Association is a good point of contact for any assistance. The Association has even produced forms that can be used for individual transactions covered by the scheme – very useful to ensure HMRC conditions are properly met.

Planning points to consider

10.32   The following planning points should be given consideration in relation to retail or margin schemes:

- A business may need to justify to HMRC why it cannot adopt a Point of Sale retail scheme by, for example, using a multi-buttoned till. The Point of Sale scheme should give the most reliable output tax calculation because the VAT liability is based on actual sales made by the business.

- Each retail scheme has potential benefits as well as potential problems for users. For example, a Point of Sale method using a multi-button till will only be accurate if the staff operating the till know how to determine the VAT position for each sale. Proper staff training is an important issue.

- Apportionment Scheme 1 avoids the need to identify the VAT liability at the point of sale. However, it is only available to businesses with annual VAT exclusive sales of less than £1m, and can produce a higher than usual tax bill for a business that has a higher mark-up on zero-rated goods. A business where the zero-rated mark-up is considerably higher than on standard rated goods should consider using an alternative scheme.

- It is important to remember that most retail schemes need to exclude the value of services provided by a business – or non-retail sales. These supplies should be accounted for outside of the scheme.

- Apportionment Scheme 2 calculates output tax using expected selling prices – so will deal with the problem mentioned above with Apportion-ment Scheme 1, ie where there is a higher mark-up made by the business on its zero-rated goods.

● Direct Calculation Scheme 2 could benefit a business that has slow moving stock of minority standard rated items. This is because the scheme makes an annual adjustment for stock so that output tax is not actually paid until the goods are sold. Direct Calculation Scheme 1 produces an output tax liability in the period that the goods are purchased.

● Remember that some smaller retailers could benefit from using the flat rate scheme if their annual taxable sales are less than £150,000 excluding VAT. The scheme produces winners and losers in terms of VAT payments – see Example 8 in this chapter which highlights a winning outcome.

● Second-hand margin schemes are very worthwhile for businesses dealing in second-hand goods. However, it is important to ensure the record keeping requirements of HMRC are fully met, otherwise it could base output tax on the full selling price of an item rather than the profit margin.

● To avoid common mistakes when operating margin scheme calculations, consider the following precautions:

    – ensure that any losses made on items are not netted off for VAT purposes against items on which a profit has been made; and
    – remember that the value of the margin cannot be reduced by any expenditure incurred to improve the condition of the item (e g restoration fees for an antique trader) but input tax can be reclaimed on such expenditure subject to the normal rules.

● A business selling high quantities of small value items could benefit from using Global Accounting – the main benefits of which relate to the reduced record-keeping requirements (compared to the main margin scheme) and the automatic loss relief available on items sold at a loss.

Chapter 11

Imports (and Acquisitions)

Key topics in this chapter:

- The difference between imports (goods brought into the UK from non-EU countries) and acquisitions (goods brought into the UK from other EU countries) and practical examples to show the VAT treatment in each case.

- Administration issues relevant to VAT on imported goods.

- The benefits of having a duty deferment account and the forms to complete to obtain an account.

- The benefits of using SIVA (Simplified Import VAT Accounting) to reduce the level of bank guarantees required for a business with a deferment account.

- Evidence needed by importers to reclaim input tax on their VAT returns (C79 certificates).

- Procedures for dealing with postal imports.

- Goods imported into the UK that are not subject to VAT, e g zero-rated goods, consignments with a value of less than £18.

- The requirement for certain businesses to complete additional declarations regarding EU transactions through the system known as Intrastat.

- The possibility of an unregistered business having to register for VAT if the value of its acquisitions exceeds the registration limits during the course of a calendar year.

- Deciding whether the importation of computer software represents an import of goods or services as far as VAT is concerned.

Introduction

11.1   An important point to remember concerning VAT on overseas goods coming into the UK is that the rules are different according to whether the goods are arriving from an EU or non-EU country:

- *imports* – for VAT purposes, only goods arriving from non-EU countries are classed as imports;

- *acquisitions* – goods arriving from EU countries are known as 'acquisitions' and it is important to be clear about which countries are in the EU.

Under HMRC rules for overseas goods arriving into the UK, the following VAT treatment applies for imports and acquisitions.

Note – the Channel Islands are not part of the EU for fiscal purposes and import VAT is therefore due on goods brought into the UK.

Imports

11.2   VAT is charged and payable at the point when the goods enter the UK – either at the port, airport, or other boundary point. The VAT payable on the goods is charged at the same rate as if the goods were supplied in the UK. This means, for example, that zero-rated goods, eg children's clothes will be imported without VAT – although there could be customs duty charged on the goods as a separate tax. As long as the goods are used by the importer for the purpose of making taxable supplies (which will usually be the case because most imported goods will be sold in the UK as an onward supply), then the VAT paid at the time of import can be reclaimed as input tax. The usual evidence for claiming input tax is import VAT certificate C79.

Note – input tax deduction on imports is subject to the usual rules that apply for domestic purchases, eg input tax cannot be claimed on a motor car available for private use.

Acquisitions

11.3   Goods bought from a VAT registered trader in another EU country will be acquired without VAT being charged by either the supplier or HMRC at the point when the goods enter the UK. The EU supplier is allowed to zero-rate his supply as long as he obtains the VAT registration number of his UK customer. However, the UK customer is then required to account for the output tax of the supplier by making a declaration in Box 2 of his VAT return. This declaration is based on the value of the goods being imported, multiplied by the rate of VAT applicable to those goods (usually 17.5% standard rate or 15% until 31 December 2009). However, the UK customer now has a source of input tax that he can reclaim in Box

4 of the same VAT return, assuming the goods are used for taxable supplies. There is a nil VAT effect with the above entries in most cases.

The rules in many situations regarding VAT and imports can be quite complicated, for example, for issues such as temporary imports and goods to be repaired in the UK etc. The aim of this chapter is to consider the main practical issues concerning VAT and overseas goods, which will be relevant to the majority of transactions that are made.

Note – the reverse charge is a concept that many advisers and taxpayers find difficult to understand. However, consider the meaning of the phrase 'reverse charge' in terms of a telephone call. In this situation, the cost of the call is being transferred from the person making the call to the person receiving the call. In VAT terms, a reverse charge results in the same outcome. That is, the VAT cost is being transferred from the person making the supply to the person receiving the supply.

Dealing with VAT on imports and acquisitions

11.4   To clarify the key principles explained above, see Examples 1 and 2 to illustrate the different VAT treatment of goods entering the UK from an EU and non-EU country.

Example 1

John is registered for VAT in the UK – his main activity is to import plant pots and sell them to garden centres throughout the north of England. He has agreed a deal to purchase 500 plant pots for £10 each from a Belgian supplier (EU) and has given the supplier his UK VAT number.

What is the VAT treatment of the arrangement?

Solution – as the Belgian supplier now holds John's UK VAT registration number, he can invoice John for the plant pots without charging Belgian VAT. This is because the deal is between two countries within the EU. However, the Belgian supplier must retain evidence that the goods have left Belgium in case the invoice is queried by a VAT officer in Belgium.

John must account for VAT in Box 2 of his VAT return relevant to the supply (£5,000 × 17.5% = £875) but he can reclaim the same amount of VAT as input tax in Box 4 of his return because he is using the goods to make a taxable supply. John must also include the net amount of the purchase in Box 7 of his VAT return (ie the inputs value) and also in Box 9 of the return (for acquisitions from the EU). When he eventually sells the goods in the UK, output tax will be declared in Box 1 of his return in the normal way, with the net value of the sale recorded in Box 6.

Example 2

John, from Example 1, has decided to import 500 special plant pots at a cost of £20 each from a supplier in Hong Kong (outside the EU). The plant pots will attract Customs duty of £10 each when they arrive in the UK.

What is the VAT position regarding this transaction?

Solution – VAT is charged and payable on the importation of goods into the UK – and the VAT is charged on the value of the goods, including customs duty. The total amount of VAT charged on the importation is £2,625 (500 × £30 × 17.5%) and John can reclaim this amount in Box 4 of his next VAT return. No entry is needed in Box 9 of the return because the purchase is not an acquisition of goods from another EU country.

Overall, therefore, the purchase of goods from another EU country is fairly simple, however, more procedures are relevant to goods purchased from outside the EU. The following points are relevant to import transactions:

(a) goods imported from abroad are declared to Customs using the Single Administrative Document (SAD) (Form C88). Import VAT is dealt with in the same way as customs duty;

(b) the import declaration must normally be accompanied by a declaration of value on Form C105, C105A, C105B or C109 as appropriate;

(c) unless the goods are placed under excise warehousing or a specified customs arrangement, then VAT must normally either be paid at the time of importation or be deferred if the importer or his agent have been approved for deferment – see **11.5**;

(d) any VAT-registered person who imports goods from outside the EU needs a Trader's Unique Reference Number (TURN). Without this number, it may not be possible to get the evidence needed to reclaim VAT paid on imports. TURNs are obtained by writing (stating full name, address and VAT registration number) to the following address:

> TURN Team
> HM Revenue and Customs
> Ty Myrddin
> Old Station Road
> Carmarthen SA31 1BT

Deferment of VAT

11.5 One very useful concession granted by HMRC allows an importer to delay paying VAT at the time the goods arrive in the UK providing he holds a Deferment Approval Number (DAN). An agent who enters goods for an importer or owner may also use the scheme.

The two main benefits for a business having a deferment account are:

(a) cash flow is improved by the delay in payment; and

(b) the process of importation is not delayed whilst payment of VAT and duty are arranged.

The key procedures for a deferment arrangement are as follows:

● charges deferred (including VAT, customs and excise duties) during a calendar month must be paid by the importer on the 15th day of the following month – payment to be made by BACS rather than cheque or cash. Form C1202 needs to be completed by the applicant to set up an appropriate direct debit arrangement with the applicant's bank;

● in order to set up a deferment arrangement, an importer must obtain a guarantee from his bank (or other approved lender) that the amounts deferred will be covered by the bank, up to a certain limit;

● the form to complete to apply for a deferment arrangement is Form C1200 – the form to be completed in order to guarantee payment of sums to HMRC is Form C1201;

● an agent making an entry can request deferment against his principal's approval number provided he is authorised to do so. This can either be executed through completion of Form C1207N or, if relevant to a 'one-off' consignment of goods, by completing Form C1207S;

● HMRC sends out 'periodic deferment statements' on a weekly basis, summarising the deferments made for the relevant period. The statement will also show the total amount of tax deferred in the month to date.

Note – deferment statements cannot be used as evidence for input tax deduction – see **11.7**.

If the tax due on imported goods during a particular period exceeds the deferment limit of the importer, then he must pay the additional tax due at the point of import.

Simplified import VAT accounting (SIVA)

11.6 The deferment system explained at **11.5** can cause problems for certain businesses trying to get a sufficient level of guarantee from their bank to cover the VAT and duty payable to HMRC in a typical month.

A concession is available for importers who hold a deferment account (or are applying for one), to allow them to reduce the level of financial guarantee required to operate it for VAT purposes only. Customs and excise duties must still be fully secured.

The new arrangement, known as SIVA, could apply if applicants can satisfy the following criteria:

- they must have been VAT registered for at least 3 years – this ensures a business has some VAT history which HMRC can review for compliance etc;

- they must have a good VAT compliance history – this will take into account issues such as the timeliness of VAT returns and payments submitted by the business, errors identified on VAT visits, the number and extent of any default surcharges;

- debtor history – traders in debt to HMRC within the 3 months prior to application will not qualify;

- payment history – the payment record of the business in connection with duty deferment will be reviewed. A business which has defaulted on its monthly direct debit payments in the 12-month period prior to application will be refused approval;

- sufficient financial means are required to meet any amount deferred under SIVA and a good HMRC offence record is necessary (ie no history of VAT fraud being committed by the company).

The SIVA application form (SIVA1) can be downloaded from the HMRC website (www.hmrc.gov.uk). The completed form needs to be sent to:

HM Revenue and Customs
6th Floor North
Portcullis House
27 Victoria Avenue
Southend
Essex SS2 6AL

The result of a successful application will be as follows:

- the business will have a deferment account limit which must be sufficient to cover all deferred charges for VAT, customs duty and excise duty;

- the business will have a deferment guarantee level which must be supported by a deferment guarantee able to cover all deferred customs and excise duties.

Evidence for input tax deduction

11.7   Import VAT can only be reclaimed by a business that is registered for VAT in the UK. If a business is not registered for VAT (for instance, because it trades below the VAT registration limits or because it is involved in making exempt supplies), then there is no scope to reclaim input tax.

Equally, input tax can only be reclaimed by a VAT-registered business if the goods are to be used to make taxable supplies and if adequate evidence is held to support the claim.

As explained at **11.5**, weekly deferment statements issued by HMRC are not acceptable as evidence to support an input tax claim. The main document for this purpose is the Import VAT Certificate (Form C79). C79 certificates are issued on a monthly basis, usually on the 12th day of the following month. They are issued to the VAT registered person whose registration number, plus a three-digit suffix, is shown on the import entry. The whole number is known as the Trader Unique Reference Number (TURN).

As far as input tax is concerned, the key date is the accounting date alongside each item, not the date when the certificate is issued. This applies even where the business uses the cash accounting scheme, as imports are excluded from cash accounting treatment.

If a monthly certificate is mislaid, replacements can be obtained (for up to 6 years) by writing to:

HM Revenue and Customs
VAT Central Unit
Section 4B
1st Floor Alexander House
Victoria Avenue
Southend SS99 1AU

An importer will often use an agent to complete the import formalities at the port of entry. If this is the case, and the agent has to pay VAT on behalf of the importer, then the agent will invoice the importer to recover this VAT. However, the VAT shown on this invoice cannot be used by the importer as evidence to reclaim input tax – only the C79 documentation is acceptable.

An important point to remember is that input tax cannot be reclaimed by a shipping or forwarding agent acting for an importer and paying VAT on his behalf. This is because the goods in question are not being used by the agent for the purpose of his business. The only exception to this rule is that there are certain times when HMRC will repay import VAT paid by an agent but not repaid to him by his client, eg if the client became insolvent. The best point of reference if this situation arises is HMRC's VAT Notice 702.

Postal imports

11.8   The procedures considered in this chapter so far assume that goods enter the UK by port or airport. There are special rules that apply if goods are imported by a postal arrangement.

- *Consignments (other than Datapost packets) not exceeding £2,000* – a VAT-registered person importing goods for business purposes does not have to pay VAT immediately on importation. Instead, he may account for the VAT due in Box 1 of the VAT return covered by the period of importation. Subject to the normal rules, the same amount of input tax can then be reclaimed in Box 4 of the return. The charge label, postal wrapper and any customer declaration attached to the package must be kept to support the claim to input tax.

- *Datapost packets not exceeding £2,000 in value* – for such imports, the Post Office require payment of the VAT when the package is delivered. The charge label attached must be kept to support any claim to input tax. It is not possible to defer payment of import charges.

- *Consignments over £2,000 in value* – for these imports, an entry (which will be sent to the consignee) must be made and returned to HMRC together with an invoice or other acceptable evidence of value. VAT and other charges due at importation are payable immediately unless the consignee is approved to use the deferment scheme. After payment, HMRC sends the consignee a copy of the entry to support any claim to input tax.

Goods not subject to an import VAT charge

11.9 There are a range of goods that can be imported into the country without VAT being charged – the obvious example being any goods that would be zero-rated if supplied in the UK. Another common example of goods that can be imported without a VAT charge are miscellaneous items where the value of the consignment does not exceed £18.

The £18 consignment limit does not apply to supplies of alcoholic beverages, tobacco products, perfumes or toilet waters.

The other main categories of reliefs that could be available apply to the following general headings – again, further detail can be obtained in Notice 702 or through the HMRC website:

- aircraft ground and security equipment;
- capital goods and equipment on transfer of activities from abroad;
- certain imports by, and for, charities;
- decorations and awards;
- electricity and natural gas;
- fuel, animal fodder and feed, and packaging necessary during transportation;
- funerals, war graves etc;

- goods for examination, analysis or test purposes;

- goods imported for sale to another EU country;

- health, including animals and biological or chemical substances for research, blood and human organs;

- inherited goods;

- personal belongings;

- printed matter;

- promotion of trade;

- re-imported goods;

- rejected goods;

- small non-commercial consignments between private individuals;

- temporary importations;

- travellers' allowances;

- United Nations visual and auditory materials;

- visiting forces;

- works of art and collectors' pieces.

Intrastat

11.10 All VAT registered businesses trading in goods with other EU countries must complete Boxes 8 and 9 of their VAT returns:

- Box 8 records the total value of sales of goods (dispatches) to other EU countries. This entry not only includes sales of goods to other VAT registered businesses in EU countries but also the value of goods despatched from the UK to a destination in another EU country, even if no actual sale is involved or the sale is being invoiced to a person located outside the EU;

- Box 9 records the total value of acquisitions of goods from other EU countries. The value to be included is the invoice (or contract) price, including directly related services such as freight and insurance. The receipt of other services should not be included.

The figures included in Boxes 8 and 9 will determine if a business needs to involve itself in the completion of Supplementary Declarations (SDs) which form part of what is known as the Intrastat system. Intrastat is the name given to the system for collecting statistics on the trade in goods between EU countries. The Intrastat system is only relevant to VAT registered businesses (ie not unregistered businesses or private individuals).

If a business has acquisitions or dispatches in a calendar year with a total value of less than £270,000 with effect from 1 January 2009 (£260,000 before this date), then no SD needs to be completed. The information recorded in Boxes 8 and 9 is then sufficient to give details of its EU trade. If a SD form needs to be completed, then a full explanation of the key issues can be found in Customs Notice 60. The £270,000 threshold applies separately to acquisitions and dispatches in a calendar year, and a SD needs to be completed from the beginning of the month when the limit is exceeded. See Example 3.

Example 3

Month (2009)	Dispatches	Arrivals
January	£20,000	£5,000
February	£30,000	£30,000
March	£80,000	£40,000
April	£50,000	£40,000
May	£100,000	£40,000
June	£50,000	£50,000
July	£20,000	£80,000

Solution – the £270,000 threshold for dispatches is exceeded in May, so SDs for dispatches are due from 1 May 2008 onwards.

The £270,000 threshold for arrivals is exceeded in July, so SDs for arrivals are due from 1 July 2008 onwards.

Registration for VAT based on value of EU acquisitions

11.11 The need to be registered for VAT is usually based on the level of taxable supplies made by a business. If the value of these taxable supplies has exceeded the relevant limits or is expected to exceed the relevant limit in the next 30 days, there is a requirement for the business to be VAT registered.

However, there is another situation when a business or person may need to be registered for VAT, based on the value of its 'acquisitions' (ie value of goods bought from other EU countries) rather than its taxable supplies.

The rules on this subject state that if the value of acquisitions made by a business at the end of any month, in the period beginning with 1 January in that year, have exceeded the annual VAT registration limit (ie £68,000 per annum with effect from 1 May 2009) or are expected to exceed the limit in the next 30 days, then the business must be VAT registered.

In the case of the annual limit being exceeded, then notification of the need to be registered must be made within 30 days of the end of the month in which the limit has been exceeded. The registration date will then be the first date of the following month.

Example – acquisitions level exceeded in May 2009 – notification to HMRC must be made by 30 June 2009, and effective date of registration will be 1 July 2009.

In the case of the 30-day limit, the date of registration is from the beginning of the period when a trader expects the monthly limit to be exceeded. See Example 4.

Example 4

On 12 June, a company that is not registered for VAT expects the value of its relevant acquisitions in the next 30 days to exceed the registration threshold. This is because a major purchase order has been raised to buy goods from Italy on 28 June.

Solution – the business will be liable to register for VAT on 12 June and must notify HMRC of its liability to register by 11 July. HMRC will register the company with effect from 12 June.

Import of computer software – goods or services?

11.12   Think of an importer's predicament as he buys the latest technology product from the USA – does he have to declare his product as an import of goods (pay VAT at the time of import into the UK and reclaim this amount as input tax on his VAT return)? Or is he making an import of services, in which case he can import the product VAT free, and deal with the VAT on his next return using the reverse charge system? (Output tax is declared in Box 1; input tax reclaimed in Box 4 – subject to normal rules). See **14.3** for further detail on this process.

The positive point is that the rules in the above situation are helpfully clarified by HMRC in Notice 702 (paragraph 7):

● If a mass-produced item is imported, this is treated as an import of both goods (the medium carrying the data, e g discs) and services (the data itself). If the value of the goods and services are not itemised separately (almost certainly they will be imported with an inclusive value), the supply is wholly treated as goods.

● If a customer designed product is imported, this is again treated as an import of both goods and services – but in this case, an inclusive price means the whole supply is treated as a supply of services.

Planning points to consider

11.13   The following planning points should be given consideration.

- It is important to recognise that different VAT rules apply depending on whether goods being acquired from overseas are imports (ie from a non-EU country) or acquisitions (ie from another EU country). Advisers should ensure that relevant clients have procedures in place to deal with the two different situations.

- It should be noted that no VAT is due on imported goods if the item in question would be zero-rated if supplied in the UK.

- In most cases, the application of the reverse charge mechanism on acquisitions will have a nil VAT effect. However, this would not be the case if the goods in question related to a non-deductible item as far as input tax is concerned, eg a car available for private use or goods relating to an exempt supply.

- Ensure that all importers obtain a TURN number so that evidence will be sent by HMRC to support input tax claims (C79 certificate).

- Be aware of the main benefits of holding a deferment account with HMRC to delay paying VAT on imports until the 15th day of the following month. However, it is important to note that periodic deferment statements are not acceptable as evidence for input tax purposes – the C79 certificate is the evidence required to support any input tax claim.

- It is worthwhile for importers with (or applying for) a deferment account to utilise the SIVA arrangements. This scheme reduces the level of a bank guarantee required for VAT on imports via a deferment account.

- If a business is not registered for VAT, it is important to regularly review the value of its EU acquisitions to ensure they do not exceed the VAT registration limits during a calendar year on a cumulative basis. If the limits are exceeded, then the business will have to register for VAT and apply the reverse charge mechanism to its acquisitions.

Chapter 12

Exports

Key topics in this chapter:

● The different VAT rules that apply depending on whether goods are sold to an EU or non-EU customer.

● The different VAT rules that apply depending on whether an EU customer is registered for VAT or not.

● The importance of obtaining proper export evidence to confirm that goods have left the UK.

● Procedures for sales to non-registered customers in another EU country – under distance selling arrangements.

● Triangulation arrangements – supplies of goods from a UK supplier to a customer's customer – where both customers are based in different EU countries.

● Procedures for completing an EU sales list – recording sales made to VAT registered businesses in other EU countries outside of the UK.

● Dealing with the situation where goods are collected from a UK supplier and exported by the customer. Cases are reviewed where export evidence has been falsified by customers.

● Practical examples of common export transactions and the VAT treatment in each case.

● The benefits of the retail export scheme.

Introduction

12.1   The VAT treatment of goods supplied outside of the UK depends on two key facts:

● whether the goods are supplied to a country that is inside or outside the EU;

- if the goods are supplied to a person that is based in another EU country, then it is relevant to consider whether the customer is VAT registered or non-registered.

In VAT terms, an export situation only applies if the goods are sold to a non-EU customer. In such cases, all sales of goods are zero-rated, irrespective of the status of the customer, as long as the exporter holds proper evidence that the goods have left the EU. This evidence must be available for inspection by an HMRC officer carrying out a VAT visit.

If the goods are sold to a customer in another EU country outside the UK, then UK VAT must be charged where appropriate if the customer is not registered for VAT in his own country. If the customer is registered for VAT, then he must give details of his VAT number to the UK supplier – the latter must then include the number on his sales invoice in order to zero-rate the supply of goods.

As with the supply of goods outside EU boundaries, a supplier of goods within the EU must obtain evidence that the goods have left the UK if no VAT is being charged.

If the value of sales to non-registered customers exceeds certain limits in specific EU countries, then a UK supplier will be obliged to register for VAT in that country through what is known as distance selling.

The other main situation where a UK supplier will become involved with an export arrangement is a retailer selling goods to an overseas customer that intends to take the goods outside of the EU. In such cases, the customer could be entitled to a refund of VAT on the goods in question through the retail export scheme.

The VAT rules regarding certain export transactions can become very complicated but the aim of this chapter is to consider the basic principles and arrangements that will apply in the majority of cases.

Difference between an export of goods and a sale of goods to another country within the EU

12.2   To illustrate the different VAT treatment of EU and non-EU sales, consider the following example.

Example 1

Jill buys plant pots in the UK and sells them to a variety of customers throughout the world. In the next VAT quarter, her sales will include the following transactions and she is keen to understand the VAT implications:

(a)   500 pots will be sold to a company in Russia (outside the EU);

(b)   5 pots will be sold to a private individual in Russia;

(c) 500 pots will be sold to a VAT registered company in Belgium (inside EU);

(d) 5 pots will be sold to a private individual in Belgium.

Solution – in situations (a)–(c) above, it is important that Jill obtains documentation to confirm that the goods have left the UK. The standard of proof is considered at 12.3.

For the goods supplied to Russia, it does not make any difference whether the customers are private individuals or business customers. All exports of goods to a country outside of the EU are zero-rated.

In the case of the 500 pots supplied to the Belgian company, the company should provide Jill with its Belgian VAT number, and Jill should show this number on the sales invoice she raises at the time the goods are sold. She can then zero-rate the supply of goods to the Belgian company.

However, in the case of the 5 pots sold to the private individual in Belgium, UK VAT (standard rate) must be charged on these goods. Jill should also record the total value of sales made to non-registered businesses in Belgium to ensure she does not exceed the distance selling levels – see 12.5.

An important point to bear in mind is that an exporter should take reasonable steps to confirm the validity of the VAT numbers given by overseas customers. Each EU country has a specific format for its VAT numbers, so it should be initially confirmed that the number provided by the customer follows this format. A telephone call to the National VAT Advice Service on 0845 010 9000 can give assurance regarding the validity of an overseas VAT number.

Evidence of exportation

12.3 HMRC is very specific about the type of evidence it requires supporting export sales, a position that is confirmed by the legislation on this subject.

Evidence may consist either of official evidence such as a Single Administrative Document (SAD) (eg Form C88 stamped by Customs) or commercial evidence concerning the transaction – the latter is more usual.

All documents retained as evidence of export must give the following details:

- the identity of both the exporter and the customer;

- the destination of the goods must be clearly given and the method of transportation;

- identification of the goods themselves.

Commercial evidence of export will either be primary evidence, eg authentication documents issued by shipping lines, air lines, railway companies etc or secondary evidence, eg documentation issued by freight forwarders exporting on behalf of a number of exporters and who will themselves obtain and retain the primary evidence.

For exports by sea, exporters should obtain a copy of the bill of lading or sea waybill. If the export process is by air, then an air waybill is required. In export methods falling outside the norm, HMRC Notice 703 should be consulted regarding the appropriate evidence in most cases.

Another important point is that proof of export to support zero-rating should be obtained within 3 months of the date of shipment. If evidence has not been obtained by this time, then the transaction becomes standard rated. Any VAT accounted for after 3 months for this reason may be reclaimed at a later date if evidence is eventually received.

An interesting situation can arise where a VAT officer raises an assessment for insufficient export evidence – where the evidence is subsequently obtained by the exporter – see Example 2.

Example 2

ABC Ltd exported goods with a value of £300,000 to a German customer on 31 March 2007. It did not charge VAT on the sale of the goods because it obtained the German VAT number of its customer.

However, it did not obtain satisfactory evidence of export and a VAT officer making a routine visit in July 2009 assessed VAT on the goods as if they had been supplied in the UK. He raised an assessment for £44,680 (£300,000 × 7/47) and HMRC calculated an interest charge of £4,000 as the assessment relates to 2007, i e more than 2 years ago.

ABC Ltd subsequently provided the officer with evidence that the goods were exported – but the officer refused to reduce the assessment, instead instructed the company to adjust the VAT on its next return.

Solution – The approach of HMRC in this situation is that the assessment is correct because at the time of the visit, the export evidence was inadequate. It is only at a later date that the evidence is produced – hence the instruction to adjust a current VAT return.

The negative outcome of this situation is that the interest charge of £4,000 will stand because the assessment has not been withdrawn.

Inadequate export evidence – case law

12.4 The exportation of goods to a non-EU country can either be a 'direct' export (where the UK supplier arranges for the goods to be delivered to the overseas customer, or through an agent he appoints) or an 'indirect export' (where the customer arranges for the collection of the goods from the UK supplier, and then takes them outside of the EU).

these customers would be taxable because the supply could not have been zero-rated without the customer's registration number. Supplies to non-registered customers in other EU countries are also excluded from the ESL (distance sales).

Goods collected in the UK by a customer

12.8 A situation may arise where an EU customer (VAT registered) collects goods himself from the UK customer, and personally arranges for the goods to be taken out of the country.

In such cases, the onus is still on the UK supplier to obtain proof that the goods have left the UK. As this type of situation is high risk (in the sense that HMRC will be keen to ensure the goods have not been diverted to the UK market), the standard of export evidence required is very high. See **12.4** to illustrate potential problems in this area that have led to court cases being necessary.

In reality, a sensible approach would probably be for the seller of the goods to take a deposit from the customer equal to the amount of VAT on the supply – this deposit to be refunded once satisfactory evidence is received to confirm the goods have left the UK. See Example 5.

Example 5

Julie sells photocopiers and is based in the UK. She has received an order from a French customer (registered for VAT in France) for 10 photocopiers costing £2,000 each. However, the customer is keen to save on delivery costs so has arranged for the goods to be collected from Julie's office himself and shipped to France.

Solution – Julie can zero-rate the sale of the photocopiers as the supply is to a business registered for VAT in an EU country outside the UK. However, this zero-rating is subject to the two key rules that she obtains the French VAT number of the customer, and proof that the goods have left the UK. It would be sensible for her to take a deposit of £3,500 from the customer (£20,000 × 17.5% VAT) on the basis that this will be refunded when satisfactory evidence has been received to confirm the goods have left the UK.

If this deposit is not taken, the French customer has no incentive to ensure the relevant evidence is forwarded to Julie. There will then be a risk that HMRC will treat the supply as standard rated on the basis that the goods could have been diverted to the UK market.

Single movement of goods but multiple transactions

12.9   As global trade becomes more sophisticated, there will inevitably be various situations arising with the movement of goods that will need to be addressed as far as VAT is concerned.

One common situation is where a single movement of goods occurs but more than two parties are involved in the sale (as with triangulation – see 12.6).

With regard to exports (excluding the triangular arrangement), if a single movement of goods is supported by two or more transactions, only the final transaction can be zero-rated – see Example 6 for an illustration of this point.

Example 6

Smith Inc is based in America and orders goods from ABC Ltd in the UK. ABC Ltd purchases the goods from DEF Ltd, also based in the UK. However, to avoid double handling of the goods, it is agreed that DEF Ltd will send the goods directly to the customer in the USA.

Solution – the supply of goods from DEF Ltd to ABC Ltd has taken place in the UK and DEF Ltd must therefore charge output tax on its sales invoice to ABC Ltd (assuming the goods are subject to VAT). However, ABC Ltd can zero-rate its supply to Smith Inc, as long as it obtains evidence of export to confirm that the goods have left the UK.

Other common export problems – is VAT to be charged?

12.10   Highlighted below are four common export problems that have been raised on many occasions over the years. They are all relevant to practical situations that could be encountered by advisers in the course of their work:

- Example 7 – customer based outside the EU but goods never leave the EU;

- Example 8 – customer based in the EU but goods are shipped outside the EU;

- Example 9 – customer based in the UK but goods are shipped to another EU country;

- Example 10 – customer is VAT registered in another EU country but goods do not leave the UK.

Example 7

A business registered for VAT in the UK receives an order from a private individual based in America, who wants the goods to be shipped to her niece in Italy as a birthday present.

Solution – in this situation, the goods have never left the EU so cannot be classed as an export. It is a requirement for zero-rating as an export that proof of export is held that the goods have left the EU. If the goods have been shipped to Italy, they have never left the EU so this condition is not met. The customer in America is not VAT registered in the EU so there is no scope to zero-rate the sale as a supply between two VAT registered businesses in different EU countries.

The American customer must therefore be charged UK VAT on her order – assuming the goods in question are not zero-rated.

Example 8

A business registered for VAT in the UK receives an order from a private individual based in Italy, who wants the goods to be shipped to her niece in America as a birthday present.

Solution – in this situation, the goods have left the EU so can be classed as an export. It is a requirement for zero-rating as an export that proof of export is held that the goods have left the EU – this should not be a problem as the business is arranging the export.

The Italian customer does not therefore need to be charged UK VAT on her order – the sale in question is zero-rated.

Example 9

A UK company based in London receives an order for goods from a business customer in Scotland. To save costs, the customer asks for the goods to be delivered directly to its customer based in France.

Solution – in this situation, the London based company is making a sale to another customer based in the UK. There is no scope to zero-rate the sale even if the Scottish customer is VAT registered because Scotland is part of the UK. However, the UK customer will forward documentation to the Scottish customer to prove that the goods have left the UK and this would enable the Scottish customer to not charge VAT to the French customer if he was VAT registered in France and supplied his French VAT number (the Scottish customer must record this number on his VAT invoice).

Example 10

A UK company receives an order for goods from a German business customer, VAT registered in Germany. However, the German customer asks for the goods to be delivered to his customer based in Wales, ie within UK.

In this situation, the goods have never left the UK, so all supplies are taking place within the UK. It is irrelevant the fact that the first customer is based in Germany.

In effect, the first outcome is that the German customer will be charged UK VAT – but can he reclaim this VAT as either input tax or by an 8th Directive claim?

The answer is 'no' in relation to the 8th Directive claim because this basically relates to VAT paid on certain services rather than goods. The German company cannot reclaim UK VAT on its own German VAT return.

If the total value of supplies made by the German company in the UK exceeds the VAT registration limits, then it would have to register for VAT in the UK on a compulsory basis. This would then create an opportunity to reclaim input tax on its UK VAT return. Equally, it could register for VAT in the UK on a voluntary basis and this would again facilitate recovery of input tax.

If the German company does not register for VAT in the UK, then the VAT it is charged by the UK supplier will form part of its cost price.

Retail exports

12.11 The retail export scheme gives the opportunity for overseas visitors coming to the UK to receive a refund of VAT paid on goods they buy in shops, as long as the goods are exported to destinations outside the EU. The onus is on the retailer to ensure that export evidence is held to support zero-rating of the goods – if this evidence is missing or unacceptable, then HMRC will treat the goods as being supplied in the UK.

There is a time limit as far as a VAT refund is concerned – the overseas customer must leave the UK for a final destination outside the EU (with the goods in question) by the last day of the third month following that in which the goods were purchased.

The retail export scheme is optional for a retailer – it gives two main advantages:

● reduced prices for eligible customers who can effectively buy goods on a VAT free basis;

● customer satisfaction – the business may attract more overseas customers if it adopts the retail export scheme.

Details about the retail export scheme, including forms to complete and procedures to adopt, are given in HMRC Notice 704.

Note – there is no problem with a retailer making an administration charge to customers for the time spent dealing with the paperwork created by the scheme.

Planning points to consider

12.12   The following planning points should be given consideration.

- Remember that an export of goods outside the EU is always zero-rated, irrespective of the status of the customer. However, the priority is to ensure that proper export evidence is held to confirm the goods have left the UK.

- Goods supplied to an EU customer can be zero-rated as long as the customer is registered for VAT in his own country and provides his VAT registration number to the UK supplier. Again, proof of export is a priority issue.

- A UK supplier should make reasonable efforts to ensure the validity of a VAT number given by an EU customer. A telephone call to the National VAT Helpline on 0845 010 9000 is worthwhile if there are reasons to doubt the accuracy of the number.

- The importance of obtaining proper export evidence to support zero-rating cannot be emphasised enough. If HMRC is not satisfied with the export evidence provided, it can treat the goods as being supplied in the UK from a VAT point of view. This could create a 17.5% output tax charge if the goods in question are standard rated.

- Be aware of the distance selling rules that may require a UK supplier to register for VAT in another EU country if the value of its sales to non-registered customers exceed certain limits. Remember that countries have the choice of adopting one of two annual turnover thresholds, ie €35,000 or €100,000.

- If goods are collected and taken out of the country by an overseas customer eligible for zero-rating, it is worthwhile to collect a deposit from the customer equal to the amount of VAT due on the supply. The deposit can then be refunded to the customer when he provides export evidence to confirm the goods have left the UK.

- The retail export scheme can offer commercial benefits to some retailers by giving certain overseas customers the chance to buy goods on a VAT-free basis.

- A UK trader whose sales are wholly or mainly exports will probably be in a repayment situation as far as VAT is concerned. The cash flow benefits of submitting returns monthly rather than quarterly should therefore be considered.

Chapter 13

International Services: Place of Supply

Key topics in this chapter:

- The importance of establishing the 'place of supply' of services as far as VAT liabilities are concerned.

- How the reverse charge works and its importance in the VAT system.

- Major changes to the place of supply rules on 1 January 2010 – and the difference between B2B (business to business) and B2C (business to consumer) sales and why this is important.

- EC Sales List to be completed after 1 January 2010 for services supplied to a business customer in another EU country if the service is covered by the reverse charge.

- Specific services where the VAT liability depends on the location of the customer or where the work is physically performed.

- Practical examples of situations where a UK supplier provides services to an overseas customer, including new procedures after 1 January 2010.

- Common questions are answered in relation to the new procedures that apply after 1 January 2010.

Introduction

13.1   The rules concerning supplies of goods and services to an overseas customer are very different as far as VAT is concerned. The VAT rules concerning the supply of goods basically involve looking at where the goods are shipped, and the status of the customer. The rules concerning the supply of services can vary according to the type of service being performed, where the work is being performed, as well as the status and location of the customer.

Important changes are being made to the VAT rules for businesses that supply or receive services to or from overseas businesses – the key date for these changes is 1 January 2010.

The main principle of the 1 January changes is that in the case of B2B (business to business) supplies, the default position for the place of supply will change from the location of the supplier to the location of the customer. The position is unchanged for B2C (business to consumer) supplies, ie the location of the supplier remains the default position.

The default position only applies when the service in question is not included within the various lists of services where the place of supply is based on:

- the location of the customer – currently known as a 'Schedule 5' service and mainly relevant to professional services; or

- the place where the service is being performed (think of a UK opera singer performing in Italy, her place of supply is Italy); or

- the location of land or goods being worked on (the place of supply for a UK based architect advising on an Irish property is Ireland).

The first challenge on this subject is to be clear about the difference between a supply of goods and services.

- *Goods* – in general terms, a supply of goods involves a change of ownership of goods from a supplier to a customer. In most cases, the supply will be for a physical product that can be touched, and the transfer of ownership will normally take place by the supplier raising an invoice and the customer providing payment to settle his account.

- *Services* – as a useful guideline, any supply that is not a supply of goods will be a supply of services. There is usually an indication of work being performed, eg a tax consultant providing advice or a decorator painting a wall. The value of the services is usually confirmed by the payment provided by the customer, which will form the basis of the VAT charge. No VAT is payable on a free supply of services.

Place of supply – basic principles and the reverse charge

13.2 The topic of international services is one of the most complicated aspects of VAT but the intention of the new rules after 1 January 2010 is to simplify procedures and hopefully improve the current system. The aim of this chapter is to look at the basic rules on the subject that can be applied in the majority of cases to arrive at a sensible conclusion regarding the VAT liability of the service being performed.

The phrase 'place of supply' is crucial because this is the country where VAT will be due. If a 'place of supply' is deemed to be in another EU country outside of the UK, then the VAT will be payable in that country – not the UK. In some cases, this VAT will be paid by the customer applying the reverse charge, on other occasions, by the UK supplier registering for VAT in that particular country.

Note – see **11.3** and **11.4** for an explanation about the 'reverse charge' and how it works. However, the relevant boxes of the VAT return for a reverse charge entry in relation to services are Boxes 1 and 4 (Boxes 2 and 4 are used for goods).

Example – A UK business receives accountancy services worth £10,000 from a Danish supplier. The Danish accountant will not charge Danish VAT (the place of supply for such services is the location of the customer) but the UK business will instead account for output tax of £1,500 in Box 1 of its own VAT return through the reverse charge mechanism. This assumes a UK VAT rate of 15%. The charge is based on the value of the service multiplied by the UK rate of VAT (£10,000 x 15%).

If the UK business is making taxable supplies and therefore able to reclaim input tax (no partial exemption problems etc) then the same amount of £1,500 will be included in Box 4 of the same VAT return. This produces a nil VAT payment overall. Entries of £10,000 (the net value of the service) will also be included in Boxes 6 and 7 of the return (sales and purchases).

The two key rules for a UK business are as follows:

- *If a UK business supplies services and the place of supply is the UK*, then UK VAT must be charged on the supply (assuming the services in question are subject to VAT). This applies regardless of where the customer belongs.

- *If a UK business supplies services and the place of supply is in another EU country*, subject to the registration limits in that country either the UK supplier or the customer is liable to account for any VAT due in that country (where the customer is liable to account for the supplier's output tax, this will be done through the reverse charge mechanism).

See Examples 1 and 2 for an illustration of the different VAT treatment of the above situations.

Example 1

ABC Ltd is VAT registered in the UK and does some work in the UK for a business customer that is based in Belgium (EU country). The customer is registered for VAT in Belgium. For this particular service, the rules state that the VAT charge will be due according to where the work is performed, rather than where the customer is based.

What is the VAT position for both the UK supplier and the Belgian customer?

Solution – ABC Ltd must charge UK VAT on the work performed (assuming the rate of VAT that applies on this particular service is standard rated). This VAT charge is made even though the customer is based in Belgium. This is because the place of supply is based on where the work is performed, ie UK.

However, all is not lost for the Belgian customer. Although he will not be able to reclaim the UK VAT on his Belgian VAT return, he may be able to make a claim to the UK to recover this VAT through what is known as an 8th Directive claim.

An 8th Directive claim gives scope for a business registered for VAT in an EU country to reclaim VAT incurred in another EU country other than its own. A full analysis of 8th Directive claims is provided in Chapter 15 at 15.3.

Example 2

ABC Ltd provides a different service to the same Belgian customer. The rules for this particular service state that the place of supply becomes the customer's location, rather than where the supplier is based.

What is the VAT position for both the UK supplier and the Belgian customer?

Solution – ABC Ltd will raise a sales invoice to the Belgian customer without charging VAT. It should be satisfied that the customer has a bona fide VAT registration in Belgium (or can provide some other evidence of being in business). The invoice will be noted along the lines of: 'this supply is subject to the reverse charge'.

However, the services are still subject to VAT and the Belgian customer will account for the output tax on his VAT return. He will apply the Belgian rate of VAT to the value of the invoice raised by the UK supplier, and include this amount of tax in Box 1 of his VAT return. As long as the service carried out by the UK supplier relates to a taxable supply (ie not relevant to an exempt or non-business activity), then the same amount of VAT can be reclaimed in Box 4 of the return as input tax.

The transaction has a nil overall effect on the Belgian's VAT return but is still declaring output tax on the transaction in question.

An important point to remember about this subject is that the performance of standard rated services by an EU supplier for any EU customer will usually include VAT at some point. VAT will either be charged in the supplier's own country (and declared on his own return), or declared in the customer's country, as in Example 2 above.

Situations when VAT charged depends on location of customer or where work is physically performed

Introduction

13.3   The basic rule to follow currently as far as VAT is concerned on this subject is this – if a UK supplier is performing standard-rated work in the UK for any customer, then UK VAT must be charged on the work, irrespective of where the customer is based, *unless the VAT liability of the work in question is specifically determined by the location of the customer or where the service is performed or, in the case of land, where the land is based.*

However, with effect from 1 January 2010, this position will change and the default position for B2B supplies will be the location of the customer and not the supplier. The default position considers the VAT position of those services that are not covered by the various lists of services that already fall into other categories. The default position will remain unchanged for B2C supplies, ie the location of the supplier is the default position.

Services where VAT liability not based on location of supplier

13.4   In effect, the VAT treatment of a supply of services can be determined by one of four issues:

• where the supplier is based;

• where the work is performed;

• where the customer is based;

• the status of the customer – in many cases, the VAT treatment will differ according to whether the customer is in business (B2B supplies), as compared to, for example, a member of the general public (B2C supplies).

For example, company A in the UK carries out work in EU country B for a customer based in EU country C. Where is the place of supply to determine the VAT liability?

The answer is – depending on the service being performed, the place of supply could be the UK or an EU country outside of the UK. This depends on whether the VAT liability for the service in question is determined by the location of the supplier, where the work is performed, where the customer is based or the status of the customer.

Note – there may be occasions when it is difficult to establish where a supplier/customer is based, eg where a business has branches and a main head office in different countries. This chapter assumes there is no confusion on this aspect, ie that it is easy to identify the location of the customer or supplier.

The basic rule that services are made where the supplier belongs (or where the customer belongs for B2B sales after 1 January 2010) does not apply for:

- services relating to land – see **13.5**;

- certain services which are supplied where physically carried out – see **13.6**;

- services falling within *VAT Act 1994, Sch 5, paras 1–8* – see **13.7**;

- transport services – see **13.8**;

- the hiring of means of transport – see **13.9**.

Services relating to land

13.5   The VAT liability of services relating to land is dependent on where the land in question is based. If the land is based in the UK, then UK VAT will be charged. If the land is located in another EU country, then the supply is regarded as taking place in that country.

The services covered by these rules include:

- any works of construction, demolition, conversion, reconstruction, altera-tion, enlargement, repair or maintenance of a building or civil engineering work;

- services such as those provided by estate agents, auctioneers, architects, surveyors, engineers and others involved in matters relating to land.

If the land in question is located outside the EU, then the supply is outside the scope of UK and EU VAT.

The main problem with the rules on services relating to land is that it could create a liability for a UK supplier to register for VAT in another EU country. However, if the customer is VAT registered in the country where the land is located, then it may be possible to avoid registering for VAT through the customer applying the reverse charge mechanism.

Note – the place of supply rules in relation to land are not affected by the new rules effective after 1 January 2010.

See Example 3 for a practical example of how VAT is dealt with on a typical land services transaction.

Example 3

ABC Construction Services Ltd is based in the UK, and has been asked to build an extension to a property in Dublin (EU country) that is owned by an

Italian company. All work will obviously be carried out where the property is located, ie Ireland. The value of the building works is £500,000.

What is the VAT position?

Solution – ABC Construction Services Ltd is making supplies in Ireland that exceed the Irish VAT registration threshold. The company must therefore register for VAT in Ireland, and charge Irish VAT to the Italian customer.

In reality, these rules are important to avoid an unfair playing field for VAT. For example, if the UK company could escape a VAT charge on the basis that it was working outside of the UK, then this would give it an unfair advantage compared to an Irish based building company that would need to charge Irish VAT. It would also be unfair if the VAT charge was based on UK rates of VAT – because these might be lower than the rates applicable in Ireland.

Services which are supplied where physically carried out

13.6   A supply of the following services is currently treated as made where the services are physically carried out (irrespective of where the customer belongs – although see the note below regarding the proposed change of rule with effect from 1 January 2011):

- cultural, artistic, sporting, scientific, educational or entertainment services and any services ancillary to any such services;

- services relating to exhibitions, conferences or meetings and any services ancillary to (including organising) any such services;

- valuation of, or work carried out on, any goods;

- ancillary transport services;

Regarding the VAT treatment of services in the above categories:

- an overseas supplier carrying out services for a UK VAT registered person will not need to account for UK VAT because this will be done by the reverse charge procedure being accounted for by the recipient of the services;

- an overseas supplier carrying out services for a person in the UK that is not VAT registered will have to register for VAT in the UK subject to the registration threshold.

Note – with effect from 1 January 2011, the place of supply in relation to supplies of 'cultural, artistic, sporting ...etc' services will be the location of the customer in the case of B2B sales. However, this change will not apply to admission charges to such events, which will remain taxable where the event takes place.

See Example 4.

Example 4

An Italian opera singer travels to the UK and performs at three top concert venues, earning a fee from the company organising the concerts. The company organising the concerts is registered for VAT in the UK.

An Australian cricketer travels to the UK and carries out some coaching at a series of amateur cricket clubs across the country. His total income is £40,000 and none of the cricket clubs are registered for VAT.

Solution – the company organising the concerts will account for the output tax of the Italian singer by adopting the reverse charge procedure, ie output tax accounted for in Box 1 of its UK VAT return and input tax reclaimed in Box 4 (as the income from the concerts is likely to be taxable).

The Australian cricketer is providing sporting services in the UK to non-registered entities. However, the total value of his supplies does not exceed the UK VAT registration limits so he has no liability to account for output tax on his fees.

Supplies based on location of customer

13.7 *VAT Act 1994, Sch 5, paras 1–8* contains a list of services (see below) which override the 'place of supply' rules in certain cases. The VAT liability is then based according to where the customer is based – and if this is outside the UK, no VAT is charged.

Note – as explained above, *Sch 5* is being repealed as part of the new place of supply rules that come into effect after 1 January 2010 and the legislation will instead be contained within a new *s 7A* and a new *Sch 4A*, as well as through amendments to *ss 7–9* of the current legislation.

The relevant rules for *Sch 5* services are as follows:

- the supply is treated as taking place where the recipient belongs if the recipient belongs outside the EU and the Isle of Man. In such cases, the supply is outside the scope of UK VAT;

- the supply is treated as taking place where the recipient belongs if the recipient belongs in an EU country other than that of the supplier and the services are supplied to him for his business purposes. In this situation, the recipient of the services will account for VAT in that country through the reverse charge procedure. With effect from 1 January 2010, a reverse charge situation will also apply to any services supplied to the customer for his non-business purposes. This is because of the new basic rule regarding B2B supplies, ie the place of supply is based on the location of the customer.

See Example 5 for an illustration of the above points in a practical situation.

Example 5

Accountancy (and tax) work is included in the list of *Sch 5* services (see below). Smith and Smith accountants are VAT registered in the UK and are currently working on three important jobs for overseas customers (all work being carried out in the UK):

● completing an audited set of accounts for a VAT-registered business based in Spain (EU customer);

● completing a UK tax return for a private individual who lives in Spain;

● completing an audited set of accounts for an American company (non-EU).

What is the VAT liability of the three jobs?

Solution – the charge to the Spanish business will be made without charging UK VAT. This is because the customer is in business in another EU country and the services are supplied to him for his business purposes. The output tax on the supply will be accounted for by the Spanish customer who will apply the reverse charge on his own VAT return in Spain, ie output tax in Box 1 of the return and input tax reclaimed in Box 4 as long as the work in question relates to a taxable supply.

The private individual in Spain is not in business, so the VAT charge reverts to the usual 'place of supply' rule which is the UK. The individual will therefore be charged UK VAT at the standard rate. This outcome will be unchanged after 1 January 2010 because this work is classed as a B2C sale, so the default position for the place of supply is still the location of the supplier. It is only B2B supplies that are affected by the changes.

The American company is outside the EU and therefore no VAT charge will be made on the services provided because the supply is outside the scope of the EU boundary. However, Smith and Smith will need to ensure they do not incur any liability to register for any sales/turnover based tax in America.

A UK supplier who treats services within *Sch 5* as being supplied where the recipient belongs must hold commercial evidence that:

● the services are received and used outside the UK; and

● in the case of business customers within the EU, proof that they are actually in business.

Note – in the case of EU businesses, the best proof is evidence of the customer's VAT registration number. The VAT number should be recorded on the sales invoice.

Some EU customers may be VAT registered and have non-business as well as business activities (eg a charity). In such cases, the supplier must be satisfied that the services supplied are being used for the purpose of its business activities before treating the supply as taking place where the

recipient belongs. However, this will not be a problem after 1 January 2010 because the non-business supplies will also avoid a UK charge of VAT (and be subject to a reverse charge entry by the customer). This is due to the new basic rule after this date that the place of supply for B2B sales be based on the location of the customer.

If the supplier cannot determine where his customer belongs, or obtain evidence of his business status, he should normally charge his customer VAT.

A list of *Sch 5* services within general categories is provided as follows (with relevant paragraph numbers also shown and an example of a service included in the category in each case):

Note – although the legislative reference for *Sch 5* services will change after 1 January 2010, the list of services covered by the legislation will remain the same. There are no plans to either restrict or expand the current list of eligible services.

Schedule 5 services	*Example of services included*	*Comments*
(1) Transfers and assignments of copyright, patents, licences, trademarks and similar rights.	The granting of a right by a photographer for one of his photographs to be published in a magazine article.	
(2) Advertising services.	The devising and undertaking of a promotional campaign by an advertising agency to launch a client's new product.	
(3) Services of consultants, engineers, consultancy bureaux, lawyers, accountants and other similar services; data processing and provision of information (but excluding from this head any services related to land).	A consultant writing a scientific report for a customer.	Note – this is an interesting category and needs to be approached with care. For example, a consultant's services are only covered by *Sch 5* if he is working in his own field of expertise. For example an engineering consultant doing consultancy work on fashion would not qualify under *para 3*.

In reality, the section requires a degree of expertise within the work being performed. For example, accountancy services do not include clerical or secretarial services. |

Schedule 5 services	Example of services included	Comments
(4) Acceptance of any obligation to refrain from pursuing or exercising, in whole or part, any business activity or any such rights as are referred to in (1) above.	Agreement by the owner of a trademark to refrain from using it.	
(5) Banking, financial and insurance services (including reinsurance but not including the provision for safe deposit facilities).	Debt collection services.	
(5A) The provision of access to, and of transport or transmission through, natural gas and electricity distribution systems and the provision of other directly linked services.		
(6) The supply of staff.	The transfer for a fee by a sports club of a professional sportsman who has a contract of service with the club, eg a professional football player.	
(7) The letting on hire of goods other than means of transport.	The hire of computer and office equipment.	Note – this paragraph contains an interesting clause that goods include all forms of movable property or equipment but not land and property or equipment and machinery installed as a fixture. It is also important to look at where the enjoyment of the goods takes place. See Example 6.
(7A)–(7C) Telecommunication services, radio and television broadcasting services, electronically supplied services.	Transmission or delivery of another person's material by electronic means.	Note – this section considers supplies made over the Internet or other electronic networks. The provisions are quite complicated and specialist advice may be appropriate to establish the correct VAT position.

Schedule 5 services	Example of services included	Comments
(8) The services rendered by one person to another in procuring for the other any of the services mentioned in (1)–(7C) above.	Services of advertising agents.	

Example 6

ABC VAT Consultants have been asked to advise on the VAT liability of the following supplies of services.

(a) An American tourist in the UK hires a video camera from a UK provider for use during her visit.

(b) A UK golf club hires out a set of golf clubs to a UK customer for use on his holiday in the USA. The clubs will be used exclusively in the USA – at no times will they be used to play golf in the UK or any other EU country.

(c) A satellite TV company based in India supplies broadcasting services to UK subscribers. The services are used and enjoyed in the UK.

Solution –

(a) VAT needs to be charged at the standard rate. This is because the use of the goods is taking place in the UK.

(b) The place of supply is outside the EU as long as the customer can demonstrate that the goods are only being used in the USA. If not, then the supply will be deemed to be taking place in the UK and subject to VAT at the standard rate.

(c) The services are used and enjoyed in the UK and are subject to UK VAT. The place of supply is the UK even though the supplier is based in India.

Transport services

13.8 As a general rule, the VAT liability of transport services depends on where the transportation is carried out. For supplies of intra-Community transport, the place of supply is based on the place of departure. However, this situation will change on 1 January 2010 and the new general rule will apply for B2B supplies, ie it is the location of the customer that counts.

Example – the place of supply for shipping goods from London to Rome for a UK customer will be the UK until 31 December 2009 (based on place of departure) but Italy after this date (default position for B2B supplies).

The hiring of a means of transport

13.9   With effect from 1 January 2010, the rules will change in relation to the hiring of a means of transport, depending on whether the hiring is long-term (over 30 days) or short-term (less than 30 days). In the case of long-term hiring, it is relevant to consider whether the customer is in business.

● Rule until 31 December 2009 – VAT charge depends on where the supplier is based.

● New rules from 1 January 2010:

— the place of supply in relation to a short-term hire to a customer (less than 30 days) is based on where the vehicle is put at the disposal of the customer;

— the place of supply in relation to a long-term hire to a business customer (more than 30 days) depends on the location of the customer;

— the place of supply in relation to a long-term hire to a non-business customer (more than 30 days) will depend on where the supplier is based.

Note – from 1 January 2013, a long-term hire to a non-business customer will also depend on where the customer is established (apart from pleasure boats where the place of supply will depend on where the boat is put at the disposal of the customer).

Example 7

A UK car hire company rents a car to a French business customer for 31 days in October 2009 and 31 days in January 2010. The car will be used in the UK. Does the company charge VAT?

Solution – the place of supply before 1 January 2010 is the location of the supplier, so UK VAT must be charged on the hiring for October. However, the French customer may be able to reclaim this VAT back through the 8th Directive system if it is for a business expense and he is VAT registered in France.

The January 2010 hiring is for more than 30 days to a business customer and the new rules apply so the place of supply is now France, ie where the customer is based.

New place of supply rules from 1 January 2010

New general rule for B2B supplies

13.10 As explained at the beginning of this chapter, a new default position takes effect from 1 January 2010 in relation to the place of supply for B2B supplies. This applies to sales of services to both EU and non-EU businesses. The new rule means that the VAT charge will be decided by the location of the customer if the service in question does not fall within the various categories where the place of supply is based on other issues such as where the work is physically performed, location of land etc.

To give an example of how a transaction will be different on 1 January 2010 compared to 31 December 2009, consider Example 8 in relation to the services of a vet.

Example 8

Pat is a vet based in Kent who has a friend called Matt based in France. Matt is a VAT registered farmer and Pat travels across the border to treat his sick and injured cows. Matt has a friend (who also lives in France) called Nat who owns a pet cat. Pat has agreed to treat her cat as a separate service when he is next in France.

Pat makes two trips to France – one on 31 October 2009 and one on 31 January 2010. What is the VAT treatment of his charges in each case?

Solution – *Up to 31 December 2009.* Under current B2B rules, Pat will add UK VAT at 15% to his fees earned before 31 December 2009 – for both Matt and Nat. He will declare output tax on his VAT return in the normal way. This is because 'veterinary services' are not included within the various services considered in the previous sections, so the place of supply is the UK based on the default position.

Matt (assuming he is VAT registered in France) then has scope to reclaim this VAT from HMRC in the UK by making an 8th Directive claim (a system of reclaiming VAT paid on expenses incurred in other EU countries which is developed further in Chapter 15).

Note – there is no scope for Nat to reclaim the VAT on the charge for treating her cat because it is a non-business expense for her and she is not VAT registered.

From 1 January 2010. The position changes dramatically with effect from 1 January 2010. From that date, the default position for 'veterinary services' and many other services (B2B supplies) will be the location of the customer, so the place of supply is now France.

This means that Pat will no longer add UK VAT to his fees for Matt (treating the cows) – and the onus is on Matt to account for the VAT on his own return using the reverse charge system. This means he will account for output tax in Box 1 of his return (Pat's fee x the French rate of VAT at 19.6%), and claim input tax in Box 4. The latter claim is not a problem because farmers are able to fully reclaim input tax because this is a taxable activity.

However, Pat will continue to charge VAT to Nat on the fee he earns when he treats her cat. This is because the supply here is B2C (business to consumer) rather than B2B so the old default position remains, ie VAT charge is based on the location of the supplier rather than the customer.

Note – the good news for Pat is that he can still claim input tax on all of his expenses even though he is no longer charging VAT on his work for Matt.

EC Sales List

13.11 A further important new regulation takes effect from 1 January 2010 – a UK business selling services to an EU business customer where the customer must account for the reverse charge must record details of all such transaction on an EC Sales List (ESL). The ESL is relevant to all services where the EU customer declares the reverse charge, not just the new situations that apply after 1 January 2010.

The ESL (VAT101) has been in place for many years and has been completed by UK businesses who sell goods to VAT registered businesses in other EU countries. The only difference for a supply of services is that a 'code 3' entry will need to be made in the end column of the form.

The aim of the new ESL is to enable the tax authorities to ensure that reverse charge entries are correctly being made by those businesses that are receiving services without being charged VAT. This is particularly relevant if the business in question is partly exempt and cannot fully reclaim input tax.

The key rules for ESL forms are as follows:

- The forms must be completed on a calendar quarter basis, either in paper format or online. An extra 7 days (21 instead of 14) are given if the form is completed online.

- It is possible that some supplies will be made to business customers in other EU countries who are not VAT registered. These sales will not be recorded on the ESL because each entry requires a VAT registration number otherwise the form will be rejected.

- The entries on the ESL only relate to the supply of taxable services not to those that are exempt from VAT.

- The ESL forms are not covered by the new penalty regime. However, a penalty of £5, £10 or £15 per day can be charged if the ESL is submitted late and a potential penalty of £100 could be charged for a material inaccuracy on the form, unless there is a reasonable excuse for such an inaccuracy.

As a final point, HMRC recognises that the completion of ESL forms is an extra challenge for UK businesses and has confirmed it will 'keep administrative burdens and VAT costs to a minimum.'

Management services

13.12 The supply of management services is another situation where the VAT rules will change on 1 January 2010 – but there are many more. The place of supply for management services is based on the default position (location of the supplier) because it is not included in either the list of *Sch 5* services or other categories.

In the case of management services, think of the implications for a UK business supplying management services to a business in Sweden that only makes exempt supplies (also remember that the rules apply both ways, i e they will affect businesses in the UK that receive management services from abroad). See Example 9.

Example 9

ABC Ltd in the UK supplies management services to Swedish Bank Ltd, the latter company is not VAT registered in Sweden because it only makes exempt supplies. The value of the management service is £100,000 per month plus VAT. What are the VAT issues?

Solution – ABC Ltd will charge UK VAT at 15% until 31 December 2009. However, the location of the customer becomes the default position after 1 January 2010, so ABC Ltd will not charge UK VAT after this date.

However, the Swedish company is now treated as making taxable supplies that exceed the VAT registration limits in Sweden because it needs to treat the services it is receiving as its own taxable income. It must therefore register for VAT on 1 January 2010 and account for the reverse charge as follows:

Box 1 = £100,000 per month x Swedish rate of VAT, i e 25% = £25,000 per month

Box 4 = £0 because the VAT in Box 1 is relevant to exempt supplies. No corresponding input tax can be claimed.

Note – the outcome here is that the Swedish company is paying an extra £120,000 VAT per year (£100,000 per month x 10% difference in VAT rates between UK and Sweden) because the irrecoverable VAT is now based on the Swedish rate of VAT rather than the lower rate of VAT in the UK.

Supplies to be used by the customer for non-business purposes

13.13   Here is another major difference between the old and new rules, again explained by a practical example. The basic principle is that the reverse charge concept will apply to services supplied to a VAT registered customer in another EU country (where the default position applies), even if the customer uses a particular service for non-business purposes.

Example 10

Jones is an accountant based in London and he has done some work for a VAT registered charity based in Denmark (EU country) in relation to its non-business activities. What is the VAT position before and after 1 January 2010?

Solution – the services of an accountant are included in *VATA 1994, Sch 5 para 3*. This means that the place of supply is based on the location of the customer if the customer is an EU business customer receiving the supply for business purposes. This does not apply to the work for the charity in this case because it is for the non-business activities of the charity. The default position applies, ie the place of supply is based on the location of the supplier before 31 December 2009 (UK) and the location of the customer after this date (Denmark).

Note – the new default position also applies in relation to non-business activities after 1 January 2010 as long as the business (charity in this case) has some business supplies. This is a further simplification measure that will make life easier for a UK business. If it receives a VAT registration number from its customer, it does not need to worry about whether it is working for the business or non-business part of the organisation.

The outcome is that:

● UK VAT will be charged at 15% on work carried out by Jones before 31 December 2009;

● No VAT will be charged on work carried out after 1 January 2010. The customer must account for VAT based on the reverse charge principle.

The new rules produce a bad result in this particular example. The Danish charity will not be able to claim VAT on the accountancy services either through the original charge by Jones or the subsequent reverse charge entry it must make after 1 January 2010 (the latter will produce an entry in Box 1 of its VAT return but no corresponding entry in Box 4). However, the reverse charge entry means its loss of tax is 25% (based on the Danish rate of VAT) compared to the lower rates that applied on the UK VAT charge (ie 15% before 31 December 2009).

Time of supply

13.14 The tax authorities are keen to ensure that there is a cross-reference facility between an entry on an ESL (EC Sales List as explained in **13.11**) and on the customer's VAT return (reverse charge entry). This is an important control to counter the risk of either VAT fraud or major errors taking place. To facilitate this process, new time of supply rules will also take effect from 1 January 2010, ie to confirm the date when the reverse charge needs to be included on the customer's VAT return.

- *Single supplies* – the key date is when the service has been completed or paid for, whichever happens first. A single supply relates to the situation when a service has a clear start and finish date, e g repairing a vehicle. The completion date will usually coincide with an invoice being raised, so this will hopefully be the key date in most cases.

- *Continuous supplies with regular billing periods* – for example, the hire of a photocopier machine. In such cases, a reverse charge entry must be made when either an invoice is raised or payment received, whichever happens first.

- *Continuous supplies that are not subject to regular billing or payment periods* – in such cases, the new regulations create an annual tax point of 31 December each year.

It may be complicated in some cases to determine the time of supply, and as such, the HMRC guidance states:

'we are aware of the difficulties, for example, in determining when a service has been completed. Events such as entry of a transaction into the accounts, receipt of an invoice or date of payment might be appropriate indicators of when that point is reached.'

Other common questions

13.15 In concluding this chapter, we will look at some other likely questions that may be raised by practitioners in relation to the new place of supply rules from 1 January 2010:

- *Does the new default position apply to services provided to a VAT registered person based in another EU country for his private purposes (as opposed to non-business services considered in **13.13**)?*

  No. To give an example, if a UK accountant is completing the private tax return of a sole trader who is VAT registered in France, then this is not classed as a B2B sale, even if the French trader gives proof of his VAT registration number in France. The service is classed as a B2C supply and UK VAT must be charged.

- *Can the same ESL be used for a business that sells goods and services to VAT registered businesses in the EU?*

Yes. The only difference is that entries on the ESL relevant to services will be given a 'code 3' entry on the form.

- *Should a UK business check that the VAT registration numbers provided by its customers are genuine?*

Yes. This can either be done by contacting HMRC's National Helpline (tel: 0845 010 9000) or by using the Europa website. Further plans are in the pipeline to make it easier to check VAT numbers through another online facility.

- *What happens if a customer is in business but not registered for VAT?*

In such cases, the customer will not be able to provide a VAT registration number as evidence of his business status. However, alternative evidence can be acquired from the customer such as business stationery, certificates from fiscal authorities, letters from the Chamber of Commerce etc. The key point is that a customer receiving services from abroad will need to take the value of these services into account when determining if he has exceeded the VAT registration limits. So a business that is not VAT registered will soon be required to register if the value of its overseas supplies are significant. See Example 11.

Example 11

A farmer in the UK has taxable sales of £65,000 per annum and is not VAT registered (his turnover is below the compulsory annual limit of £68,000). He uses a vet based in France to treat his animals and pays the vet £5,000 per year. What is the VAT position?

Note – see Example 8 to clarify the place of supply rules for veterinary services.

Solution – until 31 December 2009, the UK farmer will be charged French VAT on the fees he pays to the vet. However, he will not be charged French VAT after 1 January 2010 but must instead include the £5,000 of fees as taxable turnover in relation to his own VAT registration test. His taxable turnover is now £70,000 per annum (£65,000 + £5,000) which exceeds the current limit of £68,000. He now needs to register for VAT in the UK and will apply the reverse charge to future fees paid to the French vet.

- *What happens with services of intermediaries?*

The place of supply for the services of an intermediary is often based on where the underlying supply is arranged. From 1 January 2010, such services will be covered by the new general rule for B2B supplies, ie based on the location of the customer.

- *What about restaurant and catering supplies?*

The position is unchanged – it is where the meal is consumed that counts.

- *What about work carried out on repairing goods or valuing goods?*

  These services are covered by the new general rule, ie the place of supply depends on the location of the customer for B2B supplies after 1 January 2010.

- *The ESL form does not apply to any exempt supplies made to a business customer. How will a UK business know if a service is taxable or exempt in, say, Germany?*

  This is a question that could be quite relevant in relation to supplies of some financial services and it is worthwhile contacting the HMRC National Helpline (tel: 0845 010 9000) in areas of doubt. However, the VAT liability of most other services tends to be the same as in the UK.

- *Will reverse charge entries also apply to services bought by a UK business from business suppliers outside of the EU – say in India?*

  Yes. This has always applied in relation to many services bought from non-EU suppliers (eg the services within *Sch 5*) but will be extended after 1 January 2010. This could produce an extra source of non-recoverable VAT for exempt businesses in the UK in some cases.

  Think of an Indian business that provides bookkeeping services to a bank. Until 31 December 2009, the place of supply for such services was the location of the supplier, ie India. From 1 January 2010, the place of supply is the location of the customer for B2B supplies, ie the UK. The reverse charge entry needs to be made by the bank and this will produce a source of non-recoverable input tax if the services are relevant to its exempt or non-business activities.

- *What happens if a UK business incorrectly pays VAT to an overseas supplier after 1 January 2010?*

  An attempt to reclaim this VAT under the 8th Directive system will be rejected by the overseas authority. The correct approach will be to acquire a VAT credit note from the overseas supplier and then deal with the VAT by using the reverse charge mechanism as explained in this chapter.

Planning points to consider

13.16 The following planning points should be given consideration.

- Be aware of important new rules concerning the place of supply that take effect on 1 January 2010. It is important that the impact of the changes is recognised so that the effect on clients who provide services to overseas customers or receive them from overseas suppliers can be considered. The aim of the new rules is to reduce the number of transactions across borders that are subject to a VAT charge by the supplier. This is a welcome change that should produce cash flow and administrative savings in many cases.

- Even if an EU business outside the UK is charged UK VAT on services it receives, this is not necessarily a problem. There may be scope for the overseas customer to recover UK VAT by making an 8th Directive claim to the UK authorities. The HMRC branch in Londonderry that deals with such claims has an excellent reputation for processing claims in a timely and efficient manner.

- The VAT on services relating to land, eg building work carried out by a tradesman depends on where the land is located. This is likely to mean, for example, that a UK company providing construction services on, eg property in France, will need to register for VAT in France. However, this need to register may be avoided if the French customer applies the reverse charge to account for the output tax on his own return.

- For *Sch 5* services supplied to a business customer in another EU country, it is important that the supplier retains proper evidence to confirm that the customer is using the services for the purpose of his business. In most cases, evidence that he is VAT registered in his own country will suffice, ie confirming that output tax will be accounted for by the customer using the reverse charge mechanism.

- The list of *Sch 5* services needs to be analysed in detail to ensure that relevant services meet the various requirements of the legislation. For example, the services of a 'consultant' qualify as a *Sch 5* service but only if the consultant is providing a service in his own field of expertise. The rules concerning telecommunications supplies and Internet-based supplies also need to be considered with care.

Chapter 14

International Services – Other Issues

Key topics in this chapter:

- Territorial boundaries of the UK as far as VAT is concerned.

- The need for an unregistered business or person in the UK to take into account the value of certain services it receives from abroad in determining whether it should be registered for VAT.

- International services that are zero-rated.

Introduction

14.1 In Chapter 13 we considered the 'place of supply' rules as far as international services are concerned – which is important to determine the VAT liability of the relevant supply.

In effect, if the place of supply is considered to be outside the UK, the services are outside the scope of UK VAT. Where the place of supply is deemed to be within the UK, the services are subject to normal UK VAT rules, ie the supply will be standard rated, zero-rated or exempt (or subject to the reduced rate of VAT) as if the services were being supplied between two UK parties.

This chapter considers three main issues:

- the territorial boundaries of the UK;

- the need for an unregistered business in the UK to take into account the value of some services it receives from abroad in deciding whether it must register for VAT; and

- examples of international services that qualify for zero-rating within the zero-rated schedule, ie which are charged without VAT irrespective of the place of supply outcome.

Note – the reverse charge is given this title because it reverses the usual position of output tax being accounted for by the supplier of goods or services to the situation where output tax is accounted for by the customer receiving goods and services.

Territorial boundaries of the UK

14.2   The UK comprises Great Britain, Northern Ireland and the territorial sea of the UK (ie waters within 12 nautical miles of the coastline).

The Isle of Man is deemed to be part of the UK as far as VAT is concerned – but the Channel Islands are excluded.

UK supplier receives a Sch 5 service from a person who belongs outside the UK

14.3   A key objective of the VAT system is to create a level playing field as far as competition in business is concerned. For example, it would be totally unfair if a UK person or business could avoid paying VAT on a service it receives by obtaining this service VAT free from a supplier in another country. The rules applied throughout the EU need to avoid this situation happening – even if they are somewhat complicated in the process.

As explained above, a *Sch 5* service is one that is covered by *VAT Act 1994, Sch 5 paras 1–8* – as listed in Chapter 13 at **13.7**.

The significance of the legislation in this section is that the rules for *Sch 5* reverse charges apply to a 'person' in the UK, not a 'taxable person'. This means that anyone carrying on a business in the UK will become liable to be VAT registered if the total value of reverse charge services within these provisions and turnover from any taxable business supplies made in the UK exceed the registration limit. See Example 1 for an illustration of this point.

Note – with effect from 1 January 2010, the rules concerning supplies to a 'person' rather than 'taxable person' will also extend to those services where the place of supply is the UK through the new default position in relation to the place of supply rules. The new rules confirm that it is the location of the customer that matters in B2B (business to business) supplies. See **13.10** and Example 1 which illustrates this principle.

Example 1

John has a very successful business as an accountant in the UK and is not VAT registered. The process adopted by his business is that all accounts preparation work is carried out in India by a firm that charges John for its work. John then reviews the work and agrees the accounts with his clients.

Most of John's clients are small businesses in the UK that are not VAT registered.

The annual value of John's turnover is £50,000 and he pays £20,000 per year to the Indian company for its services.

Are there any VAT consequences with this arrangement?

Solution – the initial thinking might be that John has created an excellent business structure where there is no need to worry about VAT – good news for his customers because they are not VAT registered, so VAT would be an extra cost to their business.

However, the reverse charge rules apply to a 'person' rather than a 'taxable person' who receives a *Sch 5* service from outside the UK (the services of an accountant are included within *VAT Act 1994, Sch 5 para 3*).

John therefore has an obligation to treat the charge from the Indian business as a taxable supply for his own purposes. This means that the total value of John's taxable supplies are £70,000 per year (£50,000 from clients fees plus £20,000 through the reverse charge mechanism) meaning he must be registered for VAT as this exceeds the VAT limit of £68,000 (effective from 1 May 2009).

The other main situation where a UK business may be tempted (incorrectly) to use the services of an overseas entity is if the business is not registered for VAT in the UK because it only makes exempt supplies. See Example 2 for an illustration of this point.

Example 2

DEF Insurance Brokers Ltd is based in the UK but not registered for VAT because it only makes exempt supplies linked to insurance services.

The managing director of the company has devised a strategy that he thinks will save £21,000 VAT per annum (based on 17.5% rate of VAT):

- the company auditors in the UK charge £50,000 plus VAT for their services – he intends to use an American company to do this work for the same fee but without VAT being charged;

- the company pays £70,000 plus VAT each year for computer consultancy services. He intends to use a firm in India to carry out this work – again for the same fee but without VAT being charged.

The result of the above measures (he thinks) is that the company will save irrecoverable VAT of £21,000 – is he correct?

Solution – again, the company is affected by the fact that the reverse charge rules for *Sch 5* services apply to a 'person' in business not just a 'taxable person' already registered for VAT. If the company proceeds with the strategy being proposed by the managing director, it will be liable to be VAT registered because the value of its reverse charge services will exceed £68,000 on an annual basis.

Once registered, the company will account for output tax on the overseas services in Box 1 of quarterly VAT returns (£120,000 × 17.5% = £21,000) – but will not be able to reclaim input tax in Box 4 because the services are relevant to exempt supplies. The end result is that the company is in the same VAT position if it uses an overseas company to carry out various works as if it used a UK supplier, ie the VAT rules have ensured that a level playing field exists for all EU businesses.

Services with an EU simplification

14.4   Another opportunity to reduce the administrative burden of VAT occurs in the following situation:

● a VAT registered business in the UK provides his VAT registration number to an overseas supplier based in another EU country; and

● the overseas supplier is not registered for VAT in the UK; and

● the UK recipient is receiving services from the overseas supplier in connection with his business; and

● the services provided by the overseas supplier fall into one of the following four categories:

    (a)   valuation of, or work carried out on, any goods;
    (b)   intra-EU freight transport services and related ancillary services;
    (c)   arranging intra-EU freight transport services and related ancillary services;
    (d)   most intermediary services supplied in the EU.

Note – intermediary services are services provided to facilitate the supply of goods and services between two persons.

If all of the above rules are met, then an overseas supplier does not need to charge VAT on his services, which can again be accounted for by the UK customer applying the reverse charge mechanism. If any of the conditions are not met, eg the UK customer is not VAT registered or intends to use the services for non-business purposes, then the overseas supplier must charge VAT in the normal manner.

However, with effect from 1 January 2010, the place of supply rules are changing so that the default position becomes as a matter of course the location of the customer, ie the reverse charge calculation is made by the customer. The reverse charge also applies to supplies made to a customer for his non-business purposes, as long as he makes some business supplies (again because the VAT will be dealt with by the reverse charge).

Extension to other services supplied within the UK

14.5   The reverse charge procedure applies to all services not falling within **14.3** where:

(a)   the place of supply is the UK; and

(b)   the supplier belongs outside the UK; and

(c)   the recipient is a VAT registered person who uses the services for business purposes.

The above situation covers the following services:

*   services relating to land;

*   services supplied where physically carried out;

*   passenger transport services;

*   freight transport services not covered by **14.4**;

*   hired goods, telecommunication services, radio and television broadcasting services.

The reverse charge cannot apply to these services if the recipient is not already registered for VAT in the UK. In such cases, the supplier must account for the VAT due, which means he may be liable to register for VAT in the UK.

Note – the existence of the reverse charge procedure for the services listed above does not prevent overseas suppliers from registering for VAT in the UK under normal rules. If they do register, they must invoice UK VAT in the normal way and the recipient is not then required to account for VAT under the reverse charge procedure.

See Example 3 for an illustration of this point.

Example 3

Giovanni is a top Italian opera singer, registered for VAT in Italy. He intends to carry out a number of performances in the UK, supplying his services to ABC Production Company Ltd (VAT registered in the UK). Giovanni is responsible for finding and paying for his own orchestra within his fee and he has decided to use the services of the Lutworth Orchestra. The latter is also VAT registered in the UK. The fee for Giovanni from each concert will exceed the VAT registration limit.

What is the VAT position?

Solution – Giovanni is performing in the UK and the VAT rules concerning cultural and artistic activities state that the place of supply is where the work is physically carried out, ie the UK.

In effect, Giovanni can avoid registering for VAT in the UK, with the production company accounting for the VAT instead through the reverse charge concession described above. His services meet all of the specified conditions. In this situation, he will be faced with a UK VAT charge from Lutworth Orchestra, which he can reclaim from HMRC by making an 8th Directive claim (see 15.3).

As an alternative, Giovanni could decide to register for VAT in the UK as he is making taxable supplies in the UK. In this situation, he would charge UK VAT on his fee to the production company (not a problem because they should be able to reclaim input tax). The charge from Lutworth Orchestra would then be input tax for Giovanni in the normal way.

International services that are zero-rated

14.6 The examples considered in this chapter and in Chapter 13 have illustrated situations when VAT is not charged by suppliers in many cases because the customer has taken responsibility for paying output tax through the reverse charge procedure. The end result is still the same – an output tax declaration has been made on the services supplied (but by the customer rather than the supplier).

In other cases, VAT has not been charged on a supply because the recipient of a service has been based outside the EU.

In basic terms, the key approach is to identify the place of supply – and if this is outside the UK, then the services are outside the scope of UK VAT. If the place of supply is deemed to be inside the UK, the services are subject to normal UK rules concerning VAT.

The other occasion when a UK supplier can avoid a VAT charge to an overseas customer is if the service he is performing is specifically zero-rated or exempt under UK legislation (*VAT Act 1994, Schs* 8 and 9). See Chapter 21 for details of supplies that are exempt and Chapter 22 for an analysis of zero-rated supplies.

Specific services that will be zero-rated if supplied to an overseas customer are as follows:

- **Training supplied to overseas governments for the purpose of their sovereign activities (not their business activities).**

  The supplier must retain a statement in writing from the government concerned certifying that the trainees are employed in the furtherance of its sovereign activities, e g armed forces, public servants, police etc. The zero-rating does not extend to the business activities of a government, e g training for staff employed by a nationalised company.

- **Work on goods obtained, acquired or temporarily imported for that purpose and subsequent export.**

  The supply of services of work carried out on goods which, for that purpose, have been obtained or acquired in, or imported into, any EU country is zero-rated provided the goods are intended to be (and are) subsequently exported to a place outside the EU. Normal rules apply concerning proof of export.

  Any goods used in connection with the work performed (e g spare parts) should also be treated as part of the supply of services.

  An example of work eligible for zero-rating is a classic car imported from America, repaired by a UK company and re-exported to America. The charge by the UK repair company to its American customer will be zero-rated.

- **Services of intermediaries**

  If the place of supply is deemed to be in the UK, then the supply will be zero-rated if consisting of the making of arrangements for the export of any goods to a place outside the EU or any supply of services which is made outside the EU.

  The intermediary's services can be supplied to the supplier (in finding a customer) or the customer (in finding a supplier) or both.

  For example, Intermediary A arranges for a supply of goods to take place between UK supplier X and Russian customer Y. The fee earned by Intermediary A will be zero-rated irrespective of whether he is acting for UK supplier X or Russian customer Y.

Planning points to consider

14.7   The following planning points should be given consideration.

- It should be noted that the Isle of Man is deemed to be part of the UK as far as VAT is concerned but that the Channel Islands are excluded.

- It is important to remember that the reverse charge legislation for *Sch 5* services applies to 'persons' in the UK not just 'taxable persons'. This means that a business not registered for VAT will need to take into account the value of services it receives from abroad in calculating whether it needs to be VAT registered according to the relevant turnover limits.

- Be aware of opportunities when a UK business can avoid being charged VAT by an overseas company, i e when the reverse charge mechanism can be applied. The reverse charge mechanism can also avert the need for an overseas supplier to register for VAT in the UK.

- Certain services provided by a UK supplier to an overseas customer are zero-rated under the *VAT Act 1994, Sch 8*. In such cases, there is no VAT charge on these services, even if the place of supply is in the UK. See **14.6** for examples of zero-rated services that fall into this category.

Chapter 15

Overseas Traders and UK VAT (including 8th and 13th EC Directive Claims)

Key topics in this chapter:

- Circumstances when an overseas trader will need to be registered for VAT in the UK.

- Appointing a UK agent to deal with the VAT affairs of an overseas trader.

- Opportunities for businesses based in other EU countries to reclaim VAT paid in the UK by making an 8th Directive claim.

- Opportunities for UK businesses to reclaim VAT paid in other EU countries by making an 8th Directive claim.

- New improved procedures for making an 8th Directive claim which will take effect on 1 January 2010.

- Opportunities for businesses based in non-EU countries to reclaim VAT paid in the UK by making a 13th Directive claim (and vice versa).

- Submitting a claim to recover incorrectly charged VAT – ECJ case law example.

Introduction

15.1 An overseas trader is any person who:

- is not normally resident in the UK;

- does not have a 'business establishment' in the UK;

- if a company, is not incorporated in the UK.

As far as the phrase 'business establishment' is concerned, this normally indicates that the business actually trades from a location in the UK. In such cases, the business is not an overseas trader and must be registered for VAT in the UK at the address of its principal UK place of business (assuming the value of its taxable supplies exceeds the VAT registration limits).

If a business has a business establishment in the UK, then it must retain its books and records from this address, which must be made available to HMRC if it wants to conduct a VAT inspection. An authorised person must be responsible for handling the VAT affairs of the business from the UK address.

Important improvements are being made to the system for reclaiming VAT paid in other EU countries with effect from 1 January 2010. The procedures for making a claim (known as an 8th Directive claim) have historically been very inefficient so the proposed changes based on electronic submissions are very welcome.

Registration of an overseas trader for VAT

15.2   An overseas trader must be registered for VAT in the UK in the following circumstances:

- He makes taxable supplies of goods or services in the UK in the course of business – and the value of these supplies exceeds the VAT registration limits. The limits with effect from 1 May 2009 are £68,000 of taxable sales in any previous 12-month period – or where the business expects the value of its taxable supplies to exceed £68,000 in the next 30 days;

- He is not VAT registered in the UK but is registered in another EU country – and sells and delivers goods to non-registered customers in the UK. These sales are known as 'distance sales' and the registration threshold in the UK is £70,000 per annum on a calendar year basis. See **12.5** for a detailed analysis on the procedures for distance sales. Note that the reason why it is important for any EU country to have a threshold for distance selling is to prevent a business from locating itself in a Member State with a low standard rate of VAT (some countries have a standard rate of 15% compared to say 25% in Denmark and Sweden) and gaining a competitive advantage over countries with higher rates of VAT;

- He obtains goods from a VAT registered supplier in another EU country and brings these goods into the UK – where the total value of these supplies (known as acquisitions) exceeds the acquisition limit of £68,000 with effect from 1 May 2009. The £68,000 limit is based on transactions on a calendar year basis, rather than a rolling 12-month calculation as applies with the normal VAT registration test. Note that the acquisition rules for VAT registration are again designed to prevent distortion of competition.

For example, a non-registered business (eg a business that wholly makes exempt supplies) may gain a tax advantage by buying its goods from a country with a lower standard rate of VAT – EU rules state that where a business supplies goods to a non-registered entity in another EU country, it must charge VAT at the rate that applies in its own country;

- He makes a claim under the EC 8th Directive or EC 13th Directive and subsequently supplies, or intends to supply, the relevant goods in the UK (see **15.3–15.8** for a detailed review of 8th Directive and 13th Directive claims).

An important point to remember is that an overseas trader can also register for VAT on a voluntary basis provided he can prove to HMRC that he is carrying on a proper business and has a genuine need for registration. The most common situation when a business would want to register on a voluntary basis is where it makes mostly zero-rated supplies and wishes to benefit from recovering input tax on its expenditure.

If it has been identified that an overseas trader needs to register for VAT through the above conditions (or wishes to register on a voluntary basis) then he has three options as to how the registration is co-ordinated:

(a) he can appoint a VAT representative who will be jointly and severally liable for any VAT debts incurred by the business. However, the application of this option is limited in practice because very few representatives would be prepared to be liable for the VAT debts of an overseas trader;

(b) he may personally deal with all the VAT obligations of the business – including registration, record-keeping and completion of returns. In such cases, he should register as an overseas trader by contacting: Aberdeen VAT Office, 28 Guild Street, Aberdeen AB9 2DY (Tel: 01224 844653/4/5);

(c) he can appoint an agent to deal with his UK VAT affairs. The agent is not responsible for any debts owed to HMRC although could be held responsible for his part in any VAT fraud committed by the business.

The overseas trader must complete a VAT registration form in the normal manner – but must also submit a letter of authority to confirm the involvement of the agent. For an illustration of a suitable authority letter, see Example 1.

Example 1

ABC Inc is based in America but makes taxable supplies in the UK and has therefore been required to register for VAT in the UK. The company wishes to appoint London based accountants Smith and Smith to deal with its UK VAT affairs.

HMRC requires an authorisation letter confirming that Smith and Smith are the appointed UK agents to deal with the VAT issues pertaining to ABC Inc.

Solution –

To: HMRC

We the directors of ABC Inc, based in Las Vegas, USA, hereby appoint Smith and Smith of London to act as agent for dealing with all the legal obligations of the company in respect of UK VAT. This letter authorises Smith and Smith to sign VAT Return Forms 100 and any other documents needed for the purpose of enabling the agent or employee of the agent to comply with the VAT obligations of ABC Inc.

Signed: ......   Director authorised to sign on behalf of company

Date: ....

The VAT registration forms to complete are as follows:

- VAT 1 if in respect of taxable supplies being made in the UK;

- VAT 1A if in respect of distance sales;

- VAT 1B if in respect of acquisitions.

Refunds of UK VAT for persons established in other EU countries (and for UK businesses paying VAT in other EU countries) – 8th Directive claims

Basic principles of an 8th Directive claim

15.3   The VAT rule as far as reclaiming input tax is concerned is that a business can only reclaim input tax on its VAT return relevant to the country in which it is based. Therefore, if a UK business makes a trip to France in the course of business, and incurs French VAT, then it is not acceptable to reclaim this VAT in Box 4 of its UK VAT return.

Equally, a business registered for VAT in another EU country cannot reclaim UK VAT on its return – only input tax it incurs in its own country.

However, there is a mechanism for businesses to reclaim overseas VAT through what is known as an 8th Directive claim.

The EC 8th Directive (79/1072/EEC) is the key legislation on this subject, and basically means that a taxable person can recover VAT incurred in another EU country, provided he is not already registered in that country. However, the main point is that the VAT must be deductible under the normal VAT rules of the country where the expenditure was incurred. See Examples 2 and 3.

Example 2

ABC Ltd is registered for VAT in the UK. The managing director of the company has been on a business trip to Paris to visit a major French customer. He stayed in a hotel in the middle of Paris for three nights and incurred French VAT of €200.

What is the position regarding the French VAT that has been paid by the company?

Solution – although the trip is business related, and there is scope to recover VAT under the EC 8th Directive, one of the rules of French VAT is that input tax cannot be recovered on hotel bills. The €200 cannot therefore be reclaimed.

Note – other expenditure that is non-reclaimable in France includes entertainment, restaurant expenses, passenger transport and motor fuel (apart from diesel).

Example 3

The managing director of ABC Ltd's French customer (registered for VAT in France) now comes to the UK for three nights and stays at a luxury hotel in London for three nights. He pays UK VAT of £250. He also takes three potential customers out to dinner and incurs a further UK VAT bill of £100.

As input tax is recoverable on hotel bills in the UK (ie for UK businesses registered for VAT), then the £250 VAT on the hotel bill can be reclaimed by the French company through the 8th Directive procedures. However, business entertainment is not recoverable under UK rules, so £100 VAT on the restaurant bill cannot be reclaimed.

Procedures to reclaim overseas VAT – new rules from 1 January 2010

15.4 This section is based on the new procedures for making 8th Directive claims that will apply to any claims submitted on or after 1 January 2010. The proposed changes were announced in the 2009 Budget and are very radical in their approach. These will hopefully produce a much fairer system for reclaiming VAT paid in other EU countries.

The main features of the new system for 8th Directive claims are as follows.

● Claims must now be submitted to the country where the claimant is VAT registered, ie the UK in the case of a UK business. The previous system was based on submitting the claim to the overseas authority where the VAT was paid. The first thing a UK business will need to do is register for the scheme through the Government Gateway. This facility will apparently be in place towards the end of 2009.

- Claims will now be submitted in an electronic rather than paper format. The positive point about this situation is that it deals with the previous problem of having to complete the form in the language of the country in question. Most details on the form are completed by filling in boxes with numbers, rather than requiring any significant amount of text. In relation to text, most countries have also confirmed they will accept English as a common language.

- The deadline for submitting claims is extended with the new rules. The deadline for submitting a claim is now 9 months after the end of a calendar year rather than 6 months. A business will be able to make a maximum of five claims in a year to each relevant country where it has paid VAT. The thinking behind this limit is that four quarterly claims can be made, plus a final claim to sweep up any expenses that might have been overlooked during the year.

- The claim will be forwarded to the relevant Member State where the VAT was paid and the latter then has 4 months to process the claim. Assuming there are no problems, the claim must then be paid within 10 days of the form being processed. If further enquiries are needed, or information is incomplete, then the authority has a further 4 months to process the claim, ie a maximum of 8 months in total. If any claim is paid late, then the taxpayer will be entitled to receive interest.

Practical implications of the new claims system

15.5 The new claims system will hopefully simplify the administrative process of making an 8th Directive claim. The following are a number of practical issues that should be evident.

- By submitting a claim to its own tax authority, claimants will no longer need to provide a VAT certificate of status with each claim. This will certainly be an administrative saving for all businesses making a claim.

- As a general principle, the claim forms will be easier to complete. There is an increased emphasis on using codes and numbers rather than text.

- The claim form will require a business to record a 'Business Activity Code' – this confirms the nature of its business.

- The form will also introduce ten different 'Expenditure Codes' – which will categorise the VAT being claimed under different headings. For example, fuel will be given a code '1'. The full codes are as follows:

1   Fuel;
2   Hire of transport;
3   Means of transport;
4   Road tolls;

   5   Travel expenses;

   6   Accommodation;

   7   Food, drinks, restaurant;

   8   Fairs and exhibitions (admissions);

   9   Luxuries, amusement, entertainment;

   10 Other goods and services.

- The positive point about the ten codes is that they will give an opportunity for input tax blocks to be identified in relation to claims made for each EU country at the time the claim is being submitted.

  For example, an overseas business making a claim to recover UK VAT will need to be aware of the input tax blocks that apply to car leasing (codes 2/3), business entertainment (which could be relevant to codes 6,7 and 9). Example 2 highlighted how input tax cannot be claimed on hotel expenses in France – so a potential block would occur on code 6 claims.

- The previous system required original purchase invoices to be submitted with the claim, and photocopies were not acceptable. The new regime will require invoices to be scanned. This is another welcome improvement that should avoid paperwork being mislaid.

- As with the old system, the tax authorities will only repay VAT that has been correctly charged by a supplier in the first place. To give an example, a claim to recover VAT on advertising expenses will be rejected because the place of supply for advertising services is based on the location of the customer, ie no VAT should be charged by the supplier if he is raising an invoice to a business based in an EU country other than his own. In such cases, the correct approach is to seek a VAT credit note and refund from the supplier who has incorrectly charged VAT.

Author note – it is important that advisers also take into account the new place of supply rules that will be introduced on 1 January 2010 and are considered in Chapter 13. These changes will reduce the number of transactions where VAT is charged to a business customer in another EU country because VAT will instead be declared by the customer on his own VAT return through the reverse charge. It is much easier to get the VAT treatment right on the initial transaction than to have a circular process of submitting a claim and having it rejected and then having to go back to the supplier for a credit note.

- The HMRC office that deals with claims is based in Northern Ireland at the following address:

VAT Overseas Repayments Section
Customs House
PO Box 34
Londonderry
BT48 7AE
Northern Ireland
(Tel: 02871 376200)

Will the new system work?

15.6 HMRC has always been very efficient in processing refund claims submitted by overseas businesses based in both the EU (8th Directive claims) and outside the EU (13th Directive claims). The tax authorities in many other countries have also earned a good reputation for dealing with claims in an efficient manner, eg Denmark, Sweden, Holland and Belgium.

The new system appears to be a significant improvement on the previous regime but only time will tell if the system will provide greater certainty to UK businesses that the claims they make to certain countries will be paid promptly (if at all). It is hoped that the introduction of an interest payment for claims that are paid late will encourage improvements in certain countries that have disappointed in the past.

Overall, it is suggested that advisers acting for UK clients should still adopt a cautious approach when informing clients about the efficiency of the 8th Directive system and the length of time it will take for a repayment claim to be made in various countries. However, a successful claim now has to overcome a lot less obstacles because of the new electronic procedures (eg language issues, problems with the postal system, finding out where to send the claim in another country), so the signs are very encouraging.

Rules in particular countries

15.7 As explained earlier, each country in the EU has different rules as far as input tax recovery is concerned – as mentioned with the French rules in Example 2 above. A few other interesting points regarding specific countries are as follows (but the list is obviously not exhaustive):

- claims in Denmark must exclude hotel expenses, car rental charges and entertainment costs – these categories tend to be disallowed in most countries;

- claims in Italy must, among other things, exclude luxury items such as furs, sparkling wines and oriental carpets;

- claims to Greece must exclude, among other things, food, drink and tobacco products.

The key point is to research the rules for the country in question, and ensure that all claims for VAT comply with these rules.

Refunds of UK VAT for persons established in non-EU countries (and for UK businesses paying VAT in non-EU countries) – 13th directive claims

15.8 The EC 13th Directive (86/560/EEC) requires each EU country to adopt a scheme that allows non-EU businesses to also recover VAT.

The 13th Directive confirms that an obligation to adopt the scheme only exists with countries that have a reciprocal arrangement in their country. Obviously, this reciprocal arrangement may not necessarily involve VAT – but the similar turnover tax adopted by the country in question, for example, GST (Goods and Services Tax) in Australia.

The provisions apply to any registered trader carrying on a business established in a country outside the EU – provided that the trader meets the following rules:

● he was not registered or liable to be registered in the UK;

● he was not established in any EU country;

● he made no supplies of goods or services in the UK.

An important point to note is that there is a different time period for submitting 13th Directive claims – the 'prescribed period' is the 12-month period ending 30 June, and claims have to be made within 6 months of the 'prescribed period'.

The basic rules for 13th Directive claims are the same as 8th Directive claims, eg an overseas business cannot reclaim UK VAT on an item of expenditure that is not reclaimable under normal UK rules such as business entertainment and most motor cars.

As with 8th Directive claims, the main office for 13th Directive claims being made by overseas businesses seeking to recover UK VAT is the London-derry address given at **15.5**.

Note – if a claim is for less than 1 year, then it must be for at least £130 (unless it is for the final part of the prescribed year). No claim can be for less than £16. From an administrative aspect, 13th Directive claims are made on Form VAT 65A.

Submitting a claim to recover incorrectly paid VAT

15.9 The rules concerning VAT and international services are always complex. In the commercial world, there will inevitably be situations when a supplier wrongly charges VAT to an overseas customer (and the customer pays this VAT in good faith) – and the overseas customer then submits an 8th or 13th Directive claim to the supplier's country to reclaim this VAT. What happens if the Customs authority receiving the claim reject it on the basis that the VAT should not have been charged in the first place?

The answer is that the claimant should go back to his supplier and acquire a VAT refund – and then account for the VAT on his own return using the reverse charge procedures. However, what if the supplier in question has disappeared and there is no scope to contact him about the overcharged VAT?

In such instances, it is useful for advisers to note the outcome of the ECJ case *Reemtsma Cigarettenfabriken GmbH v Finance Minister: C-35/05* [2007] 2 CMLR 874, [2007] SWTI 543, [2007] All ER (D) 266 (Mar) which was based on the following situation:

- A German based customer received advertising services from an Italian based company – under the place of supply rules, no VAT should have been charged by the Italian company, with tax being accounted for by the German customer using the reverse charge rules (this is because the place of supply for advertising services is based according to the location of the customer, ie Germany). However, Italian VAT was incorrectly charged on the service – and paid in good faith by the German customer.

- The Italian supplier paid the incorrectly charged VAT to the Italian authorities – the German customer then tried to recover this VAT by making an 8th Directive claim to the Italian authorities.

- The Italian authorities rejected the claim on the basis that VAT should not have been charged in the first place. However, the ECJ ruled in favour of the taxpayer, on the basis that the principles of neutrality, effectiveness and non-discrimination allowed national legislation to reimburse VAT unduly paid to the tax authorities.

Planning points to consider

15.10   The following planning points should be given consideration.

- An overseas trader having business dealings with the UK must clearly establish whether it is making taxable supplies in the UK and has a potential liability to register for VAT in the UK.

- An overseas trader is entitled to register for VAT on a voluntary basis if the value of its taxable supplies is less than the compulsory registration limits.

- Remember that a UK agent dealing with the VAT obligations of an overseas trader must be properly authorised by the trader through a written letter to HMRC.

- Be aware of the new procedures that apply to 8th Directive claims made on or after 1 January 2010. The new system is based on an electronic rather than paper system, with claims being submitted via the taxpayer's own tax authority, rather than to the country where the VAT was actually paid. The new system should be more efficient than the previous regime and advisers should encourage clients to make claims where there is an entitlement.

- It is important to note that various EU and non-EU countries have specific rules about expenditure on which VAT cannot be reclaimed. Any 8th or 13th Directive claim made to an overseas country must take these rules into account.

Chapter 16

Dealing with Errors and Interest Charged on Errors

Key topics in this chapter:

- Options for dealing with VAT errors – increased error notification limits from 1 July 2008.

- The difference between an error and an adjustment.

- Error correction procedures – forms to complete and information required.

- Time limits for correcting errors – increase from 3 to 4 years by 1 April 2010.

- The importance of considering the issue of 'unjust enrichment' on any errors that have resulted in an overpayment of tax.

- The effect of charging the wrong amount of VAT on an invoice.

- Dealing with input tax claims on late purchase invoices.

- The HMRC approach to dealing with errors.

- Default interest charged on errors made by a taxpayer and occasions when HMRC may pay interest in the case of an official error.

Introduction

16.1   It is inevitable that mistakes will be made by many businesses in calculating their VAT liabilities. These mistakes will sometimes be identified before the return has been submitted, which will be helped by strong internal controls and an effective system of checking the figures. In such cases, the procedure for dealing with errors is not an issue – the figures on the return can be amended before it is submitted to HMRC.

However, there will be occasions when mistakes are identified after the return has been submitted, resulting in an underpayment or overpayment of tax. In basic terms, the following key rules apply with regard to the correction of errors:

- If an error is discovered on 1 July 2008 or later, the error can be adjusted on the next VAT return submitted by the business if the net value of all errors is less than £10,000 or less than 1% of the Box 6 outputs figure for the return when the error is discovered, up to a ceiling of £50,000.

- If the net value of errors discovered after 1 July 2008 or later exceeds £10,000 and also exceeds 1% of the Box 6 outputs figure for the return when the error is discovered or £50,000, then an error notification must be made to HMRC, giving full details of the errors and the VAT periods to which they relate.

- The monetary limit for correcting errors discovered before 30 June 2008 was £2,000.

- HMRC will usually charge interest on underpayments of tax made by an error notification, reflecting 'commercial restitution', ie the fact that tax has been paid after the due date.

Note – there has been confusion in some circles about whether the new error notification limits only apply to VAT returns relevant to July 2008 or later. This is not the case – the crucial point is the date when the error is discovered by the taxpayer, not the VAT period to which it relates. So an error discovered on 1 March 2009 that was made on the VAT return for the June 2007 quarter will still be covered by the new limits.

Difference between an error and an adjustment

16.2   A key point to remember is that there is a difference between an error and an adjustment – it is only errors that need to be corrected by making a voluntary disclosure to HMRC. See Example 1.

Example 1

ABC Ltd is a partly exempt company, with taxable supplies from selling houses on a commission basis and exempt sales from arranging financial services products.

The company has just come to the end of the tax year to 31 March 2009, and calculated its annual adjustment for partial exemption purposes. An amount of £2,400 is payable to HMRC. The company has also identified that a sales invoice it raised in July 2008 has never been paid – the VAT involved is £800 and the company wants to reclaim bad debt relief.

Finally, the company reclaimed £2,750 of input tax on the purchase of a new car in December 2007, a vehicle not exclusively for business use, and also available for private use.

What is the VAT position?

Solution – the partial exemption annual adjustment and claim for bad debt relief are not VAT errors – they are standard accounting adjustments. The partial exemption annual adjustment needs to be declared on the June 2009 return in accordance with partial exemption rules. The bad debt relief adjustment can be made at any time by the taxpayer, as long as the debt is more than 6 months overdue for payment and has been written off in the business accounts.

The positive news is that because the amount of VAT reclaimed on the car is less than the new error notification limits, the VAT can be adjusted on the next VAT return, rather than as a separate notification to HMRC.

However, some errors in accounting can occur (for instance due to invoicing errors) that result in an under or overpayment of VAT but which cannot be corrected by an error notification. See Example 2 for a typical illustration.

Example 2

X Ltd raises a sales invoice for £30,000 plus £5,250 VAT on 31 March 2008, and accounts for output tax on its quarterly VAT return for the March period, submitted on 14 April 2008.

However, the day after the return has been submitted, it is discovered that the invoice should have been for £3,000 plus £525 VAT – meaning that output tax has been overcharged by £4,725.

Solution – if the invoice clerk at X Ltd had not made the error when raising this invoice, then the cheque sent to HMRC for the March 2008 period would have been reduced by £4,725 (ie £5,250 – £525). However, the issuing of the invoice to the customer has created a tax point for VAT purposes, and the customer could reclaim input tax on this invoice. The correct procedure is for the company to raise a credit note to correct the invoicing error with a current date, and output tax will then be reduced by £4,725 in the June period as a matter of course.

Error correction procedures

New phrase – error notification rather than voluntary disclosure

16.3   The new penalty system introduced by HMRC in relation to VAT returns due on or after 1 April 2009 means that some errors could be subject to a penalty, even where the business makes a disclosure of the error to HMRC or corrects the error on its next VAT return. See Chapter 17 for further details.

The following is a summary of the key phrases that are relevant when dealing with VAT errors.

- All errors discovered by a taxpayer must be corrected as soon as they are discovered (or noted in the VAT file to be corrected on the next VAT return submitted by the business if the net value of the errors is below certain limits). This means that all errors are within the 'error correction' procedures.

- Certain errors can be corrected by a taxpayer on his next VAT return – if the net value of the errors is:

  — less than £10,000; or
  — less than £50,000 and also less than 1% of the Box 6 outputs figure on the VAT return where the errors are being corrected.

- If the net value of errors discovered by a taxpayer is above these limits, they cannot be adjusted on a VAT return. An 'error notification' must be made to HMRC to advise them of the errors – this can either be done by completing Form VAT 652 or by writing a separate letter giving full details of the various errors and the periods to which they relate.

- The phrase 'voluntary disclosure' is no longer appropriate under the new penalty system – this is because the legislation has changed the basic definition of when an error is classed as being fully disclosed to HMRC.

The new limits apply to VAT errors discovered in an accounting period commencing on or after 1 July 2008. This is the first important point to remember – it is the period when the error is discovered that determines whether the old or new rules apply, not the date when the error occurred on the VAT return.

Example – a business has VAT periods that coincide with calendar quarters. On 31 August 2008, the company accountant discovers that an error was made on the March 2008 return.

Solution – the date of discovery (31 August 2008) is the key date, and as this date is within a VAT period that begins on or after 1 July 2008 (period 1 July 2008 to 30 September 2008), the new disclosure limits are relevant, even though the error relates to a VAT period before 1 July 2008.

Example – a business has VAT periods that end on the last days of February, May, August and November. On 31 August 2008, the company accountant discovers that an error was made on the March 2008 return.

Solution – the error has been discovered by the accountant in a VAT period commencing on 1 June 2008. As this date is before 1 July 2008, the old disclosure limits are relevant. The new disclosure limits for this particular business will apply for any errors discovered after 1 September 2008.

Method of disclosure

16.4   As explained at **16.1**, it is the net value of errors that needs to be considered when deciding whether errors can be adjusted on the next VAT return submitted by a business. See Example 3 which illustrates the method of calculating the net error.

Example 3

John's accountants have just carried out their annual review of his books, and identified the following VAT errors:

* John omitted two sales invoices from his sales day book, underpaying output tax by £13,250;

* John forgot to reclaim input tax of £3,500 on the purchase of his business computer system, incorrectly thinking the expense was zero-rated.

The net effect of the errors is that John has underpaid VAT by £9,750. As this amount is less than £10,000, it can be adjusted by John on his next VAT return. However, he may still want to notify HMRC about the error to avoid or reduce a potential penalty for failing to take reasonable care. See Chapter 17.

When a business has to notify HMRC of an error for any reason, there are two alternative methods it can adopt, either to:

* complete Form VAT 652 (obtainable from the National Advice Centre on 0845 0109000 or can be downloaded from the HMRC website) – this form ensures that all relevant details are given about the error; or

* write to HMRC at the appropriate Regional Error Correction Team giving full details of the error. The location of the appropriate team is based on the postcode of the business – again, a telephone call to the National Advice Centre will provide the correct address.

In either of the above cases, information must be given about the errors as follows:

* how each error arose;

* the VAT period in which it occurred;

* if it was an input tax or output tax error;

* the VAT underdeclared or overdeclared in each VAT period;

* how the VAT underdeclared or overdeclared has been calculated;

* the total amount to be adjusted.

If an amount of tax has been underpaid, it is important to give as much detail as possible about the error.

Once the notification has been processed by HMRC, it will issue a 'statement of account', confirming the amount of tax and interest payable.

The amount payable should be remitted by the taxpayer within 30 days of the calculation date, otherwise further interest could be charged. Where a repayment is due by HMRC, it will first net the repayment off against any tax payable, and then repay the remainder by BACs or payable order.

Time limit for corrections

16.5   In general terms, errors cannot be corrected more than 3 years after the VAT period in which they arose, rising to 4 years by 1 April 2010 (in effect, the 4-year limit applies from 1 April 2009 but it is not possible for an error that was out of time under the 3-year limit as at 31 March 2009 to come back in time under the 4-year limit).

The positive point about the 3-year/4-year rule is that if a major error of principle has been discovered that results in an underpayment of tax, then a tax correction is only needed for the last 3 or 4 years. However, the disadvantage is that any overpayment of tax going back in time is also limited to the same period. See Example 4.

Example 4

The accountant at DEF Ltd has just discovered that, for the last 10 years, the company has failed to reclaim input tax on the petrol element of mileage allowances paid to employees for their business travel. However, it is also discovered that input tax has been fully reclaimed on the costs of the office Christmas party for the last 10 years, even though 50% of the guests were non-employees, ie where input tax should have been disallowed on 50% of the costs as relevant to business entertainment.

Solution – the company has made two VAT errors, one resulting in an underpayment of tax and one in an overpayment of tax. A correction can only be made for the last 3 or 4 years in both cases, which is good news for the company if the underpayments exceed the overpayments – but not such good news if it is the other way around. The correct approach is for the accountant to calculate the net tax due (or repayable) over the last 3 or 4 years. If the amount exceeds the error notification limits, HMRC must be notified of the error (by Form VAT 652 or by letter) – if it is less than these limits, an adjustment on the next VAT return can be made.

Unjust enrichment

16.6   In certain cases, a business could identify that it has made a major error of principle that has produced a significant overpayment of tax – for example, where a zero-rated product has been charged at the standard rate of VAT. This error could have been ongoing for many years.

In many cases, the taxpayer will be prevented from claiming a windfall from HMRC through the rules of 'unjust enrichment'. These rules basically state that no taxpayer can be unjustly enriched through making VAT errors – and it needs to be identified who has borne the cost of any incorrectly charged VAT. For example, in most cases where VAT has been charged to a customer on an item, the correct procedure will be for this VAT to be refunded to the customer, not to treat it as a cash windfall for the taxpayer who should not have charged tax in the first place.

A detailed analysis of the issues concerning unjust enrichment is included in Chapter 20.

Input tax claims on late purchase invoices

16.7   In an ideal world, all suppliers would submit their purchase invoices on time – not least because it will be in their own interests to get paid quicker.

However, in reality there is often a situation where a supplier submits a late purchase invoice, after the relevant VAT return has already been submitted. So the question then is: can input tax on the late purchase invoice be treated as an error notification to HMRC and be submitted as an overpayment on Form VAT 652? Or is the late purchase invoice a normal accounting adjustment to include on the next VAT return submitted?

Customs Notice 700/45 is very clear on the procedures to adopt in this situation – paragraph 6.1 states:

> 'you should claim input tax in the VAT accounting period in which it becomes chargeable. However, if you are unable to claim it in this period because you've not received the proper evidence (normally a VAT invoice), you can reclaim it once you have received the proper evidence ... either on a return for a later period or by making a voluntary disclosure'.

The ultimate decision will probably depend on the amount of tax involved for the business, and the cash flow advantage to be gained by doing a separate notification to HMRC.

Adjustments required when wrong amount of VAT is shown on a VAT invoice

16.8   It is possible that in some situations an invoice will be issued where the VAT charge has been calculated incorrectly. For example, £100 + £10 VAT instead of £100 + £17.50 VAT. It is also possible that VAT could have been charged on a zero-rated supply.

In such situations, the best option is for both the supplier and the customer to agree to a VAT adjustment being made. As long as the error occurred within the last 3 years (rising to 4 years by 1 April 2010), this can be achieved by one of the following methods:

- the original invoice can be cancelled and the supplier issues a replacement showing the correct charge of VAT;

- the supplier can issue a credit note or supplementary VAT invoice to his customer;

- the customer can issue a debit note to the supplier (in reality, this option is less likely – very few taxpayers become involved with debit notes).

If the above situation is not applied, then the priority is for HMRC to ensure it is not out of pocket by the error. There are two possible courses of action:

(a)   if the VAT shown on the invoice is too high – the supplier must account for the higher amount in his records and the customer must only include the amount which should have been charged in his records; or

(b)   if the VAT shown on the invoice is too low – the supplier must account for the amount which should have been charged and the customer must only include the lower amount actually shown on the invoice.

The essential point with errors in these situations is that there is no error notification procedure required – HMRC sets the rules to ensure that the output tax accounted for by the supplier is either equal to or greater than the input tax reclaimed by the customer.

HMRC approach to dealing with error notifications

16.9   There is often a fear among clients and advisers that if they notify an underpayment to HMRC, it will immediately result in an army of VAT inspectors arriving at the door to carry a full audit going back 3 years.

In reality, this is rarely the case, because HMRC recognises that errors will be made, even with the increasing use of computers to deal with standard VAT calculations. However, it is always useful to ensure that a 'one off' error is clearly explained as such in a letter. It would be considered a more serious problem if the errors were caused by a fundamental defect in the accounting system of a business.

Another important point is to ensure that if the notification results in money being repaid by HMRC, then as much supporting evidence about the claim as possible should be given. For example, if the notification is due to input tax not being reclaimed on a new piece of equipment, then it is worthwhile to provide a copy of the purchase invoice with the claim letter. If the error has been identified and corrected by various spreadsheet or nominal ledger reconciliations, then copies of these calculations and supporting printouts would again be useful.

In effect, the approach to adopt is to ensure that HMRC can obtain a full picture of how and why the error occurred, and also to give it confidence that the error has been corrected in an accurate manner.

Although HMRC has a responsibility to process voluntary disclosure claims promptly, it also has the right to seek further information where it is not satisfied with the figures. This can either be done through a written request for further information, or by asking to attend the premises and examine the business records.

Errors discovered on a VAT visit

16.10   The routine VAT visit where HMRC attends a taxpayer's premises and look at all records for the previous 3 years is becoming less common. Many visits are now conducted on a risk-based assessment, and may only look at one aspect of the accounting system.

If an officer finds errors during an inspection, usually resulting in an underpayment of tax, he or she will often send a letter to the taxpayer showing the calculations made to arrive at an assessment. This gives the taxpayer the chance to review the figures (possibly with an accountant or adviser) and raise any points in dispute.

In cases where the amount of VAT cannot be agreed, then the taxpayer has the right of appeal, firstly by asking for a local reconsideration. If necessary, it can then be considered by an independent VAT tribunal.

Charging of interest

16.11   In general terms, HMRC only charges interest where it considers it represents 'commercial restitution', ie compensation for the loss of use of any underpaid tax. It normally only charges interest if it has been deprived of this money for a period of time. It would not, for example, normally charge interest on an output tax underpayment that would have been reclaimed as input tax by a third party.

HMRC uses the following guidelines to decide if an interest charge for commercial restitution is appropriate, usually when either an officer assessment is raised or an error notification is processed.

(a)   Overclaimed input tax:

- Is the input tax properly reclaimable by another registered person (who is not partly exempt)? If so, then no interest will be charged as the input tax would still be recovered from HMRC.
- Is there any other reason why interest should not be charged? This

gives the officer the chance to review whether there are other reasons why an interest charge should not be made.

(b) Underpaid output tax:

- Is the underdeclaration an additional assessment, ie where HMRC has assessed for a period in the absence of a return and the true liability is later found to exceed the assessment? In such cases, interest will be charged.
- For VAT errors – is the error wholly within an accounting system, eg arithmetical and accounting errors, retail scheme errors, calculation errors? If so, interest will be charged.

An important change following the increase in the error notification limits on 1 July 2008 is that HMRC will seek to charge interest on all errors notified to it, irrespective of whether the tax could have been adjusted on a VAT return, ie errors below £10,000 or 1% of Box 6 turnover up to £50,000 etc. So the key message is to adjust an error on a VAT return if it is eligible for such treatment in order to avoid any potential interest charge. Interest is not charged by HMRC in the following situations:

- where VAT has been declared on returns but not paid;
- central assessments initially raised in the absence of a VAT return for a period;
- interest is not charged on penalties and interest;
- amendments made to VAT returns before they are fully processed.

In terms of the calculation of interest, the basic principle is that interest is charged from the date when the tax should have been paid (ie 1 month after the end of the VAT period) to the date when it was actually charged on the notice issued by HMRC. If the amount charged is not paid within 30 days from the date of the notice, then a further charge of interest is made.

Interest repaid by HMRC

16.12 A business is entitled to repayment supplement where HMRC does not make any repayment due within a specified time. However, as a general principle, HMRC does not pay interest to a taxpayer on any amounts of overpaid tax, unless it (HMRC) caused the error – see Example 5.

Example 5

ABC Ltd received a ruling from HMRC in 2006 that it could not reclaim input tax on the costs of the staff Christmas party. The director of ABC Ltd has now discovered that this ruling was incorrect, and that the company could have claimed £700 input tax on each of its December returns in years 2006 to 2008.

Solution – as well as being able to reclaim £2,100 input tax on the staff party for the last 3 years, the director can also apply for HMRC to pay interest on the input tax claimed late as the delay in the claim was due to an official error by HMRC.

Planning points to consider

16.13   The following planning points should be given consideration.

- Be aware of the increased voluntary disclosure limits that apply to VAT errors discovered on or after 1 July 2008. The increased limits will reduce the number of error notifications that need to be made to HMRC and, as a consequence, will avoid a potential interest charge on many underpayments of tax.

- It is important to ensure that all adjustments made on VAT returns are fully supported by working papers and schedules to prove the figures in the event of a future VAT visit. If a separate notification is made to HMRC, ensure supporting evidence is given where appropriate, particularly in the case of a tax overpayment.

- There is no need to be concerned about errors (underpayments or overpayments) that go back beyond 3 years (rising to 4 years by 1 April 2010) – they are out of date and cannot be adjusted.

- Always thoroughly review any assessment raised by HMRC following a VAT visit – there may be scope to request a reconsideration of the assessment if the officer has not taken important information into account within his calculations.

- It is important that a taxpayer pays error notifications or officer assessments within 30 days otherwise interest will continue to accrue on the non-payment.

- If a client is due a big tax rebate due to an error of principle, make sure that the issue of 'unjust enrichment' is fully considered before the client spends the rebate. In most cases, any overcharged VAT must be refunded to customers, not treated as a cash windfall by the business in question.

- Be aware of the impact of new penalty rules that came into effect on 1 April 2009 (see Chapter 17). For the first time, a taxpayer could be subject to a penalty, even where he has told HMRC about the error or corrected the error on a VAT return.

Chapter 17

Penalties

Key topics in this chapter:

- Default surcharge procedures that apply when tax is paid late or a return is submitted after the due date.

- The impact of payments on account as far as default surcharge calculations are concerned.

- Reasonable excuse provisions – when a penalty may not be applied.

- The new penalty regime that applies for returns that are due to be filed on or after 1 April 2009.

- Common questions relevant to the new penalty regime.

- Mitigation of penalties in certain cases, e g to reflect good levels of co-operation from a taxpayer.

Introduction

17.1   The ideal situation is for all taxpayers to pay the right tax at the right time. If this situation is achieved, then a taxpayer will not have to worry about being charged interest or penalties. All taxpayers should therefore be encouraged to adopt a simple three-point plan to ensure compliance with the regulations of HMRC:

(a)   submit all VAT returns on time;

(b)   pay tax due on the returns on time; and

(c)   have controls and procedures in place to ensure the figures on the return are accurate.

If the figures on any return are incorrect, then this indicates that one of two things has happened:

- a mistake has been made in the figures, either producing an underpayment or overpayment of VAT (See Chapter 16 for issues involved with VAT errors);

- the taxpayer has been guilty of fraud, making deliberate entries on the return to understate the amount of VAT that is due.

The powers of HMRC to deal with fraud and major errors are considerable – and follow one of two routes:

- criminal proceedings – which will only be relevant in the very serious cases of major fraud; or

- civil penalties and surcharges.

The penalty system in relation to VAT errors and fraud was radically changed with effect from 1 April 2009. Any returns to be filed on or after this date base penalties on taxpayer behaviour by introducing three different categories of penalty to punish careless errors (failing to take reasonable care), deliberate errors that are not concealed or deliberate errors that are concealed.

In effect, the misdeclaration penalty and repeated misdeclaration penalty were abolished on this date but could still apply in relation to historic VAT periods. However, the focus of this chapter is on the new system that will be the main concern of advisers.

Default surcharge system – late returns and payments

What happens when returns and payments are made late?

17.2   Many clients will sometimes face a cash flow problem – which means either paying suppliers on time (to keep the flow of goods coming into the business) or paying the quarterly VAT return on time (and keeping HMRC happy).

Note – the starting point for any business that is unable to pay its tax bill is to contact HMRC's Business Payment Support Service (BPSS) and negotiate a time to pay arrangement. See **30.6** for further details.

The question that clients often ask is: 'What will happen if I pay my VAT late?' The approach taken by HMRC in relation to late VAT returns and payments is as follows.

- *Surcharge liability notice* – on the first occasion that a return or payment is submitted late, a taxpayer will be issued with a surcharge liability notice. This notice confirms that he is in default in respect of a VAT period, and that if another default occurs within the next 12 months, he will be liable to a default surcharge penalty.

  Note – in the case of a small business with turnover of £150,000 per year or less, the first default does not produce a surcharge liability notice, but a letter from HMRC offering help and support. It is only if another default occurs within the next 12 months that the surcharge liability notice is issued. This is a generous concession – giving a small business with possibly accounting difficulties the chance to deal with its problems in liaison with HMRC (see HMRC Notice 700/50 para 3.2).

- *Default surcharge* – if the taxpayer defaults within the next 12 months, then he will be liable to pay a default surcharge penalty, as follows:

In relation to the first such period	2% of the outstanding VAT
In relation to the second such period	5% of the outstanding VAT
In relation to the third such period	10% of the outstanding VAT
In relation to each such period after the third	15% of the outstanding VAT

Note – see **17.4** for details about the phrase 'outstanding VAT'.

- *Surcharge liability extension notice* – a business only comes out of the default surcharge system when it has submitted and paid four successive VAT returns on time (assuming a business on quarterly returns). The initial surcharge liability notice covers a 12-month default period from when the first late payment or return occurs – but each additional default within this 12-month period sees a surcharge liability extension notice issued to extend the period up to the 12-month anniversary of the relevant default. Basically, to come out of the default surcharge system, a taxpayer needs to submit all returns and pay all tax on time for a full 12-month period.

There are some important points to note regarding the default surcharge penalties imposed following an offence:

- where a liability to surcharge is established, HMRC will not issue a surcharge assessment at the 2% or 5% rates for an amount of less than £400. However, a default will still be recorded, and a surcharge liability extension notice will also be issued;

- a default is not recorded if it can be shown that the return or payment was posted or despatched in such time that it would be reasonable to expect that it would have arrived by the due date, ie this issue mainly considers postal problems;

- if the taxpayer can convince HMRC (or a VAT tribunal if he takes the case to appeal) that he had a 'reasonable excuse' for the VAT not being paid (or return despatched) then the default will be withdrawn.

See Example 1 for an illustration of the workings of the default surcharge system.

Example 1

Jones Wholesalers submitted its October 2007 return late and received a default surcharge liability notice. It then submitted its January 2008 and April 2008 returns on time, but made a late payment in July 2008. The payment due for the July 2008 period was £20,500. It was also late in October 2008 (VAT due was £7,500) and again in January 2009 (VAT due was £3,500). What penalties are due?

Solution – having submitted its October 2007 return late, the company needed to be on time and fully compliant with the next four VAT returns up to and including the period ending 31 October 2008 – it did not achieve this goal.

The next default in July 2008 attracts the initial 2% penalty of £410 (£20,500 × 2%), and the next period attracts a 5% penalty of £375 (£7,500 × 5%). However, good news on this one – because the total penalty is less than £400, and it is relevant to the 5% penalty period, then no penalty is issued. The penalty for January 2009 is also less than £400 (£3,500 × 10% = £350) but this penalty is applied because we are no longer in either the 2% or 5% period – hence the £400 *de minimis* situation does not apply.

An interesting point to note: just because the 5% penalty was wavered in October 2008, it does not mean that the next default attracts only a 5% penalty – the next period still suffers a 10% rate.

When does a default occur?

17.3   The key point to remember is that the relevant date, as far as the VAT return or payment is concerned, is not the date it was posted by the trader – but the date it was received by the VAT office.

This point is confirmed by the VAT return itself, which states: 'You could be liable to a financial penalty if your completed return and all the VAT payable are not received by the due date'. As a general tip, the facility to file VAT returns online has proved of great value to many taxpayers, not only because of the extra 7 calendar days given by HMRC to file a return, but also because it averts the risk of a return being lost in the post.

Over the years, the posting issue has caused great controversy – with some interesting tribunal cases.

Basically, the aim of a business must be to ensure that the return and payment are received by HMRC before or on the due date, and this means taking postal issues into account. In reality, HMRC has confirmed that if there is proof that the return was posted 1 working day before the due date, then this will be acceptable if the return is delayed in the post for any reason. But to play safe and allow an extra day would be good advice.

Payments on account

17.4   As explained above, a surcharge penalty is based on the 'outstanding VAT' due for the period. This means that the penalty is reduced if some payment on account has been made to meet the liability – see Example 2.

Example 2

DEF Ltd is in the default surcharge system, and the next default will attract a 10% penalty. The VAT return for December 2007 shows a payment due of £30,000 but the company accountant can only pay £13,000 by the due date of 31 January 2008 because a key customer has not settled his account on time.

Solution – the 10% penalty will be based on the unpaid VAT of £17,000, ie £1,700. In effect, the company has a strong incentive to at least pay some of the VAT liability in order to reduce the extent of the penalty.

As a useful planning point, it is possible to make a part-payment to avoid a default surcharge if the penalty based on the outstanding tax is under the *de minimis* penalty of £400 for the 2% and 5% rates. See Example 3.

Example 3

JKL Ltd is in the default surcharge system and liable to a 2% penalty if it defaults in the October 2007 period. It submits the October 2007 return on time, but instead of paying the full tax due amount of £25,000 can only make a part-payment of £5,000. The company's VAT adviser suggests the part-payment be increased to £5,001.

Solution – the surcharge penalty is based on the amount of outstanding VAT for the period not paid by the due date. In this particular case, the amount is £19,999 – a 2% penalty therefore equates to £399.98 – but this will be wavered because it is less than the £400 *de minimis* limit that applies for the 2% and 5% periods. The extra pound makes all the difference!

Impact of 15% penalty charge

17.5   Once a business is paying the maximum 15% surcharge, then all future defaults within the default surcharge period will automatically be charged at 15%. This will become very costly for most businesses – and the hope by this point is that either a business has restructured its accounting system (if slow bookkeeping is the reason for defaults) or refinanced the business or its cash management procedures (if lack of cash was the problem).

For smaller businesses (taxable turnover less than £1,350,000 per annum), it may be worth considering the possible benefits of using the annual accounting scheme if bookkeeping issues are the cause of defaults being incurred. The annual accounting scheme means an eligible business will only complete one VAT return each year instead of four. See Chapter 7 for a detailed analysis of the scheme.

If a business has very high output tax (ie all standard-rated sales) and negligible input tax (eg a service-based business where the biggest overhead of labour does not produce any input tax) then the impact of the

15% penalty will be enormous. It will be a priority for the business to take measures to ensure returns and payments are submitted on time or seek a time to pay agreement with HMRC's Business Payment Support Service (see **30.6**).

Avoiding a penalty

17.6   When a business has submitted one return or payment late, then it is issued with a default surcharge notice. It then needs to submit the next four returns and payments on time (assuming quarterly returns are submitted) so that it has a clean record for the next 12 months. At this point, the business will be taken out of the default surcharge system, meaning that it can make one more return or payment late without incurring a penalty.

Some useful points to remember are as follows:

- if a repayment return (or nil return) is submitted late, then a default surcharge liability extension notice will be issued but there will be no penalty applied. This is because penalty calculations are always based on the amount of tax unpaid by the due date;

- a penalty can be avoided if a taxpayer can prove that the return and payment were despatched on time (and hence should have been received on time); or

- a penalty should not be applied because there was a reasonable excuse for not paying the tax on time – see **17.7**;

- if a business does not submit its return on time, but pays the full amount of tax due on time, then the late return will be recorded as a default but there will be no surcharge because the tax has been paid by the due date.

Reasonable excuse

17.7   As with most decisions made by HMRC, the taxpayer has the right of appeal if he disagrees with either the issuing of a default surcharge liability notice or a subsequent default penalty.

The main reason for appeal is where the taxpayer considers that he has a 'reasonable excuse' for failing to submit his return or pay his tax on time. As a general point, it is not acceptable to claim that lack of funds is a reasonable excuse for non-payment of VAT, unless the circumstances are exceptional. Equally, it is not acceptable to blame a third party for failing to carry out a task (eg 'my accountant forgot to ask me for a cheque for my VAT payment') unless exceptional events again apply, such as death, serious illness, etc.

The phrase 'reasonable excuse' is not actually defined in the legislation and therefore individual situations depend on the interpretation of the facts by HMRC or, if that fails, by the view of an independent VAT tribunal.

The following circumstances could be accepted as a reasonable excuse by HMRC.

- *Computer breakdown* – if essential records are maintained on a computer, which suffers a major breakdown, then a reasonable excuse argument could be made. However, HMRC will expect to see evidence of an engineer being called to try and solve the problem – and probably a copy of his report.

- *Illness or compassionate reasons* – if it can be shown that the person normally responsible for preparing the return was either seriously ill or recovering from such an illness, then a reasonable excuse situation could apply. However, this argument would not work for a larger organisation for example, where it would be expected that more than one person would be capable of completing the return.

- *Unexpected cash crisis* – as explained above, insufficient funds is not a reasonable excuse for a default. However, if a cash crisis was caused by the sudden non-payment of money by a normally reliable customer, then a reasonable excuse could apply. Again, however, it would have to be proved that this customer's business represented a major part of the company's trading – it would be unacceptable to say that a late VAT return by a company with £5m turnover per year was caused by a customer not paying his £1,000 invoice.

- *Loss of records* – a genuine fire, flood or burglary would certainly create a 'reasonable excuse' situation if the records for the current VAT period were lost. In such circumstances, however, there would again need to be evidence of the problem (eg insurance claim for a fire; photographic evidence of fire damage etc). The other point to bear in mind is that if records are unavailable, a business has the facility to estimate its VAT figures in the absence of records – so there is still an opportunity to submit the return and pay the tax on time.

For an illustration of when a reasonable excuse situation could apply, see Example 4.

Example 4

Smith Ltd has submitted four successive VAT returns late for different reasons. The managing director wants to know which of the following issues would be classed as a reasonable excuse:

- the first return in June 2008 was late because his bookkeeper had a week's holiday in Italy and was therefore out of the country in the last week of the month when the return was due;

- the second return was late because on 29 October, the company's computer system crashed and an engineer had to collect the computer and take it away for 4 days. As a result, the September 2008 return was not submitted and paid until 2 November 2008;

- for the December 2008 return, the bookkeeper had too much drink at an office party and posted the return in a red dustbin instead of a red post box. It was not until the default surcharge notice arrived in February 2009 that the error was realised;

- the business encountered cash flow problems in March – an important customer, accounting for 4% of the company's total turnover, did not pay his account on time. The amount unpaid equalled 50% of the VAT bill for the March quarter.

How many of the four defaults would qualify as a reasonable excuse?

Solution – in reality, the bookkeeper's holiday is a non-starter. It would be expected that she would be able to complete the return before she went on holiday or, alternatively, arrange for the company accountants to come in and do the return.

The posting of the VAT return in the dustbin is also a non-starter because it is not acceptable (as mentioned earlier) to blame another person for failing to perform a task.

The computer crash would probably be acceptable as long as there was clear evidence of the crash – and HMRC were satisfied that the circumstances were genuine.

The non-payment of money by the customer in March would not qualify as a reasonable excuse – the unpaid debt is only a small percentage of company sales.

Overall, a worthwhile approach for advisers dealing with reasonable excuse situations is to stand back and ask: 'Was my client late because of a genuine excuse, or is he trying to use this excuse to disguise the real reason for default, such as forgetting to do the return or, more likely, cannot afford to pay the tax due?'

Late registration penalty

17.8 The other main civil penalty that could apply is for belated notification of VAT registration. The rules and procedures concerning this penalty are analysed in detail in Chapter 1.

Other civil penalties

17.9 HMRC also has the power to impose a penalty in the following situations:

- penalty for the unauthorised issue of invoices;

- breaches of walking possession agreements (a walking possession situation occurs when goods have been seized and legally belong to the bailiff but remain in the possession of the original owner of the goods);

- incorrectly issuing certificates as to zero-rating (mainly relevant to the construction industry);

- inaccuracies in EC sales lists or failure to submit EC sales lists;

- failure to notify use of certain avoidance schemes.

Mitigation of penalties

17.10   The penalties described so far in this chapter can be split into two categories:

(a)   those where HMRC has power to reduce the penalty (including nil);

(b)   those where the penalty is fixed and cannot be reduced by mitigation – this applies in the case of default surcharge penalties.

The main offences where mitigation can reduce a penalty are as follows:

- civil penalty for conduct involving dishonesty;

- misdeclaration penalty;

- repeated misdeclaration penalty;

- failure to notify liability to be registered for VAT;

- unauthorised issue of invoices;

- failure to notify use of certain avoidance schemes;

- penalties relevant to the new regime considered at **17.11** below.

The basic approach to mitigation is that HMRC officers have the discretion to reduce a penalty to reflect the level of co-operation received from a trader, or the amount of work he has carried out himself to calculate any tax payable. There is a mitigation framework table to assist the officers in the process.

In reality, it is rare for a penalty to be reduced to nil, and officers are advised to consider the overall result of mitigation if the framework table produces a nil penalty.

New penalty system for returns due on or after 1 April 2009

17.11 A new penalty system was introduced on 1 April 2009 – and a business could face potential penalties if it understates its liability on VAT returns as follows:

- careless errors – a penalty of up to 30% of lost revenue;

- deliberate errors not concealed – a penalty of up to 70% of lost revenue;

- deliberate errors that are concealed by the taxpayer – a penalty of up to 100% of lost revenue.

The aim of the new penalty regime is to encourage taxpayers to comply with their responsibilities in all taxes (not just VAT). There are three clear messages:

- if a taxpayer takes reasonable care when completing his VAT returns, he will not be penalised with a penalty;

- if he does not take reasonable care, errors will be penalised and the penalties will be higher if the errors are deliberate;

- disclosing errors to HMRC as soon as they are discovered will substantially reduce any penalty that is due.

As well as penalising errors, the new system will also penalise taxpayers that do not submit a VAT return that is issued to them – and accept an HMRC assessment that is too low – see Example 5.

Example 5

John failed to submit his June 2009 VAT return – he owed tax of £100,000 for the period. In the absence of a return, HMRC estimated John's liability by issuing an assessment for £60,000. John was happy to pay the reduced assessment to help his cash flow.

Solution – John could be liable to a penalty of 30% on the tax shortfall of £40,000, ie a penalty of £12,000. A penalty assessed in situations where an assessment has been issued in the absence of a return is always classed as a 'careless' error.

Mitigation of penalties

17.12 An unprompted disclosure of an error to HMRC can produce a substantial reduction in the level of penalty applied against a business. A disclosure is unprompted if it is disclosed at a time when the taxpayer had no reason to believe that HMRC had discovered, or were about to discover, the error.

Further reductions can also be given if the taxpayer helps HMRC to calculate the total value of the underpayment and gives HMRC access to its records to check the figures.

The end result of an unprompted disclosure and subsequent co-operation with HMRC is as follows:

● the 30% careless penalty could be reduced to 0%;

● the 70% deliberate penalty could be reduced to 20%;

● the 100% deliberate and concealed penalty could be reduced to 30%;

● in some cases, HMRC has the power to suspend a careless penalty for up to 2 years and, if certain conditions are met by the taxpayer during this period, the penalty will then be cancelled once the suspension period has expired. The aim of this facility is to encourage a taxpayer to improve his record keeping in order to prevent future errors of a careless nature.

Reasonable care

17.13   An interesting sentence quoted by HMRC in their guidance on the new penalty regime is as follows (source here is Revenue and Customs Brief 19/2008):

'Each person has a responsibility to take reasonable care. But what is necessary for each person to meet that responsibility has to be viewed in the light of their abilities and circumstances.'

The paragraph elaborates further by explaining that a higher standard of care and expertise is expected from a large multi-national company compared to a self-employed and unrepresented taxpayer – but what does the reference to 'abilities and circumstances' really mean?

For example, if a taxpayer made a 'careless error' by entering £6,300 input tax on his VAT return instead of £3,600 (inversion of figures), would the interpretation of this error as far as penalties are concerned be different according to, eg whether the person completing the return had sight or health problems, or was very elderly and had problems with concentration levels? Only time will tell on this issue.

Error notification

17.14   An important point to be aware of under the new penalty system is that the correction of a previous error on a VAT return submitted by the business (ie the VAT return can be adjusted where the error is less than £10,000 or 1% of turnover up to a maximum of £50,000) does not guarantee that a 'careless error' penalty will not be issued by HMRC. Equally, an error notified to HMRC through the error correction procedures (ie exceeding £10,000 or 1% of turnover up to a ceiling of £50,000) could also be penalised.

The important issue to consider is the behaviour that caused the error and if this is deemed to be careless, then a penalty could still be issued, despite a disclosure or correction being made. In cases where a past error is corrected on a VAT return, the business should still consider writing to or telephoning HMRC to discuss the error and confirm that a 'careless error' penalty will not apply.

In reality, the new regulations mean there is no longer a guarantee that no penalty will be issued if an error is notified to HMRC (except if the mistake occurred while reasonable care was being taken) although the careless penalty could still be suspended for 2 years or reduced to 0%. There is still a very big incentive for a taxpayer to deal with errors as soon as they are discovered.

Common questions about the new penalty system

17.15

- *Does the penalty system only apply to errors on VAT returns?*

  As well as errors made on VAT returns, a penalty could also apply in the following two situations:

  (i) *HMRC estimates in the absence of a VAT return* – see Example 5;
  (ii) *8th and 13th Directive claims* – an 8th Directive claim allows an overseas trader based in another EU country to reclaim VAT paid in the UK, as long as various conditions are met. A 13th Directive claim allows an overseas trader based in a non-EU country to reclaim VAT paid in the UK, as long as various conditions are met, the main one being that an arrangement is in place between the country and the UK that allows claims to be made on a reciprocal basis.
  A penalty could be raised on the same basis in relation to 8th and 13th Directive claims as for errors made on VAT returns.

- *What VAT errors could attract a penalty?*

  There are two conditions that must be satisfied before a penalty for an inaccuracy will be charged:

  (i) The document (return) furnished to HMRC must contain an inaccuracy that leads to a VAT underpayment. This means either an underpayment of output tax or overclaim of input tax has taken place.
  (ii) The inaccuracy must be careless, deliberate or deliberate and concealed. The level of penalty will depend on which of the three categories (if any) the error belongs.

  No penalties are applied if a person takes reasonable care in his behaviour but submits an incorrect return.

• *What are the penalties for different errors and can they be reduced?*

The penalty charged will be based on a percentage of the VAT payable (known as the potential lost revenue). The rate of penalty will then be based on the behaviour that gave rise to the error. The less serious the behaviour, the smaller the penalty will be. The charges are as follows:

Behaviour	Maximum penalty	Minimum penalty
Error made but reasonable care has been taken	No penalty is applicable	
Careless error	30%	0%
Deliberate error	70%	20%
Deliberate and concealed error	100%	30%

There is a big difference between the maximum and minimum levels of penalty. There can be a substantial reduction in the level of penalty charged if the taxpayer makes an *unprompted disclosure of errors*.

A disclosure is unprompted if it is made at a time when the person making it has no reason to believe that HMRC has discovered, or is about to discover, the error.

Further reductions can be based on the quality of the disclosure. This is based on three things happening once an error is discovered:

(i) telling HMRC about the error;
(ii) helping HMRC calculate what extra tax is due;
(iii) allowing HMRC access to records to check the figures.

The reductions are available to taxpayers because HMRC wants to encourage people to voluntarily correct errors made on their VAT returns.

Note – if a disclosure is made but has been prompted (eg notice received from HMRC that it intends to make a VAT visit to check the records of a business), then the minimum penalties are as follows:

Behaviour	Minimum penalty
Careless error	15%
Deliberate error	35%
Deliberate and concealed error	50%

• *Is a penalty automatically avoided if an error is corrected on the next VAT return?*

No – and this is one of the main features of the new penalty system. An adjustment on a VAT return does not count as a full and unprompted disclosure under the new penalty regime. An 'unprompted disclosure' is only made by meeting the 'telling', 'helping' and 'allowing' conditions explained above.

So if a business has made a 'careless' error that can be included on a VAT return under the error correction procedures (and therefore avoid an interest charge), it must still make a separate disclosure by writing to HMRC to give full details of the error for penalty purposes. This will hopefully achieve a reduction in the penalty to zero in most cases.

Note – deliberate errors on previously submitted returns are not errors that can be adjusted on a later VAT return. This is because the deliberate behaviour of the taxpayer means that the error in question was known about at the outset – so cannot be an error that has been discovered.

A person should make a separate notification to HMRC of deliberate errors on previous VAT returns, irrespective of the amount of tax involved. Form VAT 652 can be used for this purpose – or a letter can be written to HMRC. The disclosure can be classed as prompted or unprompted, depending on the circumstances.

- *What is 'reasonable care' as far as VAT is concerned?*

HMRC accepts that 'reasonable care varies according to the person, the particular circumstances and their abilities.'

For example, HMRC has confirmed that it would not expect the same level of knowledge and expertise from a self-employed, unrepresented individual as from a large multi-national company.

HMRC has published detailed guidance on reasonable care in the new Compliance Handbook manual at Chapter CH80000 – paragraph CH81120 (http://www.hmrc.gov.uk/manuals/chmanual/CH81120.htm).

To give a simple VAT example, a taxpayer who incorrectly reclaims input tax on a rail fare (zero-rated expense) would not be classed as failing to take reasonable care. However, an input tax claim on a large 'drawings' figure could be classed as failing to take reasonable care.

- *What if a taxpayer is unsure if a VAT error is classed as careless?*

It is expected that most error corrections made by a taxpayer will not be due to a failure to take reasonable care. It is accepted by HMRC that many errors will be due to human error rather than careless error.

To quote from HMRC's guidance VAEC7271: 'We do not expect perfection.'

The advice to taxpayers or agents that have any doubt about whether an error comes within the definition of 'reasonable care' is to submit 'protective' unprompted disclosures when in doubt. The incentive with this approach is that most penalties will be reduced to zero as a result of the full and unprompted disclosure.

- *What happens if an agent makes a careless VAT error?*

  When an agent is acting for a taxpayer, eg completing the taxpayer's quarterly VAT returns, the taxpayer is not liable to a penalty on the basis of anything done or omitted by his agent. However, HMRC must still be satisfied that the taxpayer took reasonable care to avoid an inaccuracy.

  To give an example, if the owner of an ice-cream business received a VAT return from his agent showing a large repayment in his summer trading quarter, he would be expected to challenge why this has happened (and note his file accordingly). If the agent explains that the repayment has been caused by a large input tax claim on capital expenditure, then the proprietor has received a satisfactory explanation for the VAT figures and has shown reasonable care in his behaviour.

- *What is an example of dealing with a VAT error under the new regime?*

  The emphasis of the new regime is that to minimise a penalty (hopefully to zero in the case of failure to take reasonable care errors), a business must make an unprompted disclosure by telling HMRC about the error, helping to calculate what extra tax is due and allowing it access to business records to check the figures.

  Consider the following Example 6.

Example 6

John has submitted his September 2009 VAT return but then two weeks later discovers he made a very careless error in his calculations, meaning the liability on the return was understated by £8,000. How does John deal with this situation?

Solution – John is entitled to record the underpayment of £8,000 on his December 2009 return (because the value of the error is less than £10,000) but should make an entry in his VAT account at the time the error is discovered.

However, for penalty purposes, he must still tell HMRC about the error (giving full details) hopefully to reduce the penalty to zero. If he fails to tell HMRC about the error, and just includes it on the next VAT return, then he could be liable to a maximum 30% penalty if the adjustment is subsequently discovered by HMRC.

Default surcharge system

17.16   The default surcharge system for submitting late VAT returns and payments is unchanged. This is logical because the default surcharge system penalises the late submission of VAT returns and the late payment of tax; the new penalty system penalises careless or deliberate errors made on past VAT returns or the acceptance of low HMRC assessments in the absence of a return.

However, a positive point is that the same tax will not be subject to both penalties – see Example 7.

Example 7

Steve is in the default surcharge regime at 10% and sends in his VAT return for June 2009 on time – but without payment of the tax owing of £20,000. It is subsequently discovered that the return contained a 'careless error', producing a £5,000 shortfall of tax on the original return. The total VAT liability for the period is therefore £25,000.

Solution – a default surcharge penalty will be based on the original figures shown on the VAT return submitted by Steve ie £20,000 x 10% = £2,000. In addition, Steve will be charged a 30% penalty on his careless error, ie £5,000 x 30% = £1,500 (assuming no mitigation).

Planning points to consider

17.17   The following planning points should be given consideration.

- It is always worth checking the possibility of appealing against a default surcharge penalty if a reasonable excuse can be made – many taxpayers have won tribunal cases against the odds by putting forward their case.

- Be aware of the *de minimis* limit of £400 for a default surcharge relevant to the 2% and 5% periods. A part payment of tax could be made to reduce the chargeable penalty to less than £400, in which case no penalty will be applied.

- Consider requesting a time to pay arrangement with the Business Payment Support Service (BPSS) if a VAT bill cannot be paid. An agreed payment arrangement before the tax is due will avoid a potential default surcharge.

- Remember that in the case of some penalties, HMRC has the power to mitigate the amount of the penalty to reflect co-operation levels and the amount of work done by a taxpayer to correct errors.

- Be aware of the rules for the new penalty system introduced by HMRC for VAT returns due on or after 1 April 2009. The aim of the new system is to encourage taxpayers to take their VAT affairs seriously (and in relation to other taxes as well) and avoid making careless or deliberate errors. The best strategy at all times is to fully disclose errors as they are discovered and cooperate with HMRC to calculate the amount of any tax underpaid. This will reduce potential penalties in most cases, often to zero.

Chapter 18

Dealing with HMRC

Introduction

18.1 The title of this chapter in previous editions of this book had been 'Dealing with VAT Inspections'. The reality of the situation, however, is that very few compliant businesses now receive routine VAT visits unless their VAT affairs involve higher-risk issues such as partial exemption, complex liability issues or land and property.

Many small businesses with low tax risks (eg a baker selling zero-rated goods) will probably never receive a VAT visit, although they will still receive correspondence and other communications from HMRC. There is also scope for these businesses to develop a positive working relationship with HMRC – and these issues are considered in this chapter. The title is therefore called 'Dealing with HMRC'.

Submitting VAT returns and paying tax by due dates

18.2   This is a priority for any business.

A business gets one calendar month to submit its return to HMRC and pay any tax that is due on the return. If the return is filed online, then an extra 7 calendar days are given to submit the return.

Example – For VAT period ending on 30 April 2009, a business has until 31 May 2009 to submit the return and pay the tax that is due. This assumes the return is submitted in a paper format. If the return is filed using HMRC's online facility, then an extra 7 calendar days are given.

Many advisers and clients have been discouraged from applying to file VAT returns online because the registration process has proved to be complicated, with passwords and other information being required. However, HMRC has a dedicated telephone helpline to assist and in any case, it will be compulsory for the following businesses to file VAT returns online with effect from 1 April 2010:

- any business with annual turnover exceeding £100,000;

- all businesses that are VAT registered for the first time on or after 1 April 2010.

The following are a few important tips in relation to submitting VAT returns and paying tax:

- A business normally submits VAT returns on a quarterly basis. However, if the business regularly receives VAT repayments (e g majority of income is zero-rated) then there is scope to submit monthly VAT returns. This will improve the cash flow of the business by producing more regular repayments, although obviously means that 12 rather than 4 VAT returns will need to be submitted each year.

- A return submitted on time with full payment of tax will avoid any default surcharge being incurred by the business. The default surcharge system is analysed in Chapter 17 and can result in penalties of up to 15% of any unpaid tax being levied against a business.

- The VAT return should be signed by a senior official of the business, i e sole trader, partner or director in the case of a limited company. The person signing the return is confirming that it is correct – this is a crucial responsibility that should not be delegated.

- If it is not possible to pay the full amount of tax that is due, and attempts to raise finance have failed, then the business should approach HMRC's Business Payment Support Service (BPSS) – see **18.3**.

Business Payment Support Service (BPSS)

18.3   The BPSS was set up by HMRC in 2008 to assist businesses of all sizes that were encountering cash flow problems due to the economic downturn. It covers a wide range of taxes – including VAT, National Insurance and self-assessment tax.

The priority is to contact the BPSS before a VAT liability becomes due – if a time-to-pay agreement is then confirmed, this will avoid any default surcharge being incurred for the period in question.

Contact telephone number: 0845 302 1435

Opening hours: Monday–Friday 8am to 8pm; Saturday and Sunday 8 am to 4pm.

See **30.6** for further details about the BPSS facility.

Ensuring VAT returns are accurate

18.4   The new penalty system that came into effect on 1 April 2009 for VAT considers a taxpayer's behaviour in relation to underpayments of tax. The essential question is, did the taxpayer take reasonable care in ensuring his VAT return was accurate?

It is accepted by HMRC (and a fact of human nature) that errors will be made – but it is a responsibility of the taxpayer to minimise the risk of errors taking place by applying sensible checks on the returns before they are submitted. Here are ten basic checks that can assist this objective:

(1)   Compare the final figures on the VAT return to both the previous VAT period and possibly the corresponding VAT quarter in the previous year (the latter is particularly relevant if a business has seasonal issues). This should identify any major differences in either input tax or output tax figures that need to be considered further.

(2)   See if there is a sensible relationship between Box 1 (output tax) and Box 6 (outputs). If all sales of the business are standard-rated, then the output tax figure should be 15% (or 17.5%) of the outputs figure.

(3)   If the input tax figure is higher than average, is this because of capital expenditure or an increase in stock held by the business? If so, are purchase invoices held to support the input tax claim? Ensure the capital expenditure does not relate to a motor car that is available for private use – where the input tax is blocked.

(4) Check that the total input tax claimed in Box 4 does not exceed the value of net inputs in Box 7 multiplied by 15% or 17.5% (depending on the rate of VAT for the period). If there is a distortive relationship, this could indicate that purchase invoices have been entered incorrectly into the records, e g net and VAT figures inverted.

(5) Is the total outputs (sales) value in Box 6 consistent with the level of business that the directors know that the company has carried out during the period? Most directors will have a very good idea of the level of business they need to achieve to make a reasonable profit and how close to this figure they have been in recent months. This level of sales should be reflected on the VAT return.

(6) See whether there have been any unusual journal transactions in the period where VAT might not have been considered. For example, sales or recharges between associated companies are commonly dealt with by journals rather than by raising sales invoices. This is not a problem if there is a group registration in place and the supplies are between group members – but definitely an issue if the businesses are each VAT registered in its own right.

(7) Consider whether the business has made any zero-rated or exempt sales during the period. If so, is the liability of these sales definitely correct? To give an example, a sandwich sold by a café is zero-rated if the customer takes it away from the premises – but standard-rated if consumed on the premises.

(8) Have there been any property transactions during the period? The VAT issues of property transactions are often complex and need to be fully considered, often with professional advice being taken.

(9) Has input tax been adjusted on private or non-business use of an expense, e g scale charge applied for private road fuel; input tax apportionment on private telephone use etc.

(10) If the business using any VAT schemes, e g cash accounting, flat rate scheme, margin scheme, check whether the conditions of the various schemes are being met (the main schemes available to a business are considered in this book). To give a simple example, a condition of the cash accounting scheme is that input tax cannot be reclaimed until a supplier has been paid and this should be checked.

The main priority is to ensure that the business owner or director has confirmed the overall credibility of the VAT return submitted to HMRC. If this is the case, then the risk of a major error arising due to a 'lack of reasonable care' will hopefully be remote.

Keeping a VAT account

18.5   The record-keeping requirements of HMRC tend to be quite limited as far as VAT is concerned, as long as they are sufficient to enable accurate calculations to be made.

One legal requirement is for the taxpayer to keep a VAT account, which shows how the various figures on the VAT return have been compiled. It is sensible to keep a VAT file, which would not only show details extracted from the VAT account but also details of any correspondence received from HMRC or professional advisers on VAT rulings etc.

A typical VAT account is shown in Example 1.

Example 1

John is completing his VAT return for the quarter ended 30 June 2009. He is calculating his output figure for the period and recording this in his VAT account.

Solution – an example of how John's VAT account would look is shown as follows.

Output tax

Sales day book totals

April	£1,500	
May	£1,200	
June	£1,100	Total £3,800

Error on previous VAT return – VAT on sales invoice 345 omitted £80

Total output tax due = £3,880

Other record-keeping requirements

18.6   As explained above, HMRC's main requirement is that the records maintained by a business must enable accurate VAT returns to be completed. In reality, most computer accounting packages automatically ensure this objective is achieved, being able to produce a series of VAT reports that show a clear audit trail.

However, there are other aspects of VAT accounting that require separate records to be kept to ensure figures are accurate and can be supported with appropriate evidence:

● Paperwork in relation to export of goods – proof that the goods have left the EU;

- Paperwork in relation to sales of goods to VAT registered businesses in other EU countries – proof of a customer's VAT number and proof the goods have left the UK;

- Imports of goods – ensure C79 documents are properly retained;

- Bad debt relief claims – see **31.18** to confirm conditions for claiming bad debt relief are met;

- International services – a proper record of all work carried out for overseas customers needs to be kept, e g in some cases, the place of supply rules require that supplies are received by the customer for the purpose of his business so proof of this business status (usually a VAT registration number) needs to be kept.

Keeping up to date with VAT changes

18.7   VAT can be a fast moving tax and for practitioners with a client base in a range of different businesses, it can be a challenge keeping up to date with the many changes that take place.

As a starting point, a very useful tip is to regularly check the 'What's New' section on the home page of HMRC's website. This section highlights new information that has been published by HMRC (invariably on the website) and it will be shown in date order. The section announces details concerning all taxes, not just VAT, and will highlight newly published or amended publications such as VAT notices, HMRC Business Briefs, consultation papers etc.

HMRC only tends to announce either a change in the way it interprets legislation (e g following a court case verdict) or new legislation that is being introduced or has been introduced. For obvious reasons, it does not tend to publicise VAT planning measures or potential opportunities to reclaim tax with a wider interpretation of a court case verdict.

There are a number of ways that a practitioner can keep up-to-date on the thinking of the profession on VAT matters – reading commentary and articles in leading tax publications, attending VAT Update courses, branch meetings, online updates etc.

As a separate tip, where information is used from the HMRC website to determine the VAT treatment of a transaction, it is important to be aware that some of the information could be out-of-date or even incorrect. In cases where errors are alerted to it, HMRC will remove the information from the website or amend the details – so it is important to print out any information you use, keep it in the VAT file discussed at **18.5** and highlight the section that has been adopted.

Note – a recent example of an error on the website was that the business gift rules (no VAT is due on a gift of less than £50 given away for business purposes) did not apply for gifts of alcohol or tobacco products. This was incorrect – there is no such restriction in the legislation.

Written rulings from HMRC

18.8   This has proved a controversial subject in recent months. The basic approach of HMRC is as follows:

- The policy of HMRC is to encourage taxpayers to reach a decision about a VAT issue by making greater use of both the published public notices and guidance given on its website. Its view is that a written ruling should only be given in situations when either the law or the interpretation of the law in certain circumstances is unclear.

- As a result of the above policy, many replies will refer the taxpayer to a relevant paragraph or section of a public notice – in many (but not all) cases, this will be sufficient to enable the taxpayer to arrive at a conclusion regarding the VAT treatment of a transaction.

- In cases where the published guidance is inadequate, HMRC will give a non-statutory clearance for a business (ie a specific written ruling). However, published statistics show that the number of cases where these clearances have been given are quite limited.

It can be frustrating for advisers seeking clarification of VAT issues on behalf of a client to be referred back to public notices. What about the situation where an adviser is aware of the public notice but does not understand what it means? How can he then move forward and advise his client?

Another bizarre outcome is that any written ruling given by HMRC is neither a binding ruling nor a matter that can be appealed against. So this means that a taxpayer who disagrees with the ruling he has been given can ignore it – although the officer carrying out the next VAT visit will almost certainly raise an assessment on the basis that he is adopting HMRC's approach on the issue.

To be fair to HMRC, it is very difficult to give rulings in many cases unless all details are known about a transaction. For example, the rules about what constitutes the transfer of a going concern are very precise – but the issues in certain business sales can be very involved and complex. And what about the situation when an incorrect ruling is given by an officer not fully aware of all the facts? This could lead to a wrong approach being adopted by the taxpayer with a wide range of consequences.

One example that the author has encountered was on a property transaction in 2008 where much of the building work qualified for a 5% rate of VAT. However, the builder's accountant encouraged his client to charge 17.5% VAT – in other words, play safe and avoid any potential problems in the event of a VAT visit. The accountant advised his client to only adopt a 5% rate of VAT if he received a written ruling from HMRC, ie to 'rubber stamp' the VAT treatment.

The accountant's approach in the above situation would not have achieved anything – HMRC's written guidance in VAT Notice 708 is very clear that building work carried out to convert a house into two flats (different number of dwellings) is subject to 5% VAT. Why should HMRC repeat something that is already very clear in its written guidance? A request for a written ruling would only have produced a copy of VAT Notice 708 in the reply – and quite rightly so.

This is a subject where the issues are not clear cut but it is hoped that further liaison between the profession and HMRC will produce an improved situation for all parties.

Telephoning HMRC

18.9   It can also be a frustrating experience when attempting to speak to HMRC by telephone on its National Advice Service (0845 010 9000). A query about any technical matter of detail will again either refer the enquirer to public notices or published guidance, or ask for the issues to be put in writing.

In reality, it would be very dangerous for a taxpayer to rely on a verbal conversation in relation to any important VAT matter, especially as the meaning of words can become distorted by regional accents or badly used phrases. A written ruling or professional advice is always the best option.

One useful suggestion may be to try the search engine on the HMRC website. This facility is much improved in recent months and is now directing users to sensible links in many cases. However, as explained in 18.7, be mindful to always print off this information (and date it and retain it) just in case there is any problem with the accuracy of the guidance.

The helpline service is very effective for:

- Giving contact addresses and telephone numbers of different offices and sections of HMRC, e g where do I send a VAT 1 application to register for VAT?

- Posting public notices and giving details about where to find information on the website.

- Providing details of VAT forms that need to be completed in certain circumstances.

VAT inspections

Background

18.10   As explained at the beginning of this chapter, routine VAT visits for many businesses are now very unusual. The focus of HMRC is to adopt a risk-based approach to deciding which businesses should be visited. The following businesses tend to be considered higher risk and could receive more regular visits:

- cash traders – where there is a risk that sales (and therefore output tax) could be understated;

- traders dealing in 'relevant goods and services' – e g mobile phones and computer chips that have been the subject of widespread VAT fraud (see Chapter 19);

- land and property traders – either businesses dealing in property or providing building services that have complex liability issues;

- partly exempt businesses – this is always one of the most complicated areas of VAT and subject to detailed calculations that could produce significant VAT errors;

- businesses with a poor compliance record – i e a history of assessments on previous VAT visits, non-payment of tax/late submission of returns.

Before the visit

18.11   Before the visit is carried out, HMRC will:

- confirm who it wants to see;

- agree a mutually convenient date and time;

- advise the name and contact number of the officer carrying out the visit;

- indicate the records and relevant periods required;

- indicate the likely length of the visit;

- give the business the opportunity to indicate any matters of concern so that the officer can be better prepared; and

- give the business the option to have the above details confirmed in writing.

During a visit

18.12   For the purpose of the visit itself, HMRC officers will:

- identify themselves by name on arrival and, if requested, produce an identity card;

- explain the main purpose of the visit;

- discuss various aspects of the business at the outset so as to keep claims on staff time to a minimum (although new points may arise as they review the records);

- examine the records of the business and, where appropriate, inspect the premises;

- deal with VAT affairs confidentially;

- advise of overpayments as well as underpayments; and

- where possible, try to resolve matters during the visit.

It is possible that the officers may also want to record details of suppliers and customers of the business, to check correct VAT figures are declared in their records as well.

End of the visit

18.13   At the end of the visit, HMRC will:

- review the main work done;

- explain any areas of concern in relation to that work, discuss them and agree any future action that needs to be taken; and

- illustrate as fully as possible the size and reason for any adjustment to the VAT payable, and describe how the adjustment will be made.

After the visit, HMRC will:

- where requested, or where it feels it necessary, put in writing a summary of the visit, any rulings, agreements or recommendations; and

- where matters are unresolved, give the business a reasonable time within which to provide further information or comment.

Complaints about officers

18.14   If a taxpayer or adviser has a complaint against HMRC, and is unable to resolve it with the officer concerned, he has a number of options available to take the matter further:

- contact one of the Regional Complaints Units within the Department, giving full details of the complaint and the reasons why it could not be resolved at a local level. The local manager at the Unit will then make enquiries into the problem and aims to give a full reply within 10 days of the original complaint. Where appropriate, the Unit will consider reimbursing reasonable costs incurred by the complainant, such as telephone or postage costs. However, the compensation is unlikely to include time spent on the complaint unless loss of earnings can be clearly shown. There is also scope to make a payment to the complainant to cover distress that may have been caused – this payment tends to range from £25 to £500;

- complain to the independent Adjudicator. The Adjudicator is unconnected with the Department and will consider many different types of complaint, including complaints about delays, improper behaviour and rudeness. The Adjudicator cannot examine cases that are applicable to a VAT tribunal nor intervene once a matter is before the criminal courts. The address of the Adjudicator is:

  The Adjudicator's Office
  Haymarket House
  28 Haymarket
  London SW1Y 4SP
  Tel: 0207 930 2292

- complain to a Member of Parliament.

New appeals system

18.15   If an officer raises a VAT assessment that is challenged by the taxpayer or his adviser, then there has always been a very clear appeals process that can, in limited cases, end up with a case being considered by the European Court of Justice.

However, in most cases, appeals will be dealt with on a local basis, and the importance of local reviews was strengthened on 1 April 2009 with the introduction of a new appeals system for all taxes.

- The new system introduces a two-tier tribunal system with routine appeals being heard by the first-tier tribunal and complex appeals being heard by the upper tribunal.

- Before reaching the tribunal stage, a taxpayer has the new legal right for the decision to be reviewed at a local office level by a trained review officer who has not previously been involved with that decision. In the majority of cases, the review officer will be outside the immediate line management chain of the decision maker.

- Local reviews must be completed within 45 days (unless another period is agreed between HMRC and the taxpayer).

- The main point is that HMRC prefers to resolve disputes on a local basis without going to a tribunal if this can be avoided. Although previous regimes have always had the facility for a local reconsideration, the indications are that review officers will be better trained and more independent than their predecessors.

New powers from 1 April 2009

18.16   The way that HMRC carries out compliance checks (VAT inspections) was changed on 1 April 2009. The new system is designed to make the tax system simpler and more consistent.

From this date, HMRC will have one set of powers covering all taxes – these powers are provided by *Sch 36* of the *Finance Act 2008*.

The new legislation provides HMRC with:

- a set of powers to examine business records without a right of appeal;

- the ability to inspect business records, assets and premises;

- the ability to correct errors going back 4 years – in the case of VAT, this used to be a 3-year limit. The 20-year limit for correcting fraudulent errors remains unchanged;

- a new statutory ban on inspecting purely private dwellings without consent;

- a statutory requirement for HMRC to give at least 7 days notice prior to making a visit, unless either an unannounced visit is necessary, or a shorter period is agreed;

- a statutory requirement on HMRC to act reasonably;

- a new requirement that unannounced visits must be approved beforehand by a specially trained HMRC officer.

In practice, the rules will not impact greatly on compliant businesses – but be aware of the 4-year time limit for correcting errors and raising assessments.

Planning points to consider

18.17   The following action plan should help a business or adviser to get the most out of its dealings with HMRC and avoid any major problems:

- Always aim to pay tax and submit VAT returns on time.

- Adopt HMRC's online filing facility as soon as possible in relation to submitting VAT returns and paying tax.

- Ensure that a senior official spends time carrying out a thorough review of a VAT return before it is submitted to HMRC (see **18.4** for suggested checks). This will hopefully avoid a penalty being incurred for failing to take reasonable care.

- In the event that VAT cannot be paid, contact HMRC's Business Payment Support Service before a debt becomes due to negotiate a time to pay agreement.

- Use the 'What's New' section on the HMRC website to keep up to date on VAT developments – supported by information from other publications within the tax profession.

- Always try to solve a VAT problem by using HMRC's public notices or other written guidance. The HMRC search engine is also a useful tool to direct a user to the appropriate section. The occasions when HMRC will give a written ruling on a subject are now very limited.

- The HMRC telephone helpline service is very useful for basic enquiries – but not for detailed technical questions that should be resolved by other methods.

- VAT visits tend to be determined by risk factors. Be aware that many businesses will not receive a VAT visit for many years so it is important that procedures and systems are in place to ensure a visit does not produce any major problems.

- Be aware that VAT assessments raised by HMRC since 1 April 2009 can now be reviewed by an independent officer within the department if they are disputed by a taxpayer. The officer is trained to make a thorough review of the facts – hopefully to avoid many appeals going to a VAT tribunal.

Chapter 19

Joint and Several Liability (Missing Trader Fraud)

Key topics in this chapter:

- How Missing Trader Intra-Community (MTIC) fraud works – and the impact on government revenue collection.

- HMRC efforts to combat MTIC fraud – impact of recent cases and current approach to the problems.

- The need for a business to take 'reasonable steps to ensure the integrity of its supply chain' – practical examples of how this can be achieved.

- The reverse charge rules for supplies of mobile phones and computer chips between VAT registered traders in the UK where the invoice value of the sale exceeds £5,000.

Introduction

19.1   One of the biggest challenges faced by HMRC in recent years relates to the loss of revenue caused by Missing Trader Intra-Community VAT fraud, commonly known as MTIC VAT fraud.

The extent of the fraud has caused great concern at all levels of government. Measures have been taken to strengthen the powers of HMRC to deal with the fraudsters, the aim being to prevent fraud in the first place.

The issue of MTIC fraud is particularly relevant for advisers who have clients dealing in high-risk goods such as computer chips, telephone chargers, memory cards and mobile telephones. However, it is becoming clear that the fraudsters are extending the scope of their trade, moving to other high value, small volume goods.

The initial attempts by HMRC to deal with the problem were introduced in the 2003 Budget, and the relevant legislation is in *s 77A* of the *VAT*

Act 1994. The main thrust of the 2003 measures was that if a business bought goods from a supplier and had reason to suspect that they were part of an illegal supply chain (and that output tax might not be paid to HMRC in the normal manner), then HMRC had the power to disallow input tax claimed by the buyer, even if he met the usual rules for claiming input tax, ie holding a proper tax invoice with a VAT registration number, relevant to goods sold to him as a taxable supply. The phrase to explain this legislation is 'joint and several liability'.

How missing trader and carousel fraud works

19.2   It is important that advisers know the basis of MTIC fraud (sometimes known as 'carousel fraud' because the same goods go round in a trading circle, often many times) in order to advise clients how to avoid becoming innocently involved in an illegal trading chain.

MTIC VAT fraud basically works by the creation of a supply chain – where at some stage, a key player in the chain disappears. The chain normally involves goods being purchased from a supplier in another EU country – who does not charge VAT to his UK customer because he is given the customer's UK VAT number. See Example 1.

Example 1

ABC Ltd is VAT registered in the UK and buys 100,000 mobile phones from DEF Ltd, based in Holland for £400,000. DEF Ltd does not charge VAT on the supply of goods because it quotes the VAT number of the UK supplier on its invoice.

ABC Ltd is a fraudulent company and sells 10,000 mobile phones to ten different companies for £36,000 plus VAT (ie 10% below bulk cost). The ten companies all pay ABC Ltd £42,300 each – and reclaim input tax of £6,300 on the tax invoices issued by ABC Ltd (based on VAT rate of 17.5%). However, ABC Ltd disappears as a missing trader without ever paying HMRC the output tax due of £63,000. The company has effectively made a profit of £23,000 (£423,000 – £400,000) – wholly at the expense of HMRC.

Solution – the input tax claimed by the ten UK companies on invoices raised by ABC Ltd will be examined very closely by HMRC under the legislation (*VAT Act 1994, s 77A*). If HMRC has strong reason to suspect that the companies knew or should have known that ABC Ltd was a fraudulent company, then the input tax could be disallowed.

The above example illustrates how illegal companies can effectively sell goods at a loss and still make a reasonable profit – at the expense of HMRC. And the customers of ABC Ltd are delighted – because they have bought goods very cheaply (below cost) – which they can sell at a high price.

The development of the above scheme creates an even bigger problem for HMRC, when the same goods go round in a circular trading cycle. This means that the fraudsters have the opportunity to steal money from the Exchequer on many occasions. In one fraud case, HMRC apparently proved that the same goods went round in a circle of business deals no less than 35 times. See Example 2 for an illustration of a typical fraud situation – although there are many different variations to this main theme.

Example 2

Consider the following situation and the VAT issues arising from the chain of events.

- Company A is based in France and exports £2m of computer chips to Company B in the UK. Company B is registered for VAT.

- Company B is not charged VAT as the goods are an acquisition from another EU business. Company B sells the goods to Company C for £1.8m plus VAT of £262,500. Company B disappears without ever declaring the output tax to HMRC. As far as HMRC are concerned, Company B has never traded.

- Company C is a genuine company and sells the chips to Company D for £1.85m plus VAT. The VAT return of Company C looks sensible, with a net amount of tax payable – so the return is unlikely to be reviewed by HMRC.

- Company D is an exporter and sells the goods back to Company A for £1.9m – no VAT is charged as the supply is a despatch to another EU business that is VAT registered. Proof is held that the goods left the UK shores and arrived in France.

Solution – the end result is that Company A has bought the same goods back for a lower price than it sold them – effectively making £100,000 profit. Company B has defrauded HMRC by £262,500 – and made a profit of £62,500. Company C has made £50,000 profit and Company D has made £50,000 profit. In effect, the total profit made by the four companies is £262,500 – exactly the amount of VAT defrauded from HMRC.

And if the above chain of supply is repeated again and again (carousel) then the amount of tax lost becomes a staggering amount.

HMRC approach to the problem

19.3 The initial HMRC approach was highlighted in the well known VAT tribunal case involving *Bond House Systems Ltd v Customs and Excise Comrs* (4 March 2003, unreported) (MAN/02/534 18100), the outcome of which came as a surprise to many advisers but which has effectively been overturned by the verdict of the European Court.

In the *Bond House* case, HMRC argued that if a transaction chain was circular in nature and involved a missing trader (carousel fraud) the purpose of the chain was to defraud HMRC. The chain was not, therefore, an economic activity, and if it was not an economic activity, there was no VAT and therefore no input tax to reclaim for any transactions in the chain. The tribunal supported this view and not surprisingly the decision was appealed to the High Court, which referred it to the European Court of Justice (ECJ).

The result of the above approach was that HMRC could put pressure on legitimate traders caught in an illegal supply chain and disallow their input tax. However, the ECJ rejected HMRC's argument in its entirety. The Court found that companies such as Bond House, caught in a fraud caused by others, are fully entitled under European VAT law to receive payments of input tax, and that to deprive them of that repayment is a breach of European law.

Again, it is not allowed in European law to view a series of transactions as a whole – each transaction needs to be examined on its merits and as a separate economic activity. In effect, an innocent company cannot be held liable for the fraudulent activity of others.

The basic argument put forward by HMRC is that a person in business can only trade successfully if he is aware of the market price of goods he buys and sells. So if an unknown supplier suddenly offers him an excellent deal, he should seriously challenge the reasons for the low price on offer. To quote the phrase used by HMRC, it is expected that the buyer will 'take reasonable steps to verify the integrity of the supply chain'.

The ECJ ruling means that HMRC will now have to rely on the powers given to it in the 2003 Budget, as explained at **19.1**. It will need to look at each transaction on an individual basis and if it assesses that the buyer of the goods had reason to doubt the legitimacy of the trader from whom he was buying, then the input tax claimed by the buyer can be disallowed. The latter measure would then compensate HMRC for the undeclared output tax lost on the sale of the goods to the buyer.

Taking 'reasonable steps' to ensure the 'integrity of the supply chain'

19.4 Think of situations where you could purchase goods at genuinely low prices. For example, if an item has been superseded by more up-to-date technology, then it is likely to be sold cheaply because its place in the market has been eroded. Items that are damaged or have suddenly become unfashionable would also be sold cheaply.

In the cases above, the supplier will have a good reason for charging low prices – but equally, the onward supply by his customer will also be at a lower price to reflect the problems with the goods. Contrast this with MTIC frauds, where the goods are bought cheaply and sold at top price.

The key section to review if a company has concerns about its supply chain is section 8 of VAT Notice 726. This gives a list of key points to consider – and the main ones are as follows:

- review the supplier's history in the trade – the fraudulent companies often surface and disappear very quickly;

- ensure normal commercial practices have been adopted in negotiating prices;

- confirm the goods actually exist and the price being charged is sensible within the market place;

- verify VAT registration details with HMRC (call the National Helpline);

- seek a trade reference;

- carry out credit checks and company searches;

- ensure supplementary paperwork is completed – eg purchase orders, delivery notes, inspection reports;

- be suspicious of any payments to third parties – why is this the case?

The above measures are not an exhaustive list. HMRC takes the view that if it produced a standard checklist for all businesses to follow, then this would encourage the fraudsters to beat the system. See Examples 3 and 4.

Example 3

The Managing Director of Mobiles Phones Ltd has been approached by a newly formed company, Very Dodgy Ltd, who offer to sell him a mobile phone component that he normally pays £1.50 for on the open market. The price being proposed by Very Dodgy Ltd is £1.35 per component. The credit search on Very Dodgy Ltd shows it is a new company, and the directors are all based overseas. The company does not have any UK trading premises, and is unable to give any trade references or UK bank account details. They have asked for payment for the goods to be made direct to an overseas bank account.

Solution – there are strong indications that this company is not a bona fide organisation – it would be sensible to avoid trading with them to avoid potential problems with HMRC in the future.

Example 4

The Managing Director of Mobile Phones Ltd has been approached by an alternative supplier, Not Dodgy Ltd, who offers to sell him a mobile phone component that he normally pays £1.50 for on the open market. The price being proposed by Not Dodgy Ltd is £1.35 per component. A credit search carried out on Not Dodgy Ltd confirms they have been trading for 23 years, and have trading premises in Southampton. A reputable firm of accountants has prepared the audited accounts, and the company has net assets exceeding £1m.

The director of Not Dodgy Ltd explains why he can sell the components so cheaply – it is because the company is manufacturing the components at a new specialised factory in Southampton – pictures and manufacturing specs are seen to confirm this information. A telephone call to HMRC confirms the validity of the VAT registration number.

Solution – Mobile Phones Ltd has taken 'reasonable steps' to 'establish the legitimacy of the supplier' (Notice 726, para 4.5). It would be unlikely to be involved in a loss of input tax through an MTIC VAT fraud.

Ensuring innocent businesses are safe from the 'joint and several liability' legislation

19.5 In reality, any business that trades in either computer or mobile phone goods must now have very clear procedures in place to check out suppliers with whom they do business. Although this sounds common sense, there are always temptations to ignore procedures when a good deal appears to be on the table.

As extra assurance, however, HMRC has given some other key concessions:

● it will only issue a notice of liability if the goods in question were sold as an onward sale – there would be no problem if, for example, the equipment was adopted for the company's own use. This is because it is recognised that a company buying assets will not have the same knowledge of pricing issues as a company involved in the distribution of the goods;

● each case is independently reviewed and authorised by a central team within HMRC before further action is taken;

● HMRC recognises that the onus of proof is on itself to prove a trader had grounds to suspect there could be a problem. The actual wording in para 4.1 of Notice 726 refers to a situation where 'there is sufficient knowledge on a balance of probabilities to show the requisite knowledge';

● with regard to price, HMRC will only issue a notice if it is sure that the price paid by the company was less than the lowest price that might reasonably be expected to be payable on the open market. This would also be less than the price previously paid on the supply of the same goods.

It is important that advisers do not find themselves acting for fraudulent companies that are going to cause problems – the following questions should therefore be considered before a letter of engagement is agreed.

- Is the business being managed by young men with no indication of past business experience or a past track record in the goods with which they are trading? Do these men have any detailed knowledge about the range of goods they are selling?

- Has the company any previous history in terms of length of trading, past accounts, bank references? It is very unusual for a new business to suddenly start trading in goods worth millions of pounds – how is such trade being financed?

- Does the business have buying links with Netherlands, Spain and France and selling links with Dubai or Hong Kong? These countries are very often the start and finish points of the chains.

The list is not exhaustive and there is no substitute for having a general feel that the issues surrounding the arrangement do not look genuine.

Recent cases and current approach of courts

19.6   The last 12 months has seen a lot of court activity to determine whether HMRC was correct to disallow the input tax claimed by many companies on supplies linked to fraudulent companies.

As a starting point, the prime consideration for the courts was to consider whether a taxpayer:

> 'knew or had reasonable grounds to suspect that some or all of the VAT payable in respect of that supply, or on any previous or subsequent supply of those goods, would go unpaid' (*VATA 1994, s 77A(2)*).'

It is clear that many companies were unaware that the goods they were purchasing were relevant to fraudulent activities. However, this is not the end of the story. As the extract above explains, the consideration is to then consider whether the taxpayer ought to have known the goods were fraudulent, ie had 'grounds to suspect' etc.

The following is a summary of recent cases along with comments on the key issues.

- *Red 12 Trading Ltd* (16 December 2008, unreported) (LON/07/1345 20900) – the company exported mobile phones and claimed to have no knowledge that there was any connection with fraud. However, the tribunal referred in its report to 'the sheer improbability of these trades being genuine'. Red 12 should have known that its claim for input tax could not succeed – HMRC was correct in its action.

  Comment – HMRC was able to illustrate that the phones being traded in this case had no commercial basis or logic. The phones could not be used in the UK, were being bought in from countries where they were quite expensive to buy, and ended up in countries where they were already relatively cheap in the domestic market.

- *Blue Sphere Global Ltd* (17 December 2008, unreported) (LON/07/0934 20901) – BSG was a relatively small company with no previous trading history in mobile phones that suddenly became involved with large scale deals. For each sale, there was a customer already identified for BSG by the supplier of the phones – so if the deals were genuine, why would the supplier sacrifice some of his margin by involving another company that had little value of offer? The tribunal's conclusion was that 'BSG ought to have known that, by its purchases, it was participating in transactions connected with the fraudulent evasion of VAT'.

  Comment – as explained above, the fraudsters seem to have taken advantage of BSG's vulnerability. Why did BSG not consider the reasons it was being presented with easy deals and profit, ie because of the link with tax fraud?

- *Megtian Ltd (in admin)* (11 December 2008, unreported) (LON/07/0980 20894) – the owner of Megtian made a big mistake in his evidence by referring to 'everyone' in the supply chain, which challenged his claim that he dealt with no-one but his supplier and customer. The tribunal again concluded that Megtian knew that its transactions were connected with fraud.

  Comment – HMRC was fortunate to win this case as one of its main arguments was that an alleged 95% of trading in mobile phones was fraudulent at the time and as such, Megtian should have been aware of this and avoided getting involved with the deal. The tribunal rejected this argument. However, it was the behaviour of the taxpayer and the knowledge he should have possessed that was relevant to the case.

- *N2J Ltd* (12 December 2008, unreported) (MAN/06/0214 20895) – N2J had not verified the existence of the goods before export, not insured them and could not account for their location at any given time. It was also strange that its first customer withdrew from the deal but an identical customer was found in the same location that was prepared to pay the same price for the same quantity of goods. This outcome seemed highly improbable if the transaction had been genuine. This case was slightly different because HMRC disallowed the company's zero-rating of the goods as an export, rather than its input tax. The taxpayer's appeal was again dismissed.

  Comment – the tribunal report concluded that the transactions were 'dubious' and that N2J had 'not taken every reasonable measure to avoid becoming involved in fraudulent transactions'.

- *Livewire Telecom Ltd; Olympia Technology Ltd* [2009] EWHC 15 (Ch) – these cases were heard by the High Court and related to cases that had originally been lost by HMRC in the VAT tribunals. The outcome in both cases was that the tribunal had not properly considered whether the taxpayer ought to have known about the fraudulent trading. This was a different issue to deciding whether they knew about the fraud. In the *Olympia* case, the tribunal had focused on the knowledge of the director (Mr Habib had been described as 'naïve and gullible') but he was not the only person involved with the company trading. The tribunal should have considered the knowledge of other senior employees, ie the company as a whole rather than just one director.

Comment – HMRC will be pleased to have the original tribunal verdicts reversed. The decisions were delivered on 16 January 2009 and should make it easier for it to prove future cases.

Author note – after a series of case defeats last year, HMRC seems to have recognised the importance of looking at each individual company's trading situation to prove knowledge (or knowledge that should have been held), rather than relying on the general principle that most of the mobile phone industry was fraudulent. The cases being heard by tribunals are now showing consistent conclusions, as highlighted by those considered in this section.

Reverse charge accounting for sales of certain goods

19.7 HMRC introduced new reverse charge rules with effect from 1 June 2007 in relation to the sale of mobile telephones and computer chips between VAT registered traders in the UK. The reverse charge rules basically transfer the output tax liability in the sale of high-risk goods from the supplier to the customer. See Example 5 for an illustration of this point.

Example 5

ABC Ltd is VAT registered in the UK and buys 100,000 mobile phones from DEF Ltd, based in Holland for £400,000. DEF Ltd does not charge VAT on the supply of goods because it quotes the VAT number of the UK supplier on its invoice.

ABC Ltd then sells the goods to GHI Ltd but does not charge any output tax on the supply. It quotes the VAT registration number of GHI Ltd on its sales invoice. However, GHI Ltd must account for the output tax of ABC Ltd by making an entry in Box 1 of its own VAT return (based on the price paid for the goods × 17.5%), claiming the same amount back as input tax in Box 4 of the same return. It has applied the reverse charge mechanism by making these entries.

Solution – if ABC Ltd disappears before it has submitted and paid its VAT return, then a large VAT debt to HMRC has hopefully been avoided. This is because the output tax liability has been transferred to GHI Ltd.

The reverse charge rules contain a number of important provisions. For example, there is a *de minimis* limit if the value of the sale of qualifying goods on an invoice is less than £5,000.

Any adviser who has clients that supply computer chips or mobile telephones (and are therefore likely to be affected by the new rules) should closely study the guidance given in HMRC Business Brief 24/2007 and VAT Information Sheet 08/07. Both of these publications can be viewed or downloaded from the HMRC website www.hmrc.gov.uk. To quote from para 8.1 of VAT Information Sheet 08/07:

> 'If a customer takes no action if they are charged VAT when the reverse charge should apply, they may put themselves in a position where they could be held to be jointly and severally liable for the VAT or unable to recover the input tax on the supply.'

Reverse Charge Sales List (RCSL)

19.8 Any business making sales which are caught by the reverse charge rules must complete another return each VAT quarter, namely the Reverse Charge Sales List (RCSL).

The form is not complicated, and can be accessed through the HMRC website. The form is submitted for the same period as the taxpayer's VAT return and basically requires a declaration of sales made to VAT registered businesses which are covered by the reverse charge scheme. The declaration gives a monthly breakdown of sales to each VAT registered trader, obviously quoting their VAT registration number.

Other powers

19.9 As a final point, be aware that HMRC has two other powers to deter the activities of companies it believes could be involved in illegal supply chains. Firstly, it can ask for security (an up-front payment or guarantee) from businesses that constantly trade with other companies that go missing or become insolvent, leaving VAT unpaid. Secondly, it has the power to deny input tax for any business involved in the commodities listed if a proper tax invoice is not held. This effectively denies companies the benefit of proving an input tax claim with other supporting documentation.

Planning points to consider

19.10 The following planning points should be given consideration.

- It is important that advisers know how MTIC fraud works and the main goods used by the fraudsters. This is not only to ensure they do not act for fraudulent companies – but also to advise innocent traders of the potential risks of receiving illegal goods in a supply chain.

- Recent court cases have supported HMRC's strategy of disallowing input tax on the purchase of any fraudulent goods if it can prove that the trader had reason to suspect that the goods were part of an illegal supply chain where output tax was unlikely to be declared by the supplier. In other words, the onus is on HMRC to prove that the trader knew or ought to have known that he was dealing in goods where the intention was to fraudulently evade VAT.

- It is important that all traders in relevant high-risk goods take adequate measures to 'ensure the integrity of their supply chain'. HMRC does not produce an exhaustive list of the measures that need to be taken – but it gives very clear guidelines as to the issues that should be considered.

- Be aware of the reverse charge rules whereby the output tax liability for the sale of mobile telephones and computer chips between VAT registered traders in the UK is transferred in some cases from the seller of the goods to the buyer. This is an attempt by HMRC to eliminate MTIC fraud by preventing the seller of the goods from disappearing without declaring output tax he has received from his customer.

Chapter 20

Best Judgment and Unjust Enrichment

Key topics in this chapter:

- The powers of HMRC officers to issue best judgment assessments when records and VAT returns are incomplete or inaccurate.

- The approach adopted by HMRC when raising best judgment assessments.

- Suggested approach for tax advisers reviewing best judgment assessments.

- The key concepts of unjust enrichment and when they apply.

- Procedures for reimbursing customers in cases where unjust enrichment applies for VAT errors made.

- The difference between an error and an adjustment.

Introduction

20.1   This chapter considers two important topics that could arise for a business in its dealings with HMRC.

- *Best judgment assessments* – in the case of a business with incomplete records, or where Customs feel that returns submitted are not correct, the officer(s) has powers under the *VAT Act 1994, s 73* to assess the amount of tax due using his 'best judgment'. Unfortunately for the taxpayer, if he has no records to challenge the best judgment assessment, he will find it very difficult to claim the officer's figures are incorrect.

- *Unjust enrichment* – the concept of unjust enrichment states that no taxpayer can be financially enriched because of VAT errors that have been made in the past. For example, if output tax has been incorrectly charged to customers (eg on supplies subsequently found to be zero-rated), and this VAT has been added to the cost of the goods or services provided by the business (rather than VAT being absorbed as part of an inclusive price) then the correct procedure is for this VAT to be refunded to customers, not treated as a windfall for the business.

The main point about the topics above is that in many cases the principles are not clear-cut – for example, the judgment of one officer may forget a key point in his calculations; in the case of unjust enrichment, an officer rejecting a claim may not fully understand the way that a business fixes its selling prices.

The power of best judgment

The legislation

20.2 Before looking at some practical situations of best judgment, it may be useful to directly review the key legislation on this topic:

- *Failure to make returns*:

  'Where a person has failed to make any returns required under this Act or to keep any documents ... or where it appears to the Commissioners that such returns are incomplete or incorrect, they may assess the amount of VAT due from him to the best of their judgment and to notify it to him'. [*VAT Act 1994, s 73(1)*].

- *Evidence of supplying goods*:

  '... if he fails to prove that goods have been or are available to be supplied by him ... they may assess to the best of their judgment and notify to him the amount of VAT that would have been chargeable in respect of the supply of the goods if they had been supplied by him'. [*VAT Act 1994, s 73(7)*].

In reality, there are two main situations when an officer will use his powers to assess tax under best judgment:

- when records are incomplete or inadequate; or

- when records are fully complete, but the officer has reason to doubt the credibility of the figures.

See Examples 1 and 2.

Example 1

Bill has been trading for 1 year as a fish and chip shop and has never kept any record of his takings figures – he has also destroyed all purchase invoices and receipts. He has never submitted a VAT return, and only paid central assessments issued by HMRC, which he considers to be an accurate assessment of his VAT liability.

Bill receives a VAT visit, and the officer considers that the central assessments issued by HMRC are too low.

Solution – in this case, the officer will try to establish the correct amount of VAT he considers to be due by using his best judgment. His initial approach may be to look at the outgoings of the business to try and estimate the level of takings needed for the business to cover its costs. He will also look at profit margins and the money taken out of the business by Bill for his own needs. It is also likely that he will ask Bill to keep a record of his takings for a period of time to estimate total income since the business became VAT registered.

Overall, the officer will be interested in accurately assessing the output tax for the business – he is unlikely to give any significant credit for input tax because the main supplies will be zero-rated (food purchases) and also because Bill does not hold proper tax invoices to support an input tax claim.

Example 2

An officer of HMRC enters the premises of a fish and chip shop in the local High Street at 11.00 pm on a Friday night, just before the shop is due to close. He asks the manager on duty to cash up in front of him, which confirms takings of £1,200 for the night.

However, a routine VAT inspection carried out 6 months earlier noted that the best ever declared Friday night takings for the business was £800.

The officer is satisfied that he has evidence of underpaid output tax and, more importantly, incomplete VAT returns. He calculates average declared Friday night sales over a 12-month period (£650) and calculates a suppression of sales rate equal to 85% of declared sales (£1200 – £650 divided by £650 × 100). He applies this percentage to all declared sales made by the business during the last 3 years, and issues a very large assessment.

Solution – the officer is in a very strong position because he has clear evidence of incorrect accounting – the credibility of the taxpayer's takings records has been ruined. Has he exercised his powers honestly? The key point is that the officer has calculated the average Friday night takings figure for the last 12 months – it would not have been acceptable if he had calculated a suppression of sales rate by comparing the £1,200 figure to the lowest Friday night sales figure in the last 12 months! This would certainly have been rejected by a tribunal.

However, has he considered whether there are any reasons why the Friday night on which he entered the premises produced such a high takings figure? For example, is it a Bank Holiday weekend? Is there a local festival that would have generated extra business?

In reality, HMRC would have already researched such issues – its aim on entering the premises is to choose an average night that will not be distorted by events such as those mentioned above.

Approach adopted by HMRC officers

20.3   As explained above, officers of HMRC have extensive powers to raise best judgment assessments – and are not obliged to spend excessive amounts of time reconstructing records for every single VAT period over the last 3 years to arrive at an amount of tax due.

However, as with all aspects of VAT, the taxpayer has the right to appeal to an independent tribunal if he or she is not happy with the action taken by HMRC.

The key rules on best judgment assessments are as follows:

- HMRC must exercise its powers honestly and must have material before it on which to make its judgment;

- decisions reached must be based on factual information but the officer is under no obligation to carry out exhaustive investigations to calculate the tax he considers due;

- the officer must take into account all information presented to him – although he can obviously make a decision to ignore such information if he considers it is not relevant to his calculations;

- the role of the VAT tribunal is to act as supervisor – confirming the 'best judgment' test has been fairly applied by the officer – in other words, he has not acted in a dishonest or vindictive manner, or made unreasonable estimates when carrying out his calculations.

Decisions based on factual information

20.4   The assessment issued by the officer at Example 2 at **20.2** is based on two pieces of information – the physical cash takings after he entered the premises, and the record of daily takings declared by the business in the previous 12 months.

However, imagine if the officer had decided to add an extra 10% to the suppression rate on the basis that he felt that some of the business takings had found its way into the back pocket of the sole proprietor, ie never being entered into the till. A conclusion of this nature may be reasonable – but there is no factual information to support it, other than the gut instinct of the officer.

It is important that advisers reviewing a best judgment assessment ensure that HMRC has clearly acted on known facts and information, not on gut feelings or assumptions.

Taking account of all relevant information

20.5   The officer is obliged to take account of all information given to him although he can obviously ignore information that he considers to be irrelevant to his calculations – or where he considers the information given is inaccurate.

For example, let us assume that our fish and chip shop owner in Example 2 above suddenly reveals to the officer that for the last four Fridays, he has opened the shop for an extra 2 hours a night, eg opening hours are now 4.00 pm–11.00 pm instead of 6.00 pm–11.00 pm. At the time of the last VAT visit, the trading hours for the period in question had only been 6.00 pm–11.00 pm.

In reality, the approach of the officer will be to assess whether he is being told the truth with the statement being made. If he is satisfied on this point, he must take the information into account and readjust his figures.

Innocent until proven guilty

20.6   The key point with best judgment situations is that the onus is on HMRC to prove that an assessment is appropriate because the taxpayer has declared an incomplete return – not on the taxpayer to prove his innocence where the evidence against him is vague or incomplete – see Example 3.

Example 3

ABC Ltd trades as a confectioner, tobacconist and newsagent (CTN) in a busy High Street. The company has a routine VAT inspection and the inspector challenges the 20% gross profit margin being declared by the business. He says that he has carried out three other inspections on CTNs in the town, where the average declared gross profit margin was 28%. He tells the director of ABC Ltd that he intends to raise an assessment for the difference of 8%, going back 3 years.

Solution – in this situation, the officer has no evidence of incomplete returns being submitted by ABC Ltd – the fact that similar businesses have a higher gross profit margin is irrelevant (it could be that they are better managed or have a better location in the town).

In effect, the officer of HMRC will always need to have some tangible evidence to support his best judgment calculations – the key thinking he should adopt is: 'I have firm evidence that this trader has not declared all of his output tax – I must therefore use my best judgment powers under s 73 of the *VAT Act 1994* to realistically assess the extent of the underdeclared tax'.

Approach of tax advisers

20.7   What should be the approach of advisers when dealing with a best judgment assessment raised against a client?

- The adviser will need to obtain as much information about the client business as possible, enabling him to then make conclusions as to why the HMRC figures could be inaccurate. These factors will then need to be clearly explained in an appeal letter to the officer (local reconsideration always comes before an appeal to an independent tribunal), and the impact on the assessment needs to be established.

- Many best judgment assessments raised by VAT officers will subsequently find their way to colleagues in the direct tax part of the department. An assessment based on underdeclared takings for VAT purposes could therefore be further assessed for underdeclared Schedule D1 profits for self-assessment purposes. So there are large sums of money at stake.

- One of the questions the author is often asked by accountants is whether VAT officers deliberately make an initial best judgment assessment as high as possible, meaning that if the figures are challenged and subsequently reduced, they still end up with a good result. The answer to this question should be in the negative – officers have a duty to take all relevant information into account when raising their assessment and, in effect, should give the taxpayer the benefit of the doubt in cases where there are two sides to the argument. See Example 4.

Example 4

John and Mary Smith are partners in business, running the White Horse pub in a local village in Somerset. A VAT officer was concerned about the low gross-profit margin of the business, and carried out a mark-up exercise to calculate projected sales, based on brewery and cash and carry purchases. Projected sales are £60,000 more than declared sales over a 3-year period, so the officer raises an assessment for underdeclared output tax.

Solution – for a public house business, there are many situations where purchases made do not achieve the full selling price. For example, beer is lost through pipe cleaning, spillage and drawing off – bottled products may be broken, stolen or thrown away if they are past their sell-by date.

There are other occasions where discount could be given for, eg 'happy hour' promotions, staff discounts or own consumption for the partners. It is possible that the business may also sell bottled beer at a reduced price for take-away purposes.

John and Mary's advisers will need to review the above allowances to make sure the officer has taken them fully into account. Also, officer's projections are often based on purchases for a limited period, so unusual buying trends in this period should also be considered. Overall, there should be plenty of scope to review the content of the officer's assessment.

Unjust enrichment

Basic principle of unjust enrichment

20.8   The basic principle of unjust enrichment is that no taxable person should make a financial gain from making VAT errors. In effect, if any VAT rebate is paid by HMRC, the key question to ask is whether the rebate belongs to the taxpayer or to his customer that he has incorrectly charged VAT to in the first place. See Example 5.

Example 5

Smith Builders has just carried out some building work for a customer, and charged £5,000 plus £875 VAT. The customer pays £5,875 to settle his account. It is subsequently discovered that the work in question should have been zero-rated as it related to alterations to a Grade 2 listed building.

Smith reduces the Box 1 figure (output tax) by £875 on his next VAT return – and uses the £875 windfall to pay for a week's holiday in Spain.

Solution – the correct procedure is for Smith to issue a VAT-only credit note to his customer for £875 – as it is the customer not the business who has paid the incorrect VAT. Smith should then send the customer a cheque (or cash) for £875. He is then entitled to reduce his Box 1 figure by £875.

When unjust enrichment applies and factors to consider

20.9   The legislation for unjust enrichment is contained in the *VAT Act 1994, s 80(3)* and, as with most aspects of VAT, there can be grey areas as far as the application of the law is concerned.

The point to emphasise is that the onus is on HMRC to prove a case of unjust enrichment – not the other way round. In reality, this means it must prove that someone other than the business bore the cost of the incorrectly charged VAT.

In the case of Smith at Example 5, it is very easy to illustrate that it would be incorrect for him to pocket the £875 windfall – it is quite clearly his customer who has paid the initial VAT charge, so it is the customer who should financially gain from the zero-rating now established.

However, there are other cases where a taxpayer can benefit from the windfall – as long as he can prove that it was his business that bore the impact of the VAT rather than the customer – see Example 6.

Example 6

Mr Jones is a clothing retailer on the High Street, and has to price his goods extremely carefully because of competition from two similar shops in the next street.

His accountant has discovered that he has sold one item of clothing for the last 3 years that should have been zero-rated as children's clothing. Gross sales of the item are £30,000 per annum. What is the VAT position?

Solution – in this situation, Mr Jones can put forward a very strong case that he has priced the item in question to achieve sales in the market place – rather than on a cost plus basis where he has collated his costs, added a profit margin and then added VAT.

It would be very difficult for HMRC to prove a case of unjust enrichment – so a voluntary disclosure should be made to HMRC for a VAT rebate of £13,404 (ie £30,000 × 3 years × 7/47 – assuming a VAT rate of 17.5%).

Note – another relevant point in this example is that Jones is unlikely to issue tax invoices for the sales he has made. It is therefore unlikely that HMRC will be out of pocket through input tax being claimed by the customers buying the goods.

The examples considered so far have been very clear-cut as far as unjust enrichment is concerned, but in reality, there will be borderline cases where a full analysis of the facts will be needed. The following points are highlighted by HMRC.

- *Basis of pricing* – if the structure of a business is such that prices are mainly based on calculating costs and then adding a profit margin and then VAT, then it would be very difficult to convince an officer that an item is being costed on a VAT inclusive basis. For example, if a product was sold for £100 plus VAT in the UK, and then exported for £100 with no VAT added, then it would be virtually impossible to pocket the VAT if the item was found to be zero-rated.

- *Are customers generally VAT registered* – if a business sells mainly to other VAT registered businesses, able to recover input tax, then it will be virtually impossible to avoid an unjust enrichment situation. In reality, HMRC would be out of pocket if any overcharged output tax was kept by the taxpayer.

- *Decline in profits* – if a business that has recently become VAT registered can show that its profits have declined since it registered, then this adds to the argument that it has absorbed the VAT element, rather than added to its prices. An example of such a situation could be a mobile caterer, who needs to price his hot dogs at a certain price to achieve a sale irrespective of whether the price is VAT inclusive or exclusive.

• *Necessity of goods/addictiveness* – this is a tricky one. The basic argument is that if an item is needed by a customer for addictive reasons, eg cigarettes, then the demand for the goods is less sensitive to price. It is more likely that VAT has been added to the price rather than absorbed by the retailer.

Part refunds

20.10 It is possible to have a situation where HMRC accepts that part of a VAT charge has been 'passed on' to a customer and part of the VAT charge has been 'absorbed' within the taxpayer's pricing structure. In this situation, only the 'absorbed' VAT can be retained by the taxpayer.

Example – price charged by supplier to customer is £11.50 per unit – HMRC accepts that 30% of VAT has been absorbed within price (ie £11.50 x 7/47 x 30% = £0.51) but that the remainder of the VAT has been recharged and passed on to the customer. If the item in question is deemed to be zero-rated, the supplier will be entitled to a VAT rebate of £0.51 per unit sold from HMRC without unjust enrichment being a problem.

Note – for further details on part refunds, see HMRC's Internal Guidance V1–33 (VAT Series) entitled 'VAT Refunds – unjust enrichment – statutory interest – ex-gratia payments'.

Procedures for reimbursing customers

20.11 The worst case situation for a busy taxpayer is where he has missed out on his expected VAT windfall because of an unjust enrichment ruling, and then has to pay VAT back to his customers, giving him a lot of extra paperwork in the process.

HMRC has very tight procedures for ensuring that any VAT rebate it pays back is passed on to the correct person. In reality, HMRC will only repay any overpaid VAT if, on or before the time of making the claim, the claimant signs a written undertaking to confirm the following points:

• he is able to give the names and addresses of the customers he has reimbursed or intends to reimburse;

• the reimbursements will be paid to customers no later than 90 days after the repayment by HMRC;

• no deduction in the amount of VAT paid to customers will be made for either management or administration time;

• reimbursement will only be made by cash or cheque;

• any part of the relevant amount that is not reimbursed within the 90-day period will be paid back to HMRC;

- full records of the reimbursement will be kept, ie names, amounts etc; and

- details must be produced to a VAT officer if requested.

The aim of HMRC is very clear – to ensure a business is unable to prosper financially as a result of making VAT errors, hence the strict rules above.

Difference between an error and an adjustment

20.12 An important point to remember is that unjust enrichment (and voluntary disclosure) situations are only relevant to dealing with errors rather than dealing with normal accounting adjustments. For example, an adjustment of VAT for bad debt relief is not the correction of an error. Equally, the annual adjustment made each year for a business that is partly exempt is also an accounting adjustment rather than an error.

However, incorrectly charging output tax on a zero-rated supply is an error, as is charging output tax on a supply that should have been exempt from VAT.

Finally, note that unjust enrichment situations only apply where the taxpayer is making a financial gain from VAT errors he has made.

Planning points to consider

20.13 The following planning points should be given consideration.

- Always consider the credibility of a client's explanations regarding any best judgment assessment – how would the explanations appear in the eyes of an HMRC officer? And, more importantly, would they appear sensible reasons to an independent tribunal?

- For best judgment assessments based on outputs calculations, there are many reasons for discrepancies – advisers needs to explore issues such as stock losses, wastage, discounted sales, own consumption, theft, breakages, seasonal variations. In reality, any challenge to a Customs assessment needs to show proper evidence and realistic calculations.

- Always ensure that an officer's best judgment assessment is based on factual information and logical conclusions, not on assumptions, personal views or gut instinct.

- In cases where HMRC is claiming unjust enrichment exists, look very closely at the client's pricing structure, to see if he has actually absorbed the VAT within his price, rather than added VAT to his net costs and profit margin. It is easier to challenge an unjust enrichment ruling where sales are to the general public, rather than another VAT registered business.

- When a client has to repay overcharged VAT to customers, always ensure the correct procedures are followed. It is important that clients do not make an administration charge to customers for reimbursing VAT – this will be assessed as tax due by officers reviewing the calculations.

Chapter 21

Exempt Outputs

Key topics in this chapter:

- VAT implications for a business making exempt supplies.

- Example of how VAT exemption can improve the profits of a business.

- List of exempt supplies within the *VAT Act 1994, Sch 9*.

- Basic situations when supplies involving land are exempt or taxable.

- VAT exemptions available to non-profit making sports clubs, for example, on competition fees, membership subscriptions, fundraising events.

- Situations when a supply of goods is exempt from VAT.

Introduction

21.1 In general terms, a supply or source of income can be allocated to one of five different categories as far as VAT is concerned:

- standard-rated supply – ie VAT due at 15%, returning to 17.5% on 1 January 2010;

- reduced-rated supply – currently 5%;

- zero-rated supply – 0%. The zero-rate means that a business can still reclaim input tax on its expenses (subject to normal rules) but does not have to charge output tax;

- exempt supply – a business does not have to charge VAT on an exempt supply, but because it is not making taxable supplies, cannot register for VAT and recover input tax;

- outside the scope or non-business – e g for grant payments and donations.

In effect, a business that only makes exempt supplies does not need to register for VAT, irrespective of its level of turnover. The only exception to this statement is if it acquires goods from other EU countries and needs to register for VAT through the acquisition rules – see **11.11**.

Basic principles of exempt supplies

21.2   The goods or services that qualify as being exempt from VAT are listed under various group headings within the *VAT Act 1994, Sch 9*. See 21.3.

As explained above, a business that only makes exempt supplies is not a taxable person and cannot register for VAT. However, many large businesses that make exempt supplies also have some taxable supplies, and therefore have an obligation to register for VAT if the value of these taxable supplies exceeds the current VAT registration limits. See Example 1.

Example 1

ABC Ltd is a major insurance company with 70 offices across the UK. Its turnover from its insurance activity is £350m per year. In each office it has a vending machine for staff tea and coffee, and each vending machine has sales of £1,000 per year. What is its VAT position?

Solution – insurance income is exempt from VAT, so this activity does not create a need for the company to be VAT registered. However, the supply of catering is taxable (standard rated) and the total income from this activity is £70,000 (70 offices × £1,000 each), which exceeds the VAT registration threshold (£68,000 with effect from 1 May 2010). The company therefore needs to be registered for VAT.

Note that a business which makes some supplies that are exempt and some that are taxable is classed as being partly exempt. The issues affecting a partly exempt business (eg the amount of input tax that can be recovered) are explained in Chapters 24 and 25.

If a business only makes exempt supplies, this creates two outcomes as far as VAT is concerned:

●   no output tax is chargeable on any income received or supplies made. This can produce a competitive advantage to a business that deals with the general public or other exempt businesses because it is not making a tax charge that adds to the cost of the goods or services it provides;

●   the business does not have any opportunity to recover input tax because it is not making any taxable supplies – any costs it incurs within its business will therefore be based on the gross charge including VAT. See Example 2.

Example 2

DEF Ltd is a registered charity and is organising a fundraising dinner where the costs for meals, cabaret, venue hire etc are £20,000 plus VAT and income from ticket sales is £40,000.

JKL Ltd is a profit making company and is organising a similar event the following week, with the same income and expenditure amounts. JKL Ltd is not a registered charity or eligible body.

Solution – the income from the fundraising dinner organised by DEF Ltd is exempt from VAT under *Group 12* of *Sch 9*. The overall profit from the dinner will therefore be as follows:

Income	£40,000	(no output tax due on ticket sales – exempt supply)
Costs	£23,500	(ie gross amount because no input tax recoverable)
Profit	£16,500	

The event organised by JKL Ltd is taxable and will have a profit as follows:

Income	£34,043	(ie £40,000 less VAT of £5,957 based on a VAT rate of 17.5%)
Costs	£20,000	(ie net amount)
Profit	£14,043	

In effect, DEF Ltd has made extra profit of £2,457 – which is the difference between the output tax it has saved by making an exempt supply (£5,957) less £3,500 it has lost by not being able to recover input tax on its costs.

An important point to emphasise is that a business cannot charge VAT on exempt supplies to try and improve its input tax recovery position. It would not be acceptable to put forward the argument that because HMRC is gaining output tax on the supply, it should not worry about whether it should actually have been exempt.

An example of when a business may want to treat an exempt supply as standard rated is if a service is being performed for a business that is VAT registered and making wholly taxable supplies. The VAT charge would not be a problem for the customer, and then the supplier would try to recover the related input tax as being relevant to a taxable supply. However, this would be incorrect – an exempt supply cannot be made taxable by charging VAT on an invoice.

Exempt supplies within VAT Act 1994, Sch 9

21.3   There are 15 different group headings within *Sch 9*, as follows. The relevant HMRC public notice giving further analysis about each heading is shown in brackets, and the easiest way to view the notices is on the HMRC website at http://www.hmrc.gov.uk/thelibrary/vat.htm .

- *Group 1*: Land – see **21.4** (HMRC Notice 742);

- *Group 2*: Insurance (701/36/02);

- *Group 3*: Postal services (701/8/03);

- *Group 4*: Betting, gaming and lotteries (701/26/04, 701/27/02, 701/28/03);

- *Group 5*: Finance (701/49/06);

- *Group 6*: Education (701/30/02);

- *Group 7*: Health and welfare (701/2/07, 701/31/07,701/57/07);

- *Group 8*: Burial and cremation (701/32/06);

- *Group 9*: Subscriptions to trade unions, professional bodies and other public interest bodies (701/5/02);

- *Group 10*: Sport, sports competitions and physical education – see **21.5** (701/45/02);

- *Group 11*: Works of art (701/12/02);

- *Group 12*: Fundraising events by charities and other qualifying bodies – see **21.8**;

- *Group 13*: Cultural services etc – admissions to museums, exhibitions, zoos and performances of a cultural nature supplied by public bodies and eligible bodies (701/47/03);

- *Group 14*: Supplies of goods where input tax cannot be recovered – see **21.9**;

- *Group 15*: Investment gold (701/21/02).

The key VAT issues and some planning points on some of the more commonly used groups are now considered in more detail.

Land

21.4 The grant of any interest in, or right over, land and licence to occupy land is exempt under *Group 1* – subject to certain exceptions. This means, for example, that most rental arrangements are exempt from VAT, unless the option to tax election has been made. However, there are certain exceptions where a right over land situation is evident, but the supplies made are mostly taxable:

- the first grant of a major interest in a 'qualifying building', ie a dwelling or building intended for use for a relevant residential or charitable purpose; a dwelling converted from a non-residential building; a substantially reconstructed protected building – these supplies will be zero-rated for VAT purposes;

- the sale of the freehold interest in a new completed or uncompleted non-qualifying building or civil engineering work, eg sale of the freehold interest in a new warehouse – these supplies will be standard-rated for the first 3 years after the building has been completed;

- certain supplies that form part of the transfer of a going concern – these supplies will be outside the scope of VAT if they meet the relevant rules;

- gaming and fishing rights;

- hotel/holiday accommodation and similar establishments. This includes furnished flats and houses that are used by or advertised as suitable for use by visitors or travellers, even if provided with board or facilities for preparing food;

- caravan and tent pitches and camping facilities;

- parking facilities;

- timber rights;

- storage, mooring of aircraft, ships etc;

- boxes, seats or other accommodation at a sports ground, theatre, concert hall or other place of entertainment are standard rated;

- sports facilities, in most cases. There is an exception if the facility is hired for exclusive use as a series of at least ten lets for the same activity, at the same place, with intervals of not more than 14 days – and the hirer is a club, school or association (ie not a private individual).

In certain situations, there can be practical problems in deciding whether a supply is a right over land situation, ie exempt from VAT or standard rated as a supply of services. It needs to be carefully considered what benefits the tenant is receiving from the landlord and whether this is a clear right over land arrangement. See Example 3.

Example 3

John owns a hairdressing salon and is VAT registered. He decides to rent out some of his chairs to self-employed hair stylists to generate extra income. The stylists will benefit from the use of clean towels in the salon, equipment such as hairdryers and curling tongs and the services of a receptionist who will make bookings and collect money from customers. John decides the income is exempt from VAT under *Group 1* as a right over land arrangement.

Solution – the reality of the supply is that John is giving the self-employed stylists a package of benefits, and this is not just a simple right over land or license to occupy land situation. HMRC (and almost certainly a VAT tribunal) would rule that the main supply is the package of benefits beings enjoyed by the stylists such as the equipment and towels, and that the rental of the chair is incidental to this main supply. The income would therefore be deemed to be standard rated.

Note – the positive point for John is that because the income is taxable, this means that he will be able to recover any relevant input tax on costs associated with the salon. This will hopefully avoid the need for him to become involved in the complicated issue of partial exemption.

Sport, sports competitions and physical education – fundraising events

21.5   Many accountants and tax advisers find themselves involved with sports clubs, either on a client basis or through a voluntary arrangement by being treasurer of, for example, the local golf club. This section will therefore focus on some important planning points to consider which may benefit such clubs as far as exempt supplies are made.

Entry fees for competitions

21.6   An entry fee for the right to enter a competition is normally standard rated. However, there are circumstances where the income can be classed as exempt if the following conditions are met:

- the 'competition' must be in 'sport or physical recreation';

- it must be organised by an 'eligible body' established for the purposes of sport or physical recreation;

- the entry fee must be wholly allocated towards prizes or prizes awarded in that competition.

HMRC gives a very clear definition as to what it considers to be a competition: 'a structured and organised contest, tournament or race where prizes or titles are awarded'.

As far as the definition of sport or physical recreation is concerned, HMRC accepts any activity recognised as a sporting activity by Sport England. The obvious sports include football, cricket, golf and tennis, but less obvious ones include angling and dancing (chess, card games and dominoes are excluded).

Finally, an eligible body means a non-profit making body which cannot distribute any profit it makes otherwise than to another non-profit making body or its own members on winding up or dissolution.

Example 4 demonstrates how a competition organised by a golf club can qualify for VAT exemption on its entry fees.

Example 4

Big Town Golf Club is a non-profit making body organising its annual handicap competition for 150 players at an entry fee of £30 each. The gross receipts of £4,500 are used to purchase trophies at £35 each for the top ten players, and then a large cup for the winner worth £500. The winner also receives a cheque for £2,500 and the runner-up receives a cheque for £1,150.

Solution – the income from this event is exempt becomes all of the entry fees have been allocated to prizes and trophies.

Membership subscriptions and playing facilities

21.7 VAT exemption applies to the supply of services closely linked with, and essential to, sport or physical recreation supplied to individuals who are taking part in the activity where the supplies are being made by an eligible body. However, exemption only applies to a membership body providing facilities to its qualifying members or a non-membership body, such as a charity, to individuals.

Note – there is a view (not accepted by HMRC and therefore likely to be subject to a lengthy appeal process) that all supplies of sport made by an eligible body are exempt from VAT under EU law, ie including those facilities enjoyed by non-members such as green fee income in the case of a golf club. This opinion is based on the outcome of the ECJ case *Canterbury Hockey Club v Revenue and Customs Comrs: C-253/07* [2008] STC 3351. Readers with a potential interest in this subject should closely monitor the progress of the appeal process and any HMRC announcements in the coming months.

HMRC has produced a list of activities that qualify for exemption in Notice 701/45 – the key condition is that the activity must comprise some element of physical activity intended to improve physical fitness. A few unusual examples that are included are: octopush, tang soo do, kabaddi and unihoc. Interestingly, snooker, billiards and motor sports are also included as designed to improve physical activity.

The following sources of income are exempt from VAT if supplied by an eligible body as being closely linked to playing sport:

- membership subscriptions and joining fees covering active participation in sport;

- use of changing rooms, showers and playing equipment;

- court hire costs, pitch or green fees;

- refereeing, umpiring, judging services;

- coaching, training, physical education services.

See Example 5 to consider the VAT liability of some of the main sources of income for a members' club.

Example 5

Big Town Golf Club has 300 playing members paying an annual subscription of £2,000 and social members who enjoy the bar and catering facilities paying £50 a year. In addition, the club has three other sources of income:

- it allows non-members to play a round of golf for £35;

- it charges members £5 a week for the use of a locker in the club changing rooms;

- it produces a quarterly magazine charging £5 a copy.

Solution – the VAT liability needs to be considered in each case. The playing subscription is exempt from VAT, however, the social membership is standard rated because the use of the bar is not closely linked to sport. The fee charged to non-members for playing a round of golf is currently standard rated because it is not supplied to members (but see the note above regarding a potential challenge to this conclusion). The locker facility for members qualifies for exemption because it is linked to the participation in sport. Finally, the magazine is zero-rated as reading matter (*VAT Act 1994, Sch 8, Group 3*).

Fundraising events

21.8 Since 1 April 2000, the supply of goods or services in connection with an event where the primary purpose is to raise money and which is promoted as such is exempt from VAT when organised by an eligible body. The key point is that HMRC needs to be convinced that the aim of the function is to raise money. This can be proved by minutes of meetings, costings and publicity material. An eligible body for this section of the law also includes charities and their trading subsidiaries.

The scope for exemption is very wide, and includes income received from admission charges, the sale of advertising space in brochures and items sold at the event, eg auctioned goods. Examples of events that could qualify for exemption include dinner dances, discotheques, concerts, fêtes, dinners and lunches – see Example 6.

A few rules exist that limit the scope of exemption, for example, there is a maximum number of events of the same kind that can be held at the same location (ie 15 maximum in a financial year).

Similar kinds of events held in different locations qualify for exemption provided all the other conditions are met, for example, 30 dinners held by a national charity in different towns in the same financial year would all qualify for exemption.

Example 6

Big Town Golf Club needs to raise £5,000 to purchase a new tractor to improve the grass cutting on the greens. The committee decides to organise a dinner for 250 people with a top quality guest speaker talking about an entertaining topic. A profit of £20 will be made on each ticket to produce the £5,000 needed for the new machine.

Solution – the event is clearly being organised for a fundraising purpose by an eligible body, and the income from the ticket sales will be VAT exempt.

Supplies of goods where input tax cannot be recovered

21.9   A supply of goods is an exempt supply where the following conditions are all met:

- the person making the supply incurred input tax on the item in question; and

- all of the input tax incurred on the item was not reclaimed because it was classed as 'non-deductible input tax'.

Non-deductible input tax comprises three main categories:

(a) input tax used on goods to make exempt supplies;

(b) input tax which is wholly excluded from credit under the provisions relating to non-deductible items such as business entertainment, motor cars and non-building materials incorporated in a building or its site;

(c) VAT incurred by the person concerned when he was not a taxable person (ie when he was not registered or liable to be registered).

See Example 7 for an illustration of how this principle works in a practical situation.

Example 7

ABC Ltd supplies computer software and is registered for VAT. In March 2008, the company bought a brand new car for the sales director and did not reclaim input tax of £3,500 on the purchase because the car is not wholly used for business purposes and is also available for private use. The car was used by the director for only 12 months and then sold by the company for £10,000 in March 2009.

DEF Ltd is an insurance broker making exempt supplies, and purchased two computers in March 2008 for £50,000 each. They were used by the company for 18 months until September 2009, but now need to be upgraded. The company has been offered £35,000 for each of the computers. The directors are concerned that these sales may be taxable and will take the company above the VAT registration limits and the company may need to register for VAT.

Solution – the money received from the sale of the car in the first situation is exempt from VAT because no input tax was claimed on the original purchase of the car. The sale of the computers in the second situation is also exempt from VAT because there was no input tax claim on the original purchase because the expenditure was wholly relevant to an exempt supply.

General comments about other categories

21.10   The group headings covered at **21.4–21.9** mainly focused on areas where businesses are likely to have some VAT issues to consider, ie there are 'grey' areas as to whether income in many cases is exempt or taxable.

For many of the other categories, a relevant business is likely to have income which is wholly exempt income and the business is therefore unlikely to be registered for VAT, eg insurance broker, private school or children's nursery. In such cases, VAT is not a concern, unless the business diversifies its activities to include supplies that are taxable, eg vending machine sales as in Example 1 at **21.2**.

Planning points to consider

21.11   The following planning points should be given consideration.

- It is an advantage for supplies to either the general public or other exempt businesses to be exempt from VAT because there is no tax charge to customers that they cannot recover. In most cases, this situation will outweigh the disadvantages of the input tax relevant to the supply not being reclaimable.

- There are occasions when a standard rated supply being incorrectly treated as exempt could prove costly for a business. For example, a VAT charge to another registered business would not be a problem if the business could reclaim the charge as input tax. The supplier can then recover related input tax on its own expenses because it has made a taxable supply.

- For supplies involving land, it is important that the benefits being received by the tenant from the landlord are closely analysed to confirm the liability for VAT purposes.

- Output tax is not payable on the supply of goods where the original input tax was not reclaimed because it was either non-deductible or relevant to an exempt supply.

- For non-profit making sports clubs, it is important that HMRC rules are closely followed if a source of income is to qualify as exempt from VAT. For example, there are strict conditions concerning exemption for membership subscription income, entry fees and fundraising events.

Chapter 22

Zero-rated and Reduced-rated Outputs

Key topics in this chapter:

- Goods or services that qualify for zero-rating within *VAT Act 1994, Sch 8.*

- Situations when zero-rating applies on supplies of food and printed matter.

- The importance of accounting for VAT correctly if a business makes both standard and zero-rated sales.

- The impact of the flat rate scheme, cash accounting scheme and annual accounting scheme for a business that wholly, or mainly, sells zero-rated items.

- Potential benefits of a business making zero-rated supplies registering for VAT on a voluntary basis.

- Procedures to adopt if VAT is incorrectly charged on a zero-rated item (unjust enrichment).

- The aim of the 5% rate of VAT and supplies within *VAT Act 1994, Sch 7A.*

- The opportunity for a business that wholly or mainly makes zero-rated sales to avoid registering for VAT.

Introduction

22.1 If a supply is zero-rated, then tax is still chargeable – but at 0%. Therefore, a zero-rated supply is still a taxable supply, and input tax is reclaimable on costs related to the supply. This means that a business wholly making zero-rated supplies will have no output tax to pay on its VAT returns – but will be able to recover input tax on costs and overheads it incurs in the business.

If a business is in a repayment situation on a regular basis, it has the option to submit monthly rather than quarterly returns. Although this requires extra administration time (twelve VAT returns to complete each year instead of four), there is a cash flow advantage in receiving money from HMRC on a monthly basis.

Another key point to remember is that even if a business only makes zero-rated supplies, it must still register for VAT if the value of these supplies exceeds the registration limits. However, in many cases, a business making zero-rated supplies will want to register for VAT on a voluntary basis in order to benefit from input tax recovery on its costs and overheads.

Supplies that are zero-rated

22.2   There are 16 different groups of zero-rated supplies, specified in the *VAT Act 1994, Sch 8*. The groups are listed below. For advisers who have specific queries regarding any of the categories, the relevant HMRC public notice reference is shown in brackets against each group heading. The easiest way to view the notices is on the HMRC website at http://www.hmrc.gov.uk/thelibrary/vat.htm .

- *Group 1*: Food – see **22.3** (HMRC Notices 701/14/02; 701/15/05);

- *Group 2*: Water and sewerage services (701/16/02);

- *Group 3*: Books and printed matter – see **22.4** (701/10/03);

- *Group 4*: Talking books for the blind and handicapped and wireless sets for the blind;

- *Group 5*: Construction of buildings – see Chapters 26–28 (708);

- *Group 6*: Protected buildings – see Chapter 26 (708);

- *Group 7*: International services – see Chapters 13 and 14 (744D);

- *Group 8*: Transport (744A);

- *Group 9*: Caravans and houseboats (701/20/04);

- *Group 10*: Gold and precious metals (701/21/02);

- *Group 11*: Bank notes;

- *Group 12*: Dispensing of drugs, reliefs for people with disabilities (701/7/02; 701/59/02);

- *Group 13*: Imports, exports etc – see Chapters 11 and 12 (702; 703; 704);

- *Group 14*: Withdrawn on 1 July 1999;

- *Group 15*: Charities – see Chapter 35 (701/1/04);

- *Group 16*: Clothing and footwear (714).

The most commonly used categories within the above list are covered in detail in other chapters of this book. This chapter therefore focuses on two other categories that may be quite common for an adviser, namely food and books (printed matter). Both of these categories are useful to be aware of because many businesses spend money on food, for example, for business entertaining and subsistence and on printed matter, eg printing of business cards, letterheading and annual reports etc. It is therefore useful to be aware of the key rules to assist with claims for input tax recovery.

Food

22.3   A basic principle of VAT is that food is zero-rated if it is of a kind used for human consumption – however, there are a number of exceptions to this ruling, which is why there can sometimes be complications. The main exceptions are:

- any supply of food for consumption on the premises where it is supplied is always standard rated;

- any supply of hot food for consumption off those premises is also standard rated.

The two exceptions above are classed as supplies of 'catering' rather than food, hence the reason they are standard rated. The other main exceptions to the rule about zero-rating apply to specific products which are always standard rated, the main ones are as follows:

- ice cream and similar products;

- confectionery, eg chocolate, sweets, certain biscuits;

- alcoholic drinks, including beer, wine, cider, spirits and liqueurs;

- beverages such as fruit drinks, lemonade, cola and bottled waters;

- crisps, roasted and salted nuts.

However, the main everyday food items are almost invariably zero-rated, including raw meat, fish, vegetables, fruit, cereals, cakes (but not some biscuits), tea, coffee and milk.

From a practical aspect, there are two main challenges facing a business that sells food items as far as VAT is concerned:

(a)   identifying the correct liability of the product being sold;

(b)   where goods are sold at both standard and zero-rates of VAT, it is important that there is an accurate method of recording the split – a two button till is the most common method.

See Example 1.

Example 1

ABC Ltd trades as a bakery shop. It sells sandwiches for take-away purposes (zero-rated) and also has a seated area in the shop which serves tea, coffee and light meals (standard rated). What is the best way of recording the amount of output tax payable by the company?

Solution – one possible option could be to have separate tills for the two activities – this would also be useful from an internal management aspect because it would then be easy to identify the level of sales being achieved by each part of the business. All sales from the café area would be standard rated, and all take-away sales by the bakery would be zero-rated. However, this situation assumes that all take away sales are for cold food – any hot food supplied would be standard rated as well.

When visiting a business as in Example 1, HMRC officers will look carefully at the overall split between standard rated and zero-rated sales. Their main concern will be to ensure that a business is not trying to gain an unfair advantage by overstating its zero-rated sales. It is therefore important that taxpayers have strong accounting controls in place to minimise the risk of error.

With regard to identifying the correct liability of goods, it is important to remember that there are a number of food items that are standard rated, even though they would appear to be classed as an everyday food item. Since VAT was introduced in 1973, the interpretation of zero-rating for food has been challenged at many tribunals, and this has led to some interesting decisions. For example, a biscuit is generally zero-rated – but a biscuit wholly or partly covered with chocolate or some product similar in taste and appearance is standard rated.

Books and reading matter

22.4   With regard to printed matter, the following main supplies are zero-rated:

- books and booklets;

- brochures and pamphlets;

- leaflets;

- newspapers;

- journals and periodicals;

- children's picture books, music and maps.

The legislation does not specifically define any of the above items – but the words are to be given their everyday meaning. This means, for example, that goods containing text in other formats, eg audio or video cassettes or CD-Rom are standard rated because they cannot be deemed to be a book. For example, the supply of text by electronic means (eg via the Internet) is standard rated because the supply is for a service rather than goods. In the case of the supply of services, different rules apply.

The main situation where an adviser will need to look closely at whether a printer has applied the correct rate of VAT is if his client is either a business making exempt supplies or a business that is not registered for VAT. In both cases, an incorrect VAT charge will cause an adverse impact on the bottom line profits of the company – see Example 2.

Example 2

DEF Ltd trades as an estate agent, making 30% taxable supplies (sale of houses on a commission basis) and 70% exempt sales (fees from selling mortgages). The company has produced a new colour brochure advertising all of its services and has paid Smith Printers an amount of £7,000 plus VAT for producing 1,000 copies of the brochure.

Solution – the brochure produced by Smith Printers is zero-rated for VAT – therefore, no VAT should have been charged on the supply to DEF Ltd. As the latter company is partly exempt, it would only be able to reclaim 30% of the VAT charged as input tax (based on the standard method of partial exemption) and therefore have lost 70% of the VAT, ie £857.50.

Note – it is common practice for many suppliers to play safe and charge VAT where they are unsure about the correct liability. This principle does not produce a problem for a business that is VAT registered and able to recover input tax, but it impacts heavily on exempt, partly exempt or unregistered businesses.

Many items produced by printers are standard rated, mainly relevant to supplies that are not classed as reading matter. For example, business cards, compliment slips, letter headings, invoices and calendars are all standard-rated items and commonly purchased by most businesses. In such cases, input tax can be claimed on these items subject to the normal rules.

One of the more difficult issues involving supplies of goods is where there are two different supplies within a package, the two items attracting VAT at different rates, eg supply of zero-rated magazine with a standard-rated CD. A full analysis of the approach to adopt with mixed supply situations is given in Chapter 23.

Zero-rated supplies and schemes for small businesses

Flat rate scheme

22.5 The flat rate scheme is available for use by a small business with taxable turnover of £150,000 per year or less (VAT exclusive). The basic aim of the scheme is that a business does not reclaim input tax on its costs, but just applies a flat-rate percentage calculation to its VAT inclusive sales, and this is the amount of VAT that will be paid each quarter. The flat rate percentage depends on the trade category of the business (see Chapter 8 for further details).

For a business that wholly makes zero-rated supplies, there will be no benefit in using the flat rate scheme. This is because there is no flat rate that has a 0% rate – and even if there was a 0% rate, this would be a negative result anyway because the business would not get any input tax recovery.

However, where the flat rate scheme may prove a winner is where a business sells a mixture of standard and zero-rated items, and the trade category percentage to be applied within the flat rate scheme produces a good result. See Example 3.

Example 3

Jenny Smith trades as a confectioner, tobacconist and newsagent. The location of her shop means that the majority of her sales are confectionery items (standard rated), closely followed by cigarettes (standard rated), and finally, newspapers (zero-rated). Her taxable turnover is £145,000 per year excluding VAT and she is considering whether it would be worthwhile using the flat rate scheme.

Solution – the flat rate percentage for a business of this nature is 2%. This may be a very favourable rate for Jenny because the mark-up on confectionery (her main selling item) is higher than cigarettes, and therefore the normal method of accounting may produce a higher tax bill than the flat rate scheme.

However, if the nature of Jenny's business meant that the majority of her sales were zero-rated newspapers, then the flat rate scheme would probably not be worthwhile for her to use.

Cash accounting scheme

22.6 The cash accounting scheme is available to any business with taxable supplies of £1,350,000 per year or less (excluding VAT), and has the main advantage of basing VAT calculations (output tax and input tax) on cash book accounting rather than day book accounting. In effect, this means that output tax is not due on a sales invoice until payment has been received from the customer (instead of the earlier date of the invoice under normal VAT accounting). However, input tax cannot be reclaimed on a supply until payment has been made to a supplier (see Chapter 6 for a full analysis of the cash accounting scheme).

For a business that wholly or mainly makes zero-rated supplies, the cash accounting scheme is unlikely to be a winner. This is because the delay in accounting for output tax does not give the business a big cash flow advantage, but it would lose out by not being able to reclaim input tax until the date of payment.

Annual accounting scheme

22.7   The annual accounting scheme has a number of features, the main one being that only one VAT return per year is submitted instead of four, and that payments on account are made throughout the year to pay tax to HMRC based on the previous year's returns (see Chapter 7).

For a business that makes wholly or mainly zero-rated sales, there will be no payments on account (on the basis that the business will almost certainly be a repayment trader) but the problem will be that the business will not benefit from any VAT repayment until the annual return has been submitted. This causes a lengthy cash flow delay, so the annual accounting scheme is not worthwhile, unless the business owner is particularly keen to benefit from the advantage of only submitting one VAT return each year.

Voluntary registration

22.8   As explained at **22.1**, a business making wholly (or mainly) zero-rated sales may benefit from registering for VAT on a voluntary basis. Voluntary registration is available to a business that makes taxable supplies below the compulsory VAT registration limits (the compulsory limit increased to £68,000 with effect from 1 May 2009).

The advantages of registering for VAT on a voluntary basis are as follows:

- the business will not suffer a competitive disadvantage on its sales because no output tax will be charged if supplies are zero-rated;

- the business will be able to reclaim input tax on costs and overheads, which will produce a reduction in its total expenditure and therefore an improvement in its overall net profit.

Registration for VAT on a voluntary basis will be particularly worthwhile for a business that has standard-rated purchases and zero-rated sales – see Example 4.

Example 4

Ruth makes children's clothes and sells them to members of the public on the Internet. Her annual sales are £50,000 and her biggest cost is the purchase of material – a total of £25,000 per year plus VAT. She has learned that she may be able to register for VAT on a voluntary basis and that it could be in her interests to do so. What is the position?

Solution – Ruth is entitled to register on a voluntary basis because she is making taxable supplies. Her sales will be zero-rated as children's clothing (*VAT Act 1994, Sch 8, Group 16*) but she will be able to reclaim input tax of £4,375 on the purchase of material. Her net profit will therefore increase by £4,375 as a result of being VAT registered (and there may be other costs on which input tax could be claimed, eg accountancy fees, motor costs, machine repair costs, etc).

Avoiding VAT registration

22.9   A business that makes zero-rated sales is normally very pleased to be registered for VAT because the returns it submits usually produce a repayment from HMRC (input tax exceeding output tax).

However, in a limited number of cases, the administrative cost of being VAT registered could outweigh the benefits of these repayments. In this situation, it may be worthwhile for the business to either deregister or seek permission from HMRC to avoid being VAT registered in the first place (eg if taxable sales have exceeded the registration limit for the first time, creating a need to register). HMRC needs to be convinced that the business will always be in a net repayment position as far as VAT returns are concerned.

See **1.10** for further details on this opportunity, including a worked example of one particular business that could benefit from this concession.

Incorrectly charging VAT on a zero-rated supply

22.10   There may be occasions when a business has charged VAT on goods or services supplied to a customer, and then belatedly discovered that the item in question should have been zero-rated. This situation can be particularly common for some of the more complex groups. For example, the liability of children's clothing (*Group 16*) is based on garment measurements and how items are held out for sale, and *Group 1* (food) can also include some interesting rulings on products that may qualify for zero-rating.

A taxpayer who discovers he has incorrectly charged VAT on a zero-rated item should bear the following points in mind.

●   It needs to be considered who has paid the incorrect VAT that has been charged. In many cases, this will be the customer, namely when VAT has been added to a cost price. The rule of 'unjust enrichment' states that no taxpayer can make a financial gain from making a VAT error – the correct procedure in most cases will be to refund the incorrectly charged VAT to customers who have paid the tax. The procedures for unjust enrichment are considered in depth in Chapter 20.

• Note that any adjustment for overcharged VAT can only be made by going back 3 years (rising to 4 years with effect from 1 April 2010) – any tax beyond this period is out of date.

Reduced-rated supplies subject to 5% VAT

22.11 A development in the VAT world over the last ten years has been the extended use of the reduced rate of VAT. It seems that a moderate extension of the 5% rate has become a feature of many budgets and pre-budget reports.

The attraction of the 5% VAT rate is that it ensures the Treasury collects some tax on relevant supplies (as opposed to the complete loss of tax evident with zero-rating) – but obviously produces a healthy saving for the taxpayer compared to 17.5%.

A list of items subject to 5% VAT is contained in *VAT Act 1994, Sch 7A* (*Groups 1–11*) – the groups are shown below, along with the relevant HMRC Notices that give more detail on each category:

Group 1	Supplies of domestic fuel or power (HMRC Notice 701/19/02)
Group 2	Installation of energy saving materials (708/6/06)
Group 3	Grant-funded installation of heating equipment or security goods or connection of gas supply (708/6/06)
Group 4	Women's sanitary products (701/18/02)
Group 5	Children's car seats (701/23/02)
Group 6	Residential conversions (708)
Group 7	Residential renovations and alterations (708)
Group 8	Contraceptive products (Business Brief 7/706)
Group 9	Welfare advice or information (701/2/07)
Group 10	Installation of mobility aids for the elderly (HMRC Business Brief 47/07)
Group 11	Smoking cessation products – see **22.12**

Note – the most common supplies that advisers will encounter on a regular basis are probably relevant to building works (construction services). See **26.10** for further detail about services that can benefit from the 5% rate of VAT.

Smoking cessation products

22.12   It was initially announced in the 2007 Budget that the reduced rate of VAT would apply to smoking cessation products sold over the counter for the 12-month period from 1 July 2007 – but the 2008 Budget announced that the measure would apply on an indefinite basis.

The 5% rate applies to supplies of pharmaceutical products designed to help people to stop smoking tobacco. However, smoking cessation products dispensed by a pharmacist on prescription by a medical practitioner are zero-rated and unaffected by the 5% rules. The 5% rate applies to all other supplies of smoking cessation products by retailers including supplies made over the internet. Examples of products included are:

- patches (e g nicotine patches);

- inhalators;

- gums.

However, the rate applies to any product where the primary purpose is to help people in their efforts to stop smoking.

Planning points to consider

22.13   The following planning points should be given consideration.

- A business making wholly or mainly zero-rated supplies will almost certainly benefit from registering for VAT on a voluntary basis if its taxable turnover is less than the compulsory registration limits.

- If a business makes both standard-rated and zero-rated sales, it is imperative that systems and procedures are in place to correctly record the correct amount of output tax to charge.

- VAT incorrectly charged to a business on a zero-rated item will produce reduced profits for the business if it makes some exempt supplies or if it is not VAT registered. A review of possible items of expenditure where a supplier has incorrectly charged VAT (e g in relation to printed matter) could be worthwhile.

- It is unlikely that a business making zero-rated sales will benefit from using the cash accounting scheme or annual accounting scheme. However, there may be occasions when the flat rate scheme could be worthwhile if the percentage of zero-rated sales for a business is quite low.

- If VAT has been incorrectly charged on a zero-rated supply, then the issue of unjust enrichment needs to be fully considered before trying to obtain a VAT windfall from HMRC. No business is able to make a financial gain from making VAT errors.

- There is scope for a business that makes wholly or mainly zero-rated sales (net repayment situation) to avoid being VAT registered or to deregister if it feels this approach is worthwhile.

- The 5% rate of VAT has been extended in recent years. It is important that advisers are aware (in principle if not in detail) of possible situations when the 5% rate may apply to goods or services supplied to or by clients. This is particularly important if the person receiving the supply is unable to reclaim input tax, as more tax will obviously be paid if VAT is incorrectly charged at 17.5%.

Chapter 23

Mixed Supplies at Different Rates of VAT

Key topics in this chapter:

- The rules to consider when determining whether a single or multiple supply situation exists for VAT – and guidelines given by the European Court on this issue.

- Examples of single and multiple supply situations.

- Examples of case law to highlight the principles of single and mixed supply situations, including the recent case of *Revenue and Customs Comrs v Weight Watchers (UK) Ltd.*

- Methods of apportioning income in mixed supply situations using one of two methods approved by HMRC (cost based or revenue-based calculations).

- The HMRC approach to apportionment situations – ensuring the taxpayer's calculations give a fair and reasonable result.

Introduction

23.1   One of the more controversial subjects involving VAT in the last ten years has been the interpretation of the rules when a business sells two or more different items within one supply, and these individual items attract different rates of VAT. In such situations, the suggested approach is as follows:

- it needs to be identified whether each of the supplies constitutes an aim in its own right – if so, there is more than one supply;

- if one of the supplies is classed as being insignificant or incidental to the main supply, then it can be ignored for VAT purposes – the liability will then be determined by the rate of tax applicable to the main supply (or supplies).

In this chapter, we will consider the best approach to adopt as far as dealing with mixed supplies is concerned, looking at some useful examples where tribunals have had the difficult job of mediating in cases which are less obvious to determine.

Key principles of mixed supply situations

23.2 The case involving *Card Protection Plan Ltd v Customs and Excise Comrs* [1999] 2 AC 601, [1999] ECR I-973, [1999] 3 WLR 203, [1999] STC 270 (C-349/96) found its way to the European Courts in 1999, and is regarded as the landmark ruling in this subject, because the court gave clear guidance on whether a transaction was a single or mixed supply. HMRC considers that the tests laid down in this case will be appropriate in the majority of situations.

The following rules emerged from the *Card Protection Plan* decision. However, the background to the case and the verdict that was reached is not really of importance, it is the guidance given by the court following this decision that has been the basis for most mixed supply issues in the last ten years.

- Where a transaction comprises a bundle of features, the question to ask is whether each supply constitutes an aim in itself, or whether there is one main supply, with the other supplies being incidental to the main supply.

- It needs to be considered whether the aim of the secondary supply (or supplies) is to enhance the enjoyment of the main supply. For example, a customer could pay to hire a box at a football club for a big match (standard-rated supply) and then receive a match day programme as part of the facility (zero-rated). The match day programme is not an aim in itself, but a way of helping the customer to enhance his enjoyment of the main supply, which is the game itself.

- If there is only one main supply, then this will determine the VAT liability of the entire charge to the customer. So if the main supply is zero-rated, the entire charge to the customer will also be zero-rated – if the main supply is standard rated, then VAT will be due on the whole payment.

- The perception of the customer should also be taken into account about what he expects to receive when he makes payment for goods or services. This conclusion was very important in the recent case of *Revenue and Customs Comrs v Weight Watchers (UK) Ltd* [2008] EWCA Civ 715, [2008] STC 2313, heard by the Court of Appeal – see **23.10**. For example, in the previous situation, if the match day programme was not provided, then this would not have created a situation where he would have complained to the club about not receiving something he has paid for. In effect, he is paying for the box to watch the game, ie this is clearly the main supply.

To illustrate the points above, consider Examples 1 and 2.

Example 1

John takes a flight from London to Edinburgh (supply of zero-rated air travel). During the journey, he receives a cup of tea and a biscuit (supply of standard rated catering). Does the money paid by John for his ticket need to be apportioned so that output tax is paid on the value of the tea and biscuit – the balance being zero-rated as air travel?

Solution – in this case, the purpose of John's expenditure is to benefit from the air travel. The cup of tea and biscuit serves no other purpose than to make the flying experience more comfortable for him, ie it is incidental to the main supply. The whole of the payment made by John will be zero-rated as far as VAT is concerned.

Again, would John have cancelled his flight to Edinburgh if the tea and biscuit had not been available? Would the absence of the tea and biscuit cause him to write a strong letter of complaint to the air company and request part of his money back? The answer is almost certainly 'no'.

Example 2

John and Jean have booked a day trip on the Orient Express. As well as the comfortable rail journey, their trip also includes a sumptuous five-course meal with wine and champagne. The rail journey is zero-rated for VAT – catering supplies are standard rated. Is there a single or multiple supply situation in this example?

Solution – imagine the likely response of John and Jean if they boarded the train and were suddenly told that the five-course meal was not available and they were only going to benefit from the train journey. They would almost certainly complain to the rail company and demand a refund of part of their fee. In other words, they expect to receive two very distinct benefits – the rail journey and the meal.

The five-course meal is an aim in itself, and cannot be dismissed as incidental to the rail travel. The rail company must account for output tax on the value of the catering supply – the rail travel can be zero-rated. See 23.14–23.18 for methods of apportioning output tax.

In this situation, the customer has paid for two very clear benefits – and would feel short-changed if the meal and champagne were suddenly unavailable. In this situation, there needs to be an apportionment of the supply between standard rated catering and zero-rated rail travel.

The key point to remember about mixed supply situations is that they only become a problem if the goods or services within the supply attract different rates of VAT. See Example 3.

Example 3

Steve has decided to go and watch a football match at the ground of Hale Town. Hale Town is VAT registered and charges Steve £10 for admission and, as a special offer just for today's match, his admission fee includes two hamburgers and a portion of chips.

Solution – in this situation, the supplies involved (admission fee to watch a football match and supply of catering when inside the ground) are both standard rated. No VAT problem here – output tax of £1.49 is due on the full price (£10 × 7/47 – assuming a VAT rate of 17.5%).

Tribunal decisions in borderline cases

23.3 The examples given above were clear as far as the mixed supply situation is concerned. However, there have been many tribunal cases on this subject over the years and a few have been included in this section to give readers an indication of the approach to adopt when reviewing similar situations.

Multiple supply decisions

Medical Aviation Services Ltd

23.4 In the case of *Medical Aviation Services Ltd v Customs and Excise Comrs* (30 September 1997, unreported) (LON/97/016 15308), the question concerned the supply of an air ambulance (helicopter) and pilots to two Air Ambulance Trusts.

The supply of the helicopter would be zero-rated as the hire of goods (*Sch 8, Group 15, Item 5* via notes 3(*b*) and 9), the hire of the pilots being standard rated.

The taxpayer argued that there was one overall supply of a transport service (ie zero-rated) whereas Customs argued that there were two distinct supplies, the transport and the pilots. The tribunal clearly ruled in favour of a mixed supply.

Cairngorm Mountain

23.5 In the case of *Cairngorm Mountain v Customs and Excise Comrs* (20 May 2002, unreported) (EDN/01/208 17679), the customer's payment entitled him to ski passes and also the train journey to get from the bottom of the mountain to the top. The argument put forward by HMRC was that the train journey was incidental to the main supply of the ski passes, on the basis that it was a service that made the skiing experience more pleasant, ie enhancing the enjoyment of the main supply.

The tribunal concluded that the aim of the rail travel was to get a person from 'A' to 'B' as is the aim of any transport facility. On this basis, it must therefore form an aim in its own right, confirming that the arrangement was a multiple supply with zero-rated travel and standard-rated skiing facilities.

Note – this is an interesting case because the two supplies are both for services rather than goods. The apportionment of output tax will be quite an interesting calculation – see **23.14–23.18** for the different methods that could be adopted.

Single supply decisions

Sky Broadcasting Group plc

23.6   In *British Sky Broadcasting Group plc v Customs and Excise Comrs* [1999] V & DR 283 (LON/98/889 16220), Sky provided broadcasting services to customers in return for a monthly subscription. However, as part of the deal, the customer also received a regular copy of a magazine (zero-rated as printed matter), giving the customer details about the television programmes and their times.

Sky argued that the magazine constituted an aim in itself, and therefore the subscription payment made by the customer should be apportioned for VAT purposes. HMRC argued (successfully) that the magazine was incidental to the main supply of the subscription payment and that the whole supply was standard rated.

Note – following the *Card Protection Plan* ruling (see **23.2**), it will be very difficult in most cases involving printed matter to convince a tribunal that the printed matter is an aim in its own right. This is supported by the findings in the *Weight Watchers (UK) Ltd* case – see **23.10**. A similar decision was reached in the case of *Manchester United plc v Customs and Excise Comrs* (11 June 2001, unreported) (MAN/00/371 17234), where the tribunal concluded that a match day programme supplied as part of a hospitality package was not an aim in its own right but a means of better enjoying the main supply of hospitality.

Byrom (t/a Salon 24)

23.7   In *Byrom (t/a Salon 24) v Revenue and Customs Comrs* [2006] EWHC 111 (Ch), [2006] STC 992, [2006] SWTI 378, [2006] All ER (D) 75 (Feb), the High Court upheld a decision of the VAT tribunal that supplies by the taxpayers, who operated a massage parlour from which they let rooms to individual masseuses, were standard rated supplies of facilities for VAT purposes and not licenses to occupy land that would have been exempt from VAT.

The benefits enjoyed by the masseuses in return for their payment to the salon, included:

- provision of laundry services;

- use of a day room;

- provision of receptionist services;

- a telephone system and credit card payment facility.

The court concluded that the facilities offered by the taxpayer were all intended to assist the masseuse in running her business (ie an aim in their own right), not a means of better enjoying the room itself.

The next question concerned the hire of the room – could that be a supply in its own right and benefit from being exempt from VAT? If so, this would mean that the payment by the masseuses would need to be apportioned as a mixed supply.

The court ruled that the room was incidental to the main supply of the services provided by the parlour – therefore the whole payment to the taxpayer was standard rated.

Note – in a simple sentence, the court ruled that the taxpayer was making a 'supply of massage parlour services' not the 'rent of a room as a license to occupy land'. This interpretation can apply to similar arrangements in other business structures (eg hairdressers) and advisers need to look closely at the reality of a situation, not just how it is described by a taxpayer to avoid VAT being charged on his supplies.

Tumble Tots UK Ltd

23.8 (Note – this is an interesting case because the original decision of the tribunal was that a mixed supply situation was evident – the High Court overturned this verdict and ruled that there was just a single supply).

In the case of *Tumble Tots UK Ltd v Revenue and Customs Comrs* [2006] SWTI 1711 (LON/05/0028 19530) the company is franchiser of a chain of play centres for children. In order to take part in a play session, the child must be a member of the National Tumble Tots Club. An annual fee is payable, and this was the subject of the appeal. In return for the annual fee, a member receives the following benefits:

- membership card;

- special yellow Tumble Tots T-shirt;

- DVD and CD of nursery songs;

- members' handbook and gym bag;

- various newsletters and booklets.

HMRC argued that there was one main supply of membership (standard rated), entitling the children to take part in activity sessions at Tumble Tot premises. All other supplies were considered to be incidental to this main supply.

Tumble Tots argued that the main supplies were the zero-rated supplies of printed material and children's clothing (T-shirt), so overall it was making a zero-rated supply.

The tribunal concluded that the membership was the main benefit, and all other supplies were incidental apart from the T-shirt that had some monetary benefit and importance to the child.

However, HMRC appealed to the High Court ([2007] EWHC 103 (Ch), [2007] SWTI 293, [2007] All ER (D) 274 (Jan)), which ruled that the aim of the payment made by the customer was to secure attendance at the classes. Other benefits such as the t-shirt were incidental to this main supply. The entire payment made by the customer was therefore standard rated.

Recent cases and current thinking

23.9   As explained at the beginning of this chapter, the subject of VAT and mixed supplies has kept the courts busy in recent years.

In the last twelve months, the main court case that has created interest was *Revenue and Customs Comrs v Weight Watchers (UK) Ltd* [2008] EWCA Civ 715, [2008] STC 2313, a case that was heard by three different courts before being concluded at a Court of Appeal hearing – see **23.10**.

The main conclusion there was to show the importance of looking at a supply from the point of view of the customer rather than the supplier. What does the customer expect to receive for his money? What would his reaction be if he did not receive a specific benefit? Example 2 earlier in this chapter considered this process – how would John and Jean have reacted if the five-course meal they were expecting had been absent from their trip on the Orient Express?

Weight Watchers (UK) Ltd

23.10   The case of *Revenue and Customs Comrs v Weight Watchers (UK) Ltd* [2008] EWCA Civ 715, [2008] STC 2313 was finally concluded in the Court of Appeal. It concerned the VAT liability of payments made by customers to attend weight loss meetings. The following questions were considered:

● Did the payments made by the customers wholly relate to the standard rated attendance at weight loss programme meetings?

● Did some of the payments relate to the zero-rated supply of printer matter – booklets provided to the customers to assist with their weight-loss efforts?

The Court of Appeal effectively overturned the thinking of both the VAT tribunal and High Court by ruling that there was a single supply of standard-rated weight loss services. The lower courts had concluded that there was some zero-rated element of printed matter supplied to the customer.

The Court of Appeal concluded that the handbook given to new members when they first enrolled on a weight loss course, plus the subsequent monthly newsletters and leaflets, were all supplies that were incidental to the main supply of the standard-rated course. In effect, this conclusion supports the findings of the other cases involving printed matter mentioned in this chapter. The aim of printed matter is usually to enhance the enjoyment of another supply, ie it rarely forms an aim in its own right.

David Baxendale Ltd

23.11   The High Court delivered a ruling in this case that was consistent with the *Weight Watchers (UK) Ltd* case considered at **23.10**: *Revenue and Customs Comrs v David Baxendale Ltd* [2009] EWHC 162 (Ch), [2009] STC 825.

The court held that the provision of a weight loss programme through replacement food packages supported by counselling and advice was a single composite supply of services which was standard-rated for VAT purposes. The zero-rated supply of food was incidental to the main supply of the weight loss programme.

The court ruled that it would be artificial to split the different elements of the supply and this meant it was therefore necessary to consider whether the consumer considered that he was paying for zero-rated food or standard-rated services. The main character of the supply was of services, ie standard-rated.

Note – this case has again emphasised the importance of looking at a supply from the point of view of the customer rather than the supplier. It is also interesting that this is another case where two courts have reached different conclusions, as the VAT tribunal had acknowledged an element of zero-rating, ie mixed supply conclusion.

Leisure trusts providing all-inclusive membership schemes

23.12   Following the *Weight Watchers (UK) Ltd* case, HMRC sensibly issued Revenue and Customs Brief 13/09, which finally settles the VAT liability of membership schemes supplied by leisure trusts (the latter are charitable organisations so their services qualify for a range of VAT exemptions).

HMRC's previous stance was that if one benefit of a membership scheme was standard-rated (eg the right to use a sauna) then the whole of the membership payment received from the customer would be standard-rated, even if the majority of facilities were exempt from VAT if supplied in their own right (participation in sport provided by an eligible body).

The Brief confirms that in cases where the customer's main motive for purchasing an all-inclusive membership package is to use the range of available sports facilities, the single supply is exempt. It is irrelevant if a small proportion of the benefits would be standard-rated if sold in their own right (eg sauna use) – it is the overall package that counts. This policy will hopefully end the situation where some trusts were providing free saunas or closing saunas completely because of the VAT problem – common sense has won the day.

Strategy for advisers

23.13   So what is the key message for practitioners from the three recent cases analysed above?

It is very difficult in the current climate to obtain an official ruling from HMRC on a mixed supply situation. The written enquiry teams are reluctant to give a ruling on any subject unless it is felt that HMRC's own published guidance is unclear about the matter. However, there are plenty of court cases to refer to about mixed supply situations – the challenge is often to remember the conclusion reached by the final appeal court when decisions have fluctuated.

The following are four key questions to consider in each case. The answers to these questions should give a strong indication about whether a single or multiple supply is evident.

- What does the customer perceive he is paying for – one main supply or a combination of two or more supplies?

- How are supplies advertised or marketed – do adverts promote one main benefit or a range of benefits, each of which will be of interest to the customer?

- What is the contractual position between the buyer and seller – is the seller obliged to provide a range of different services to the customer, eg to supply both rail travel and catering as in Example 2 considered at **23.2**?

- What are the monetary values of the supplies in question? Although not totally conclusive, if a supply only forms a small element of the overall cost of the product, then it can usually be ignored as incidental to the main supply. For example, a cheap standard-rated pen supplied with an expensive zero-rated book could be ignored on the basis of cost.

Apportionment of output tax

23.14   Having decided that a supply comprises two or more elements that attract different rates of VAT, the next challenge is to apportion the customer's payment to account for output tax on the standard rated element. Obviously, if both elements of the supply attract VAT at the same rate, then there is no problem.

The HMRC rule in such cases is that the business must allocate a fair proportion of the total payment to each of the supplies. There is no prescribed method of carrying out this apportionment – but the emphasis is on fairness and achieving a reasonable result.

In practice, there are two main methods of apportioning output tax – one based on the cost of the supplies, and the other on normal selling prices.

Apportionment of output tax using cost based method

23.15   The basic principle of apportioning output tax using a cost-based method is to calculate the total cost of the standard-rated supply compared to total cost, and apply this percentage to the total selling price for output tax purposes. See Example 4.

Example 4

Item A sells for a VAT-inclusive price of £200 and includes a standard-rated element and a zero-rated element. It has been confirmed that each of the supplies represents an aim in itself – rather than one of the supplies being ancillary to the main supply.

The cost of producing the standard-rated part of the supply is £80 (excluding VAT) and the zero-rated supply £40. How much output tax is due?

Solution – the key point to remember for this example is that the ratio of standard rated costs compared to total costs needs to include VAT – this is because the selling price is also VAT inclusive (the figures that follow are based on a VAT rate of 17.5%):

(£80 + VAT)/(£80 + VAT) + £40 = £94/£134 × £200 × 7/47 = £20.89 output tax to pay.

In effect, the total selling price can be split as follows:

Standard rated goods	£119.41
Zero-rated goods	£59.70
VAT	£20.89

In Example 4, the apportionment was easy to carry out because it was possible to calculate the costs of both elements of the supply. As long as all costs were calculated correctly (with no major exclusions from the standard-rated costs) then the method is unlikely to deviate from the fair and reasonable test.

However, problems can occur if it is only possible to calculate the cost of one element of a supply, for example, where standard-rated goods are supplied with zero-rated services (or vice versa).

In such cases, HMRC has approved a calculation method as follows:

- calculate the total costs of the supply that can be worked out;

- apply a mark-up to this cost figure to give a selling price;

- the balance of the selling price will then be for the goods/services supplied at the different rate of VAT.

Another acceptable calculation for mixed supply situations where only one element can be costed is for a mark-up to be applied that relates to the mark up achieved for the overall business.

The onus is on HMRC to disprove the method of apportionment used by a business, and by and large, it will accept calculations given to it as long as a fair and reasonable approach has been taken.

For example, if a 200% mark-up is applied to costs relevant to a zero-rated item, but the overall business is only achieving a 50% mark-up, then the business would have to justify why it felt a 200% mark-up was reasonable (obviously the high mark-up applied greatly reduces the output tax due on the item in question). The high mark-up could clearly be a deviation from the fair and reasonable approach. HMRC would be justified in challenging the accuracy of the 200% mark-up figure being adopted.

A useful indicator concerning the accuracy of the applied mark-up could be to look at the profit margins being achieved by similar products within the company. Again, the business may be trading in goods where there are generally accepted mark-ups and profit margins, although individual variations will have to be taken into account.

Apportionment based upon normal selling prices

23.16　This method of apportionment considers the prices charged by the business for separate supplies of the item in question, and uses these amounts to make a sensible apportionment. See Example 5.

Example 5

Item B includes a standard and zero-rated item, sold jointly for £10. The standard-rated item is sold on its own for £5 including VAT, and the zero-rated item is sold for £7.

Solution – in this situation, the standard rated element would be 5/12, giving an output tax liability of: £10 × 5/12 × 7/47= £0.62 (based on VAT rate of 17.5%).

Retrospective apportionment

23.17　A frequently asked question is whether it is possible to go back to earlier VAT periods, and adjust calculations that have already been made.

In reality, the answer to this question depends on the circumstances of the proposed amendment and the approach taken by HMRC once the changes are analysed. Without being too controversial, it is fair to say that most requests for retrospective adjustment are intended to reduce output tax previously paid – rather than increase it.

One situation where a business could clearly go back 3 years and recalculate its output tax liability is if an error was discovered in relation to the specific method being used. For example, it might be discovered that a key cost component has been omitted from the zero-rated item, which would create an output tax overpayment on any method of calculation linked to cost.

Again, it is possible that a business has made an item wholly standard rated in the past, unaware that part of it is eligible for zero-rating under the mixed supply rules. Again, there would be no problem doing a historic adjustment. However, all adjustments must fully consider the issue of unjust enrichment and whether the taxpayer or his customer is entitled to any VAT repayment (see **20.8**).

The situation where it would be more difficult to make a retrospective adjustment would be if a business has correctly applied one of the methods in the past (and paid the correct output tax each quarter) but has now discovered that an alternative method would give a better result in terms of paying less output tax. There is no doubt that HMRC would view any request to backdate a calculation using a different method with suspicion – it would be up to the business to clearly justify why the outcome of the previous method was unfair.

HMRC approach to fairness

23.18 There may be occasions where a business has correctly carried out an apportionment calculation for many years, but HMRC then decides on a VAT visit that it is unfair, ie the output tax paid is too low. In such circumstances, HMRC would adopt the sensible approach of seeking to change methods from a current date, rather than assessing any underpaid output tax on a retrospective basis. This conclusion assumes that the taxpayer has adopted one of the approved methods highlighted in this chapter. As with most aspects of VAT, the taxpayer would have a right of appeal if he disagreed with the ruling made by the officer.

The other situation that might apply on a VAT visit is where errors in the method of calculation are discovered by the officer – in such cases, an assessment would be raised to correct the errors, going back a maximum of 3 years (or 4 years from 1 April 2010). Examples of errors could be where incorrect selling prices are used if the method is based on sales values; there could be errors of calculation between the VAT exclusive/ inclusive figures; for cost apportionment methods, key components of the cost price could have either been omitted or incorrectly calculated.

Planning points to consider

23.19   The following planning points should be given consideration.

- When assessing whether a single or multiple supply situation exists, it is necessary to consider whether each supply constitutes an aim in itself, or whether it is incidental to the main supply.

- Remember that an analysis of mixed supply situations is only relevant if goods or services within the supply attract VAT at different rates.

- Be aware of the two different methods of apportionment in mixed supply situations (ie cost-based and revenue-based calculations) and identify if one of the methods gives a fairer result.

- Any errors of principle in apportioning output tax on mixed supplies can be adjusted by going back 3 years and correcting the error. This time period extends to 4 years by 1 April 2010. If the amount of tax involved is less than £10,000 (or 1% of the Box 6 figure on the relevant VAT return up to a maximum of £50,000), this can be done by adjusting the next VAT return, otherwise, a separate disclosure must be made to HMRC.

- It is unlikely to be acceptable for a taxpayer to readjust his method of output tax apportionment on a historic basis, unless the method adopted was totally unfair. HMRC will be rightly suspicious about recalculations that are made just to try and get a better result in terms of output tax paid in the past.

- Several court cases in the last twelve months (considered in this chapter) have emphasised the importance of looking at mixed supply situations from the perspective of the customer rather than the supplier. In other words, whether the customer considers that he is only paying for one main benefit (single supply outcome) or a range of benefits subject to different rates of VAT (multiple supply).

Chapter 24

Partial Exemption – Introduction

Key topics in this chapter:

- The allocation of expenditure between taxable, exempt and residual input tax and the importance of adopting an assertive approach to the allocation process.

- Calculating the amount of residual input tax that can be reclaimed using the standard method of calculation.

- Important changes to the standard method from 1 April 2009.

- The need to make an annual adjustment for all partial exemption calculations and declare tax on the relevant VAT return.

- The *de minimis* rules for partial exemption – a business that is *de minimis* for partial exemption purposes can reclaim all of its input tax in a tax year.

- The standard method override provisions effective from 18 April 2002.

- Partial exemption issues concerning foreign income, specified and incidental supplies

- The 'clawback' and 'payback' provisions which deal with a situation where the actual use of an item is different to the intended use when expenditure was first incurred.

- An important concession for house builders who temporarily rent out properties they cannot sell.

Introduction

24.1   Partial exemption is one of the most complicated aspects of VAT, and becomes relevant to a business that makes some supplies that are taxable and some that are exempt. It should be remembered that taxable supplies include zero-rated and lower-rate goods or services – not just those that are standard rated.

In basic terms, three common situations will be evident as far as supplies made by a business are concerned:

(a) *Taxable supplies only* – a business that wholly makes taxable supplies is able to recover all of its input tax, subject to normal rules. If most or all of these supplies are zero-rated, then this is likely to mean that the business will be a repayment trader for VAT purposes.

(b) *Exempt supplies only* – a business that only makes exempt supplies will not be able to register for VAT – because it is not making taxable supplies. In effect, this means that it has the advantage of not having to charge output tax on its income, but the disadvantage that it will not be able to reclaim input tax on expenditure that it incurs. The VAT element of any expense will therefore form part of the cost of the item. For example, expenditure for £100 + £17.50 VAT, the gross amount of £117.50 will be charged to the profit and loss account.

(c) *Taxable and exempt supplies* – a business that makes both taxable and exempt supplies is able to benefit from input tax recovery to the extent that the input tax relates to taxable supplies. This is where the subject of partial exemption becomes relevant. Any input tax that relates to exempt supplies is known as exempt input tax, and cannot be reclaimed for VAT purposes.

There are two ways of apportioning input tax for a partly exempt business:

- standard method of calculation – which is adopted by most partly exempt businesses and is considered in this chapter;

- special method of calculation – a taxpayer can make a request to HMRC to adopt a special method, usually when it feels that the standard method does not give a fair and reasonable result as far as input tax recovery is concerned. Special methods of calculation are considered in Chapter 25.

Input tax apportionment

24.2 In basic terms, a business that is partly exempt needs to split its purchases invoices into three distinct categories as far as VAT is concerned:

(a) invoices that wholly relate to exempt supplies made by the business;

(b) invoices that wholly relate to taxable supplies made by the business;

(c) invoices that cannot be attributed to either activity, for example, head office expenses, overhead items, computer expenditure etc.

There are three key phrases that emerge following the above split as follows.

● *Exempt input tax* – input tax relevant to exempt supplies. In most cases, this input tax will not be claimed by a business, unless the business qualifies as being *de minimis*, in which case it can recover all of its input tax in the normal way (see **24.7**).

● *Taxable input tax* – input tax relevant to taxable supplies, and wholly reclaimable, subject to normal rules.

● *Residual input tax* (sometimes known as non-attributable input tax or the 'pot') – input tax that is not wholly relevant to taxable or exempt supplies, e g general overhead items.

See Example 1 for an illustration of the principles of input tax allocation.

Example 1

Verity Ltd trades as an estate agent in the local High Street. It makes some taxable supplies (sale of houses on a commission basis) and some exempt supplies (sale of financial products such as mortgages on a commission or fee basis).

For VAT period ended 30 June 2008, it makes the following payments:

● an advert in the local newspaper for £1,000 plus VAT to advertise its mortgage based products;

● the vehicle exclusively used by one of the property negotiators has a major service costing £700 plus VAT;

● the pool car used by the company and available to all employees also needs a service costing £800 plus VAT;

● the office telephone bill is paid for £3,000 plus VAT;

● the auditors are paid for completing the annual audit, a fee of £2,000 plus VAT;

What is the input tax position on each of these expenses?

Solution – the advert in the local newspaper is deemed to be exempt input tax because it wholly relates to the exempt activity of the company – an amount of £175 cannot be reclaimed (assuming a VAT rate of 17.5%). However, good news for the service to the first vehicle – the property negotiator's work is wholly linked to the taxable activity of the business, so this input tax can be fully reclaimed.

The final three expenses in this example cannot be directly attributed to either the taxable or exempt activities of the business, so the input tax will be only partly reclaimed. See 24.3 to see how this partial claim is made under the standard method of calculation.

Calculation of reclaimable input tax – the standard method

24.3   In reality, most of the problems caused by partial exemption concern the amount of 'residual input tax' that can be claimed by a partly exempt business. This is because the other two categories of input tax give a clear result, ie no input tax can be claimed on costs relevant to exempt supplies, and all input tax can be reclaimed on costs relevant to taxable supplies.

A business must calculate the amount of residual input tax to be reclaimed using the standard method (no permission required by HMRC) unless it makes a request to adopt a special method of calculation – see Chapter 25.

The standard method means that residual input tax is reclaimed using the following formula:

$$\text{Reclaimable \%} = \frac{\text{Value of taxable supplies in the period (excluding VAT)}}{\text{Value of all supplies in the period (excluding VAT)}}$$

Some important points to remember:

- the percentage calculation is always rounded up to the next whole number, eg 43.1% calculation means that 44% residual input tax can be recovered. The exception is when the amount of residual input tax to which the calculation is applied exceeds £400,000 per month on average. In such cases, the reclaimable percentage needs to be rounded up to two decimal places, eg 43.656% means 43.66% input tax is reclaimed;

- the above calculation is carried out at the end of each VAT period, however, monthly or quarterly calculations are always made on a provisional basis, and an annual adjustment must be made at the end of each tax year – see **24.6**;

- the tax year ends on 31 March, 30 April or 31 May, depending on when the VAT periods end for the business in question;

- any sum receivable for capital goods must be excluded from the calculation, eg sales of fixed assets;

- any supplies which are 'incidental' to the business can also be ignored. The main situation when this would tend to apply is relevant to bank interest income, which is not an activity in its own right but income that is dependent on the bank balance held by the business;

- the value of any supply made by the business which is neither taxable nor exempt should also be excluded, eg proceeds from the transfer of a going concern payment which is outside the scope of VAT;

- the value of certain imported services subject to the reverse charge should also be excluded;

- remember that the formula for calculating the percentage of reclaimable input tax (residual) works on VAT exclusive figures, not inclusive figures.

See Example 2 for an illustration of the principles of the standard method of calculation.

Example 2

Following on from Example 1, our estate agent company is about to complete its June 2008 return – it has summarised the key figures as follows:

Standard rated sales for quarter excluding VAT	£80,000
Exempt sales for quarter	£20,000
Taxable input tax (input tax wholly relevant to taxable supplies)	£7,000
Exempt input tax (input tax wholly relevant to exempt supplies)	£2,000
Residual input tax (non-attributable)	£3,500

How much VAT will the company pay on this particular return?

Solution – output tax is simple: £80,000 × 17.5% = £14,000.

With regard to input tax, the total amount reclaimed will be £9,800 as follows:

Taxable input tax – reclaim in full £7,000.

Residual input tax – claim 80% based on percentage of taxable supplies compared to total supplies, ie £2,800 (£80,000 ÷ £100,000 × £3,500).

Net VAT payment for period = £4,200, ie £14,000 less £9,800.

Note – if the company is using the cash accounting scheme then all relevant figures for sales and purchases will be based on payments made and received, not invoices raised or received.

In Example 2, the company had a high percentage of input tax recovery on its residual input tax. This was because the income for this particular business was mainly taxable rather than exempt. This is one of the key outcomes of partial exemption calculations – a business with higher taxable income as a proportion of its total income gets a better rate of residual input tax recovery than a business which has mainly exempt supplies.

Potential problems with allocation of input tax

24.4   One of the key skills for an accountant dealing with a partly exempt business is to be very clear about the correct way of allocating purchase invoices to one of the three categories of input tax, ie taxable, exempt or residual.

In most cases, the allocation process is straightforward – but in a commercial situation, there can be certain expenses that need to be very closely analysed. For example, if a business has 80% exempt income, then the decision to post a purchase invoice to residual input tax rather than taxable input tax will cost the company £800 if the total VAT on the invoice is £1,000.

See Example 3 for some interesting allocations.

Example 3

Nortons Golf Club is a partly exempt business (non-profit making golf club with exempt income from playing subscriptions and taxable income from a bar and restaurant). It has a clubhouse where the ground floor is allocated to changing room facilities for the players, and the first floor is allocated to a purpose built bar and restaurant. The club has two sources of income – membership subscriptions paid by cheque or direct debit, and bar or restaurant sales paid by cheque, cash or direct debit.

It incurs the following expenses in the period to 30 June 2008:

- the disabled lift that takes customers from the ground floor to the first floor bar area has been serviced at a cost of £2,000 plus VAT;

- the club has just bought a safe in the office to store cash at a cost of £1,000 plus VAT.

The purpose of the disabled lift is to take customers to the bar area, so the cost of servicing it is wholly related to taxable supplies. It may be tempting to code the expense as residual because it relates to a general building expense but this would not be correct. Input tax of £350 can be reclaimed in full.

In the case of the safe, this input tax is also taxable – the purpose of the safe is to store cash held on the premises, and the only source of cash income is the bar area (because membership subscriptions are only paid by cheque or direct debit). Again, it may have been tempting to code this expense as residual because it is located in the office, and office overheads tend to be residual by nature.

As a general observation, it is important that advisers fully consider the VAT allocation of each item of expenditure, and avoid the easy option of playing safe and choosing the allocation which results in the lowest input tax claim.

Case law examples of input tax allocation

24.5   *Town and County Factors Ltd v Revenue and Customs Comrs* (20 April 2006, unreported) (LON/04/0791 19616).

In this particular case, the company was the representative member of a VAT group that operated about 2,000 licensed betting offices throughout the UK – each shop having a mix of exempt income (placing of bets) and taxable income through gaming machines and catering. The exempt income was about 73% of total income.

The expenditure item that was the subject of the appeal related to the costs paid to SIS, Sky TV and Sabrinet – relevant to the TV screens placed in each betting shop. Sky TV provided the basic broadcasting service plus sports coverage and SIS provided racing information and television broadcasts to all of the appellant's betting offices.

The question at stake was whether the television costs wholly relate to the exempt part of the business (ie the placing of bets) or do they relate to all aspects of the business – on the basis that customers passing the shop may be tempted to enter the premises to watch the TV, and then as a result of this decision, spend money on all parts of the shop, ie including the gaming machines and catering outlet.

The latter argument was put forward by the taxpayer, ie that the TV costs should be classed as residual input tax. HMRC maintained that the link between the expenditure and the taxable income was tenuous and that the input tax was wholly relevant to exempt supplies.

The result? The tribunal agreed with the taxpayer. It was satisfied that the presence of the TV screens was enough to draw customers into the shop, who were then likely to spend money on both the betting activity (exempt) and the gaming machines (taxable).

Cheshire Racing Ltd v Revenue and Customs Comrs [2007] V & DR 345, [2008] SWTI 194 – HMRC did not accept defeat lightly in the *Town and County Factors Ltd* case, concluding that the significance of this case was that the televisions generated taxable advertising revenue. The HMRC policy team dismissed the argument about the TV presence attracting customers into a betting shop, and decided to challenge another case in the courts, ie where no advertising revenue was generated by the televisions.

The outcome was the same – another defeat for HMRC, based on the argument that the presence of the TV screens was enough to draw customers into the shop, who were then likely to spend money on both the betting activity (exempt) and the gaming machine (taxable). The tribunal chairman observed that the televisions provided a comprehensive coverage of many sporting and gaming activities, coverage was not just restricted to horse and dog racing alone.

HMRC has now accepted this argument – and confirmed its revised policy in Revenue and Customs Brief 01/08 issued on 3 January 2008.

Annual adjustment

24.6 Many businesses have seasonal variations in their trading levels – or periods when the exempt or taxable income can be artificially high.

Consider the situation of the non-profit making golf club in Example 3. It is likely that all of its exempt membership receipts will be received in one

VAT period (date when annual fees are due for renewal) and this will create an exceptionally high percentage of exempt sales in this one period. If the club has a very high residual input tax figure in this period, then the percentage recovery will be very low because of the exempt income.

The way that HMRC ensures a fair and reasonable recovery rate is by requiring all partly exempt businesses to make an annual adjustment for input tax purposes. The result of this annual adjustment is to even out the effect of any periods where the split between taxable and exempt income creates an unfair result (either too much or too little VAT paid to HMRC).

The annual adjustment needs to be made for the 12-month period to 31 March, 30 April or 31 May, depending on when the trader's VAT periods end.

When the annual adjustment has been calculated, the amount payable or repayable needs to be adjusted in the following VAT period, ie the return ending 30 June, 31 July or 31 August. This is a useful concession – giving taxpayers 3 months to make the calculations and declare the difference. However, see **24.12** concerning the opportunity to include the annual adjustment on the return for the same VAT return as the annual adjustment is calculated.

See Example 4 for a full calculation of an annual adjustment.

Example 4

Vickery Ltd from Example 2 has now come to the end of its tax year to 31 March 2009.

It has calculated the following figures in relation to the four VAT periods up to this date:

Taxable supplies for the year excluding VAT	£330,000
Exempt supplies for the year	£90,000
Residual input tax for the year	£16,000
Residual input tax claimed to date	£12,500

Solution – the percentage of taxable income for the year (rounded up to nearest whole number) is 79%. This means that residual input tax of £12,640 can be claimed, ie £16,000 × 79%. The actual amount of residual input tax claimed on a quarterly basis is £12,500 – so the business can reclaim an additional amount of £140 in Box 4 of its June 2009 VAT return.

One important point to note is that the annual adjustment calculation does not represent the correction of a VAT error – it is a normal VAT adjustment appropriate to the rules of partial exemption.

De minimis limits

24.7   The calculations made so far in this chapter have worked on the basis that all exempt input tax is not reclaimed by a business, plus a proportion of residual input tax based on the value of taxable and exempt income. In other words, a partly exempt business always suffers some loss of input tax.

One important rule of partial exemption is that a business can reclaim all of its input tax if the total value of exempt input tax (and remember, exempt input tax also includes the proportion of residual input tax that is not reclaimed) is less than the following amounts:

(a)   £625 per month on average and £7,500 per year; and

(b)   50% of the total input tax.

The quarterly calculations are again superseded by an annual adjustment – so it is possible to have the situation where a business is partly exempt in a VAT quarter but *de minimis* for the year as a whole.

See Example 5 which gives an example of a business that is *de minimis* in a VAT quarter.

Example 5

ABC Ltd is about to complete its September 2008 return – it has summarised the key figures as follows:

Standard rated sales for quarter excluding VAT	£80,000
Exempt sales for quarter	£20,000
Taxable input tax (input tax wholly relevant to taxable supplies)	£7,000
Exempt input tax (input tax wholly relevant to exempt supplies)	£1,000
Residual input tax (non-attributable)	£3,500

Solution – output tax is simple: £80,000 × 17.5% = £14,000.

With regard to input tax, the total amount reclaimed before consideration of the *de minimis* rules will be £9,800 as follows:

Taxable input tax – reclaim in full £7,000.

Residual input tax – claim 80% based on % of taxable supplies compared to total supplies, ie £2,800.

However, the total exempt input tax for the period is £1,700 (£1,000 directly related to exempt supplies plus 20% of residual input tax, ie £700). The amount of £1,700 is less than £625 per month, and also less than 50% of the total input tax figure of £11,500.

The company is *de minimis* for this period and is therefore entitled to reclaim input tax of £11,500 in Box 4 of its return. However, it is possible that the company will not be *de minimis* for the overall tax year, so the recovery of exempt input tax in this period could be only temporary.

Standard method override

24.8   In most cases, the standard method gives a fair and reasonable result. However, in some very rare cases (which in general only apply to large businesses) the standard method gives an unfair input tax recovery rate.

To combat this situation, HMRC introduced override provisions with effect from 18 April 2002 to address these difficulties. Except in cases of deliberate abuse (eg through complex VAT planning schemes), the application of the override provisions is very limited. As a general principle, the override provisions could be used if the standard method gives a level of input tax recovery on an expense that is widely different to the extent to which it is used in the making of taxable supplies.

The override only applies if the adjustment required to correct the distortion exceeds:

* £50,000; or

* 50% of the residual input tax, and £25,000.

The limits above mean that any adjustment that is less than £25,000 can be ignored. It can also be ignored if it is between £25,000 and £50,000 and less than 50% of the residual input tax figure.

An interesting case on the standard method override rules is the recent *Abbeyview Bowling Club v Revenue and Customs Comrs* [2008] SWTI 1685. Input tax was claimed by the club on the construction of a new rink next to its clubhouse. HMRC felt that the input tax claimed on the rink was excessive (unfair) when a turnover based calculation was adopted and it applied a calculation based instead on use. This produced an input tax adjustment that exceeded the £50,000 limit (ie the difference between the two calculation methods).

The tribunal accepted an alternative calculation put forward by the taxpayer that produced an input tax difference of less than £50,000 and therefore the override provisions did not apply. This case shows the importance of not always accepting an HMRC basis of calculation and looking at the wider issues of a transaction.

Foreign income and specified supplies

24.9   The subject of VAT and international services is very complex. However, without going into detail, there is a concession in the legislation that means that input tax can still be fully recovered (subject to normal rules) on any costs relevant to:

- 'foreign supplies' – defined as supplies made outside the UK which would be taxable supplies if made in the UK (eg accountancy services to an American or German business client);

- 'specified exempt supplies' – applies when exempt supplies of insurance (*VAT Act 1994, Sch 9, Group* 2) and finance (*VAT Act 1994, Sch 9, Group 5, Items 1–8*) are made to a customer outside the EU, but the rules do not apply to a customer inside the EU;

Example – banking services to a German customer are outside the scope of VAT (place of supply is Germany) but no input tax can be reclaimed on related costs because Germany is in the EU. A banking service to an American customer is a specified exempt supply and input tax can be reclaimed on any related costs because America is outside the EU.

If a cost is partly used for the above supplies and partly for exempt supplies in the UK (or non-specified exempt supplies to an EU customer), then an apportionment of input tax must be made on a 'use' basis.

Example – if the cost relates to the fees of a consultant, then timesheet records may be appropriate to determine use. Any method of calculation is acceptable to HMRC as long as it is fair and reasonable. The standard method of calculation is applied in the usual way – but the income from non-specified exempt supplies (ie banking/financial services to EU customers) must also be included in the income calculation. The income from specified exempt supplies and foreign income is excluded from the calculation because input tax has already been dealt with on a 'use' basis.

Incidental transactions

24.10   When applying the standard method of calculation, it is important to be clear about the sources of income that are excluded from the figures – as well as those that are included. The aim of the calculation process is that the percentage of residual input tax that is reclaimed by the business should be 'fair and reasonable', ie an amount that reflects the level of taxable supplies made by the business.

The following sources of income should be excluded as being incidental transactions:

- sale of capital assets of the business, eg sale of car, plant and machinery etc;

- exempt supplies of finance where these supplies are incidental to the business, eg bank interest received;

- with effect from 1 April 2007, any 'real estate transaction' (sale of a building etc) where such supplies are again incidental to the main activities of the business.

Example – a firm of accountants sells the freehold of the building from which it trades and rents a new office in the next street. The proceeds from the sale of the building (exempt if no option to tax has been made on the building) are excluded from the partial exemption calculation:

- the value of certain imported services specified in *VAT Act 1994, Sch 5*, which are subject to the reverse charge in the UK;

- proceeds from the sale of any business (or part of a business) as a going concern.

Non-business input tax

24.11   The basic principle with regard to non-business input tax, for example private expenditure, is that it should be excluded from any calculations before partial exemption issues are considered. This would also relate to input tax on any non-business activity as well. See Example 6.

Example 6

John trades as a sole proprietor and is VAT registered, making taxable and exempt supplies. The percentage of taxable supplies is 80% of total supplies.

He has just purchased a piece of equipment for £20,000 plus VAT of £3,500 that will be used for non-business purposes for 20% of the time. For the remainder the time, the equipment will be used for both parts of his business, ie taxable and exempt activities. What is the input tax position?

Solution – an initial amount of input tax will be disallowed to reflect the non-business use, an amount of £700 (ie £3,500 × 20%). The remaining input tax of £2,800 will be treated as residual input tax and included within the partial exemption calculations for the business. If 80% of income is taxable for the relevant period, then the input tax recovery will be £2,240.

Note – this example ignores an alternative method of dealing with expenditure that has a non-business element, known as the *Lennartz* mechanism – see further, Chapter 32 at 32.17.

New standard method procedures – 1 April 2009

24.12   HMRC issued Business Brief 19/09 and VAT Information Sheet 04/09 in March 2009 to explain important changes in relation to businesses that use the standard method. The aim of the measures is to simplify the partial exemption calculations for a business, ie to produce administrative savings in many cases. The new procedures took effect from 1 April 2009 and included three optional measures and a fourth measure that is compulsory.

The three optional measures are as follows:

(1) *A provisional input tax recovery percentage can be adopted throughout the tax year, based on the previous year's annual adjustment calculation.*

This recovery percentage will be relevant to input tax claims on expenses where some taxable and some exempt use is evident (ie residual input tax). The actual recovery percentage will then be established when the annual adjustment calculation is made at the end of the tax year.

Example – ABC Ltd uses the standard method and reclaimed 75% of its residual input tax in the year to 31 March 2009. It will reclaim the same percentage of residual input tax in relation to VAT returns submitted during the year ending 31 March 2010. It will then calculate its annual adjustment for the year and reclaim additional input tax if the percentage of taxable income exceeded 75%, ie the provisional recovery rate was too low. It will repay tax to HMRC if the percentage of taxable income was less than 75%, ie the provisional recovery rate was too high. The percentage of taxable income for year ended 31 March 2010 will then form the basis of quarterly calculations during year ended 31 March 2011.

Advantage of the new measure – the adoption of an in-year recovery percentage will avoid any significant fluctuations in the percentage of residual input tax claimed on a quarterly basis because of, for example, big fluctuations in income levels (as in the earlier example of a golf club that received all of its exempt membership subscription income in one VAT period). It will also be easier for a business to complete its quarterly VAT returns, knowing that the percentage of residual input tax it will claim will not change each period during the year.

How it will work – a business does not need HMRC permission to apply this new measure. Its intention to adopt the concession will be confirmed by the first VAT return it submits in the new tax year, ie if this return is based on the previous year's recovery percentage, the business must then adopt the same method for the remainder of the tax year.

(2) *A business has the option of including the tax that is payable or repayable as a result of the annual adjustment calculation on the VAT return at the end of the tax year rather than the first return of the new tax year.*

This measure means that the tax payable or repayable as result of the annual adjustment calculation can be included on the VAT return ending 31 March, 30 April or 31 May rather than the subsequent return.

Example – ABC Ltd has a partial exemption year that ends on 31 March 2010. The annual adjustment for the year has produced a VAT overpayment of £13,000. It would be sensible to include this adjustment on the March 2010 return, as allowed by the new legislation, because this brings forward the repayment by three months, ie a useful cash flow benefit.

Advantage of the new measure – there is potential for a business to help its cash flow position if the annual adjustment calculation produces a rebate situation. If a business has a financial year that is the same as its partial exemption year (eg 31 March is a common year end for many businesses) then the inclusion of the adjustment on the earlier VAT return will also avoid the need to include the amount of the annual adjustment as a VAT debtor or creditor figure in the accounts.

How it will work – the new measure is available to any business with a partial exemption year that ends on or after 30 April 2009. There is no need to apply to HMRC to adopt this measure.

(3) *A 'use based' basis of input tax recovery can be made in certain circumstances, rather than the usual standard method calculation based on income.*

The new rules enable a new partly exempt business to recover input tax on the basis of 'use' in the following circumstances:

- During its registration period – ie from the date when it first became VAT registered to either 31 March, 30 April or 31 May, depending on when it completes its VAT returns.
- During its first tax year – normally the first period of 12 months commencing on 1 April, 1 May or 1 June following the end of the registration period. However, this concession only applies if the business did not incur any exempt input tax during its registration period.
- During any tax year – provided it did not incur any exempt input tax in its previous tax year.

The principle of 'use' means that input tax recovery is based on how an expense will be used in the future rather the percentage of taxable income generated in the period when it is incurred.

Example – a business registered for VAT on 15 July 2009 and its registration period ends on 31 March 2010. During this period, it incurred input tax of £50,000 on setting up costs. These costs relate to future income that is both taxable and exempt, ie the input tax is classed as residual input tax. The business expects that its taxable income will be 70% of total income in its first three years of trading and that this would be a fair and reasonable basis to claim input tax on the £50,000 of setting up costs. This will produce an input tax claim of £35,000, ie £50,000 x 70%.

Advantage of the new measure – the measure will produce a fairer and probably improved input tax recovery rate by considering the principle of use. It will be particularly relevant for a business with negligible income in its registration period, ie where the standard method calculation could give a distortive result.

How it will work – the calculation made on quarterly VAT returns during the relevant period must also be applied to the annual adjustment calculation at the end of the tax year, ie to ensure consistency. However, a business that did not make a use based calculation on its quarterly returns can still do so for the annual adjustment calculation. This gives a new partly exempt business the maximum flexibility to ensure it can reclaim a fair amount of input tax.

Note – it is possible that the partly exempt business in the last example could benefit from the other concessions after the end of its registration period. This means it could use the 70% recovery rate on a provisional basis in its next tax year, although the annual adjustment calculation would need to be based on a standard method calculation based on income.

Compulsory measure

24.13   The three measures considered above are all optional. A fourth measure announced in the Brief is compulsory and relates to those businesses that make:

● supplies of services to customers outside the UK; or

● certain financial supplies such as shares and bonds; or

● supplies from establishments located outside the UK.

The main situation encountered by practitioners will be in relation to those clients who do some work for overseas customers, eg a UK based consultant who does some work for a Swedish client. Example 7 gives a practical example of the rule change.

Example 7

A UK business provides consultancy services to UK and non-UK business customers. It also has some exempt income in the UK from selling insurance services. No VAT is charged on the consultancy work carried out for overseas customers (place of supply is where the customer is based).

What is the input tax position under current and new rules?

Solution – under the partial exemption procedures that applied until 31 March 2009, a business was required to make a separate calculation to work out how much input tax could be reclaimed on costs relevant to the overseas consultancy income. This was achieved by making a calculation based on use.

For VAT returns commencing on or after 1 April 2009, the rules are simpler and the amount of residual input tax claimed is based on an income based calculation (usual standard method calculation) ie to include the consultancy income as taxable income irrespective of the location of the customer.

Note – even though consultancy work for an overseas client is outside the scope of UK VAT (because the place of supply is where the customer is based) it is classed as taxable income for partial exemption purposes because the services would be taxable if supplied in the UK.

Author note – HMRC's previous stance was that the inclusion of overseas income within the standard method could produce a distortive result. The new rules reverse this approach and recognise the fact that such income is based on normal commercial principles and does not warrant special treatment. However, a taxpayer who preferred the previous method based on use can still apply to HMRC to adopt a special method.

Input tax adjustments for change of intended use – 'clawback' and 'payback' provisions

24.14   Consider the following two examples:

(a)   A building company builds a new house and intends to sell the freehold of the property once it has been completed. This is a zero-rated supply for VAT purposes, so input tax of £20,000 incurred on building costs can be fully reclaimed as it relates to a taxable supply. However, when the building is completed 6 months later, the company decides to change the intended use and rent the house to a tenant on a 15-year lease. The rental income paid by the tenant is an exempt supply for VAT purposes (and because the property is residential there is no scope to waiver the exemption with an option to tax election).

(b)   A building company builds a new house and intends to rent it out to a tenant once the property has been completed. This is an exempt supply for VAT purposes, so input tax of £20,000 incurred on building costs cannot be reclaimed as it relates to an exempt supply. However, when the building is completed 6 months later, the company receives an excellent offer from an individual who wants to purchase the freehold of the property, ie generating a zero-rated (taxable) supply.

In the first example, the company is correct to reclaim input tax on the initial expenditure because at the time of incurring the expenditure, it intended to make a taxable supply. However, the change of use means it is affected by the 'clawback' provisions, which apply in the following situations:

• input tax was originally reclaimed because the taxpayer intended to use the goods or services for the purposes of taxable supplies. However, within a period of 6 years from the beginning of the period covered by the VAT return in which the original intention was formed, the use or intention to use is changed to making either exempt supplies or both taxable and exempt supplies;

- input tax was originally treated as residual input tax because the goods or services were intended to be used for the making of taxable and exempt supplies. However, within a period of 6 years from the beginning of the period covered by the VAT return in which the original intention was formed, the use or intention to use is changed to making exempt supplies.

In effect, the 'clawback' provisions apply because the initial input tax deduction based on intended use has proved to be excessive, and an amount is now payable to HMRC. The payment must be made on the return for the tax period in which the use occurs or the revised intention is formed.

There may be occasions when an item is actually used for the making of taxable or exempt supplies (or both) but then the use changes in future years. In such cases, no adjustment to the original allocation is normally needed unless the item in question needs to be adjusted over a 5 or 10-year period under the capital goods scheme (see Chapter 9).

In the second example at (b) above, the change of use from an intended exempt supply to an actual taxable supply means the business will benefit from the 'payback' provisions. This situation is the opposite to the 'clawback' provisions, as it means additional input tax can be reclaimed from HMRC.

The 'payback' provisions apply in the following situations:

- a business has not reclaimed input tax on relevant expenditure items because it was intended to use them in the making of exempt supplies. However, there is now a change of use or intended use so that they are either used in making taxable supplies or taxable and exempt supplies;

- a business has treated input tax on certain expenditure as residual input tax because it intended to use them in the making of taxable and exempt supplies. However, there is now a change of use or intended use so they are to be used only in the making of taxable supplies.

In the case of 'payback' situations, it is not acceptable to just make an entry on the next VAT return – approval has to be firstly granted by HMRC. Once approval has been received, the amount of VAT involved can be entered as an overpayment on the next return.

Note – with both 'clawback' and 'payback' provisions, the revised input tax calculation must use the same method of calculation as the original claim. Also, the provisions do not need to be corrected by a voluntary disclosure because the situation does not reflect the correction of any error – but a change in the basis for reclaiming input tax due to a change of intended use.

House builders and rental income

24.15 The downturn in the UK property market means that many house builders have been unable to sell their properties and have instead rented them out on a temporary basis in order to generate cash flow.

A potential input tax problem is caused by the fact that the first sale of a new dwelling (flat, house, bungalow etc) is a taxable supply (zero-rated) so input tax can be fully reclaimed on related expenses. But income from renting out a dwelling is exempt from VAT, so related costs cannot be reclaimed. If a house builder rents out a property for even a short period of time, the costs then relate to both taxable and exempt supplies – and an input tax adjustment could be needed.

HMRC took the opportunity to clarify its policy on the input tax challenges facing house builders in the above situation and full details are explained in Business Brief 44/08 and VAT Information Sheet 07/08. Both documents were issued on 15 September 2008.

The process for a builder is as follows:

- For past VAT returns, he must carry out a test called 'a simple check for *de minimis*' – this test identifies the past exempt input tax for relevant properties based on the expected number of letting years (out of a 10-year total period).

- If an adjustment of past input tax is then needed because the business is not *de minimis* for partial exemption purposes (exempt input tax less than £625 per month on average and 50% of total input tax) then HMRC will allow the business to adjust its input tax by using any method that 'fairly reflects the use of costs in making taxable supplies'. This could be based on income figures (expected letting income compared to expected sale proceeds from the property) or the number of letting years compared to a 10-year economic life of the building.

- For current and future VAT returns, the business must either adjust its input tax (if appropriate) by using the standard method of calculation for partial exemption (based on income) or formally request a special method from HMRC.

Note – any adjustment of past input tax is made on the VAT return relevant to when the decision was taken to rent out the property rather than sell it – there is no error notification issue because the original input tax was correctly claimed at the time.

The 10-year economic life figure quoted by HMRC is based on the same period that tax needs to be adjusted for property within the capital goods scheme and Lennartz mechanism.

The Information Sheet issued by HMRC gives full details and worked examples about input tax adjustments needed by builders for past, current and future VAT returns.

See Example 8 to show how input tax can be adjusted under the new rules.

Example 8

New Homes Ltd exceeded the 'simple check for *de minimis*' for year ended 31 March 2009 (it has decided to rent out properties (flats) it cannot sell for four years and sell them in 2013).

The company now needs to adjust some of the input tax originally claimed on the cost of the flats – an HMRC concession explained in VAT Information Sheet 7/08 means this can be done by any method that 'fairly reflects the use of costs in making taxable supplies.' (this assumes the taxpayer does not already have an agreed partial exemption special method in place – unlikely for smaller house builders).

The directors decide to make the input tax adjustment (amount not claimed) based on the following formula:

$$\frac{\text{Expected rental income}}{\text{Expected total income}} \times \text{input tax claimed on properties}$$

Note – expected total income = expected rental income + expected selling price of flats.

The current projections are that each of the six flats in question will sell for £200,000 in four years time, and will generate rental income of £10,000 per annum in the meantime.

Input tax to be adjusted:

$$\frac{(£10,000 \times 6 \text{ flats} \times 4 \text{ years})}{(£200,000 \times 6 \text{ flats}) + (£10,000 \times 6 \text{ flats} \times 4 \text{ years})} \times £30,000 = £5,000$$

Planning points to consider

24.16 The following planning points should be given consideration.

● An accurate partial exemption calculation can only be made if an accountant (or relevant staff) clearly identifies whether an expense should be coded as taxable, exempt or residual as far as input tax recovery is concerned. A major invoice incorrectly coded as residual instead of taxable (or exempt instead of residual or taxable) could cost a business a lot of money.

- Most businesses use the standard method of calculation as far as partial exemption is concerned. However, be aware that a special method of calculation can be applied for (as long as HMRC approval is obtained) if the standard method does not give a fair and reasonable result (see Chapter 25).

- Be aware of the need to make an annual adjustment for all partial exemption calculations – the adjustment is then declared on the first VAT return following the end of the tax year.

- Always check to see if a client is *de minimis* as far as partial exemption is concerned. In such cases, all input tax can be reclaimed, however, it is the annual position that matters, any quarterly calculations being made on a provisional basis.

- Optional procedures were introduced on 1 April 2009 that could benefit many partly exempt businesses by giving the opportunity to use an in-year recovery rate in relation to residual input tax. The measures also give the option to bring forward the annual adjustment declaration by 3 months and could also improve input tax recovery in some VAT periods by adopting a use rather than income based method of calculation.

- Compulsory rules were introduced on 1 April 2009 that effect businesses supplying services to customers outside the UK, certain financial supplies and supplies from establishments located outside the UK. It is important advisers consider these changes for any clients involved in such activities.

- A change of intended use of an item or actual use being different to intended use means that input tax originally claimed on goods or services could be affected by the 'clawback' or 'payback' provisions. In the case of a 'clawback' situation, extra VAT will be payable to HMRC – the opposite applies in a 'payback' situation, with a rebate being due.

- Special concessions were introduced in September 2008 to help the input tax position of house builders that temporarily rent out properties they have been unable to sell. The procedures are very flexible as long as a 'fair and reasonable' basis of calculation is used.

Chapter 25

Partial Exemption – Special Methods

Key topics in this chapter:

- Reasons why a special method could be appropriate for a business.

- Different methods that could be proposed, eg based on floor area, inputs, staff numbers and transaction numbers.

- HMRC approach to approving or rejecting special method proposals.

- The requirement for applicants to make a 'fair and reasonable' declaration when applying for a special method.

- Proposed methods likely to be rejected by HMRC, eg floor area applications where a large proportion of the floor area is excluded from the calculation as a non-attributable area.

- The importance of notifying HMRC of any changes in business circumstances that might affect a special method calculation.

Introduction

25.1   In Chapter 24, we considered the key issues for a partly exempt business as far as input tax restriction was concerned on costs relevant to exempt supplies. The main principle of input tax recovery is that it can only be recovered to the extent that it relates to taxable supplies.

The assumption made in Chapter 24 was that a business was using the standard method for partial exemption purposes, which basically works as follows:

- input tax relating wholly to taxable supplies can be reclaimed in full;

- input tax wholly relating to exempt supplies cannot be reclaimed;

- residual input tax to reclaim – apportioned according to:

$$\frac{\text{value of taxable supplies excluding VAT}}{\text{value of taxable and exempt supplies excluding VAT}}$$

(Note – residual input tax is relevant to those costs that cannot be directly attributed to either taxable or exempt supplies, eg general overhead items.)

The main principle of partial exemption is that the input tax reclaimed by any business with taxable and exempt supplies should be 'fair and reasonable'. Although calculation methods can never be totally exact, and are always based on an estimated situation, it is important that advisers (and HMRC) look at the overall result of a calculation to determine if it is reasonable.

For example, if a business has 90% exempt supplies and 10% taxable supplies, then it will recover 10% of its residual input tax using the standard method. But what if, for example, the business has an office where 50% of the staff in the building are working for the exempt part of the business and 50% of the staff in the building are working for the taxable part of the business? Would it then be fair for this particular business to only reclaim 10% of the input tax on its office costs?

The above situation is an example of where the standard method of calculation does not give a fair result. In such situations, a business has the opportunity to write to HMRC to request the use of a special method of calculation.

When a special method should be requested

25.2   The reason that a partly exempt business would want to adopt a special method of calculation is solely due to the fact that it considers the standard method does not give a fair and reasonable result in terms of input tax recovery on residual expenditure.

In cases where it considers that the standard method is unfair, the approach of the taxpayer (or his adviser) should be as follows:

- identify why the standard method is considered to be unfair;

- consider alternative methods of calculation that would give a fairer result;

- make a written application to HMRC to request formal approval to use this proposed method for future VAT periods.

The situation in Example 1 below highlights one arrangement where the standard method does not give a fair result.

Example 1

ABC Ltd has two activities – both generating equal levels of income (ie 50% taxable and 50% exempt). The main expenditure of the business on which input tax is incurred is linked to its property. The taxable activity is the organisation of fitness classes which takes up 80% of the premises; the exempt activity is the sale of insurance which takes up 20% of the premises. Is the standard method fair and reasonable in this situation?

Solution – most of the input tax for this particular business relates to the property from which it trades – and 80% of this property is used for taxable activities. But in reality only 50% of the input tax will be recovered on property costs using the standard method of calculation based on income.

In this particular situation, the business should write to HMRC to apply for a special method of calculation based on floor area.

Different types of special method

25.3 There are many different special methods that could be proposed by a business – the following are the main alternatives to the standard method.

Alternative methods

Floor area method

25.4 The situation in Example 1 identified a common basis of calculation, namely, an apportionment method based on floor area. This method is very simple to operate and is widely used by many businesses.

For example, a major cost of most non-profit making golf clubs is the cost of their clubhouse. In many cases, the percentage of the floor area allocated to the bar activity (taxable) will be a very high proportion of the total floor area in the building, but the percentage of bar income may be quite low compared to total income (which would include membership and entry fees, exempt from VAT). In such cases, it may be worthwhile to request a floor space method to apportion the input tax on clubhouse expenses.

Inputs method

25.5 The most common methods based on inputs are:

(a) taxable input tax divided by total input tax;

(b) taxable input tax divided by taxable input tax plus exempt input tax;

(c) taxable inputs (net of VAT) divided by taxable inputs plus exempt inputs (both net of VAT).

Note that method (a) above effectively includes any input tax on non-business supplies in the denominator part of the fraction; by increasing the denominator part of the fraction, this is effectively reducing the percentage of residual input tax that will be reclaimed with this method.

In reality, a special method based on inputs may produce a fairer result when the use of an overhead is more closely linked to costs than revenue. The limitation of the standard method in many cases is that it assumes that overhead and cost proportions are incurred in the same ratio as income percentages.

Staff numbers

25.6 This method is based on staff numbers and may be appropriate for a head office of a company in the case of expenses. Alternatively, a method based on the floor space occupied by staff involved in the taxable and exempt parts of the business may also be appropriate. See Example 2 for a practical situation when a staff number method may be appropriate.

Example 2

DEF Ltd is a national company with 50 estate agency branches throughout the UK. It uses the standard method of calculation for partial exemption purposes, but feels this method does not give a fair input tax recovery on its head office costs. The key figures for the year ended 31 March 2008 are as follows:

- the percentage of taxable income for the company is 40%;

- there are 120 staff at its head office, with 60 staff working on the taxable part of the business, 30 staff working on the exempt part of the business and 30 staff in sections that encompass both parts, eg finance.

The business wants to calculate its residual input tax based on employee numbers. What is the situation?

Solution – a key point is that a special method for partial exemption purposes cannot be made on a retrospective basis. It would not be acceptable for HMRC to allow a business to backdate a method just because an alternative calculation gives a better result in terms of input tax recovery.

As far as a special method is concerned, the company has two options:

- it could request a method of calculation that gives input tax recovery based on staff directly involved in taxable supplies (60) compared to total staff (120). This would give a recovery rate of 50%, which is still better than the standard method recovery rate of 40% (based on income);

- it could request a method of calculation that gives input tax recovery based on staff directly involved in taxable supplies (60) compared to total staff involved in taxable and exempt supplies (90). This calculation would give a recovery rate of 66.7%, which is the best result of all.

Note – the approach of HMRC to dealing with special method applications is considered at **25.8**. However, one of HMRC's main concerns is where a special method proposal attempts to ignore a large non-attributable element, eg as in the case of the 30 employees above who work on both taxable and exempt activities.

Number of transactions

25.7   A proposal could be made to base a special method calculation on the number of taxable transactions carried out by a business compared to the total number of transactions, ie including exempt sales. For example, this method could apply to a shop where the number of taxable and exempt transactions can be clearly identified and there is a sensible link between the volume of transactions and the input tax recovery overall.

However, it would not be sensible to propose a method based on the number of transactions if each taxable transaction was small in value, eg the sale of a bar of chocolate, whereas the exempt transactions were less frequent and higher value. See Example 3 for an illustration of this point.

Example 3

DEF Ltd, from Example 2, now wishes to propose a special method of calculation to deal with the input tax it can reclaim on the cost of its branch expenditure. For the year ended 31 March 2009, it made the following transactions:

● it sold 250 houses on a commission basis (taxable);

● it arranged 200 mortgages for clients and received a fee from the mortgage lender (exempt);

● it sold 3,000 books on how to be a property millionaire at £9.99 each (taxable).

It feels that an apportionment based on the number of taxable transactions to total transactions would be appropriate.

Solution – the proposed method would give an input tax recovery rate of 94.2% based on the number of taxable transactions (3,250) compared to total transactions (3,450). In reality, the proposed method would almost certainly be challenged by HMRC as it does not produce a fair and reasonable recovery rate.

A fairer method would be to propose a method that excludes the book sales – as these supplies are really incidental to the two core business activities of house sales and mortgage services. Even if accepted by HMRC at the application stage, the company would be wise to reconsider the proposed method if it was applied for after 1 April 2007. This is because of the potential comeback on the taxpayer through rules that require him to certify that the proposed method is 'fair and reasonable' in terms of input tax recovery. See 25.9.

HMRC approach to special methods

25.8   The key aim of any officer reviewing a special method application, or subsequent review of the method on a VAT inspection, should be to ask the simple question: does this method give a fair and reasonable outcome as far as residual input tax recovery is concerned?

In recent years, officers have looked very closely at applications, mainly because they feel that tax advisers are putting forward schemes that produce an excessive input tax recovery for certain clients. However, rules effective from 1 April 2007 put the onus on the taxpayer to certify that his proposed method is 'fair and reasonable' in terms of input tax recovery. If it is subsequently found to be unfair (and HMRC considers the taxpayer knew it would be unfair at the time of the application), then HMRC has the power to raise an assessment to correct any unfair recovery of input tax. Before this date, HMRC's powers were limited to preventing a taxpayer from using an agreed special method from a current date only. The power to issue a retrospective assessment of tax means it is now essential that taxpayers critically review their proposed methods before an application is made.

An officer will look at the bigger picture of any application and ask questions such as: is it reasonable that a business with 90% exempt income puts forward a special method application that produces an 80% input tax recovery on its residual costs.

The officer will confirm the method in writing – giving clear instructions as to how the method should be carried out. The following points should be noted:

- with a special method, the ratio of any calculation should be made to two decimal places – not rounded up to the nearest whole number as is the case with the standard method;

- all special methods should have an annual adjustment calculation – exactly the same as with the standard method. The aim of the annual adjustment is to even out any unfair results that can often occur with quarterly calculations;

- HMRC should be informed of any change in the business that has a substantial effect on the amount of input tax reclaimable. The special method will then be reviewed and, if no longer suitable, a direction to stop using the method will be issued.

A key point regarding special method applications is that they can only be effective from the date the method is approved – there is no facility in the legislation for retrospective approval. The reason for this is simple; if a business was allowed to go back and recalculate its partial exemption figures because it secured a better result in terms of input tax recovery, then advisers could exploit this loophole at every opportunity.

HMRC rules for special method applications approved after 1 April 2007

25.9 A key point to remember is that a special method application can appear to be based on a fair and reasonable proposal but contain a clause or section that distorts the overall result. This distortion may not be identified by HMRC at the time that the proposal is made, giving the taxpayer a very good outcome in terms of input tax recovery. It is probable that an officer will identify the distorted result on the next VAT visit but until 1 April 2007, he only had the power to revise the method from a current, rather than historic, date.

An important change was introduced on 1 April 2007 – any special method application now requires the taxpayer to certify that his proposed special method is 'fair and reasonable'. This declaration must be made before the application is approved for use.

The exact wording of the new special method declaration is as follows:

'As the taxable person, I hereby declare that to the best of my knowledge and belief, the proposed special method fairly and reasonably represents the extent to which goods and services are used or to be used in making taxable supplies. I also confirm that I have taken reasonable steps to ensure that I am in possession of all relevant information before making this declaration.'

A responsible person within the organisation must sign the declaration – or the sole trader or partner in the case of unincorporated businesses.

The change in the legislation means that HMRC now have powers to set aside a special method which the business should have known was not fair and reasonable. This enables retrospective recovery of VAT in such situations, a strong incentive for businesses (or advisers) not to make special method proposals that could be challenged in the future.

For a practical example of the impact of the rules, see Example 4.

Example 4

DEF Ltd operates a 24-hour call centre in a big office in London. Virtually all of its residual input tax relates to office costs – the landlord has opted to tax the property so rent is a major source of input tax.

The company employs 25 full-time staff processing applications on behalf of a large insurance company (which has been ruled as an exempt activity) and 50 part-time staff dealing with tax queries on behalf of a large firm of account-ants, which has been ruled as a taxable activity. It has been identified that the standard method gives unfair input tax recovery for the business – so the directors have put forward a case to HMRC that a special method should be approved, based on the number of employees involved in taxable and exempt activities, ie 66.67% input tax recovery (50 divided by 75).

Solution – HMRC would probably accept this proposed method at the application stage. However, there is a key piece of information that it might not fully appreciate. This is the fact that the tax staff are working part-time and the insurance staff are working full-time. This means that the actual staff usage of the building by the two activities is the same if the tax staff are working 50% of full-time hours – the proposed method gives the taxpayer a very good result.

Note – under rules effective from 1 April 2007, HMRC would probably impose a calculation method that either provides a split based on staff hours or staff numbers on a full-time basis. It would put forward the case that the company directors should have recognised the unfairness of their proposed method when they signed the declaration at the time of their application that 'to the best of their belief, the proposed special method is fair and reasonable'.

A fair result for input tax apportionment would probably be a 50% recovery rate – not the 66.67% initially proposed. An assessment of tax would be raised from the date the method was adopted by the taxpayer (assuming approval date after 1 April 2007) up to the VAT period when the unfairness was recognised by a visiting officer. The period of assessment is subject to the usual 3-year time limit, rising to 4 years on 1 April 2010.

Methods likely to be refused by HMRC

25.10   One of the main reasons why an application for a special method based on floor area can sometimes be rejected by HMRC is if it considers that the method proposed ignores a large part of the building because it is not wholly used for either taxable or exempt activities – in other words, a majority of the building is used for general purposes and is taken out of the proposed calculation.

This can mean that a business could propose a special method where, say, only 10% of the actual floor space is used in the computation – the balance of the building being ignored because it is not specific to either taxable or exempt activities. In such cases, HMRC could rule (probably with some justification) that the proposed method does not give a fair and reasonable result. This view (which has often been proposed in the past for opticians' businesses) has been supported by tribunal decisions. See Example 5.

Note – the tribunal chairman in the case of *Optika Ltd v Customs and Excise Comrs* (12 December 2003, unreported) (LON/00/1281 18627) made the comment in his case assessment that 'partial exemption methods based on floor area are seldom fair and reasonable'. However, this view was not shared by the chairman in the case of *Auchterarder Golf Club v Revenue and Customs Comrs* (3 November 2006, unreported) (EDN/06/28 19907) who concluded that a floor based method was effective in many situations, giving a fair and reasonable result in terms of input tax recovery.

Example 5

IC Clearly Ltd trades in the local high street. Its taxable activity is the sale of non-prescription glasses (taxable income) and it is calculated that about 60 square metres of the premises is allocated to glasses stock. The company also carries out sight testing (exempt income) and has a 20 square metre area for this activity. The rest of the premises (1200 square metres) consist of corridors, common areas, or areas linked to both parts of the business.

An application is made to HMRC for a special method based on the square footage ratio of the taxable activity to the taxable plus exempt activity. This effectively gives a recovery rate of 75% (60 divided by 80).

Solution – in reality, the method would be refused because the common areas represent too big a proportion of the overall premises, ie 93%. The use of only a small percentage of the land for specific purposes can hardly be expected to give a fair and reasonable result.

With regard to methods proposed on an inputs basis, a similar outcome could be evident, namely, that the proposed method gives an unfair result because of the high proportion of expenses that come into the residual input tax or inputs category.

Changes in circumstances

25.11 A special method approval letter from HMRC will include a paragraph that any significant change in the nature of the business must be notified to it if it has a notable effect on the amount of input tax being reclaimed. The method will then be reviewed, and if the fair and reasonable argument no longer applies, then a direction will be issued to stop a business from using the special method. It is then up to the taxpayer to propose an alternative special method, or accept the standard method instead.

One important power that HMRC holds is the option to issue a special method override direction.

Basically, it is recognised that if HMRC tells a business that a special method is no longer appropriate, there could be a time delay between the withdrawal letter and the date that the new method is agreed. In this case, for all VAT periods after the date of the notice, the business has to calculate the difference between the amount of input tax deductible using its current special scheme, and the amount of VAT that would be deductible in accordance with the principle of use. The difference between the two figures must then be declared by the business on its VAT returns.

In effect, the special method override direction ensures that a business cannot continue to benefit from an advantageous special method – due to delays in negotiating a new method with HMRC.

Opportunities for tax planning

25.12 One useful technique for a company to consider is whether it can legitimately plan its expenditure to produce a better than expected input tax recovery rate.

This technique would mainly apply if an expense that would be categorised as residual for input tax purposes could be split in advance so that direct attribution is feasible. Consider the circumstances at Example 6 below, which shows how thoughtful planning can produce a VAT saving as far as partial exemption is concerned.

Example 6

ABC Ltd has decided to carry out a major advertising campaign to promote its business – £20,000 plus VAT of £3,500 (based on VAT rate of 17.5%). The advert in question will promote both parts of its business (estate agency and mortgage sales) – but 80% of the advert will promote its estate agency activity. The business is on the standard method of partial exemption – 50% of its income being exempt and 50% of its income being taxable.

In this case, the cost of the advert will be categorised as residual input tax – producing a recovery of £1,750 VAT out of the total VAT charged of £3,500.

However, if the business had taken out two separate adverts, one to wholly promote its property sales (taxable) and one to wholly promote its exempt activity (mortgages), then the cost of these adverts would have been £16,000 plus VAT and £4,000 plus VAT respectively (assuming a charge based on the size of the advert).

The VAT recovery position has now improved – £2,800 being reclaimable on the taxable advert and only £700 being lost on the wholly exempt advert. The result? A saving of £1,050 in VAT.

As a general point, the time and effort spent on reviewing and applying for special methods will largely depend on the amount of residual input tax that is relevant to a particular business. The principle of direct attribution applies to both standard and special methods so if a business is able to allocate 99% of its input tax to wholly taxable or wholly exempt supplies, then the remaining input tax will be insignificant (unless it is a very large business). In such cases, the overall recovery percentage of the residual input tax is not an important issue.

Planning points to consider

25.13   The following planning points should be given consideration.

- It is important to regularly review the position of all partly exempt businesses and identify whether to apply to HMRC for a special method. These applications are appropriate when it is considered that the standard method does not give a fair and reasonable recovery of residual input tax.

- In many cases, the standard method gives a perfectly fair result – and overall is easy to calculate. However, it is important to be aware of alternative methods of calculation, particularly those based on inputs, square footage or staff numbers.

- The key principle of any partial exemption calculation is to ensure methods proposed are fair and reasonable. HMRC introduced regulations on 1 April 2007 that now require a taxpayer to make a 'fair and reasonable' declaration at the time he submits the application. HMRC has the power to recover tax on a historic basis if this declaration is incorrect.

- Any change in circumstance for a business that could affect the fair and reasonable result of its special method calculations should be immediately notified to HMRC. A revised special method may then be appropriate.

- Remember that it is only appropriate to spend time and effort proposing a special method if a business has a significant amount of residual input tax. If most (or all) input tax can be directly attributed to taxable or exempt supplies, there are negligible benefits to be gained by adopting a special method of calculation.

Chapter 26

Construction Services

Key topics in this chapter:

- The type of work that qualifies for zero-rating.

- The importance of the completion date for a new dwelling or qualifying building.

- Identifying what constitutes a new dwelling or qualifying residential/charitable building.

- The VAT liability of supplies made by subcontractors.

- Situations when a VAT certificate needs to be issued to enable a main contractor to zero-rate his supplies to a developer on a relevant new residential or charitable building.

- Supplies that are subject to the reduced rate of VAT (5%).

- Supplies of building materials that are always standard rated if supplied in the course of construction of a new dwelling, e g electrical appliances such as a fridge or dishwasher.

- The opportunity to obtain some zero-rating on professional fees through a 'design and build' arrangement.

Introduction

26.1   The services supplied in the construction of a new or existing building are normally standard rated. However, there are a number of exceptions to this rule:

- certain supplies may qualify for zero-rating – mainly in the case of new residential dwellings or other qualifying buildings. Certain alterations (but not repairs) to protected buildings are also zero-rated providing the building will remain as, or become, an eligible dwelling, or be used solely as a relevant residential building or relevant charitable building;

- in recent years, certain works have qualified for a reduced rate of 5%. This reduced rate is mainly relevant to work carried out in the course of certain residential conversions, or in carrying out work on altering certain buildings that have been empty for at least 2 years (3 years before 31 December 2007).

In many cases, services are supplied by subcontractors to a main contractor – the latter then works for the client who is receiving the benefit of the work. In certain cases, the work of the main contractor can be zero-rated if he receives a certificate from his client to confirm the building qualifies for zero-rating in accordance with the legislation. (Note – the main legislation concerning the zero-rating of construction services is contained in *VAT Act 1994, Sch 8, Group 5*.) However, the work of the subcontractor on the same building will be standard rated. This is an important principle to remember – the work of the subcontractor is not zero-rated because he does not hold a certificate from the main client.

Another important point to remember is that some of the VAT legislation relevant to construction services is largely dependent on the interpretation and meaning of certain key words, for example, 'dwelling', 'relevant charitable purpose', 'completion'. There will inevitably be occasions when appeals are made to VAT tribunals regarding the HMRC interpretation of these terms, which could extend the range of services that qualify for zero-rating. It is therefore worthwhile to read relevant articles and VAT tribunal decisions on this subject.

Zero-rated supplies

Main categories of zero-rated work

26.2   Zero-rating applies to the following supplies:

- services supplied in the course of construction of new qualifying dwellings and certain other new relevant residential properties and relevant charitable buildings. In the case of work on a new dwelling, zero-rating also applies to the construction of a garage if it is built at the same time as the dwelling and it is intended to be occupied with it;

- services supplied in the course of construction of civil engineering work for the development of a new permanent residential caravan park;

- services supplied to housing associations in the course of converting non-residential buildings into residential buildings;

- certain approved alterations to protected buildings;

- building materials and certain electrical goods incorporated into a building by a builder who is also supplying any of the above zero-rated services;

- certain goods and services supplied to disabled persons;

- the first time connection of gas or electricity mains to dwellings and certain other residential buildings.

An important point to remember is that building materials are only zero-rated if jointly supplied to the customer with services from the same builder – see Example 1.

Example 1

Smith Builders Ltd is installing kitchen units into a new house being built by Mr Jones. Mr Jones suggests that he buys the units himself from Kitchen Furniture Ltd and that Smith Builders Ltd just charges him for labour. Mr Jones is not registered for VAT – but Smith Builders Ltd has been registered for many years.

Solution – if Smith Builders Ltd bought the units from Kitchen Furniture Ltd, it would be able to recover input tax on the cost of the units. The company is then making an onward supply of labour and materials for work on a new residential building, and the full charge will be zero-rated.

However, if Mr Jones buys the materials himself from Kitchen Furniture Ltd, he will be charged VAT by the company, even though the units are for a new residential property. This is because Kitchen Furniture Ltd is supplying materials only, and zero-rating would only apply if the company was supplying relevant services as well. In this case, Mr Jones will have an unnecessary VAT bill (although he could possibly recover this VAT under the DIY scheme – see Chapter 29).

Type of work that qualifies for zero-rating – and relevance of completion date

26.3   A key point about zero-rating on qualifying dwellings is that it is only supplies made directly in the course of construction that can be zero-rated, not related services such as the following:

- services of architects, surveyors, consultants or supervisory services;

- the hire of goods on their own, e g plant and machinery without an operator, scaffolding without erection/dismantling.

In effect, therefore, the legislation means that the building work carried out on the building itself will be zero-rated – and this includes all work carried out until the building is completed. Once completed, any subsequent work is standard rated. The usual time when a building is deemed to be 'complete' is when a Certificate of Completion has been issued. However, there can be other relevant issues, such as, the date when the building is sold, the intentions of the developer, when the building is occupied. See Example 2.

Example 2

John has bought a 'shell' apartment from a developer, on which he has obtained a special deal because he is responsible for fitting out the property himself. He makes contact with builders covering a wide range of trades – carpenters, plumbers, kitchen fitters, electricians – and they perform a range of services on the apartment to make it a property that John can then live in. What is the VAT position of the supplies made by the builders?

Solution – even though the builder sold the property to John, it was sold before it was completed. The work carried out is therefore zero-rated as construction services carried out on a new dwelling before it has been completed. In effect, the completion date would be when John moves in to the property.

From a tax planning point of view, it is therefore important for as much work as possible to be carried out before the building is completed so that it can qualify for zero-rating. For example, if a customer agrees to buy a new house from a developer and agrees to pay an extra £10,000 for the property to have a conservatory fitted, then this payment will form part of the consideration to buy the house and will be zero-rated. However, if he bought the property without the conservatory and then asked a builder to subsequently build him a conservatory, this work would then be standard rated because it has taken place after the relevant completion date.

Note – a tribunal case *Mr and Mrs James* (30 October 2007, unreported) (LON/07/328 20426) considered the VAT liability of plastering work carried out after the completion date of a new dwelling, but with the aim of correcting defective plastering work caused by the original builder.

HMRC claimed that the work was standard rated as the alteration of an existing house, but the tribunal supported the taxpayer and confirmed the work should be zero-rated. The tribunal's approach was that the new plastering work was supplied in the course of the construction of the building because the old plastering work was inadequate and dangerous.

Scope of new qualifying dwellings, qualifying charitable buildings and other relevant residential properties

26.4   As explained at **26.1**, zero-rating mainly applies if work is being carried out on a new dwelling, a new qualifying charitable building or other new properties used for a relevant residential purpose.

New dwelling

26.5   In basic terms, a new dwelling must have the following main features if the work is to qualify for zero-rating:

- it must consist of self-contained living accommodation;

- there must be no provision for direct internal access to any other dwelling;

- the separate use, letting or disposal of the dwelling is not prohibited by any legal clause or other provision. This means, for example, that the construction of a granny annex to an existing house is not classed as a new dwelling;

- statutory planning consent has been granted in respect of that dwelling and its construction or conversion has been carried out in accordance with that consent.

In most cases, it will be fairly obvious to identify if a project is both 'new' and a 'dwelling' – a key exclusion will always be if a project is for commercial purposes, eg new office, warehouse, factory, industrial unit.

An example of when a new dwelling is created is if an additional flat (or flats) is built on top of existing flats, ie to create an additional floor(s) with new units. However, the conversion of two flats on an existing floor to create three smaller flats on the same floor would not be classed as the construction of a new dwelling but the conversion of two existing dwellings.

Building for a relevant charitable purpose

26.6 A key point is that building work carried out by the main contractor (not subcontractor working for the main contractor) on a new building being constructed for a charity will only qualify for zero-rating if it is being used by the charity 'otherwise than in the course or furtherance of a business'.

The phrase 'business' does not necessarily relate to 'profit' – it is possible for a charity to have a loss making business activity.

Examples of *qualifying* buildings would therefore be:

- places of worship;

- offices used by charities for administering non-business activities such as the collection of donations.

Examples of *non-qualifying* buildings would be:

- child nurseries where a fee is charged;

- school buildings where a fee is charged for the provision of education;

- offices used by charities for administering business activities such as fundraising events where an entrance fee is charged.

Note – where a building has business and non-business use, there is an HMRC concession that the business use can be ignored if it is less than 10%. The 10% figure can be calculated on a floor space, staff numbers or time basis, however, once a method of calculation is chosen, it cannot be changed. A calculation method using floor space or staff numbers must be approved by HMRC.

With effect from 21 March 2007, the charity must certify that there is no intention at the time of zero-rating that the building will be used for business purposes in excess of 10% of total use within 10 years. So if, for example, a building is finalised in June 2009, the charity must not have an intention to have a business use of the building that exceeds 10% of total use before June 2019. It would not be a problem if the 10% use was exceeded between these years, as long as the intention in June 2009 was for less than 10% business use to be achieved.

The other main situation where zero-rating would apply is if the new building is being constructed as a 'village hall or similarly in providing social or recreational facilities for a local community'. This particular aspect of the legislation has been the subject of various tribunal decisions in recent years – the main principles being challenged have related to the scope of the facilities being offered by a building and the extent to which it is being used by the local community.

The obvious situation where zero-rating would apply is in the case of a new village hall being built solely for the use of residents in a particular area. Such buildings must be available for use by the community at large, not just isolated sections of the community. This clause would therefore exclude the construction of a theatre, swimming pool or child nursery. See Example 3 which highlights the importance of the building being intended for local community use.

Example 3

ABC Charity Ltd is a registered charity owning a property that is used by an independent fee paying school. The charity has arranged for the construction of a new building to be used as a sports hall for the school, which will be available for general community use at specific times, ie weekends, school holidays, evenings. The company trustees consider that the building work should benefit from zero-rating.

Solution – the sports hall could be available for general use, so the nature of the building is not a problem. However, the main beneficiaries of the hall are the pupils at the school, not the local community at large. The community use is effectively a secondary purpose of the building, not its main aim. The construction services will therefore be standard rated.

Recent case law – building for relevant charitable purpose

26.7 The question of whether a new building was intended for use solely for a relevant charitable purpose was considered by the VAT Tribunal in the case of *Quarriers* (EDN/07/120 20660).

The issue for the tribunal was whether a new epilepsy centre being constructed by Quarriers was eligible for zero-rating on the construction costs or whether the actual use of the building was to be for business purposes, ie the building work would be standard-rated. The tribunal ruled in favour of the building being for non-business purposes.

- Although fees were received from local authorities towards the costs of caring for patients at the centre (fee income usually indicates a business purpose), these fees were not determined by reference to going rates in the market but were based on what Health Boards were willing to pay for the unique services provided by Quarries.

- The activities carried out by the charity were at the heart of its charitable purposes.

- The tribunal did not feel that the activities were carried out on a commercial basis which might justify them being described as a business activity.

- The appeal was therefore allowed, with costs awarded to the charity.

Other properties used for a relevant residential purpose

26.8   This part of the legislation (*VAT Act 1994, Sch 8, Group 5, Note 4*) secures zero-rating for work carried out by the main contractor (not subcontractors working for the main contractor) on the following new buildings:

- a home or other institution providing residential accommodation for children;

- a home or other institution providing residential accommodation with personal care for persons in need of such care by reason of old age, disablement, past or present dependence on alcohol, drugs or past or present mental disorder;

- a hospice;

- residential accommodation for students or school pupils;

- residential accommodation for members of any of the armed forces;

- a monastery, nunnery or similar establishment;

- an institution which is the sole or main residence for at least 90% of the residents.

Note – the legislation makes an exception where use of a building is as a hospital, prison or similar establishment or an hotel, inn or similar establishment.

See Example 4 for an illustration of when zero-rating applies on this part of the legislation.

Example 4

Barry is the chief surveyor for BCD Construction Services Ltd. He is currently submitting quotes for three jobs and has asked his VAT advisor to confirm the VAT liability in each case:

(a) the company has been asked to build a new bedroom block comprising 10 bedrooms in the grounds of a registered care home;

(b) the company has been asked to build a new home for people with mental disorders – the home will be for the people to use on a temporary basis only, while they recover from their illnesses;

(c) the company has been asked to construct a new property which will comprise 50 apartments for nurses to live in on a permanent basis as their main residence, and 4 apartments that will be rented out on a short-term bed and breakfast basis.

Solution – only (c) will qualify for zero-rating. In this case, the four apartments being rented out on a short-term basis is not a problem because at least 90% of the residents will be using the building as their sole or main residence.

The mental home will almost certainly be classed as a hospital, which is excluded from zero-rating. The new bedroom block is not eligible for zero-rating because it is not classed as the construction of a new home for a relevant residential purpose in its own right – but part of a larger home or institution.

Services of subcontractors and issuing of certificates for qualifying buildings

26.9 At 26.4–26.8, it was identified that zero-rating could be relevant to construction services carried out on three different types of new building:

(a) a new dwelling, eg a house, flat or bungalow;

(b) a new building for a relevant charitable purpose, eg a church;

(c) a new building for a relevant residential purpose, eg a home for elderly persons.

In the case of a subcontractor working for the main contractor (or for any other person apart from the person who intends to use the building), it is only work being carried out on a new dwelling that could qualify for zero-rating. All work carried out by a subcontractor for a main contractor on a new building for a relevant charitable purpose or a new building for a relevant residential purpose is always standard rated.

As an additional clause, the work carried out by a main contractor on a new building for a relevant charitable or residential purpose (ie excluding new dwellings) cannot be zero-rated unless he receives a certificate from the user of the building (his customer) confirming that the building in question is being used for a relevant residential or charitable purpose.

Regarding these certificates, the following points should be noted:

- the customer can either copy the certificate from HMRC VAT Notice 708, or create his own certificate provided it contains the same information;

- the certificate must be issued before the supplier makes his supply;

- the customer providing the certificate could be liable to a civil penalty if it is found by HMRC that it should not have been issued, ie work should have been standard rated rather than zero-rated or subject to VAT at the reduced rate;

- the supplier has a responsibility to take reasonable steps to ensure the certificate is valid, including correspondence with the customer to confirm the use of the building;

- as long as the supplier has taken reasonable steps to ensure the certificate is valid, then HMRC will not seek to recover any VAT from the supplier if it is found that VAT has been undercharged on the work in question.

See Example 5 for a practical example of how the above chain of events works in practice.

Example 5

ABC Ltd has secured work as a main contractor on two new projects:

- the construction of a new home for the elderly for Claywell Housing Association;

- the construction of three new four-bedroom detached houses for a national house builder.

ABC Ltd intends to use the services of DEF Ltd to carry out all roofing work on these two projects. What is the VAT position for the two companies?

Solution – ABC Ltd and DEF Ltd can both zero-rate the work carried out for the national house builder, as long as the work is relevant to the construction of the property and carried out before its completion. In this case, there is no need for any certificates to be obtained from the housebuilder to confirm zero-rating.

The new property for Claywell Housing Association is classed as a new building for a relevant residential purpose, which means the services of DEF Ltd as the subcontractor must always be standard rated.

However, as long as Claywell Housing Association issues a certificate to ABC Ltd as the main contractor confirming that the building will be used for a relevant residential purpose, then ABC Ltd can zero-rate its charges to the Association.

The other positive point is that because ABC Ltd is making a zero-rated supply (ie taxable) it can reclaim the VAT charged by DEF Ltd as input tax.

Note – there is still widespread ignorance of these rules within many construction companies. Many surveyors working for main contractors think (incorrectly) that their subcontractors should zero-rate supplies to them if they give the subcontractor a copy of their certificate from the final customer. Other surveyors think (incorrectly again) that the certificate from the final customer only becomes relevant if requested by HMRC. The main contractor should receive a proper certificate from his customer before work is carried out on the project.

Work that is always standard-rated

26.10 A basic rule of VAT is that a supply is always standard rated, unless it is specifically zero-rated, exempt or outside the scope of VAT. There are also other supplies that can qualify for a reduced VAT charge of 5%.

The approach to adopt for dealing with a liability query from a construction industry client is to identify under which section of the legislation the work could qualify for zero-rating, and then see if it qualifies within that section.

However, as a general principle, the following categories of work are always standard rated for VAT purposes:

- repair or maintenance work – but see **26.11** regarding residential conversions and the reduced rate of VAT;

- alterations to an existing building – unless the building is a protected building;

- the reconstruction of an existing building – a building only ceases to be an existing building when it is demolished completely to ground level or the part remaining above the ground level consists of no more than a single façade (double façade where a corner site), the retention of which is a condition or requirement of statutory planning consent or similar permission;

- any work on a non-residential building unless it is a new qualifying building for a relevant charitable purpose;

- work on new and uncompleted non-qualifying buildings and civil engineering works, eg commercial buildings such as offices;

- extensions to existing buildings.

Reduced rate supplies (subject to VAT at 5%)

26.11   The main categories of construction work that can qualify for a reduced rate of VAT are as follows:

- qualifying services supplied in the course of certain residential conversions;

- qualifying services supplied in the course of renovating and altering certain buildings that have been empty for 2 or more years (the previous limit was 3 years until 31 December 2007);

- building materials and certain electrical goods incorporated into a building by the builder who is also supplying the above services;

- installation of energy-saving materials and the grant-funded installation of heating equipment or security goods or connection of a gas supply.

With regard to residential conversions, work on the following projects would all qualify for the reduced rate of VAT:

Type of conversion	Examples
A single household dwelling into a multiple occupancy dwelling, or a building for a relevant residential purpose.	Converting a four bedroom detached house into two bedsits; converting a private house into a residential home for elderly people.
A single house dwelling into two or more single house dwellings.	Conversion of a house into two flats; converting a four bedroom detached property into two semi-detached properties.
A number of single house dwellings into a different number of single house dwellings.	Conversion of property with five large flats into seven smaller flats.
A multiple occupancy dwelling into a single household dwelling or a building for a relevant residential purpose.	Converting a property with four bedsits into a large detached home; converting a property with four bedsits into a residential home for elderly people.
A relevant residential purpose building into either a single household dwelling or a multiple occupancy dwelling.	A residential home for elderly people is converted to a four bedroom house; a residential home for elderly people is converted to six bedsits.
Any other building into a single household dwelling, multiple occupancy dwelling or building for a relevant residential purpose.	Conversion of office block into flats; conversion of a public house into a four bedroom detached house. In these cases, the number of dwellings is being changed from zero to a positive number of one or more.

The main exclusion from the reduced rate of VAT is where a property starts as a multiple occupancy dwelling, and is converted into another multiple occupancy dwelling – even where the number of units has changed. This means, for example, that work carried out on the conversion of a property comprising four bedsits into a property that comprises six smaller bedsits will be subject to VAT at the standard rate.

The reduced rate would not apply if a relevant residential building was converted into another relevant residential building, eg a conversion of a home for the elderly into a children's home.

Qualifying services mean either of the following:

- carrying out work to the fabric of the building or part of the building being converted;

- carrying out work within the immediate site of the building in connection with the means of providing water, heat, power or access to the building; the means of providing drainage or security to the building; the provision of means of waste disposal for the building.

Note – the qualifying services include all works of repair, maintenance or improvement to the fabric of the building where the work forms an intrinsic part of changing the number of dwellings.

The rules concerning conversions of single/multiple occupancy dwellings can sometimes be somewhat complicated and a useful situation to highlight this point is shown at Example 6.

Example 6

Manor House is a property that comprises 12 self-contained flats, with four flats on each floor. Work is carried out to create three large flats on the first floor (instead of four) but the ground floor is altered so that this floor accommodates five smaller size flats.

Solution – although the number of units remains unchanged at 12, the reduced rate of VAT can still be applied for the work carried out in connection with the conversions because the number of flats on the ground and first floors has changed.

Empty property rules

26.12 The reduced rate of VAT can also be applied (as explained above) to supplies of qualifying services on the renovation or alteration of single household dwellings, multiple occupancy dwellings or buildings to be used for a relevant residential purpose as long as the building in question has not been lived in for 2 years or more (3 years until 31 December 2007).

The reduced rate charge will also apply to any building materials installed by the builder as part of his work.

The rules concerning empty building conditions are very specific (see VAT Notice 708) and there is some responsibility on the supplier of the services to have reasonable evidence that the property has been empty for at least 2 years. In assessing whether a property has been lived in, any illegal occupation by squatters and non-residential use can be ignored, for example, if the building had been used for storage by a business.

Supply of building materials and other goods

26.13   The supply of goods by a builder also providing services will qualify for zero-rating if the work being performed is zero-rated, and the goods in question relate to the services being supplied.

For example, a builder installing kitchen units to a new dwelling would be able to zero-rate the supply of both the goods and his services. However, if he also supplied a television to his customer, then this would not be zero-rated because it is not linked to the service being performed.

In general terms, the phrase 'building materials' relates to goods that are 'ordinarily' incorporated or installed as fittings by builders in a building of that description.

For example, HMRC accepts that an item is incorporated into a building if its removal would require the use of tools but they would not accept that free-standing appliances or furniture would qualify. This would therefore exclude from zero-rating the supply of plugged-in appliances and free-standing furniture such as sofas, tables and chairs.

In terms of the phrase 'ordinarily' installed, HMRC accepts that certain properties have items which it would be expected would be included within the building, for example, air conditioning, burglar alarms, fire-places and surrounds, electric showers.

However, there are a number of items that are excluded from the general rules and which would always be standard-rated (or subject an input tax block) if supplied by a builder. These items are listed in VAT Notice 708 – but the main exclusions are as follows:

- electrical or gas appliances such as refrigerators, cookers, washing and dish-washing machines, tumble dryers;

- carpets or carpeting material such as carpet tiles or underlay. However, floor coverings such as linoleum, ceramic tiles and wooden floor systems are building materials and could therefore qualify as zero-rating.

Note – if the builder installs non-building materials into a new dwelling (such as carpet) then it is only the supply of the goods that is standard-rated. If he makes a separate charge for his installation services, the latter would still be zero-rated.

Other matters

26.14   The VAT issues involving construction industry supplies are very extensive, and this chapter has focused on the main practical situations which advisers could be faced with on a day to day basis. A few useful issues to consider are now given to conclude the chapter:

- *Design and build supplies* – as explained at **26.3**, the supply of professional services is always standard rated. However, there may be occasions when a main contractor is engaged to carry out both the design and construction elements of a project. In such cases, the VAT liability of the overall project depends on the liability of the building work. If the building work is zero-rated, the design element will also be zero-rated, which could produce a potential tax saving for the client if he is not in a position to reclaim input tax. The main contractor will be able to reclaim input tax on any fees charged by an architect or surveyor because he is making a zero-rated supply.

- *Authenticated receipts and self-billed invoices* – both of these documents are issued by the customer rather than the supplier and are very common in the construction industry. The main principle is that the customer issues the authenticated receipt or self-billed invoice at the time that he makes payment to a supplier – and these documents form the basis of output tax declared by the supplier and input tax reclaimed by the customer. The procedure is particularly useful in the construction industry where amounts actually paid for, e g work in progress based on a valuation figure, can be different to amounts requested by a supplier on his sales invoice. In both the case of authenticated receipts and self-billed invoices, a tax invoice should not be issued by the supplier.

- *CIS deductions* – in many cases, a main contractor is required to deduct income tax from his payments to a subcontractor under the Construction Industry Scheme (CIS) arrangements. If the subcontractor is VAT registered, then VAT charges must be based on the gross value of the work carried out, not the amount remaining after the income tax has been deducted by the main contractor.

- *Protected buildings* – the basic VAT rule is that work on protected buildings can be zero-rated if it relates to an approved alteration and is carried out on a building that will remain, or become, an eligible dwelling, or the building will be used solely for a relevant residential purpose or for a relevant charitable purpose. Any work of a repair or maintenance nature cannot be zero-rated. The supplier should have evidence that the building is protected. Any unapproved alteration work carried out on a protected building will be standard rated.

- *Work for disabled persons* – certain work carried out for disabled persons can qualify for zero-rating. However, zero-rating will depend on two main issues, namely the status of the person receiving the work (i e the extent to which he is disabled and whether this will be acceptable to HMRC) and the nature of the work being carried out ie the goods or services being supplied. A good reference point on this subject and the procedures to adopt is VAT Notice 701/02.

- *Retentions* – it is common practice in the construction industry for a customer to hold back part of the payment for services performed, usually for 6 months or 1 year. In such cases, output tax is not payable to HMRC by the supplier until either he receives payment for the retention from his customer, or he raises an invoice to the customer (whichever happens sooner).

- *Incorrect VAT charge* – there is a tendency for many builders to adopt a play safe approach and charge VAT at the standard rate. If you think that work should be zero-rated or subject to a reduced rate VAT charge, then it is sensible to agree this position before the work begins. There could be problems recovering VAT from a builder if he has already received his payment. In such cases, if zero-rating is subsequently agreed, the builder should refund any incorrectly charged VAT by issuing a VAT credit note. He can then reduce his output tax liability on the VAT return covered by the date of the credit note or VAT refund to the customer.

Planning points to consider

26.15 The following planning points should be given consideration.

- Building materials are only zero-rated if they are also supplied with a service that is eligible for zero-rating.

- It is advisable for people buying a new residential dwelling to fit out the property to their requirements before it has been completed. The work will then be eligible for zero-rating in most cases – once the completion date has passed, the work will be standard rated.

- Remember that supplies made by a subcontractor to a main contractor are only zero-rated if relevant to a new dwelling. All supplies involving a relevant residential building or qualifying charitable building are standard rated when supplied by a subcontractor.

- A main contractor is only able to zero-rate work carried out on a new relevant charitable building or new relevant residential building if he obtains a certificate from his client confirming the building is eligible for zero-rating. This certificate should be received before the building supplies are made.

- There are a wide range of services that qualify for the 5% reduced rate of VAT in relation to many residential conversions – or work on residential properties that have been empty for at least 2 years. The difference between the reduced VAT rate and standard VAT rate is considerable so there is scope for considerable savings if reduced rate work is correctly identified in advance.

- Most goods supplied by builders as part of their work on a new dwelling will be zero-rated. However, there are certain goods where the supply is always standard rated (or subject to an input tax block), and it is important to be aware of such items, e g fridges, washing machines, dishwashers.

- There are opportunities to save VAT on professional fees if a developer enters into a 'design and build' arrangement with a main contractor. In such cases, the liability of the design services will follow the same liability as the building work, ie possibly zero-rated. Design fees and professional services supplied on their own are always standard-rated.

Chapter 27

Property Transactions – Introduction

Key topics in this chapter:

- What constitutes a licence to occupy land.

- Examples of exempt and standard rated supplies involving a licence to occupy or use land.

- The approach to adopt when identifying whether a licence to occupy land arrangement is exempt or standard rated as far as VAT is concerned.

- Assessing whether an arrangement is for an exempt licence to occupy land or a standard rated supply of services (illustrated by example of self-employed hair stylist).

- Exceptions to the rule that the grant of an interest in or right over land is exempt from VAT, ie standard-rated (eg sale of new commercial building) or zero-rated (eg sale of new dwelling).

- Apportionment of output tax where the sale of a new building includes a standard rated and zero-rated element, eg the sale of a new first floor flat and a ground floor shop.

- Temporarily renting out new dwellings that cannot be sold by a house builder.

Introduction

27.1   The main focus of Chapter 26 was to consider the VAT issues concerning construction industry services, ie situations where work performed by a builder would be zero-rated, standard rated or, in some cases, subject to VAT at the 5% lower rate of tax.

In this chapter, we consider actual supplies involving property, ie the sale of a freehold or leasehold property and the VAT issues therein – or the letting of property to receive rental income.

There are two main situations as far as land and property are concerned:

- the granting of an interest in or right over land, eg the sale of property on a freehold or long leasehold basis;

- the granting of a licence to occupy land, eg where a landlord sublets his interest in the property to a tenant in return for payment of rent.

Property transactions are quite unique from a VAT aspect because the landlord/user of a property has the right to waive exemption in certain cases by making an election to tax the property, ie exempt supplies will become standard rated and subject to VAT. The decision to opt to tax a property has major implications and is considered in Chapter 28.

Exempt supplies – licence to occupy land

27.2   The basic legislation in *VAT Act 1994, Sch 9, Group 1* states that, subject to certain exceptions, the 'grant' (see **27.3**) of any 'interest in or right over' land (see **27.4** and **27.10–27.12**) or 'licence to occupy' land (see **27.5** and **27.8**) is exempt as far as VAT is concerned.

Grant

27.3   A grant of land is a sale of the freehold or other interest, or a lease or letting of land. It includes the surrender of the land (eg where a tenant renting the land returns its use back to the landlord) and assignment of the land, ie the transfer of a lease by an existing tenant to a new tenant.

Interest in or right over land

27.4   'Interest in or right over land' means that the person using the land has either a legal interest in the land (ie formal ownership of the land such as a freehold or leasehold interest in it), or a beneficial interest (that is, the right to receive the benefit of supplies of the land, eg sale proceeds or rental income). Rights over land include rights of entry and easements.

Licence to occupy land

27.5   HMRC regards a licence to occupy land as being created when the following criteria are met:

(a)   the licence should be granted in return for a consideration paid by the licensee;

(b)   the licence must be to occupy a specific piece of land;

(c)   the licence is for the occupation of the land by the licensee;

(d)   another person's right to enter the specified land does not impinge upon the occupational rights of the licensee; and either:

(i)   the licence allows the licensee to physically enjoy the land for the purpose of the grant (eg to hold a party in a hall); or

(ii)   the licence allows the licensee to exploit economically the land for the purpose of its business (eg to run a nightclub).

It is important to recognise when a licence to occupy land situation applies – see Example 1 for an illustration of a practical situation.

Example 1

Smitherton Golf Club is looking to generate extra funds to pay for some improvement projects. The committee has therefore decided to rent out the kitchen area to a self-employed caterer, who can then sell light meals and snacks for members in the bar area. The rental arrangement will include full use of all the kitchen equipment.

As a separate transaction, they allow a local company to come to the club office at any time in order to use the club's photocopying machine and fax machine. The company will pay a fixed monthly fee for this facility.

What is the VAT position of the two transactions above?

Solution – going back to the four main rules as to when a licence to occupy land exists:

• *Is the licence granted in return for a consideration paid by the licensee?*

The answer in both situations is 'yes' as both the caterer and the local company are paying rent to the golf club.

• *Does the licence give the licensee a specific piece of land to occupy?*

In the case of the caterer, the answer to this question is 'yes', ie he has use of the kitchen area to develop his activities. The answer is 'no' in the case of the company using the office equipment – the main users of the office will be the golf club staff, and the supply being enjoyed by the company is the use of the office equipment, ie standard rated.

• *Is the licence for the occupation of the land by the licensee?*

In the case of the caterer, a 'yes' reply is again applicable.

• *Does the licensee have the right to enjoy the land or to exploit it for economic gains?*

The caterer is trading from the premises he is occupying, ie he meets the economic gains clause.

Overall, the catering arrangement has met all four of the licence to occupy land rules and therefore the rental payment to the golf club will be exempt from VAT. However, if the golf club had opted to tax their premises, then the supply would become standard rated – see Chapter 28.

Examples of exempt supplies under licence to occupy land rules

27.6 Listed below are some examples of exempt supplies under the licence to occupy land rules.

- *The provision of office accommodation* – however, this would have to be a specified bay, room or floor, and an agreement would often include the right to use shared areas such as reception, lifts or leisure facilities. The key point is that the tenant occupying the land is obtaining his own area of land from where he can conduct his business.

- *A shop-in-shop arrangement* – this situation occurs when a business is granted a specific area in a shop or store from which to trade. This situation is particularly common in large department stores, where there are a number of different entities trading from the premises in their own names.

- *Granting space to erect advertising hoardings* – this situation applies at, for example, a sporting ground where there are advertising boards around the ground to promote various companies. The company that is advertising through the board pays a rent to the sports club for the board to be displayed. The board should be fixed in its own area, i e not a mobile board that moves around the ground to different locations.

- *Hiring out a hall or other accommodation for meetings, parties etc* – this can be a difficult area as far as VAT is concerned, because sometimes the hire of a hall includes other benefits such as catering arrangements and the supply of staff to, for example, entertain delegates. In such cases, the overall supply could be standard rated. However, the basic hire of a hall/room for an event will qualify for exemption.

- *Granting a catering concession, where the caterer is granted a licence to occupy specific kitchen and restaurant areas, even if the grant includes the use of kitchen or catering equipment* – see Example 1 above.

- *Granting traders a pitch in a market or at a car boot sale* – this example illustrates the point that a short-term let can still qualify for VAT exemption – it is the principle of a licence to occupy land that counts, not the length of time that it is used.

Approach to adopt in identifying if an arrangement is exempt

27.7 The above examples of exempt supplies in licence to occupy land situations all meet the four key rules identified at **27.5**.

A useful approach to adopt when assessing the VAT liability of an arrangement is to ask three key questions as follows.

(a)   In reality, what is the main supply being enjoyed by the person paying his money to the landlord? If this is clearly the right to occupy a specific area of land for his own benefit or enjoyment, then the supply will usually be exempt from VAT.

(b)   Does it appear that the main benefits being enjoyed by the person paying his money are related to specific services rather than the right to occupy land, eg the use of photocopying facilities as in Example 1 above.

(c)   Is there an indication that an arrangement is not for a specific area of land, for example, the fee paid for an ice cream van to be allowed into a sports venue to sell ice creams would not be exempt because the van driver has the opportunity to move his van to different parts of the ground (eg to place it in the area where there are most potential customers). In such cases, his payment is standard-rated as the right to sell ice-creams, not a licence to occupy land.

See **27.8** for examples of arrangements that would be standard rated for VAT purposes because a licence to occupy land situation does not exist.

Standard rated supplies – in relation to use of land

Examples of standard rated supplies

27.8   At 27.6, examples and situations were given to illustrate when a supply involving land was exempt from VAT on the basis that the owner/user of the land is providing another party with a 'licence to occupy the land'.

In commercial situations, there are many examples of a business 'using' the land of another person or party for various reasons – but the arrangement falls short of the 'licence to occupy' arrangement that qualifies for exemption. In such cases, the charge to the user of the land will be standard rated.

The following examples illustrate when an arrangement is standard rated rather than exempt:

●   sharing business premises where more than one business has use of the same parts of the premises without having their own specified areas – the key feature here is that the business does not have its own land to enjoy, only on a shared basis;

●   providing another person with access to office premises to make use of the facilities – as in Example 1 above;

- granting an ambulatory concession, e g ice cream vans on the sea front, hamburger vans at sporting events. The key point here is that it would be impossible for these vehicles to have their own specified area of land, in reality, they are paying for access to a potential market in which to sell their goods;

- allowing the public admission to premises or events – again, there is no licence to occupy land situation – the member of the public is gaining access to premises in order to enjoy the entertainment or other facilities on offer;

- allowing the public to tip rubbish on land;

- storing someone else's goods in a warehouse without allocating any specified area for them;

- any grant of land where the land is incidental to use of the main facilities that can be enjoyed – see **27.9** which illustrates this situation with the example of a hairdresser.

Hairdresser arrangement

27.9 Many practitioners have hairdresser clients, so in this section the rules on hairdresser arrangements will be considered. The situation highlighted could apply to many other different types of business as well.

A common arrangement for hairdressers is as follows:

- many stylists will trade on a self-employed basis, using the facilities within a hairdressing salon (the scope of whether a person is employed or self-employed is beyond the scope of this book);

- the stylists will make payment to the landlord/main owner of the hairdressing salon – to compensate him for the facilities they enjoy in the salon;

- on occasions in the past, the payment for these benefits has been described as for 'rent a chair', i e an attempt to make the supply exempt from VAT as a licence to occupy the land covered by the chair;

- in reality, the stylists receive many other benefits for their payments – laundry services, the use of a rest room, the services of a receptionist employed by the salon owner, towels and linen, shampoos and other materials.

The key question to ask is: what is the main supply (or supplies) being enjoyed by the stylist – and does this represent an exempt licence to occupy land (the chair space), or a standard rated supply of related services such as those described above? This question has been considered by a number of well publicised tribunal cases in recent years – including the case of *Byrom (t/a Salon 24) v Revenue and Customs Comrs* [2006]

EWHC 111 (Ch), [2006] STC 992, [2006] SWTI 378, [2006] All ER (D) 75 (Feb). This particular case related to a massage parlour, but with a similar arrangement to the hairdressing example.

The conclusion reached was that the payment to the massage parlour owner (equivalent to a salon owner in hairdressing situation) represented a standard rated supply of various services provided for the masseurs – not an exempt supply of a licence to occupy land. The renting of the room to the masseurs (chair in hairdressing example) was incidental to the main supply of services and effectively ignored.

An important point to remember is that it is not possible to escape the reality of a situation by producing a contract between the stylist and salon owner that says the stylist is only paying for the rent of the chair. Equally, it is not acceptable to raise a sales invoice describing payment as being for the rent of the chair. In effect, the commercial reality of the situation and the actual benefits being enjoyed by the stylists are the important factors – not the wording of a sales invoice or contract.

Exempt, standard rated and zero-rated supplies – grant of an interest in or right over land

What constitutes the grant of an interest or right over land?

27.10   As explained at 27.3, the grant of any interest in or right over land is, subject to certain exceptions, an exempt supply. The grant of an interest in, or right over, land is different to a licence to occupy land. See Example 2.

Example 2

Bill owns the freehold of a four-story office block – he agrees to rent the third floor of the block to Ben and sell him the second floor on a 999-year lease.

Solution – in the first situation, Ben has a licence to occupy the land on the third floor. In the second situation, he has an interest in and right over the land on the second floor.

Situations when the grant of an interest in, or right over, land is standard rated

27.11   The supply of an interest in, or right over, land is exempt from VAT in most cases – but standard rated in the following main situations.

- *New and uncompleted non-qualifying buildings and civil engineering works* – if a new or uncompleted building does not qualify as a 'dwelling' or number of dwellings and is not intended for use solely for a 'relevant residential purpose' or a 'relevant charitable purpose' then its sale will be standard rated. The sale of a new building as a 'dwelling' or a number of dwellings or for a 'relevant residential purpose' or 'relevant charitable purpose' is zero-rated.

This means, for example, that the freehold sale of new or uncompleted office blocks, factories, warehouses and industrial units would all be standard rated. A building/civil engineering work is to be taken as 'completed' when an architect/engineer issues a certificate of practical completion in relation to it or it is fully occupied/used, whichever happens first. It is to be treated as 'new' if it was completed less than 3 years before the grant.

Note – the sale of a building means the freehold sale, not the assignment of a lease at a premium. Once a building is three years old, any future sales of the building will be exempt from VAT unless an option to tax election is in place.

The issue of what is classed as a building for a 'relevant residential purpose' or a 'relevant charitable purpose' is considered in Chapter 26 – the person buying the building in these cases is obliged to provide a certificate confirming the intended use of the building. See Example 3 for an illustration of this point.

- *Gaming and fishing rights.*

- *Hotel/holiday accommodation* – the grant of any interest in or right over or licence to occupy holiday accommodation, e g a chalet, caravan or house-boat, is standard rated if the accommodation is held out as holiday accommodation or suitable for holiday or leisure use.

- *Caravan and tent pitches and camping facilities.*

- *Parking facilities* – the granting of facilities for parking a vehicle is always standard rated – this would include the letting or licensing of garages or designated parking bays or spaces. However, the letting of a garage as part of the letting of a dwelling for permanent residential use is exempt from VAT because the letting of the garage is incidental to the letting of the main property.

- *Boxes, seats etc at entertainment venues* – this has become increasingly more common in recent years, e g a company may rent a box for a season at a football ground. In such cases, the main benefit being enjoyed by the users is the opportunity to see the sporting or entertainment activity taking place (standard rated), rather than an exempt right over land situation.

Example 3

Jones Builders Ltd has purchased a plot of land and intends to build two office blocks on the land and then sell the freehold interest. The first office block is built and sold to a national stationery company to use as its head office. The second property is to be sold to a national charity for them to use for non-business purposes.

What is the VAT position in each case?

Solution – the sale of the new office block to the national stationery company is standard rated because it is a new building that is not being used as a dwelling or number of dwellings, or for a relevant residential or relevant charitable purpose.

The sale of the second property to the national charity can be zero-rated because it is being used by the charity for non-business purposes. However, the charity will need to issue a certificate to confirm the use to which the property is being put. Without the certificate, it would not be possible for Jones Ltd to zero-rate the sale.

Situations when the grant of an interest or right over land is zero-rated

27.12   The examples above illustrated when grants in or rights over land are standard-rated – zero-rating would apply in the following circumstances.

- *New dwellings* – the first grant of a major interest in a new dwelling is zero-rated, i e the freehold sale of the building or a long lease exceeding 21 years (20 years in Scotland). Any second sale or subsequent long lease sale will be exempt from VAT. See Example 4.

- *New residential and charitable buildings* – the first grant of a major interest in a building to be used by the buyer for a 'relevant residential purpose' or a 'relevant charitable purpose' is also zero-rated. In these situations, it is necessary for the buyer of the property to issue a certificate to the seller confirming his intended use of the building. An example of a standard certificate layout can be found in HMRC's VAT Notice 708. For a list of the main types of properties that would be classed as being for a relevant residential or charitable purpose, see Chapter 26 at **26.4–26.8**.

- *Conversion of non-residential buildings* – if a building has been converted from non-residential into residential use, then the first grant of a major interest in the building will be zero-rated. An example of a qualifying project, quite common in this country, is for an agricultural barn to be converted into a house or bungalow. Commercial buildings (e g office blocks) may be converted into blocks of flats or a home for elderly persons (the latter is an example of a new building for a relevant residential purpose, which are also covered by these rules).

- *Substantial reconstruction of a protected building* – the first grant of a major interest in a protected building that has been substantially reconstructed will qualify for zero-rating. A protected building is substantially reconstructed when:

  - reconstruction takes place that involves major work to the building's fabric, including the replacement of much of the internal or external structure; and

  either:

  - at least 60% of the total cost of the reconstruction (including materials and other items to carry out the work but excluding the services of an architect, surveyor or other person acting as consultant or in a supervisory capacity) could be zero-rated as 'approved alterations'; or
  - the reconstruction involves 'gutting' the building – that is no more of the original building is retained than an external wall or walls, or external walls together with other external features of architectural or historic interest.

Note – A protected building is not 'substantially reconstructed' where the only major alteration is the addition of an extension. However, work to extend a protected building could be zero-rated as an approved alteration if supplied by a builder. This means that if you carry out major works to reconstruct a building, then the construction of an extension can count towards your 60% 'substantial reconstruction' calculation.

Example 4

Smith Ltd is a property development company working on two projects:

(a) the company purchased a plot of land for £50,000 and has spent £100,000 on labour and materials to construct a new four-bedroom detached house. It intends to sell the freehold interest in the house for £200,000;

(b) the company also bought an existing residential property for £120,000 in the next street. It intends to spend £30,000 refurbishing and repairing the property – and will then sell the freehold interest in the property for £200,000.

What is the VAT position in each case?

Solution – The first property is a new dwelling so the first sale of the freehold will be zero-rated. This has the double advantage for the company in that no output tax is payable on the proceeds of the sale but any related input tax on the project, for example on building materials, can be reclaimed. As the property in question is a new dwelling rather than for a relevant residential or charitable purpose, then zero-rating can be applied without the need for a certificate to be issued by the person buying the property.

The second property relates to the sale of an existing dwelling – it is only new dwellings that can qualify for zero-rating so the sale of this property will be exempt from VAT. This situation has an advantage in that there is no VAT to charge on the sale of the property – but a disadvantage in that the related costs of improving the property will be classed as relevant to an exempt supply and the input tax would not be reclaimable (unless the amount of input tax is small and the *de minimis* rules could apply). See Chapter 24 for an analysis of the issues concerning what is known as partial exemption.

Note – the above situation is very common for many property development companies and it is important that advisers fully appreciate the difference between a sale being zero-rated and exempt as far as input tax recovery is concerned.

Sale of new buildings with a mixed use

27.13   Consider the following situation: a property developer builds a new property on land that he has bought, which comprises a shop on the ground floor and a first floor flat. The shop is clearly for a commercial purpose and therefore standard-rated as the sale of a new non-qualifying building. The sale of the flat is zero-rated as the first time sale of a new dwelling.

In many cases, it is possible that the two separate properties will be bought by different people, in which case the VAT treatment will be straightforward, ie zero-rating will apply for the flat and the shop sale will be standard-rated.

However, it is possible that the same person might buy the combined property and, in such cases, the consideration received from the buyer needs to be apportioned on a fair and reasonable basis so that output tax is correctly paid on the part of the deal relating to the shop.

Another common situation that occurs for housing associations is where they sell a percentage of a new dwelling to an individual(s) and retain ownership of the rest of the property. This type of transaction is known as a shared ownership arrangement – the intention being that the tenant will eventually buy the entire interest in the property. The tenant will pay rent to the housing association for the percentage of the property that he does not own.

In such cases, the initial payment by the occupier for his share of the new equity in the new property can be zero-rated but the subsequent rental payments and any additional payments for equity are exempt from VAT, ie not zero-rated.

Temporarily renting out new houses

27.14   A common situation that has emerged in recent years is where new house builders (or builders of any new dwellings) have been unable to sell their properties because of the downturn in the property market. In such cases, they have often decided to temporarily rent out these properties to generate short-term rental income.

The challenge for house builders is that the sale of a new dwelling is zero-rated as far as VAT is concerned (input tax can be claimed) but rental income is exempt from VAT (no input tax can be reclaimed on related costs). The decision to generate rental income therefore has implications in relation to partial exemption and means that input tax already claimed may need to be repaid.

Any adviser who has a client faced with this situation should refer to HMRC's Business Brief 44/08 and VAT Information Sheet 07/08 issued on 15 September 2008. These notes explain the potential input tax adjustment needed for a house builder generating short-term rental income. The positive news is that the procedures recognise that although a business is making exempt supplies (rental), the overall intention is to still make an eventual zero-rated supply – so not all input tax is disallowed. In fact, many house builders could be *de minimis* after the various calculations have been made and not need to repay any input tax.

Planning measure

27.15   A possible measure to protect the input tax claimed on the cost of constructing new dwellings is to form a connected company or business and sell the completed property to this business (zero-rated sale) – the latter then generates the exempt rental income. The zero-rated sale made by the first business protects all input tax it has claimed on the construction costs. HMRC has confirmed in Business Brief 54/08 that such a measure is not considered to be abusive because the legislation always intended for input tax to be claimable on the costs of building new dwellings for sale.

It is important to consider the direct tax and SDLT (stamp duty and land tax) implications of such a measure and the other key issue relates to the amount of input tax actually involved in the project. For example, many house builders use subcontractors to carry out building services and these services (and any materials provided by the subcontractor) are zero-rated. So the only input tax incurred by the house builder could be relevant to professional fees only, which may produce the outcome where he is *de minimis* as far as partial exemption is concerned, ie able to fully recover all of his input tax.

Note – the issues considered in this section are quite complex and professional advice may be needed to ensure all relevant matters are fully considered.

Other matters

27.16   Other situations to be taken into account are as follows.

- *Option to purchase or lease land* – it is quite common for a property developer to make a payment to a landowner for the opportunity to purchase an interest in his land or buildings at a future date for an agreed price. The payment represents the right to an interest in land and the liability of the payment will be the same as the liability of the land or buildings when it is eventually purchased. In most cases, the purchase of the land and buildings will be exempt so the option payment will also be exempt.

- *Landlord inducement payments* – there may be occasions when a landlord will make a payment to a tenant in order to encourage the tenant to take out a lease on his property. In reality, such payments are outside the scope of VAT as long as there is no obligation for the tenant to give benefits to the landlord in return for the payment. For example, if it was an obligation of the payment for the tenant to carry out some building improvement work on the property, this would constitute a standard rated supply of services.

- *Reverse surrenders* – it is possible that a tenant wishes to escape from a lease and pays a sum of money to the landlord to accept the surrender. In most cases, this payment will be exempt from VAT (following the same liability as the rental payments) unless the option to tax has been taken in which case the payment will be standard rated.

- *Dilapidation payments* – many lease agreements will contain a clause that a landlord can charge a tenant at the end of an agreement for the cost of any necessary repairs to return the property to its original condition. In effect, such payments reflect a claim for damages by the landlord to the tenant and are therefore not a supply for VAT purposes. The payment is therefore outside the scope of VAT.

- *Rent-free periods* – the grant by a landlord of a rent-free period is not a supply for VAT purposes except where the rent-free period is given in exchange for something which the tenant agrees to do, eg carry out works for the benefit of the landlord. In the latter example, the supply would then be standard rated, with output tax due on the value of the rent that has been sacrificed.

- *Services charges* – a service charge generally applies to a leased property where common areas are shared between more than one tenant. For example, a block of flats will often incur a service charge arrangement, so that each leaseholder contributes to the cost of upkeep of common areas, buildings insurance, gardening services to communal land etc. The VAT liability of the service charge usually follows the liability of the main rental payment to the landlord, ie exempt in most cases but standard rated if the option to tax election has been made.

Planning points to consider

27.17 The following planning points should be given consideration.

- The supply of a licence to occupy land is generally exempt from VAT. However, it is important to ensure that an arrangement qualifies for exemption by meeting the four key rules explained at **27.5**.

- Some supplies can be exempt from VAT if the supply is only to occupy land, e g hire of a hall. However, the supply could become standard rated if the hirer receives significant other benefits as well as the hire of the hall. In such cases, it is important to charge VAT if appropriate.

- Many businesses have tried to describe arrangements as being relevant to an exempt supply of land – whereas the reality of a situation is that they are providing a package of services subject to VAT at the standard rate. In such situations, it is important to remember that the commercial reality of an arrangement takes precedence over how an arrangement is described in a contract or on a sales invoice.

- Remember that the sale of the first freehold (or long leasehold) interest in a new dwelling is zero-rated but the sale of an existing dwelling is exempt from VAT. Although there is no output tax charged in either case, the input tax issues between the two different transactions are very different, ie no input tax is reclaimable in relation to an exempt supply.

- Certain payments relating to a property are outside the scope of VAT or exempt from VAT so it is important to recognise these situations when they arise to avoid an unnecessary output tax charge (particularly to a person that cannot recover the VAT charged, eg a business making exempt supplies). For example, dilapidation payments and landlord inducement payments are outside the scope of VAT and service charges are usually exempt too because they follow the VAT liability of the main rent payment.

- House builders need to be aware of the VAT implications of temporarily renting out any new dwellings they cannot sell, ie the potential input tax restriction because exempt supplies are being made. A possible measure could be to sell the completed property to a connected company (zero-rated sale) to protect any input tax claimed on the construction of the dwellings.

Chapter 28

Property Transactions – Option to Tax

Key topics in this chapter:

- The consequences of making an option to tax election.

- How to notify HMRC of an option to tax election.

- The opportunity to revoke an option to tax election on certain properties after 1 August 2009.

- The benefits of opting to tax a property – enhanced input tax recovery because supplies become taxable rather than exempt.

- Potential problems of opting to tax a property – creating a VAT charge to some tenants or property buyers who are not able to reclaim input tax.

- Failing to notify an option to tax election to HMRC – Business Brief 13/05.

- Situations when the option to tax is overridden, e g when the buyer of an opted property intends to convert it into a dwelling.

- Rules to follow when an opted property is sold as part of a transfer of a going concern arrangement.

- The different forms to complete since 1 June 2008 in relation to various situations involving land and property and the option to tax election.

Introduction

28.1   The VAT liability of goods and services is determined by relevant legislation – and will either be standard rated, zero-rated, subject to the reduced rate of VAT, exempt or, in some cases, outside the scope of VAT.

There is an extra dimension to consider as far as land and property transactions are concerned – namely that there is an opportunity for certain exempt supplies to become standard rated through making what is known as the 'option to tax'.

The option to tax (or 'election to waive exemption') is a decision taken by a person owning or renting land or buildings and has the effect of making all supplies relevant to his interest in that property taxable rather than exempt. It is a very important decision to make because the option cannot be revoked for 20 years once it has been made (apart from a limited cooling-off period).

The main reason for making an option to tax election is to facilitate input tax recovery on either capital or revenue expenditure – if a supply is exempt, then input tax cannot be reclaimed in relation to that supply.

However, the option to tax election means that all supplies relevant to the land or property (eg rental income from subletting; proceeds from selling the building) will become standard rated rather than exempt. This means that tenants or purchasers will be faced with a 15% or 17.5% extra charge – no problem if they can reclaim input tax on their own VAT returns, but definitely a problem if they are either an exempt or partly exempt business or not registered for VAT.

An important point to note is that the option to tax election can only be made on commercial properties – for example, it is not possible for the owner of a three-bedroom house to opt to tax the property and charge VAT on future rents to tenants.

Implications of opting to tax a property

28.2 As explained above, the decision to elect to tax a property has major consequences as far as VAT is concerned, and is one that should not be taken lightly. The amounts of tax involved in land and property transactions are considerable and a hasty decision to tax a property could potentially create an extra VAT cost to tenants or prospective buyers of the property who cannot reclaim input tax.

Equally, the decision to opt to tax the property could exclude a large number of potential buyers or tenants (eg businesses with exempt income such as insurance brokers) from having any interest in the property, for instance because it will be more cost effective for them to pursue an interest in a property where the option to tax has not been made.

Once a business has opted to tax its interest in land or property, it must charge VAT on all future supplies it makes in relation to that property:

- if the property is let or sublet to tenants, then VAT must be added to any rent charge;

- if the property is sold, then VAT must be added to the disposal proceeds.

Note that there are some situations where the option to tax a property is overruled by other legislation – see **28.6**.

An important point to remember is that it is only the taxable person's interest in the property that is subject to the option to tax – not the interests of other people also connected with the property – see Example 1.

Example 1

ABC Properties owns the freehold of a building at 67 High Street. It lets the building to a VAT registered firm of accountants, DEF Ltd, who sublet two of the four floors in the building to a training firm called GHI Ltd. ABC Properties decides to opt to tax its interest in the property. How will this situation affect DEF Ltd?

Solution – once ABC Properties has made the decision to tax the property, all rent that it charges to DEF Ltd will include VAT at the standard rate. However, the option to tax the property only relates to the supplies made by ABC Properties – there is no compulsion for DEF Ltd to also tax its own interest in the property.

However, DEF Ltd may also decide to opt to tax its interest in the property – otherwise some of the VAT charged by ABC Properties could be disallowed because it relates to an exempt supply, ie the sublease to GHI Ltd. This decision should not be a problem if GHI Ltd is also registered for VAT and able to reclaim input tax on its expenditure.

Procedures for taxing a property

28.3   There are two stages in opting to tax:

- making the decision to opt to tax an interest in land or a building and recording this decision, for example, in board meeting minutes or other relevant correspondence (ie this is the internal decision confirming there are benefits in making the election);

- making a formal notification in writing to HMRC of the decision.

The notifications to HMRC are now dealt with centrally from one office:

Option to Tax National Unit
HM Revenue and Customs
Cotton House
7 Cochrane Street
Glasgow G1 1GY
Telephone: 0141 285 4174/5

The notification should be made by using Form VAT 1614A (which can be obtained from the National Advice Service or downloaded from the

HMRC website). It is acceptable to fax a notification (0141 285 4454) or send it by e-mail to: optiontotaxnationalunit@hmrc.gsi.gov.uk.

The written notification to HMRC must be made within 30 days of the decision to tax the property being made and cannot be made on a retrospective basis.

Important points to bear in mind as far as the option to tax notification is concerned are as follows.

- In most cases, it will be clear as to the extent of the land or property subject to the election. To use the situation from Example 1 above:

    'We, the partners of ABC Properties, wish to apply the option to tax to our freehold interest in the property we own at 67 High Street. We wish to make the election with effect from xx/xx/xxxx.'

    However, in some cases it may be necessary for a taxpayer to clarify his exact interest in a property by including a map or plan with his notification form.

- Form VAT 1614A is used where no previous exempt supplies have been made in relation to a property. In simple terms, this means that the property has not been rented out before the election was made. If a business has generated exempt income in the past, then it may need HMRC's permission to opt to tax the property, ie permission is not automatic. In such cases, VAT 1614H needs to be completed instead of VAT 1614A. To decide whether you need HMRC's permission, it is necessary to review HMRC Notice 742A, section 5 (Permission to opt to tax).

- Once made, the option to tax cannot be revoked until at least 20 years have elapsed since the date on which it had effect. The only exception to this rule is if a business meets conditions of the 'cooling off' regulations, which give limited opportunities to revoke an option within 6 months of the election being made (3 months before 1 June 2008). See **28.18** for further details on the 'cooling off' rules.

- HMRC expects Form VAT 1614A to be signed by a person with the appropriate authority, eg a director in the case of a limited company; the sole proprietor or one of the partners in a non-corporate entity. If a business submits an election via a third party, eg a solicitor or accountant, then HMRC must receive confirmation that the third party has been authorised to act on behalf of the business.

Benefits of opting to tax land or property

28.4   As explained at **28.1,** the main benefit of opting to tax land or property is that input tax relevant to an exempt supply and not reclaimable would become relevant to a taxable supply and therefore reclaimable subject to the normal rules. See Example 2 for an illustration of this point in a practical situation.

Example 2

ABC Properties have purchased a commercial property for £500,000 plus VAT of £87,500. They intend to rent out the property on a 10-year lease to a firm of solicitors for £25,000 per year. ABC Properties will also be responsible for any property repairs (landlord repairing lease), estimated to be £5,000 per year plus VAT. The solicitors taking on the lease are VAT registered and only making taxable supplies, ie no exempt income.

Solution – this is a clear situation of when the option to tax should be adopted by ABC Properties. Failure to opt to tax the property will mean that the £87,500 of VAT on the initial purchase of the property will be lost (as being relevant to an exempt supply) because the income generated by the property will be exempt. Equally, the £875 of VAT on the repair costs each year (£5,000 × 17.5%) will also be not reclaimable because it relates to an exempt supply. The total VAT lost in 10 years will be £96,250 (ie £87,500 plus £875 × 10).

However, if the option to tax is made at the time the property is purchased, then all input tax will be reclaimable because all supplies relating to the property are now taxable. There is no problem with VAT being added to the rent charge to the solicitors because they can reclaim it as input tax.

The situation given at Example 2 was a 'win:win' arrangement. The landlord of the property was able to benefit from a significant input tax saving by electing to tax his interest in the property; the tenants were not inconvenienced by the subsequent VAT charge on the rent because their business allows them full input tax recovery.

However, in some business arrangements, the facts may not be as clear cut and the overall benefit of opting to tax the property will need to be assessed. Consider the following circumstances:

● it is possible that a business may want to sell property at some time in the future. If the option to tax election has been made in respect of that property, then VAT will need to be added to the sale proceeds – this may deter certain prospective purchasers not able to recover input tax – see **28.5**;

● it is possible that future tenants of a property may not be registered for VAT, e g because they only make exempt supplies. The VAT charged on the rent will then become an extra cost to the business, which reduces the competitiveness of the letting arrangement;

- it is possible that an existing lease may preclude a landlord from adding VAT to his rental charge. In such cases, the landlord would have to treat rent received as VAT inclusive if he opted to tax the property in question – directly affecting his bottom line profit.

Disadvantages of opting to tax land or property

28.5 There are two main disadvantages of opting to tax an interest in land or property:

(a) a tenant who is paying rent to use the property may not be able to recover any VAT charged as input tax; and

(b) the purchaser of the land or property may also be unable to reclaim VAT charged as input tax.

See Example 3 for an illustration of this point.

Example 3

ABC Properties now decides to sell the property in Example 2 for £800,000. It has forgotten that the proceeds of the sale must account for output tax because it elected to tax its interest in the property.

There are two businesses interested in buying the property – an insurance broker to use as its head office and a clothes retailer, also interested in using the property as a head office function. What is the VAT situation as far as the sale of the property is concerned?

Solution – the option to tax situation will almost certainly come to light before the deal is finalised, which means that £140,000 VAT will be added to the sale value (based on standard rate of 17.5%).

For the clothes retailer, this should not be a problem (apart from the increased stamp duty cost it will face – stamp duty is charged on the gross proceeds of the sale) – because the sale of clothing is a taxable activity, so input tax should be reclaimable on the acquisition of the building. However, the insurance company will have a problem – insurance services are mainly exempt from VAT, so the VAT charge will almost certainly add an extra £140,000 to the cost of the building, with no scope for input tax recovery.

Note – the insurance company may be happy to buy the property for £800,000 including VAT – in which case ABC Properties will be out of pocket, effectively only receiving sale proceeds of £680,852 (£800,000 × 40/47) instead of £800,000.

Situations when the option to tax is not applied

28.6 There are certain situations when an option to tax arrangement is effectively overridden, ie the sale of the interest in the land or property will be exempt rather than standard rated (even though the property owner has made an option to tax election). See **28.13** for new certification procedures now required in many cases. The main situations when the override would apply are as follows.

- *Dwellings* – any supply in relation to a building (or part of a building) intended for use as a dwelling or a number of dwellings or solely for a 'relevant residential purpose'. If an opted building is being sold and converted into dwellings by the buyer, the latter must complete Form VAT 1614D and give it to the seller before the price of the deal is legally fixed (usually before exchange of contracts). This means the sale of the building will then be exempt rather than standard-rated. However, this may present some input tax problems for the seller – hence the need for VAT 1614D to be issued before exchange of contracts. If the form is issued after this time, the seller can reject the request to override the exemption if he wishes.

- *Charitable use* – a supply in relation to a building (or part of a building) intended for use solely for a 'relevant charitable purpose' other than as an office. (See Chapter 26 for an explanation about what constitutes a 'relevant residential purpose' or 'relevant charitable purpose'. An example of a relevant residential property is a residential home for children; a building for a relevant charitable purpose is a building used as a village hall or similar.)

- *Residential caravans* – a supply of a pitch for a residential caravan.

- *Residential houseboats* – a supply of facilities for the mooring (including anchoring or berthing) of a residential houseboat.

- *Housing associations* – a supply to a relevant housing association which has given the supplier Form VAT 1614G stating that the land is to be used for the construction of buildings or a building for use as a dwelling or number of dwellings or solely for a 'relevant residential purpose'.

- *DIY builders* – a supply of land to an individual where the land is to be used for the construction of a building intended for use by him as a dwelling (not as a business venture).

- *Certain supplies affected by anti-avoidance measures* – HMRC has detailed anti-avoidance measures in place, mainly to prevent a business that has some or mainly exempt supplies obtaining an unfair recovery of input tax in a land or property transaction. Any adviser or business that thinks it will be affected by the provisions (unlikely in most cases) can review the detailed rules in VAT Notice 742.

For an illustration of a situation when an option to tax election is overridden, see Example 4.

Example 4

JKL Properties Ltd owns the freehold of a public house that has been rented out for the last 10 years to a publican. The company opted to tax the property when it first bought it in 1997 and is now selling the freehold interest in the property to MNO Ltd, who intend to convert the entire property into eight self-contained flats.

Solution – in normal circumstances, JKL Properties Ltd would need to charge output tax on the disposal of the property because it made the option to tax election within the last 20 years. However, no output tax is due on the proposed sale because the conversion by MNO Ltd means the building is intended to be used as a 'dwelling or a number of dwellings'. With effect from 1 June 2008, MNO Ltd must issue Form VAT 1614D to JKL Properties Ltd to confirm its intended use of the building and that the option to tax is therefore overridden. This certificate must be issued by MNO Ltd before the price of the sale if legally fixed, ie usually exchange of contracts.

Registering for VAT as a result of making an option to tax election

28.7 It is possible that a previously unregistered business may need to become VAT registered as a result of opting to tax land or property. This need to register may be on a compulsory basis (ie value of taxable supplies exceeding registration limits) or on a voluntary basis because the business wishes to benefit from input tax recovery on its costs.

If this situation applies, then the business will need to submit Form VAT 1 and its option to tax election (Form VAT 1614A or VAT 1614H) at the same time to the relevant VAT Registration Unit appropriate to its postcode. It may need to support the application with other evidence concerning the land or property in question – correspondence, plans, minutes of meetings confirming intentions etc.

Forgetting to tell HMRC about an option to tax election

28.8 As explained earlier, there are two stages to carrying out a successful option to tax election:

- taking the decision to opt to tax ie internal action through board meeting minute, correspondence with advisers, charging VAT on income generated by the property, claiming input tax on costs etc;

- formally notifying HMRC of the election in writing.

A common VAT problem occurs when the business making the election forgets to tell HMRC about its option – ie the second stage above. In such cases, this is not usually a problem as long as the business can prove its original intentions ie it has taken the decision to opt to tax and acted accordingly. A belated notification can then be made in accordance with the terms of HMRC Business Brief 13/05.

However, a problem would be evident if the taxpayer is attempting to gain a VAT advantage by trying to backdate his option. Any such request for backdating would then almost certainly be refused by HMRC.

Transfer of a going concern arrangements

Buyer must opt to tax the property as well

28.9   The transfer of a going concern is normally outside the scope of VAT – as long as various rules are met – as explained in Chapter 4. The transfer of a business will often include land and buildings, and the seller may have opted to tax these buildings.

There is potential for the part of the sale relating to the land and buildings to also be outside the scope of VAT, even where the seller has opted to tax the property. The basic rules are as follows:

- the buyer must have opted to tax the land or buildings concerned and must have given written notification of the election to HMRC. The option must be notified to HMRC in writing and no later than the time of the deal;

- with effect from 18 March 2004, the buyer must also notify the seller that his option to tax the land or buildings concerned will not be disapplied. This notification should be in writing.

Note – the seller is responsible for ensuring the correct amount of output tax is charged on a property sale, so it is prudent for him to ask the buyer for evidence that his option to tax is in place by the relevant date, eg copy of the notification letter.

If the above conditions are not met, the transfer of the land and buildings is a supply and output tax will be due at the standard rate.

Property rental business

28.10   A situation that has become quite common in recent years is where a property has been sold to a third party, but with an existing lease in place with a tenant. In these situations, the sale can qualify as a transfer of a going concern (sale of a property rental business).

However, if the seller has opted to tax the property in question, then the buyer must also elect to tax the property himself before the deal is completed. If this election is made without any problem, the VAT charge can be avoided.

Practical challenges with option to tax procedures

20-year rule – revoking an option to tax

28.11   The option to tax regulations were introduced on 1 August 1989, so this means that it will be possible for some options to be revoked for the first time after 1 August 2009 under the 20-year rule.

A taxpayer will be able to automatically revoke his option in most cases (no HMRC permission needed – completion of Form VAT 1614J).

However, in completing VAT 1614J, a taxpayer needs to pass three anti-avoidance tests shown as Conditions 3 to 5 on the form. If any of the conditions are not met, then HMRC permission is needed before the election can be revoked, ie it is not automatic. The aim of the anti-avoidance tests is to prevent a business gaining an unfair tax advantage.

An important point for advisers to appreciate is that all of the tests at Conditions 3 to 5 must be met in order to revoke an option without HMRC permission, as well as Condition 2 regarding the 20-year time limit. Example 5 illustrates a situation where all of the conditions are met. The four conditions are:

- 20-year time period (Condition 2) – the taxpayer must have held a relevant interest in the building or land at the time when the option first took effect and more than 20 years have now passed;

  Note – if this condition is not met, then the other issues are irrelevant. The option to tax election cannot be revoked.

- no input tax adjustments are needed under the capital goods scheme (Condition 3) – the capital goods scheme mainly applies in relation to the purchase of certain buildings and building works exceeding £250,000 – input tax is adjusted over a 10-year period;

- valuation condition (Condition 4) – in the 10-year period before the option to tax is revoked, there must have been no supply of a relevant interest in the building that was made at less than open market value (eg undervalued rents);

- prepayments condition (Condition 5) – no payments have been made in relation to the property that relate to a period that is more than 12 months after the option is revoked – see Example 6.

Example 5

Alan owns the freehold of an office block in Southampton. He made an option to tax election on the property when he first bought it on 1 January 1993. In the last 22 years, the property has been rented out to a firm of accountants who have been able to reclaim input tax on the rent charged by Alan.

It is now 1 January 2015 and Alan wishes to revoke his option to tax election because the accountants are vacating his premises and the new tenants are a firm of insurance brokers (exempt activity – input tax cannot be reclaimed).

Alan's advisers establish that he has always charged a proper market rent to the accountants in the last ten years; he has not prepaid any expenses in relation to the property; there are no capital goods scheme issues … and more than 20 years have passed since Alan made his option to tax election with HMRC (or Customs and Excise in those days).

Solution – Alan can automatically revoke his option to tax election without prior permission from HMRC but must still notify it by completing Form VAT 1614J.

Example 6

Alan from Example 5 suddenly has a bright idea. Just before he revokes his option to tax election (December 2014) he decides to make a payment of £200,000 plus VAT to the maintenance company that carries out all repair work on his property in Southampton. The £200,000 payment will cover all repair works for the next five years up to 31 December 2019. Alan thinks this payment will allow him to claim £35,000 input tax on his December 2014 return because it has been incurred in a period when income from the property is still taxable, ie before the option to tax election has been revoked.

Solution – in this situation, the prepayment means that Alan cannot revoke his election without prior permission from HMRC. However, all is not lost. If he does not reclaim input tax on the maintenance payment (on the basis that it relates to a period when only exempt supplies of the property will be made), then HMRC will almost certainly grant permission to revoke the option. He will need to write a letter to HMRC, giving the full facts of the transaction, at the time he submits Form VAT 1614J.

Motives for revoking an option – including SDLT savings

28.12   Alan in Example 5 had an excellent motive for wishing to revoke his option to tax. The new tenants renting his building are not in a position to reclaim input tax on the rent he charges, creating an extra VAT cost to their business.

The other main situation when Alan might wish to revoke his option is if he wants to sell the property – and potential buyers might also have an exempt activity (financial services, insurance, health etc) where input tax claims are restricted. A 17.5% VAT charge on a £1m property is a lot of tax. Keep in mind that SDLT (stamp duty land tax) is also charged on the VAT element of any sale proceeds. See Example 7 which illustrates a useful SDLT saving if an option to tax election is revoked.

Example 7

Jones Chartered Accountants are buying a building from Smith Chartered Surveyors for £230,000 plus VAT on 1 September 2009. Smith made an option to tax election on the building on 1 August 1989. Jones can fully reclaim input tax on their VAT returns (no partial exemption problems) so are there any benefits in Smith revoking the option to tax election (as 20 years have now passed)?

Solution – as well as a cash flow saving for Jones (avoiding the need to pay out VAT and then wait possibly three months to claim it back on a VAT return), there is a big saving in SDLT if the option to tax election is revoked:

- £230,000 + VAT at 15% = £264,500; SDLT = £264,500 x 3% = £7,935 (because purchase price exceeds £250,000, SDLT is charged at 3% rather than 1%)

- £230,000, no VAT; SDLT = £230,000 x 1% = £2,300

SDLT saved = £7,935 – £2,300 = £5,635

Certificates to be issued for buildings to be converted into dwelling(s) or used for a relevant residential purpose and land supplied to housing associations

28.13   The option to tax is disapplied if a building is sold and will be converted for use as a dwelling (or number of dwellings), or for use for a relevant residential purpose (providing the purchaser has confirmed his intention to the seller). The sale of land to a housing association is also treated as exempt from VAT, assuming the association will build new dwellings or a relevant residential building on the land.

The buyer of an opted building (or land) in such cases will need to confirm his intentions by issuing the following certificates to the seller:

- Certificate to disapply the option to tax: Land sold to Housing Associations (VAT 1614G);

- Certificate to disapply the option to tax: Buildings to be converted into dwellings etc (VAT 1614D).

The above certificates give the seller the right to waive the option and treat the sale of the building as exempt.

Note – the option will continue to apply in relation to any parts of the building that will not be converted into dwellings or used solely for a relevant residential purpose. These parts of the building will be unaffected by the issue of the certificate. The certificate must describe the parts of the building that are affected by the override, and the percentage, on the basis of floor space, that they represent of the whole building. See Example 8.

Example 8

Property Ltd owns the freehold of an office block, which is sold to New Homes Ltd, which intends to convert 60% of the property into a block of flats with a view to selling them – the other 40% will be maintained as office accommodation. Property Ltd has opted to tax its interest in the building.

Solution – the intention of New Homes Ltd to convert the property into dwellings means the option to tax made by Property Ltd is disapplied in relation to this part of the building. New Homes Ltd must issue a certificate to Property Ltd confirming its intention to build dwellings. The certificate (which must follow a format produced by HMRC) must be issued before the price paid for the grant is legally fixed, ie exchange of contracts, the signing of heads of agreement etc.

Note – be aware that the regulations effectively mean the option will be maintained if New Homes Ltd does not issue a certificate to Property Ltd. This might not be a problem for New Homes Ltd if it is constructing the dwellings for resale (zero-rated supply) because the input tax will be relevant to a taxable supply. However, it would be a problem if New Homes Ltd rented the flats to tenants (exempt income) because the VAT charged by Property Ltd now relates to an exempt supply.

Supplies made by a 'relevant intermediary'

28.14   It is possible that a business will acquire a property on which an option to tax election has been made, with the sole intention of reselling the building to another person that intends to convert it into a dwelling or use it for a relevant residential purpose. In more complicated transactions, there may be more than one intermediary involved in the process.

If the above situation applies, the business reselling the property can be classed as a 'relevant intermediary' and issue VAT 1614D (Condition 3 applies) to the seller to enable the option to tax to be overridden. The relevant intermediary can only issue a certificate if one of the three conditions has been met in relation to his own resale of the property:

● he has received a certified VAT 1614D from his buyer confirming his intention to convert the building for use as a dwelling or solely for a relevant residential purpose;

● he has received a certified VAT 1614D from his buyer confirming his intention to sell the property to a person who intends to convert the building for such use;

● he has received a certified VAT 1614D from his buyer confirming his intention to sell the property to a person who will, in turn, sell the property to a person who intends to convert the building for such use.

See Example 9 to illustrate the new rules.

Example 9

> ABC Ltd is seeking to sell a building that it opted to tax. Its customer DEF Ltd has already found a buyer GHI Ltd (the recipient) for the property which intends to convert the building into a dwelling (or number of dwellings) or for a relevant residential purpose. What are the VAT issues?
>
> *Solution* – GHI Ltd provides a certified VAT 1614D to DEF Ltd confirming the intention to convert the building. Once DEF Ltd has this certificate, it can then issue a certified VAT 1614D to ABC Ltd confirming that it intends to dispose of the building to a person GHI Ltd who will convert it into a dwelling (or number of dwellings) or for a relevant residential purpose. Once ABC Ltd has the certificate, it can exempt its supply of the building to DEF Ltd and DEF Ltd can exempt its supply of the building to GHI Ltd.

'Real estate election'

28.15   A company has always been able to make a 'universal' or 'global' option to tax election in the past, meaning that all properties it acquires become subject to an option to tax ie avoiding the need to make a separate election for each property. The new regulations give the same facility (but with some amendments to the rules) through what is known as a 'real estate election'. This can be achieved by completing Form VAT 1614E (Opting to tax land and buildings: Notification of a real estate election).

In reality, most property owners (or other parties with an interest in property) will prefer to make an option to tax election on an individual property basis, having analysed the advantages and disadvantages of making an election. The issues concerning real estate elections are therefore not considered further in this chapter.

Automatic revocation of an option after 6 years

28.16   Under the new rules, an option to tax election is treated as being automatically revoked where the opter has held no relevant interest in the building for 6 years.

Example – building sold by opter in June 2004 (and no other use or occupation of the building has been made since then) – option automatically revoked in June 2010 (there are some exceptions to this clause in relation to group companies).

Future options apply to land and buildings

28.17   The new regulations make it clear that an option to tax land applies equally to a building upon the land (including a building that has yet to be built). This withdraws HMRC's previous policy of allowing land and buildings to be separately opted.

However, if a taxpayer has an existing option in place where land and buildings have been subject to separate options (or non-options) then there are transitional rules in place to help taxpayers. There is also a new ability to exclude a new building and land within its curtilage (as long as the building is separate from any existing building) from an option to tax election even though the land has been subject to a previous option. In such cases, a taxpayer will need to complete Form VAT 1614F (Opting to tax land and buildings: New buildings – exclusion from an option to tax).

Changes to 'cooling off' period rules

28.18   The opportunities for a taxpayer to revoke an option to tax election are very limited, the main opportunity being when the election was made 20 years ago (revocation date 1 August 2009 at earliest – as considered above).

Until 31 May 2008, an option to tax election could also be revoked under the 'cooling off' regulations but only if:

- less than 3 months had passed since the option to tax election took effect;

- no supplies (on which VAT would be charged) had been made in relation to the building since the election was made;

- no input tax had been claimed on costs in relation to the building as a result of the election;

- the property had not been sold together with a business as a transfer of a going concern.

The 3-month cooling off period was extended to 6 months with effect from 1 June 2008. The new regulations also maintain the transfer of a going concern rule. However, an election can only be automatically revoked within the 'cooling off' period if:

- no tax has become chargeable as a result of the option;

- no use has been made of the land since the option had effect;

- any input tax claimed as a result of the election has been repaid – see section 8.1.2 of HMRC Notice 742A (Box F).

If the conditions above are met, then a business will need to complete Form VAT 1614C (Option to tax land and buildings: Revoking an option to tax within six months (the 'cooling off' period)). HMRC can then give permission for the option to be revoked. The certificate must be sent to HMRC within 6 months of the date of the original election.

Note – if the input tax condition is not met, then a letter should be sent to HMRC with the form explaining the details and, in some cases, a request to revoke the option could still be granted.

The priority of HMRC will be to ensure no net tax gain has been acquired by the incorrect election, and there are no anti-avoidance motives to worry about.

Revised rules for 'relevant associates'

28.19   The rules that apply since 1 June 2008 introduce the new concept of a 'relevant associate'. This situation applies to group structures and anti-avoidance issues when a corporate body is 'connected to the opter'. The revised legislation imposes new conditions for a body corporate to cease to be treated as a relevant associate of an opter. In such cases, Form VAT 1614B (Opting to tax land and buildings: Ceasing to be a relevant associate) needs to be completed.

Summary of relevant forms

28.20   The various forms that need to be completed since 1 June 2008 have been considered in each relevant section above. They can be summarised as follows:

- VAT 1614A – Notifying an option to tax election;

- VAT 1614B – Ceasing to be a relevant associate;

- VAT 1614C – Revoking an option to tax within 6 months ('cooling off' period);

- VAT 1614D – Certificate to disapply the option: Buildings to be converted into dwellings etc;

- VAT 1614E – Notification of a real estate election;

- VAT 1614F – Notification of the exclusion of a new building from the effect of an option to tax;

- VAT 1614G – Certificate to disapply the option: Land sold to housing associations;

- VAT 1614H – Application for permission to opt;

- VAT 1614J – Revoking an option after 20 years (1 August 2009 is the earliest possible date for a revocation to take effect).

Note – be aware of the difference between Forms VAT 1614A and VAT 1614H. Form VAT 1614A is used when an option to tax election can be made without HMRC permission. However, there may be situations when HMRC's permission to opt to tax a property is required, usually when exempt supplies have been in connection with the property in the previous ten years. See paragraph 5.2 of HMRC's Notice 742A for further details on this issue.

As a final point, all of the forms mentioned above have the force of law and must be used where appropriate.

Planning points to consider

28.21   The following planning points should be given consideration.

- Remember that once an option to tax election on land or a building has been made, it cannot usually be revoked for 20 years. It is therefore important to take all relevant factors into account before making the option (and a long-term view as to the likely use and potential sale of the property).

- The main reason for making an option to tax election is to enhance input tax recovery by making a supply taxable rather than exempt. However, this enhanced input tax recovery needs to be balanced against the possibility that potential tenants or purchasers of the property may not be able to claim input tax. eg if they are in a business that is exempt from VAT. In such cases, the option to tax creates an additional 17.5% charge on supplies relevant to that property.

- The option to tax election can only be made on commercial properties. If a property is residential, the option to tax cannot be applied.

- A common mistake made by many tenants renting a property is to assume that because their landlord has opted to tax the property in question, they must also opt to tax their own interest as well. This is not correct – each VAT registered entity must make its own decision as to whether an election is in its own interests.

- If there are any doubts at all regarding the boundary of a property being elected, then a map or plan of the premises/land should be sent to HMRC at the time the election is made. This avoids any ambiguity in the future.

- Remember there are certain situations where the option to tax is overridden. eg if an opted property is going to be used as a dwelling. Also, the option to tax is overridden if a building is sold as part of the transfer of a going concern – but only if the transferee has also elected to tax the property before the deal is finalised.

- The option to tax rules were introduced on 1 August 1989, so the first opportunities to revoke an option became available on 1 August 2009. This is because once an option to tax election has been made, it cannot be revoked for at least 20 years. As well as saving VAT for businesses unable to reclaim VAT, a decision to revoke the option to tax could produce significant savings of SDLT.

Chapter 29

DIY Refund Scheme

Key topics in this chapter:

- Purpose and aims of the DIY scheme.

- What constitutes the construction of a new dwelling that qualifies for a refund under the scheme.

- Rules to be aware of when converting a non-residential property into a residential property, eg 10-year rule for non-residential use.

- Situations when a claim cannot be made under the scheme, eg commercial ventures, speculative development projects.

- Costs that can and cannot be reclaimed under the DIY scheme.

- Rules for claiming VAT on costs where partly residential and partly non-residential buildings are converted.

- When the 5% rate of VAT applies to building works – and the importance of only claiming correctly charged VAT under the DIY scheme.

- Procedures for making a DIY claim – Form VAT 431 to be completed within 3 months of completion date and forwarded to HMRC office in Birmingham.

Introduction

29.1   The aim of the DIY (do-it-yourself) Refund Scheme is to give private individuals not in business or registered for VAT the chance to recover VAT on the relevant costs of certain building projects. The main works where a claim could be made are as follows:

- the construction of a building designed as a dwelling or number of dwellings;

- the construction of a building for use solely for a relevant residential purpose or for a relevant charitable purpose; or

- a residential conversion, ie the conversion of a non-residential building or the non-residential part of a building into either a building designed as a dwelling or number of dwellings or a building intended solely for a relevant residential purpose or anything which would fall into either of those categories if different parts of a building were treated as separate buildings.

The criteria for what constitutes a relevant charitable purpose or relevant residential purpose are considered in Chapter 26. However, most DIY claims tend to be relevant to dwellings, where private individuals obtain a plot of land and build a house on the land for their own occupation.

All work carried out on the property must be lawful, ie proper planning permission must have been obtained and there are formal procedures and deadline dates that must be followed in order to obtain a refund from HMRC.

Objectives of the DIY scheme

29.2 In basic terms, the DIY scheme is intended to ensure that people who build their own houses or convert non-residential properties into dwellings are not disadvantaged in VAT terms compared to housebuilders or other VAT registered businesses who buy and sell properties as a trading activity – see Example 1.

Example 1

Smith Housebuilders Ltd buys half an acre of land at Potters Farm and builds a new house, which is subsequently sold. The company is VAT registered.

Mr Jones is a local tax consultant, who has also bought half an acre of land at Potters Farm to build a new house to live in himself. He is VAT registered as a tax consultant.

What is the position in these two situations as far as recovering VAT is concerned?

Solution – Smith Housebuilders Ltd has made a taxable (zero-rated) supply and can therefore reclaim input tax on any related costs such as building materials, fittings etc associated with the new property.

Mr Jones is VAT registered but cannot reclaim input tax on his VAT return because the cost of the house is a private expense relevant to him, not relevant to his taxable supplies as a tax consultant. However, he is eligible to make a claim to HMRC under the DIY scheme by completing Form VAT 431.

The end result is that both Smith Housebuilders Ltd and Mr Jones recover VAT on their costs – but by different methods.

The DIY scheme has clear and simple rules – and the main HMRC guidance is recorded in a very well written VAT 719 Notice.

Definition of 'constructing a building'

29.3 Many DIY claims will be relevant to dwellings or qualifying buildings built on empty land and it will therefore be obvious that the project relates to the construction of a new building. However, there will be other occasions when a project utilises part of an existing building and this is where great care is needed to ensure the project is still eligible for a DIY refund.

The key rules are as follows:

• a building can still be classed as new if it makes use of no more than a single façade (or a double façade on a corner site) of a pre-existing building; and

• the pre-existing building is completely demolished before work on the new building is started; and

• the façade is retained as an explicit condition or requirement of statutory planning consent.

In determining whether a building has been demolished, the party walls relevant to a neighbouring property that is not being developed can also be ignored.

In addition, the construction of a self-contained semi-detached property will be classed as a newly constructed building, and also if an existing building is enlarged or extended and the enlargement or extension creates an additional dwelling.

For example, a new qualifying flat built on the top of an existing block of flats would be eligible for a claim – but the conversion of a loft space into a flat would not qualify.

Definition of a 'non-residential conversion' and who can use the DIY scheme

29.4 In most cases, it will be very easy to identify when a conversion from a non-residential to residential property has taken place. For example, a very common example of a conversion is where an agricultural building such as a barn is converted into a house or bungalow. Equally, a commercial building such as an office, warehouse or shop may be turned into new flats.

Again, an important point to remember is that situations such as those above are only covered by the scheme if the project is for a non-business purpose. For example, if an individual proposes to buy an office block, turn it into six flats and sell the flats, this is a clear business venture. The correct route is to complete Form VAT 1 and register for VAT in the normal way. In effect, therefore, the following individuals cannot use the DIY scheme:

- speculative developers looking to buy and sell property at a profit;

- landlords seeking to rent out properties for commercial gain;

- bed and breakfast operators;

- care home operators who make a charge (even if not for a profit) to their residents;

- membership clubs and associations;

- theatres; and

- child nurseries where a fee is charged.

Note – in the case of the child nursery and care home examples, it is the 'business' aspect of the arrangement that creates the exclusion from the DIY scheme.

One important rule that applies to non-residential conversions is the 10-year rule. This rule states that a building only qualifies for DIY relief if it has not been lived in for at least 10 years. For example, if an office block is being converted into a freehold dwelling, this project will qualify for a refund (subject to the normal rules). However, if the building in question has only been an office block for the last 5 years, and was previously a dwelling, then a claim is excluded by the 10-year rule.

Costs that can be claimed under the DIY scheme

29.5 The first priority is to be aware of what services provided by a builder are zero-rated or chargeable at the lower VAT rate of 5%. This is important for two reasons:

- from a cash flow angle, it is better not to pay VAT in the first place, rather than pay it to the builder and then have a time delay before it is recovered from HMRC with a DIY claim; and

- under the DIY scheme, HMRC will only refund correctly charged VAT. If a builder charges VAT at 17.5% instead of 0%, this is not correctly charged VAT – and the claim to HMRC under the DIY scheme will be rejected. See Example 2.

Example 2

Mr C employed a builder to do all of the bricklaying works at his new house in Wilstead. The builder is also supplying all of the materials. He does a good job on the building but is not sure of the VAT rules for the work he has carried out. He invoices Mr C for £20,000 plus VAT of £3,500 (based on VAT rate of 17.5%) – which Mr C agrees to pay because he can recover the VAT from HMRC under the DIY scheme.

Solution – HMRC will reject the claim for £3,500 – as this is incorrectly charged VAT. The supply should have been zero-rated. The correct course of action is for the builder to issue a VAT only credit note to Mr C for incorrectly charged VAT – and refund the VAT to him. The adjustment is therefore made through the builder's VAT return, rather than by making an incorrect claim under the DIY scheme.

Another important point about the DIY scheme is that VAT can only be recovered on 'building materials'. This means that no claim can be made on items such as washing machines, carpets, doorbells, freezers, etc. A detailed list is included in Notice 719.

As far as the definition of 'building materials' is concerned, the main guideline is that the items in question tend to be permanent in the building. For example, a carpet can be lifted and moved to another room or building – wood flooring permanently fixed to the ground cannot. Therefore, the VAT on wood flooring costs can be claimed – but not carpets.

On a positive note, all goods or services relevant to making the building suitable for construction can also be claimed, including:

- drainage;
- main paths on the site;
- driveways;
- retaining walls and boundary walls and fences.

The cost of building a garage is also eligible under the scheme, as long as the dwelling and garage are constructed at the same time and the garage is intended for occupation with the dwelling (or one of the dwellings)

Examples of works and materials that cannot be claimed

29.6   One common situation is where a 'granny' annex is constructed to an existing property, for example, to give independent living to an elderly relative but close to, or attached to, the main property. In such cases, a claim cannot be made unless the annex can be disposed of separately to the main house. In most cases, this is not possible so a DIY claim cannot be made.

The other main exclusion from the DIY scheme is that VAT cannot be recovered on certain services associated with the project. These exclusions mainly relate to professional and supervisory services – architects, surveyors, design fees, solicitor costs. Also, VAT cannot be recovered on the hire of plant, tools and equipment (generators, scaffolding etc).

In reality, the professional fees exclusion is slightly unfair, taking the argument that the aim of the scheme is to ensure that the DIY builder does not lose out to the main housebuilders. In the latter case, housebuilders are able to recover costs for professional fees – because they all relate to the final zero-rated supply made when the new dwelling is sold. However, the argument against this is that such costs are included as part of the builders' costs anyway – and added to his final mark-up to the end user.

Other costs that are excluded relate to detached workshops, playrooms or swimming pools constructed in the grounds of a new dwelling. These exclusions would also include other leisure facilities such as tennis courts, as well as fishponds, rockeries and other ornamental works.

An important point to remember is that the best way of dealing with the exclusions is for a builder to separately invoice for works carried out, for example, on a playroom built above a detached garage. If the builder raises an invoice for his total works on an inclusive basis, this could lead to an excessive amount of VAT being disallowed by HMRC. See Example 3.

Example 3

Jane Smith is having a new four-bedroom detached house built on a plot of land she has bought, and intends to live in the property herself (ie the nature of the scheme qualifies for a VAT refund under the DIY scheme). The project includes a snooker room being built above the garage – the garage being detached from the property. She buys all building materials and fittings from a local merchant at a total cost of £70,000 plus VAT. The new house is 3,000 square feet and the playroom is 600 square feet. What is the VAT position regarding the snooker room?

Solution – HMRC could seek to disallow 1/6 of the VAT claimed on the materials relevant to the snooker room by making an apportionment calculation on a square footage basis (600 divided by 3,600). This could lead to the claim being reduced by £2,041 (£70,000 × 17.5% divided by 6). However, this could produce an unfair result for Jane because the building materials in the snooker room are likely to have cost considerably less on a pro-rata basis than, for example, the kitchen, bathroom or bedrooms. It would almost certainly produce a better result for Jane if she isolates the material costs for the snooker room, and reduces her initial claim by this amount, ie only making a claim for the costs that qualify under the DIY scheme.

Buildings that are partly commercial and partly residential

29.7   One topic that has caused some difficulty in recent years concerns the amount of VAT that can be claimed under the scheme to reflect the situation where a building that was partly residential and partly non-residential is converted into a residential building.

HMRC now accepts that, for the purposes of the DIY scheme, the conversion of a building that contains both a residential part and a non-residential part comes within the scope of the scheme so long as the conversion results in an additional dwelling being created. It is no longer necessary for the additional dwelling to be created exclusively from the non-residential part. However, VAT recovery is restricted to the conversion of the non-residential part and the project would also be outside the scope of the DIY scheme if the owner had a business motive, ie to sell or rent out the property. See Example 4 for an illustration of this point.

Example 4

Phil has purchased a public house that includes a three-bedroom flat on the first floor (living quarters). He has obtained planning permission to convert the property to a private residence but is unsure whether to convert the pub into one large detached house or two flats. He needs some advice about the VAT position.

Solution – if Phil converts the flat into a detached house, then he cannot recover any VAT under the DIY scheme because he has not created an additional dwelling, ie the property will comprise one dwelling before and after the conversion.

However, he will be able to obtain relief for the costs of converting the non-residential part of the building if he takes the option of converting it into two flats. This is because he has created an additional dwelling. He will not be able to recover any VAT on the costs of converting the residential part of the building. However, Phil must ensure the project is a non-business venture and live in the property to qualify for a refund of VAT under the DIY scheme.

The change in HMRC policy is explained in Business Brief 22/05, and reflects the Court of Appeal ruling in the case of *Revenue and Customs Comrs v Jacobs* [2005] EWCA Civ 930, [2005] STC 1518, [2005] SWTI 1316, [2005] All ER (D) 326 (Jan).

Lower rate VAT charge (5%)

29.8   As explained at **29.4**, it is only possible to reclaim correctly charged VAT under the DIY scheme. Certain construction services supplied by a builder will be eligible for a VAT charge at 5% rather than

17.5%. An example of such a situation would be when a non-residential property is converted into one or more single house dwellings (although any non-residential to residential conversion work for a housing association will be zero-rated).

If the builder is unaware of the reduced rate charge, and adds VAT at 17.5%, then HMRC will reject the DIY claim because they can only repay correctly charged VAT. See Example 5.

Example 5

John has bought the freehold of a public house and has obtained planning permission to convert it into a five-bedroom detached house to live in himself (there was no living quarters within this pub, so the accommodation was wholly non-residential). ABC Builders Ltd carry out all of the building work and charge John £100,000 plus £17,500 VAT. He submits Form VAT 431 to HMRC to recover this VAT under the DIY scheme.

Solution – John is correct to make a DIY claim on the basis that the scheme represents the conversion of a non-residential building into a dwelling. However, the correct amount of the claim is only £5,000, ie ABC Builders Ltd should have charged VAT at 5% instead of 17.5%. John will need to obtain a VAT only credit note from ABC Builders Ltd for £12,500 to ensure he is not out of pocket.

Claim procedures under the DIY scheme

29.9 Form VAT 431 needs to be completed and sent to HMRC in order to obtain a VAT refund under the DIY scheme. The form is made up of four different parts and it is important to give plenty of detail in the relevant parts to support the application.

The first key point is that there is a time limit for making the claim, namely 3 months after the construction or conversion is completed. If this deadline date cannot be met, then a letter needs to be sent to HMRC, advising the reasons for the delay and when a claim form will be submitted. As long as the reason for the delay is sensible, there are unlikely to be problems gaining a time extension.

Form VAT 431 is user friendly, and can either be obtained from the National Advice Service (Tel: 0845 010 9000) or downloaded from the HMRC website (www.hmrc.gov.uk).

As with most aspects of HMRC administration, the local office structure no longer applies, and all claims need to be submitted to:

HM Revenue and Customs
2 Broadway
Broad Street
Five Ways
Birmingham B15 1BG
(Tel: 0121 697 4000)

As well as Form VAT 431 being submitted, it is also necessary to send original invoices and supporting documents with the claim. Finally, the claim also needs to include a copy of the planning permission approval for the project, as well as evidence that the project is completed. This is to meet the HMRC objective that it will only provide refunds to a project if it is carried out lawfully.

In reality, the evidence of completion will usually be a certificate or letter of completion from the local authority. However, alternative evidence could be a valuation rating or Council Tax assessment – or a certificate from the bank or building society involved with lending money against the project.

As with all claims, HMRC has the right to make any enquiries about any relevant issue, and the taxpayer has the right to appeal to a VAT tribunal if he disagrees with a decision that affects his claim.

When a claim is submitted, the DIY section in Birmingham will acknowledge receipt of the claim in writing (within 10 working days), and usually give a date when they expect to make a repayment. As a general guide, a refund is normally made within 30 days of receiving the claim.

Planning points to consider

29.10   The following planning points should be given consideration.

- A building can still qualify as a new dwelling under the DIY scheme if a single façade is retained from the existing building or a double façade in the case of a corner site. Party walls can also be ignored. However, the façade can only be retained if this was a requirement of planning consent.

- The construction of a new flat on top of an existing block of flats will qualify under the DIY scheme because it creates an additional dwelling, capable of being sold as a single unit in its own right.

- Remember that the conversion of a non-residential to residential property will only qualify under the scheme if a property has not been lived in for at least 10 years. It is important to check this point before making a DIY claim.

- The DIY scheme excludes any claim linked to a commercial venture. In such cases, the claimant will need to register for VAT in the normal way (assuming he makes or intends to make taxable supplies) and recover VAT costs by claiming input tax on his VAT returns.

- It is important to ensure that builders charge the correct rate of VAT on works carried out on a project. If a builder charges standard rate VAT on a zero-rated supply, then HMRC will reject the DIY claim. In such cases, it will be necessary to get a VAT only credit note from the builder. Be aware that most building services on non-residential to residential conversions attract VAT at the reduced rate of 5%.

- The DIY claim can include most building material costs that are permanently fixed to the building – however, be aware of exclusions relevant to items such as washing machines, freezers and carpets. VAT Notice 719 gives a detailed list of items that can and cannot be claimed.

- Be aware that certain aspects of a project cannot be reclaimed under the scheme, eg the costs relevant to a detached playroom. In such cases, it may be more profitable to directly exclude the VAT costs relevant to these aspects, than to allow HMRC to make an overall deduction of a claim based on an alternative method, eg square footage basis.

- Rules concerning the conversion of a property that partly included a residential element and partly included a non-residential element changed in 2005. The rules only allow a DIY claim to be made if an additional dwelling is created through the conversion project (eg a pub with one flat being converted into two flats) and only on the costs of converting the non-residential part of the building. There may be benefits in considering these rules before a project is started.

Chapter 30

VAT Planning Tips to Survive the Recession

Key topics in this chapter:

- The benefits of using the cash accounting scheme.

- Rules for claiming VAT on bad debts and dealing with subsequent payments from a customer where the debt has been written off.

- Opportunities to delay raising a sales invoice – 14-day rule and applications for payment.

- Filing VAT returns online.

- Utilising HMRC's Business Payment Support Service if a business is unable to pay some or all of the tax due on its VAT return.

- Input tax treatment of leased vehicles.

- The benefits of deregistration if sales have decreased.

- Saving tax with the flat rate scheme.

- The scope to reduce interim payments for users of the annual accounting scheme.

- Repaying input tax on unpaid purchase invoices more than 6 months overdue for payment.

Introduction

30.1   As far as VAT is concerned, it is fair to say that both advisers and clients will be faced with different challenges when cash and profits are in short supply. For example, questions such as 'Can I claim input tax on my new personalised number plate?' may be replaced by questions like 'What happens if I can't pay my VAT bill on time?' or 'What happens if my customers haven't paid their invoices for the last three months?'

In this chapter, we will consider some practical measures that could help to save some VAT for clients during the economic downturn.

Rules for VAT on bad debts and cash accounting scheme

30.2   An inevitable consequence of an economic slowdown is that many businesses will suffer bad debts.

If a business uses the cash accounting scheme (available to a business with annual taxable sales of £1.35m or less – see Chapter 6), then bad debt relief on unpaid sales invoices is automatic. This is because the main feature of the scheme is that output tax is not due on a VAT return until payment has been received from a customer. For a business that does not use cash accounting, VAT is due on a return when either a sales invoice is raised or payment received, whichever happens sooner. This usually means that output tax is payable according to the invoice date. See Example 1 for an illustration of this point.

Example 1

John is VAT registered as a surveyor with annual sales of £300,000. He has very little input tax to claim and completes his VAT returns on a calendar quarter basis.

It is 30 June 2009 and John has unpaid sales invoices of £45,000 plus VAT of £6,750. What are the implications for John's VAT return for this quarter?

Solution – John is eligible to use the cash accounting scheme because his annual taxable sales are less than £1.35m. He can adopt the scheme at any time without HMRC approval. This means the output tax on his June 2009 VAT return will decrease by £6,750 if he adopts the scheme because all unpaid sales invoice as at 30 June will be excluded. This produces a worthwhile cash flow saving.

Note – the one negative aspect of the scheme is that input tax cannot be reclaimed until payment has been made to a supplier – but this is not a major issue for John because, like many service related businesses, he has very little input tax to reclaim.

As explained above, if a business is not using the cash accounting scheme, then output tax is usually payable on a VAT return according to the date of the sales invoice, ie before payment has been received from the customer. However, in the event of non-payment of the invoice, there is scope to reclaim this VAT under the bad debt relief rules as long as the following conditions are met:

• the debt must be at least 6 months overdue for payment;

- the debt has been written off in the company accounts, eg credit entry to customer's sales ledger account and debit entry to a 'bad debt' account;

- output tax was charged on the original invoice and accounted for by the taxpayer on a previous VAT return;

- the debt must not have been paid, sold or factored under a valid legal assignment.

An essential point to remember is that a bad debt cannot be adjusted by issuing a credit note to either reduce or cancel the unpaid invoice. A credit note can only be used to correct pricing errors or situations where a customer has returned goods and an invoice correction is needed.

A common misunderstanding (or out-of-date understanding because the rule was in place until 31 December 2002) is that a supplier claiming bad debt relief must also write to his customer and instruct him to adjust his input tax claim on the unpaid invoice(s) in question. This is no longer correct. The change is a welcome one because otherwise, a customer may be encouraged not to pay his dues if he thinks his supplier has written off the debt in his accounts.

Future payment of bad debts written off

30.3   If a customer makes a future payment in relation to a debt that has been written off, then output tax must be accounted for on the amount of the payment. This payment could be a part-payment in which case it is treated as VAT inclusive, assuming that all sales were standard-rated.

However, what happens if a part-payment is made and some of the original sales invoices were either zero-rated or exempt? See Example 2.

Example 2

Susan is owed £5,525 from a particular customer as follows:

Invoice date	VAT exclusive	VAT	Total
30/6/08	£1,000	zero-rated	£1,000
20/7/08	£1,000	£175	£1,175
31/7/08	£2,000	£350	£2,350
14/8/08	£1,000	exempt	£1,000

She has claimed bad debt relief on all of the above invoices but has now received a part payment of £3,500 from the customer on 30 June 2009. What is the VAT position?

Solution – assuming that the customer has not specified which invoices he is paying, then for VAT purposes, the payment must be matched against the oldest invoices. This means that output tax of £175 is due on the first two sales invoices (which are effectively fully paid within the £3,500 payment).

The remainder of the payment relates to the invoice raised on 31 July 2008 (£3,500 – £1,000 – £1,175 = £1,325). Output tax payable on this invoice in relation to the payment is: £1,325 x 7/47 = £197.34.

In effect, Susan's original claim for bad debt relief of £525 has now been reduced to £152.66 because of the customer's part payment.

Delaying issuing a tax invoice

30.4   There is an old phrase in business that 'cash is king'.

A possible method of delaying a VAT payment to keep money in a client's bank account a bit longer is to delay issuing a tax invoice for ongoing contracts – instead issuing an alternative document such as a 'request for payment' or 'application for payment'. This is a common and perfectly legal technique, eg in the construction industry.

The reason why this approach is only appropriate for ongoing jobs is because the normal tax point rules for VAT require an invoice to be issued within 14 days of a supply being made. If no invoice is raised (referred to as an actual tax point), then VAT becomes due on the date when the supply was made (known as a basic tax point). See Example 3.

Example 3

Jack supplies goods to Jill on 30 June 2009 (basic tax point). Jack does not raise an invoice for the goods until 31 July 2009. Jack completes VAT return on a calendar quarter basis. When must he include the sale on his VAT return?

Solution – the actual tax point of 31 July 2009 has taken place more than 14 days after the basic tax point. VAT is therefore payable on 30 June 2009, ie the basic tax point and should be included on Jack's June 2009 return. If the sales invoice had been raised on 13 July, this would have delayed the VAT payment until the September return because the invoice has now been raised within 14 days of the supply taking place.

Note – the phrase tax point has been used in this section, whereas the wording used in the legislation (*VATA 1994, s 1(2)*) is 'time of supply'.

However, if a contract or job is being carried out on an ongoing basis, and involves interim payments, then a sensible strategy could be to issue an application for payment (not a tax invoice) and then advise the client that a tax invoice will be issued once payment has been received. This approach is covered by the continuous supply of service rules in VAT, whereby output tax is due according to invoice date or receipt of payment, whichever happens sooner. In other words, an application for payment is not an invoice – so output tax is not due until payment has been received. See Example 4.

Example 4

Decorators Ltd has annual turnover of £2m and is currently working on a large contract to paint all the rooms in a big office, a job which could last for many months. The company's VAT periods end on calendar quarters and they raise tax invoices at the end of each calendar month to charge the customer for work completed during the month. The customer pays the invoice at the end of the following month. It is 31 December 2008 and the company is about to raise an invoice for £100,000 plus VAT of £15,000. Can the company improve its VAT cash flow management?

Solution – if the company raises an application for payment instead of a tax invoice, output tax will not be payable on this charge until the March 2009 VAT quarter (assuming payment is made at the end of January by the customer) rather than the December 2008 period if an invoice was raised. This is because the tax point becomes the payment date in January. A tax invoice will also be issued when payment has been received. The company gains a useful 3-month cash flow benefit on £15,000.

Filing VAT returns online

30.5   A useful tip is to take advantage of HMRC's online facility to file VAT returns, which can give up to 12 additional days to pay the tax due on a return. To prove this statement works in practice, this is how the online payment arrangement worked for a taxpayer who completed a March 2009 return:

- the normal due date for filing the March 2009 return was 30 April 2009;

- an extra 7 calendar days were given to file the VAT return online;

- an extra 3 working days were then given before the direct debit payment was taken from a taxpayer's account – and because 9 and 10 May were weekend dates, this meant a payment day of 12 May.

Note – online filing of VAT returns will be compulsory for many businesses with effect from 1 April 2010, ie those with annual sales exceeding £100,000 and those who are newly VAT registered after this date. It is therefore sensible to encourage clients to register with HMRC to file returns online as soon as possible.

HMRC's Business Payment Support Service (BPSS)

30.6   During an economic downturn, many businesses will be faced with the decision as to whether they pay their suppliers on time (to keep the flow of goods coming into the business) or the quarterly VAT return on time. The positive news is that HMRC have introduced a new facility that could ease this dilemma by giving the opportunity for businesses to spread the liability due on their VAT return over a number of months.

The BPSS deals with payments of VAT, National Insurance and other taxes managed by HMRC and is open 7 days a week (telephone number 0845 302 1435).

Its opening hours are:

- Monday to Friday: 8am–8pm

- Saturday and Sunday: 8am–4pm

The key challenge is to contact the BPSS before the liability on a VAT return is due and make a time-to-pay proposal as to how a particular VAT debt can be settled. Most proposals are instantly agreed by HMRC staff within the telephone call and this will also avoid any potential default surcharges being levied if the payment terms are agreed in advance.

The approach to dealing with the BPSS is as follows:

- ensure you have your VAT registration number available to quote at the beginning of the telephone call;

- clearly identify the VAT that cannot be paid – this might relate to the balance due on a VAT return if a part payment has been made;

- quantify basic income and expenditure details of the business to show to HMRC that the VAT debt can be paid within future profits.

Note – HMRC's policy in the BPSS is to 'enter into realistic time to pay arrangements as a temporary option tailored to your business needs.' The main situation when an arrangement would be appropriate is if a business has encountered cash flow problems because of a major bad debt or late payment from a major customer.

Leasing rather than buying vehicles

30.7 One decision taken by a company with cash flow difficulties could be to lease vehicles in the future rather than buy them as an outright purchase.

The implication of leasing an asset is that VAT is usually charged on monthly hire payments made to the leasing company rather than when the asset is initially purchased by the business. The leasing company will often issue an annual tax invoice in advance, which serves as evidence for the lessee to reclaim input tax on each monthly payment. Be sure to resist the temptation to claim all of the year's input tax when the first payment is made!

The important point with leasing cars is that a 50% input tax restriction applies, unless the car is used exclusively for business purposes and never available for private use (unlikely ... think for example, of the emergency trip to the supermarket) or is primarily used by a business involved in car hire, taxi work or driving instruction. The 50% restriction recognises the fact that the vehicle will be partly used for private or non-business purposes.

Author note – occasionally, there are queries from practitioners asking why a 50% restriction on input tax is needed in relation to car leasing charges if a business also pays output tax each VAT period using the scale charge system. The key point is that the scale charge adjustment only relates to private fuel usage – not to the private use of the actual vehicle.

Deregistration

30.8 The VAT registration threshold increased by £1,000 to £68,000 with effect from 1 May 2009 – the same increase was applied to the deregistration threshold (£65,000 to £66,000).

In a slowing economy, many businesses will suffer a decline in sales, and could therefore be eligible for deregistration. If the nature of their businesses means they are selling standard-rated goods or services to the general public (most retailers), then deregistration would probably be a sensible move. However, it is necessary to remember that output tax may be due on the value of stocks and assets held at the date of deregistration – this could be a crucial factor in the decision making process (see **2.10**).

A business can deregister from VAT if it expects its taxable sales in the next 12 months to be less than £66,000. See Example 5.

Example 5

Andy is a self-employed bricklayer, earning £75,000 per year. As a result of the economic downturn, he expects to only work 4 days a week for the next couple of years.

Solution – Andy's expected sales in the next 12 months will be £60,000 (£75,000 x 4/5), so he could request deregistration. However, this may not be a sensible move if he is working on new houses (zero-rated sales) or for commercial companies that are able to reclaim any VAT he charges as input tax. In such cases, deregistration gives him a loss of input tax without any output tax gains. The main benefits of deregistration would be if his work is for the general public where the VAT charge cannot be reclaimed by his customers.

Benefits of the flat rate scheme

30.9 The flat rate scheme is available to a small business with annual taxable sales of less than £150,000. It has proved to be very popular in recent years and is used by more than 180,000 businesses in the UK.

The scheme is analysed in Chapter 8. The main message is that the scheme can save tax for a lot of businesses, depending on their circumstances, as well as making it easier to maintain accounting records and complete quarterly VAT returns. The savings that could be made with the scheme may prove crucial to the survival of a business in the current economic climate.

Annual accounting scheme – review payments on account

30.10 The annual accounting scheme involves the completion of one annual VAT return and is considered in Chapter 7. A feature of the scheme is that payments on account are made throughout the year and these payments are based on the tax paid on the previous year's annual return.

The reality of the current economy is that business profits and sales are declining for many businesses. This could mean that payments on account based on the previous trading year are too high. There is scope to contact HMRC (initial contact should be the National Helpline Service on 0845 010 9000) and reduce these payments on account. This would produce an important cash flow saving for the business.

Repaying input tax on unpaid purchase invoices

30.11 We considered how a business could claim bad debt relief in relation to sales invoices that were more than 6 months overdue for payment at 30.2. To compensate the loss of output tax, HMRC also requires a business to adjust its input tax on purchase invoices that are more than 6 months overdue for payment. See Example 6.

Example 6

Jack owes Jill £1,000 + VAT of £175 on an invoice due for payment on 31 December 2008. It is now 30 June 2009 and Jack has so far only made a part-payment of £500 to Jill.

Solution – Jack must make an input tax adjustment on 30 June as follows:

Input tax to repay = £175 x £675/£1175 = £100.53

Note – Jack will reduce the Box 4 (input tax) figure on his VAT return relevant to 30 June 2009. If Jill decides that Jack is a bad debt (unlikely), then Jill would claim bad debt relief by increasing the Box 4 figure on her VAT return when (or if) she writes off the debt in her accounts.

Planning points to consider

30.12   The following planning points should be given consideration.

- A review of a client's sales ledger when producing year end accounts might identify bad debts that are unlikely to be paid and where bad debt relief can be claimed for VAT purposes.

- Consider the potential benefits to clients of adopting either the cash accounting scheme (cash flow benefits) or the flat rate scheme (tax savings in certain cases).

- A tax point (time when VAT is due on a return) can be delayed in some cases by raising a document such as an application for payment, fee note or payment request, ie any document other than a sales invoice. This could produce important cash flow benefits for the business by delaying the payment of output tax until perhaps the next VAT period.

- Consider the benefits offered to a business through filing VAT returns online. The reality is that online filing gives a business at least 10 extra days to pay its VAT (compared to a paper VAT return) and 12 extra days if a weekend is involved.

- In cases where a business is unable to pay its tax, there is scope to negotiate a time to pay arrangement with HMRC's Business Payment Support Service. However, contact should be made before a VAT debt becomes overdue for payment, ie to avoid a potential default surcharge being levied.

- There may be scope for many businesses to deregister from VAT if their expected sales in the next 12 months will be less than £66,000. The reality of the current economic climate is that many businesses have experienced a reduction in both sales and profits. However, be sure to remember that output tax might be due on the value of stock and assets held by a business at the time it deregisters. This could mean that deregistration is not a viable option.

Chapter 31

Supply of Goods and Services

Key topics in this chapter:

- The difference between a supply of goods and services.

- Key issues to consider concerning computer software supplies, hire purchase agreements and leasing arrangements.

- Procedures relating to goods supplied on a sale or return basis.

- Tax point rules – basic and actual tax points.

- Warranties, samples, compensation payments, lost or stolen goods, discount deals, part-exchange transactions.

- Mixed supplies – basic introduction to deal with the situation where goods are supplied which attract different rates of VAT.

- VAT invoices – when they should be issued and what information they should include.

- Electronic invoicing – the need for HMRC approval.

- Credit and debit notes – when they should be issued and what information they should contain.

- Bad debt relief – conditions for reclaiming bad debt relief on supplies made.

- Business gifts – £50 limit to avoid a VAT liability.

- Recharge of zero-rated expenses to a customer – form part of main supply.

- Continuous supplies of services.

- Sales between related parties.

Introduction

31.1   For a transaction to be within the scope of UK VAT, there are four key conditions that need to be satisfied:

(a)   it is a supply of goods or services;

(b)   it takes place within the UK;

(c)   it is made by a taxable person; and

(d)   it is made in the course or furtherance of any business carried on by that person.

The principle of VAT being a tax on the 'supply' of goods and services is in contrast to many other taxes – where calculations are based on money in and money out.

An outcome of this basic rule is that tax can sometimes be due, even where no money has changed hands. This can cause confusion among clients and tax advisers, who struggle to understand the concept that a transaction can have nil proceeds but still produce a VAT bill.

Another important point is that, by definition, a supply can only be of goods or services.

This chapter considers some of the important issues as to whether goods or services are being supplied to a customer.

Difference between goods and services

31.2   The HMRC definition of a supply of services is 'something other than supplying goods' (VAT Notice 700, para 4.5).

However, the definition is extended to include the phrase 'done for a consideration', which means there is no VAT to worry about on a free supply of services.

The difference between goods and services is clear in most cases because goods are usually tangible and can be clearly seen by the customer.

To give everyday examples, a washing machine, television and dishwasher are clearly goods. In contrast, a hairdresser, opera singer and VAT lecturer are obviously supplying services because the customer is receiving no goods and is enjoying the skills of the individual in question.

However, there are a number of borderline situations, usually when computer related supplies are involved – see Example 1.

Example 1

DEF Ltd produces a monthly newsletter for £600 per year that gives UK subscribers advice and tips on marketing. The newsletter has always been posted to subscribers in paper format but with effect from 1 June 2009, it will be e-mailed to each subscriber on a monthly basis. What is the VAT position?

Solution – the paper copy of the newsletter qualifies as a supply of goods, eligible for zero-rating as printed matter under *VAT Act 1994, Sch 8, Group 3*. The e-mail arrangement means the customer is now receiving a supply of electronic services – and the supply is standard rated. The subscription should be increased to £600 plus VAT from 1 June 2009.

Computer software supplies

31.3 The VAT situation regarding computer software supplies can sometimes be difficult.

To give a simple example, if a person buys a copy of a standard accounting software package from the shelf of his local store, this is a supply of goods. This is because the software is a mass-produced item that is freely available to all customers. In effect, personal and home computer software, game packages etc are all classed as a supply of goods.

In contrast, if someone orders a 'specific' software product for his own requirements (ie to create a unique programme), this is clearly a supply of services. The expertise of the person(s) producing the package means payment has been made for a supply of services.

Transfer of ownership – HP or lease?

31.4 A supply of 'goods' applies when a transaction involves:

- any transfer of the whole property in goods;
- the transfer of possession of goods.

A common situation encountered by practitioners concerns the VAT treatment of hire purchase (HP) and leasing agreements.

The key point with an HP agreement is that the intention of the agreement is that ownership of the goods will pass to the hirer at some point in the future, usually when the final payment has been made. The transaction therefore relates to a supply of goods.

The first instalment paid to the HP company usually includes a deposit on the asset and full payment of the VAT on the value of the goods. The hirer can reclaim input tax (subject to normal rules), even though he is paying for the goods over a longer period of time.

Contrast the above situation with the common lease hire arrangement for a car:

Example – Jim pays £400 per month to lease a car for 3 years and then return it to the leasing company at the end of the period.

In this situation, there is neither a transfer in the property of the goods, nor in the possession of the goods. The intention was always for the goods to be returned to the owner after 3 years. The monthly instalments of £400 therefore relate to a supply of services and should charge VAT at 17.5%, ie £70 (or 15% until 31 December 2009). As long as the vehicle has some business use, HMRC allows 50% input tax recovery (£35), again subject to normal rules (see **33.10**).

The above examples are very clear – but the approach to adopt in any difficult situation is to study the written agreement in detail and the intention of the scheme as far as ownership is concerned. To give a legislative reference, Directive 2006/112/EC, Art 14(2)(b) rules there is a supply of goods where 'in the normal course of events' ownership will pass at the latest upon payment of the final instalment.

Land

31.5 Another situation when a supply of goods is evident relates to a supply that involves 'the grant, assignment or surrender of a "major interest" in land'. A major interest in the UK relates to either a freehold sale or a lease exceeding 21 years (20 years in Scotland).

In effect, this means that the rental of a property (landlord and tenant basis) involves a supply of services.

Sale or return

31.6 This situation arises when a customer receives goods from a supplier – but the supplier retains ownership of the goods until the point when they are adopted by the customer. In effect, this means the customer has the right to return them at any time.

A common example of where this type of supply may occur is when a manufacturer provides a demonstrator product to a retail outlet – allowing the latter to display the goods in his shop and show the benefits to potential customers.

The main rules to remember with supplies on sale or return are as follows:

- as the goods remain the property of the supplier, then no tax becomes due until they are formally adopted by the customer;

- if no formal adoption takes place, then the adoption date will automatically become 12 months after the goods were first received – creating a tax point for VAT purposes.

An interesting situation occurs when a supplier receives some payment for these goods – in advance of the adoption date. Such transactions will be looked at very closely by HMRC because payment normally indicates a transfer of ownership, ie confirming a supply has taken place. However, if it can be clearly shown that the adoption of the goods has not taken place, and that the payment made is a refundable deposit, then no VAT is due.

With regard to the 12-month adoption deadline, output tax will be due at this point on the market value of the goods. In the case of an item that has been sitting on the shop floor for a year, going through various demonstration procedures, this value is likely to be considerably less than for a brand new item. It is also possible that the item could have been superseded by a more up-to-date product, again eroding its open market value.

Slow invoicing procedures – tax point rules

31.7 This is very common in business – a busy client working hard to supply goods to all of his customers – but forgetting to raise tax invoices promptly.

In these circumstances, it is useful to return to the basic tax point rules that apply as far as VAT is concerned.

- *Basic tax point* – this occurs at the time the supply of goods actually takes place, ie the point when goods are delivered to the customer. This transfer of ownership creates a supply as far as VAT is concerned – and a liability to the tax. However, the basic tax point is overridden if an 'actual' tax point is created.

- *Actual tax point* – this is created when either a supplier raises a tax invoice or payment is received from the customer. As long as one of these situations arises within 14 days of the basic tax point, then the actual tax point becomes the date when the VAT is due.

See Example 2.

Example 2

ABC Computers Ltd supplies a new computer server to DEF Ltd for £1,500,000 plus VAT on 15 March 2009. The VAT period of ABC Computers Ltd ends on 31 March 2009. The Finance Director of ABC Ltd has decided that in order to boost the cash flow of the company, he will not raise an invoice for the supply until 1 April 2009, ie so that the VAT will be paid on the return for the June quarter instead of March. The 3-month delay in the VAT payment will be very welcome for the company. The payment date from the customer has already been agreed at 30 April 2009.

Solution – the actual tax point (invoice date) occurs more than 14 days after the basic tax point. This means that VAT is due on 15 March 2009, ie the March rather than June quarter. If HMRC identified this anomaly on a VAT visit, then interest and potential penalties could apply.

Note – the logical solution would have been for ABC Ltd to delay the supply of goods until 18 March, so that the invoice date would then have been within 14 days of the supply.

As a final point, an application to HMRC can be made to extend the 14-day rule – but it is necessary to show why the 14-day period is inadequate. This could be, for example, that a price negotiation period takes place with a customer that always exceeds 14 days. There are several trades that have an agreement in place with HMRC to extend the 14-day period.

Warranties

31.8 A warranty arrangement is very common with the supply of many goods and, in the case of extended warranties, has proved particularly profitable for companies that trade in electrical goods.

The first situation that normally occurs is where the manufacturer or supplier gives a guarantee, for example, for the first 12 months that any repair or defect to the goods will be repaired without charge. In this situation, all parts and labour supplied by the manufacturer or supplier are not charged to the customer – and no VAT is therefore due.

The situation that can cause complications is where a company sells an 'extended warranty arrangement', ie the customer receives assurance that if the goods break down after the standard warranty period expires, then he will still have repairs carried out without charge – apart from the cost of the extended warranty.

As far as VAT is concerned, the key question to ask is: does the supply to the customer involve a contract of insurance (and is a contract that would be recognised as insurance by the Financial Services Authority)? If the answer is in the affirmative (unlikely in most cases), then the charge to the customer will be exempt under the *VAT Act 1994, Sch 9, Group 2*. However, the supply of a non-insurance warranty by a UK business will be standard rated.

Samples

31.9 Basically, the rule as far as samples are concerned is that no VAT is due, unless identical supplies are given to the same person. In such cases, only the first sample is deemed not to be a supply – see Example 3.

Example 3

ABC Computers Ltd has now introduced a new print accessory that the directors think could prove very popular with customers – and profitable for the company. It is sold to retail outlets throughout the country at £100 plus

VAT. A deal is agreed with one retailer, GHI Computer Stores, that a free print accessory will be given to them every week, as a sample to show customers and, if they are very persuasive, to sell as well.

Solution – the above example is a situation where no money changes hands on a supply – but a VAT liability is created.

In effect, the correct outcome for ABC Computers Ltd would be to raise a nil tax invoice for the first sample (assuming it is needed to record the movement of goods for stock control purposes) but then a VAT-only invoice for future samples, ie so that output tax can be paid on each sample after the first one. In most cases, this should not prove a problem because the VAT charged will be claimed as input tax by retailers/wholesalers.

Compensation

31.10   The compensation culture is always a potential problem – and almost every business will, at some time, have to deal with a situation where something has gone wrong, and a distraught customer is looking for financial recompense.

The basic principle as far as VAT is concerned is to consider whether the compensation payment relates to a specific taxable supply of goods – or whether the payments are compensatory, eg for distress caused. See Examples 4 and 5.

Example 4

Garage Doors Ltd supplied a customer with a garage door for £1,000 plus VAT that had a loose nut in it. As a consequence, the garage door collapsed on the customer's head when she was opening it – she had to have hospital treatment for cuts and bruises. Garage Doors Ltd pays her £500 compensation and reduces its output tax by £74.46 (ie £500 × 7/47 with a VAT rate of 17.5%).

Solution – Garage Doors Ltd is incorrect to adjust its output tax figure. The payment to the injured customer is compensation for her inconvenience and suffering – it is not linked to the taxable supply of goods. The payment is outside the scope of VAT.

Example 5

Garage Doors Ltd supplies another customer with a red painted door for £1,000 plus VAT. However, after 2 weeks the customer notices that the paint is peeling from the door and she demands compensation for the poor quality of the product. Garage Doors Ltd pays her £500 compensation and reduces its output tax by £74.46 (ie £500 × 7/47 with a VAT rate of 17.5%).

Solution – in this case, the output tax adjustment is correct because the payment directly relates to the goods supplied. In effect, the customer is receiving a reduction in the original price because the goods are sub-standard – there is no compensation for damage or injury suffered (apart from the embarrassment of the neighbours noticing that she has bought a cheap garage door).

A further situation where compensation could be evident is where a supplier actually receives compensation from, for example, a local authority for loss of trade suffered as a result of the local authority's action. However, it is again important to research the reason for the repayment being made.

In the case of the local authority carrying out path improvement works outside a supplier's premises, causing a loss of trade to the supplier, any payment made will be outside the scope of VAT as compensation. However, if, for example, the local authority pay the supplier a sum of money for allowing them to store their plant and machinery on his land overnight, then this payment is consideration for a supply of services and is therefore taxable.

Note – an interesting ECJ case ruled that deposits paid by hotel guests who booked rooms in advance did not represent a taxable source of income for the hotel if the guests failed to arrive (or cancelled their booking) and lost their deposits.

It was ruled by the ECJ that the money retained by the hotel represented compensation for the loss suffered as a result of the cancellation – the money had no direct connection with the supply of any service for a consideration. The deposits retained were therefore outside the scope of VAT (*Societe thermale d'Eugenie-les-Bains v Ministere de l'Economie, des Finances et de l'Industrie: C-277/05* [2007] 3 CMLR 1003, [2007] SWTI 1866, [2007] All ER (D) 273 (Jul)).

Lost or stolen goods

31.11   It is important that any client who suffers a loss of goods for any reason, eg theft, fire, employee error or accident, retains full records concerning the circumstances of the loss. This is to reduce the risk of a problem with HMRC on a VAT visit. Consider the situation at Example 6.

Example 6

An officer from HMRC is carrying out a routine VAT visit, and notices that ABC Computers Ltd purchased 50 computers on a special shipment from America. The officer identifies that 30 have been sold (and output tax correctly charged on sales invoices), nine are still in stock and one is actually being used by the company in its own office. What about the other 10 computers?

The instant reaction of the officer will be that the ten missing computers have been sold as an off-record sale and he will be reluctant to believe any alternative explanation such as theft, accidental loss, fire damage etc.

The officer will not only try to assess output tax on the market value of the 10 missing computers – but at worst, he could try to formulate an argument that the company is suppressing 20% of all of its sales, and raise an even bigger assessment of tax due. This would be on the basis that he is using the powers of 'best judgment' given to him under the *VAT Act 1994, s 73* (see 20.2).

Solution – the end result is a feast of problems, which could largely be avoided if the client retains supporting evidence of, for example, insurance claims (for damage or theft situations), police crime reports (for theft), notes of dates, people involved, action taken etc.

In the worse case scenario, the case could go to a VAT tribunal – where the tribunal panel would have to decide if they consider the defendant to be a witness of truth regarding the explanations given.

Discount deals

31.12 It is common practice for many businesses to offer a bulk discount deal – where the customer pays the full price for a quantity of goods, but is then entitled to a further quantity of goods free, eg three for the price of two. See Example 7.

Another common form of discount is settlement or prompt payment discount. In this situation, a customer receives discount (usually 2.5%) if he settles his account within a certain period of time, eg 14 or 28 days. The VAT rule as far as settlement discount is concerned is that VAT is always charged on the discounted amount, even if the customer does not take advantage of the discount being offered.

For example, if an invoice is for £100 plus VAT, and there is 2.5% settlement discount available, the invoiced amount will be £100 plus VAT of £17.06, ie total charge of £117.06 (these figures again assume a VAT rate of 17.5%).

Example 7

JKL Ltd manufacturers wood tables, selling goods to retailers throughout the country. In order to encourage bulk purchases, they give customers the chance to purchase ten tables at a standard list price – but then supply another table free of charge. In other words, '11 for the price of 10'.

On sales invoices raised for this type of deal, the eleventh table is recorded as a free sale.

Solution – VAT officers may be tempted to go down the route of assessing output tax based on the market value of the eleventh table. However, the correct outcome is that output tax is only due on the total price paid by the customer, ie the 10 tables at list price. It is the consideration from the customer that is the basis of the VAT charge in this situation.

Mixed supplies

31.13   In most cases, the VAT liability of goods supplied will be very straightforward. However, an area of VAT that has always caused a few complications (although the ECJ decision in the case of *Card Protection Plan* has clarified the position to a large extent) is when a bundle of goods are sold as part of a supply – and the goods attract rates of VAT at different rates.

Chapter 23 is devoted to this topic, but the key principle of mixed supplies is explained here as it is an important issue for traders supplying goods.

The main question to ask with mixed supply situations is: 'Am I making two or more separate supplies – or one main supply with an ancillary supply to enhance the enjoyment of the main supply?' In effect, this question looks at the importance of each of the supplies in question, to consider whether there is only really one main supply, with other incidental supplies that can be ignored. It is also important to consider this question from the viewpoint of the customer – what does he perceive that he is receiving for his money?

If there is only one main supply, then the whole of the VAT charge depends on the liability of this main supply. See Example 8.

Example 8

ABC Computers Ltd supplies a new computer to DEF Ltd for £10,000 plus VAT. However, the supply also includes a detailed manual explaining how the computer works, which cost ABC Computers Ltd £30 to produce. The manual is zero-rated for VAT purposes (reading material – *VAT Act 1994, Sch 8, Group 3*) so they only charge VAT on £9,970.

Solution – in this situation, the aim of the manual is to assist the use and understanding of the main supply, ie the computer. The manual is not a supply in its own right – if the customer was not purchasing the computer, he would have no reason to buy the manual. The whole supply for £10,000 is therefore standard rated.

Part exchange transactions

31.14   The basic VAT principle of part-exchange transactions is that there are two separate supplies taking place. It is important that amounts are not netted off against each other – VAT is due on the full value of supplies made. See Example 9.

Example 9

> High Street Motors is VAT registered and sells a van to Mr Smith for £2,000 cash plus Mr Smith's Vauxhall car worth £3,000. High Street Motors account for output tax of £297.87 (ie £2,000 × 7/47 with a VAT rate of 17.5%).
>
> *Solution* – this is incorrect – the sale of the van is effectively taking place at £5,000 and output tax needs to be accounted for on this amount (£5,000 × 7/47 = £744.68). In effect, the value for VAT purposes is based on the monetary and non-monetary consideration.

Note – VAT also needs to be accounted for on barter transactions. For example, consider a VAT registered business selling lawnmowers that agrees to give the local football club (not VAT registered) a free lawnmower in return for an advert in its match day programme. In effect, there are two supplies taking place, and the value of these supplies would be the open market value of the lawnmower. The lawnmower business has an output tax liability to declare on its VAT return.

The valuation of part exchange items can cause some difficulties, and a useful tribunal case on this subject is *CCE v Ping (Europe) Ltd* [2002] EWCA Civ 1115.

Here, the company offered to buy back illegal golf clubs it had sold to customers in return for a new club that complied with the regulations of the golfing authorities. The new club had a retail value of £72 and a wholesale price of £50. The customer's payment was £22 in cash plus his old club. HMRC contended that output tax was payable on the wholesale price of £50, giving the old club a value of £28 in part-exchange. Ping contended that the old club had a nil value because it was illegal and could not be used, so output tax was only payable on the monetary payment of £22 received from the customer. The courts agreed with Ping, ie the old club had a nil value.

VAT invoices

31.15　A VAT invoice is an important document because it is essential evidence to support a customer's claim for input tax. In effect, therefore, a registered business must issue a VAT invoice to all customers who are also registered for VAT. However, there is no obligation to issue an invoice in the following circumstances:

- if the supplies in question are zero-rated or exempt;

- supplies where the customer cannot reclaim input tax, eg in relation to motor cars or business entertainment;

- supplies on which VAT is charged but the goods are provided free of charge, eg as in the case of gifts and goods put to private use;

- supplies where the customer operates a self-billing arrangement. Self-billing is an established practice where the customer prepares a VAT invoice in the name of the supplier and then sends it to the supplier, usually with payment. It is very common in the construction industry;

- supplies by retailers unless the customer requests a VAT invoice;

- supplies by one member to another in the same VAT group.

A VAT invoice must show certain basic details, including:

- an identifying number;

- the time of the supply (tax point), name, address and VAT registration number of the supplier;

- name and address of the person to whom the goods are being supplied;

- a description to identify the goods or services being supplied;

- the rate of VAT and amount of VAT payable.

Where the registered business is a retailer, there is no requirement to issue a VAT invoice unless requested by a customer. Also, if the gross amount of the sale is less than £250, and the supply is not to a person in another EC country, the VAT invoice can be less detailed – to include just the following information:

- name, address and registration number of the retailer;

- the time of supply;

- a description sufficient to identify the goods or services supplied;

- the total amount payable including VAT; and

- for each rate of VAT chargeable, the gross amount payable including VAT, and the VAT rate applicable.

Note – in effect, the main benefits of being able to issue a less detailed tax invoice (compared to a full tax invoice) are that the customer's name and address do not need to be shown, and the gross amount paid by the customer can be recorded, rather than a separate split of net and VAT amounts.

With effect from 1 October 2007, HMRC introduced new invoicing regulations, which are explained in VAT Information Sheet 10/07:

- as well as having an identifying number, a sales invoice number must also be unique and sequential – see below;

- if a supply relates to a second-hand scheme, the sales invoice should be noted along the lines of – 'this is a second-hand margin scheme supply';

- a reference is also needed on any invoices relevant to the Tour Operators Margin Scheme (TOMS) – again along the lines of – 'this is a Tour Operators Margin Scheme supply';

- any intra-EU supply where the customer needs to account for the reverse charge on his own VAT return (e g in relation to a supply of goods between VAT registered businesses in different EU countries) needs a reference along the lines of – 'this supply is subject to the reverse charge'.

In relation to the new numbering regulations (unique and sequential), think of a small business that might buy a number of duplicate invoice books where each book is numbered from 1 to 100. The previous regulations allowed the business to issue the same invoice number on more than one occasion (eg invoice number 1 will be issued on each occasion that a new duplicate book is started) – but the new rules mean the numbering system should be adjusted so that each different series is unique (eg by adding a letter of the alphabet so that the first duplicate book is 1A to 100A; second book is numbered 1B to 100B etc).

Electronic invoicing

31.16   Electronic invoicing is the transmission and storage of invoices by electronic means – as an alternative to the delivery of paper documents.

Any business which intends to begin invoicing electronically must advise HMRC within 30 days of beginning to do so, by contacting the National Advice Service or in writing to its local office.

Basically, an electronic invoice should contain the same information as a paper invoice – HMRC also specifies a number of other conditions that must be met by a business. An important condition is for HMRC officers to have full access to the system being adopted, and to be able to carry out their usual checks on VAT visits to verify the accuracy of returns submitted.

Note – a business can also send invoices by fax or e-mail as an alternative to post; invoices sent in either of these two ways are acceptable as evidence for input tax deduction.

Credit and debit notes

31.17   A credit note is issued by the supplier of goods to make any adjustments to invoices previously raised. This can apply if the goods are returned, if a pricing error on the invoice has occurred or if discounts need to be applied to a customer's account.

A debit note fulfils the same need as a credit note – but is issued by the customer rather than the supplier. A valid debit note places the same legal obligations on both parties as a valid credit note.

To be valid for VAT purposes, a credit or debit note must reflect a genuine mistake or overcharge and must be issued within one month of this overcharge being discovered or agreed.

In cases where a credit or contingent discount is allowed to a customer who can reclaim all the VAT on the supply as input tax, there is no obligation to adjust the original VAT charge provided both parties agree not to do so. If the customer is not VAT registered, then the original VAT charge must be adjusted.

A valid credit note should include the following details:

- identifying number and date of issue;

- supplier's and customer's name and address;

- supplier's registration number;

- description identifying the goods for which credit is given;

- quantity and amount credited for each description and reason for credit, eg 'returned goods';

- total amount credited excluding VAT;

- rate and amount of VAT credited;

- number and date of the original VAT invoice – in other words, this will enable HMRC to verify that VAT has been accounted for on the original supply.

As far as VAT returns are concerned, a credit note issued by a supplier (or debit note received) will result in a reduction of his Box 1 figure for output tax – the net amount will also be subtracted from the Box 6 figure for outputs.

For a customer receiving a credit note, or issuing a debit note, the boxes affected by the transaction will be Boxes 4 and 7 (ie input tax and inputs respectively).

Note – the rate of VAT to be used for a credit or debit note is the one in force at the tax point of the original supply.

Bad debts

31.18 A credit note cannot be issued to a customer on the basis that the customer has refused or been unable to pay the amount charged on an invoice.

In such cases, the correct way of recovering unpaid VAT is by reclaiming bad debt relief. The basic rules are as follows:

- the debt in question must be at least 6 months overdue for payment – in the case of an invoice issued on 30-day payment terms, this would mean the debt can qualify for bad debt relief 7 months after the date of the original invoice;

- the whole or part of the debt has been written off in the accounts as a bad debt – and transferred to a specific bad debt account;

- output tax on the original invoice must have been accounted for and paid to HMRC.

A claim for bad debt relief is made by increasing the Box 4 (input tax) figure on the VAT return.

A business also has an obligation to repay input tax to HMRC on any purchase invoices that are more than 6 months overdue for payment. This provision is applicable even in cases where the supplier of the goods has not made a claim for bad debt relief. The basic principle is that it is unfair for a business to reclaim input tax on invoices that have remained unpaid over a long period of time. There could be a genuine reason for non-payment (eg dispute over goods or services provided on the invoice) but it is also possible that a balance remains unpaid on the ledger because a credit note has been mislaid. This would then account for why the supplier is not chasing payment of the outstanding invoice.

As a potential planning point, it is worth considering whether clients could be eligible to use the cash accounting scheme, ie where output tax and input tax entries on the VAT return are based on payments received and made rather than the date of sales and purchase invoices. The scheme is available to a business with annual turnover of £1.35m or less and is considered fully in Chapter 6. An advantage of the scheme is that bad debt relief is automatic because output tax is never declared until payment has been received from a customer.

Note – if you are acting for clients who are behind with payment of their VAT liabilities to HMRC, there might be some restriction in the amount of bad debt relief they can claim on their VAT returns. This situation will apply in very few situations so is not developed further in this book. Revenue and Customs Brief 18/09 gives full details of the procedures and calculations that need to be made.

Business gifts

31.19   An item is a gift when the donor is not obliged to give it and the recipient has provided no goods or services in return for receiving the gift.

A gift of goods can be made without accounting for output tax (and input tax still claimed on the purchase of the goods in question) if:

- the cost to the donor of acquiring or producing the goods is less than £50; and

- the gift is made in the course of business, eg gift to recognise loyal customers or hardworking staff; and

- the total value of gifts given to the same person in the same year is less than £50.

Note – the same year means in any 12-month period that includes the day on which the gift is made.

If a business gift does not meet the above criteria, then the gift becomes a taxable supply, and the value of the supply becomes the price the recipient would have to pay (excluding VAT) to purchase identical goods. Where that value cannot be quantified, the price for the purchase of goods similar to those in question (same age and condition) becomes the relevant figure. Assuming the goods in question are standard rated, output tax is then payable by the donor on the value of the goods.

Note – where a business makes a gift of goods on which VAT is due, and the recipient uses the goods for business (taxable) purposes, that person can recover the VAT as input tax (subject to normal rules). The donor cannot issue a tax invoice (because there is no consideration) but may instead issue a 'tax certificate', which can be used as evidence to support a claim for input tax.

The tax certificate is similar to an invoice in presentation (ie showing full details of goods being supplied) and will be worded along the lines of – 'no payment is necessary for these goods. Output tax of £x has been accounted for on the supply'.

Recharging zero-rated expenses to a customer

31.20   A common point of misunderstanding with clients and advisers relates to the recharging of zero-rated expenses to a client. These expenses do not form part of a separate supply to the customer but part of the main supply of services. Example 10 illustrates this principle with a simple situation.

Example 10

Mike is a tax lecturer and has agreed to carry out a lecture on tax for an insurance company for a fee of £1,000 plus VAT. Mike is based in London and the lecture is in Scotland so Mike will travel by first class rail and pay a return fare of £200. Rail travel is zero-rated as far as VAT is concerned. Mike itemises the £200 zero-rated rail travel on his invoice to the insurance company, and only charges output tax on the balance of his fee, ie £800 x 17.5% = £140. Is he correct?

Solution – in this situation, the £200 rail fare is not relevant to the insurance company because the supply of rail travel is between Mike and the rail company. Mike's supply to the insurance company is for a tax lecture (not rail travel) so output tax must be charged on his full fee of £1,000.

Continuous supplies of services

31.21   The temporary reduction in the rate of VAT from 17.5% to 15% on 1 December 2008 created a lot of queries about when a tax point was created in relation to a continuous supply of services.

The basic VAT principle to be aware of is that a tax point is only created in such cases when either an invoice is raised by a supplier or payment is received from a customer. This situation tends to cover, for example, most supplies of services provided by an accountant to a client where a standard letter of engagement is in place. This is because the accountant is deemed to be supplying services throughout the year as part of an ongoing relationship with the client. It is irrelevant that there might be a number of different jobs performed by the accountant with a clear start and finish date, eg submitting a tax return to HMRC.

The delay in paying output tax can be legitimately extended by raising a 'fee note' or 'request for payment' document rather than a tax invoice – and then only issuing the invoice when the customer has made payment. The customer will often need a tax invoice in order to claim input tax, so the alternative documents such as 'fee notes' are delaying his potential to claim input tax until he has paid for the service.

The challenge for advisers is to identify when a continuous supply of service arrangement has taken place.

Example of a continuous supply – Jones Solicitors provides ongoing legal services by acting as a trustee for a particular client. A tax point will occur when either an invoice is raised by Jones or payment received from the customer.

Example of a non-continuous supply – Smith Decorators are painting the rooms in a large office block – a job that started on 1 May 2009 and will finish on 31 July 2009.

In this situation, there is a single supply of services and the normal tax point rules will apply, ie a basic tax point is created on 31 July 2009 when the work is completed. VAT will be due on this date unless a sales invoice is raised or payment received within 14 days (before 14 August 2009), ie to create an actual tax point. This scenario assumes that no advance invoices have been raised or payments on account received in relation to this job. If so, then each advance invoice or payment also creates a tax point.

Sales between related parties

31.22   Imagine that Company A buys goods for £10,000 plus VAT and reclaims input tax on its VAT return. The goods are sold to Company B (a wholly owned subsidiary of Company A) for £1 plus VAT. The reason for this valuation is because Company B only makes exempt supplies and therefore cannot reclaim input tax. Is there a problem with this arrangement?

The answer is that there is indeed a big problem because HMRC has anti-avoidance rules in place which means it can direct that the value of a supply is the 'open market value'. The conditions are:

- the monetary consideration paid is less than the open market value – this is clearly the case in our example;

- the supplier and customer are connected – the 'connection' is based on the provisions of *Income and Corporation Taxes Act 1988, s 839*. This includes relatives of an individual and the spouse and relatives of the individual; partners in a partnership and their relatives and spouses; companies that are controlled by the same person or controlled by persons connected with each other, ie as with Company A and Company B;

- the customer is not entitled to fully claim input tax because he is either not VAT registered or is making some exempt supplies.

Output tax is therefore due based on the amount that would be payable if there was no relationship between the parties. If it could be argued that the goods supplied by Company A in the above example are genuinely only worth £1 (because of damage, wear and tear, obsolescence etc), then there would not be a problem – but this is very unlikely.

Planning points to consider

31.23   The following planning points should be given consideration.

- Remember that a tax point is created for VAT purposes when goods supplied on a sale or return basis have been held by a customer for 12 months.

- The basic tax point for goods (date of supply) is overridden if an invoice is raised or payment is received within 14 days of the supply – this can possibly create a cash flow benefit for a business by moving the output tax liability to the next VAT period.

- When dealing with compensation payments to customers, output tax can be reduced on a payment if it relates to a specific problem with goods supplied, eg compensation to reflect the poor quality of a product.

- Clients should be encouraged to keep full details of any goods that have been lost, stolen or destroyed. This could avoid problems on VAT visits if an officer tries to assess output tax on goods he cannot trace.

- If prompt payment discount is offered to a customer, then VAT is only charged on the discounted amount of the invoice, irrespective of whether the customer takes advantage of the discount. This could produce a small VAT saving for customers that are unable to reclaim input tax, eg the general public.

- Always ensure that clients treat part exchange transactions as two separate supplies, and do not just account for output tax on the net amount of any payment received.

- Retailers can benefit from issuing less detailed tax invoices if they supply goods where the total consideration is £250 or less.

- Be aware of the potential opportunity to reclaim bad debt relief on any sales invoices that are overdue by more than 6 months – as long as certain conditions are met. Equally, input tax claims need to be adjusted on any unpaid purchase invoices that are overdue by more than 6 months as well.

- Do not forget that bad debt relief is not an issue for any business that uses the cash accounting scheme. See Chapter 6 for details of the scheme.

Chapter 32

Input Tax Issues – Non-Deductible Items and Pension Funds

Key topics in this chapter:

- Input tax can only be reclaimed on genuine business expenses linked to the making of taxable supplies.

- Examples of when HMRC considers expenses to be private and non-deductible for VAT purposes.

- Rules for claiming (and not claiming) input tax on business entertaining expenses – and a possible opportunity to claim input tax on the cost of entertaining overseas customers.

- Rules for claiming input tax on specific employee benefits, domestic accommodation costs and farmhouse repairs.

- Procedures for reclaiming input tax on costs related to sporting events or leisure interests – the 'business purpose' test considered by HMRC.

- Input tax and motor cars.

- Apportioning input tax for an expense only partly used for business – rules to deal with private use of home computers provided by employers to employees.

- Accounting for output tax using the *Lennartz* mechanism as an alternative to input tax apportionment.

- The need to consider whether a supply is made to a business.

- Input tax issues for costs relevant to a funded pension scheme.

Introduction

32.1   The basic rule for reclaiming input tax is simple: if the VAT on an expense relates to taxable supplies, then input tax can usually be reclaimed; if it relates to non-taxable supplies or exempt supplies, eg private expenditure, then no input tax can be reclaimed.

There are a couple of notable exceptions when input tax cannot be reclaimed:

- business entertaining is a non-deductible expense, unless the expenditure relates to the entertaining of staff;

- motor cars are also non-deductible in most cases – unless it can be proved that the car is wholly used for business purposes (ie not available for private use, which is difficult to prove);

- input tax cannot be reclaimed on certain goods incorporated into a new residential dwelling by a developer, eg carpets, fridges, dishwashers (the latter two items are classed as 'white goods', and all white goods are subject to the input tax block).

In reality, however, HMRC is generous in allowing much expenditure relevant to employees and business owners to be classed as business – and some items will be considered in this chapter.

The business argument

32.2   A key method to adopt when considering input tax deduction on an expense is to ask the question: why was the expenditure incurred? Is there a clear business link? Was the expenditure made specifically to benefit the business? Or was it primarily made for private purposes – but the owner is trying to justify a business argument? See Example 1.

Example 1

Mr Jones is a sole trader (management consultant) and has claimed input tax on three expenses.

(a) He has renewed his golf club membership for £4,000 plus VAT. He has reclaimed £700 input tax because the golf club gives him important business contacts. He can prove that his biggest job last year was obtained through a golf contact.

(b) Mr Jones employs three other management consultants, and because the business has traded so well, he has decided to take them all out for the day – to watch the British Open Golf Championship. He incurs expenditure on tickets for the event, food and drink in a restaurant, plus petrol for his car – and has claimed input tax on all costs.

(c)   Mr Jones has decided to hire an executive box for another day at the British Open Golf Championship. This will be used for entertaining key business customers – the charge is £10,000 plus VAT and he has reclaimed £1,750 as input tax.

Solution – the second expense is the only cost that can be reclaimed for input tax purposes.

In example (a), although Mr Jones can clearly illustrate the business benefits of his golfing activities, the key point is that in reality he has joined the club because he enjoys playing golf. Think of the arguments that would be put forward across the country if input tax could be reclaimed on costs associated with every hobby or sporting interest.

Example (b) illustrates a key principle of VAT, namely, that input tax can be reclaimed on costs associated with entertaining staff. As an alternative justification, ask the question: if the business had traded badly, and made losses, would Mr. Jones have taken them out for the day to reward their efforts? Unlikely – proving a clear link between the business and the motive for the expenditure.

Finally, example (c) highlights one of the main non-deductible items as far as VAT is concerned, namely, business entertainment for any non-employee.

Business entertainment

General rules for input tax deduction

32.3   The basic rule for VAT purposes is that input tax cannot be reclaimed on business entertaining expenses, unless it relates to employees of the taxable person. For an event that includes both employees and non-employees, the input tax on the employee costs cannot be reclaimed if their function is to act as hosts for the non-employees.

The definition of business entertainment is extensive and HMRC regards entertainment as including all of the following facilities:

* provision of food and drink;

* accommodation in hotels;

* theatre, concert or sporting tickets; and

* the benefits of using capital assets such as yachts and boats for entertaining.

There are a few important concessions where input tax can be reclaimed on costs relevant to non-employees:

* self-employed persons (subsistence expenses only) who are treated in the same way for subsistence purposes as the employees of a company;

- helpers, stewards and other people essential to the running of sporting or similar events;

- accommodation provided by airlines to delayed passengers;

- entertainment provided by local authorities at civic functions – this is not business entertainment because the function is a non-business activity.

Entertaining of staff

32.4　However, the opportunity to reclaim input tax on staff entertaining is considerable – expenditure of this nature is regarded as a genuine business expense to boost staff welfare or reward staff success. It needs to be remembered, however, that input tax cannot be reclaimed on staff entertaining when the role of the staff member is to act as host to non-employees.

Charge to guests

32.5　One important principle established over the years is that the rules concerning input tax and business entertainment only apply if entertainment is provided free of charge.

In many cases, it is common for a staff function to be organised whereby the staff are allowed to attend free of charge, but any guests they bring must pay a per head contribution. This contribution may not be enough to cover the full cost to the company, but still represents a deviation from the 'free lunch' concept. However, it is important to note that output tax must be accounted for on the contributions from the guests. See Example 2 for an illustration of this point.

Example 2

Jones Ltd has decided to organise a Christmas party for 30 employees and 30 guests at a cost to the company of £40 plus VAT per person, ie a total charge for the evening of £2,400 plus VAT of £420 (based on 17.5% rate of VAT). This charge includes all food and cabaret. The employees can attend without charge but the guests must help with the costs by paying £15 each for their tickets.

Solution – the charge to the guests means that the whole of the input tax can be reclaimed (£420). This is because the company is not providing free hospitality to non-employees, which is a condition of the business entertaining rules. Output tax of £67.02 will be declared to HMRC (£15 × 30 guests × 7/47) – a net VAT rebate of £352.98 overall.

Entertaining for directors and business owners

32.6　As explained above, there is a block on input tax recovery for staff acting as hosts when non-employees are being entertained. The other exception to the rule of input tax on staff entertaining being reclaimable is where directors, partners or the sole trader of a business incur entertainment costs that do not involve other staff members. In this case, the input tax is not classed as being relevant to business purposes (eg directors' day out at the races).

However, where directors and owners attend staff parties together with other employees, HMRC accepts that all of the input tax on the event can be reclaimed, including the costs relevant to the directors.

Entertaining overseas customers – window of opportunity?

32.7 A recent verdict in the ECJ in the Danish case *Danfoss A/S v Skatteministeriet Case C-371/07* [2009] STC 701, [2009] All ER (D) 107 (Feb) could create an opportunity for UK businesses to reclaim input tax on the costs of entertaining overseas customers.

The details of the Danish case are not relevant but the outcome has questioned the legality of a decision taken by the UK government in 1987 to create an input tax block on costs relevant to the entertaining of overseas customers. HMRC is reviewing the position and it is likely that tribunal cases will follow if it does not allow claims to be made.

The *Danfoss* case has also created the opinion in some circles that input tax can be claimed on the cost of business meetings involving non-staff members, as long as the purpose of the meeting is exclusively for business ends. It will be interesting to see how this view is developed in the coming months.

To quote from the HMRC press release issued on 23 March 2009:

> 'HMRC do not consider that this decision has any implications for the input tax block on expenditure on entertaining UK business clients. Nor dos it have any impact on input tax that can be claimed on expenditure on meals and other entertainment provided to employees – business can continue to claim this input tax subject to the normal rules.'

Employee benefits

32.8 A happy employee is a productive employee – so input tax can be reclaimed on many benefits and perks provided to employees. However, in some cases, output tax must be accounted for on the onward supply of the goods to the employee. The following is a brief summary of the benefits where input tax can be reclaimed.

- *Computers supplied for home working* – see **32.16**.

- *Sporting facilities available to all staff* – corporate membership of a local gym may be taken out by a company, and this will be deductible for input tax purposes as long as the facility is available to all staff. If a facility is available to only specific employees, then input tax can still be reclaimed but output tax must be declared for the same amount, i e nil tax gain. See Example 3.

- *Canteen and recreational facilities* – there is no output tax charge on the free supply of services to employees – and input tax can be reclaimed on all costs relevant to a staff canteen, recreational room etc. However, the key point is again that it must be available to all employees.

- *Relocation expenses* – employers may provide assistance to employees or future employees relocating to be nearer to their main job. In such cases, input tax can be reclaimed on costs paid by the employer – as long as it is directly associated to the house move. For example, this rule would allow input tax to be reclaimed on estate agent's fees, removal costs, short-term accommodation in a hotel – even carpets and curtains. It would not allow input tax deduction on installing new windows to the property, or a new television and video.

- *Clothing* – many clients feel input tax recovery is justified on the basis that it is important to look presentable and smart to impress clients or suppliers. Unfortunately, this is not the case. Clothing is normally a private expense – and the only time when input tax can be recovered is if the clothing relates to a uniform or protective clothing, worn by an employee in the perform-ance of his duties. A barrister can therefore reclaim input tax on the cost of his wig and gown.

- *Mobile phones* – in basic terms, HMRC has agreed that input tax can be recovered by an employer on all standing charge costs or costs of purchasing the phone for an employee, even if the phone is used by an employee for private calls. However, if the employee is allowed to make private calls without charge, then the input tax on the calls must be apportioned on a fair and reasonable basis.

- *Gifts* – a gift to an employee for long service can be reclaimed as far as input tax is concerned, e g a clock for 20 years' service. However, the business must then account for output tax on the supply – creating a nil tax gain.

Example 3

Jones Ltd has recruited a new office manager on a salary of £30,000 per year. However, the employee is a keen golfer and instead of taking a company car as part of his remuneration package, he requests that the company pays his annual golf subscription at the top local club, £5,000 plus VAT (if the club was non-profit making, then the subscription would be exempt).

Solution – as far as input tax recovery is concerned, there is no problem. However, the golf membership is effectively put to private use by the individual concerned and, therefore, output tax must be declared. The end result is the same as if the input tax had been blocked – a nil tax gain.

Money for sport or hobbies – private or business expense?

32.9   Many business owners have a strong interest in sport or other pursuits, and there will inevitably be occasions when they will question the possibility of linking these interests to their business activity in order to gain VAT benefits.

The HMRC approach largely revolves around applying the 'business purpose' test to the expenditure. This often means trying to determine the intention of the person at the time of incurring the expenditure. Although it is often easy to justify the 'business benefit' of an expense, this does not necessarily mean that the 'purpose' of the expenditure was for the business.

Overall, the aim of HMRC, as far as input tax on sponsorship costs is concerned, is to ensure that a business gets recovery on the legitimate costs incurred promoting the business – but avoiding the situation where recovery is given to a business in respect of its own favoured sporting or recreational facility.

For example, as explained at Example 1 at **32.2**, the sole trader of a business cannot justify reclaiming input tax on his golf club membership on the basis that he obtains important business contacts at the club. His primary motive (or purpose) for the expenditure is that he enjoys playing golf.

In general terms, a suggested three-stage process to consider this issue is as follows:

(a)   consider the likely HMRC view on expenditure of this nature (ie how it will look in the eyes of a VAT officer carrying out a routine inspection);

(b)   clearly analyse the arguments in favour of the expenditure being business, and those that suggest it could be private;

(c)   research past tribunal cases – all 'grey' areas of VAT tend to have some useful case law to assist the process.

With regard to the approach adopted by HMRC, there is useful guidance in Manual VI-13, Ch 2A, paras 16.1–16.4 and Ch 3, Table 11. The questions considered in this section are as follows.

● Is the owner of the business actively participating in the sport?

● Does any of his family actively take part in the sport?

● Is there a connection between the sport and the business?

- Is there related advertising or promotional material?

- Does the business name appear on the merchandise, equipment or venue of the entity receiving the sponsorship?

- Can the business produce any evidence of research into the benefits to be obtained by the advertising?

As with other aspects of the UK taxation system (eg the definition of someone being employed or self-employed), the decision will be based on an assessment of the overall package of the arrangement. For example, it would not be sufficient for just one of the above tests to be met – it is the overall picture that counts.

A good example of a sponsorship arrangement that would have no problems meeting the HMRC tests is the sponsorship of the Premier League in football by, eg a top bank. The exposure of such an arrangement is worldwide and there is no personal involvement in the benefits of the deal from the business owners, ie the shareholders.

See Example 4.

Example 4

John is the sole trader of a butcher's shop and is a keen motor racing competitor. It is a very expensive hobby – but he has decided that he will advertise his business on the side of his racing car; include a reference to his business in all press articles, race programmes and other literature; he will also advertise the race wins on his business literature. The question is: can he reclaim input tax on all of the costs of the activity – or would it be classed as a non-business expense, not relevant to taxable supplies?

Solution – the whole picture needs to be taken into account when making a decision regarding input tax deduction. If the circumstances are still not conclusive, a written ruling from HMRC may be the best approach.

The points in favour of the expense being for the 'purpose of the business' are as follows:

- the business is being actively advertised on the car and in various items of literature;

- the 'winning' link would certainly be a good marketing tool for the business;

- spectators at events would read details about the business – and this could have trading benefits.

The issues against the business argument are:

- the sole trader is actively participating in the sport – indicating a motive based on personal interest rather than business promotion;

- if he cannot compete because of injury, there is no substitute driver to take his place;

- the races could take place many miles away from his business (eg would an event in the north of the country benefit a local shop in the south?);

- it would be difficult to show that the venture produced a direct boost to either business turnover or profits.

Overall, it is unlikely that HMRC would allow input tax deduction on the motor racing expenditure in this particular situation because it is too closely linked to the personal interests of the business owner.

Note – an interesting tribunal case that ruled against the taxpayer is *Independent Thinking Ltd* (25 November 2008, unreported) (LON/08/927 20884). The director put forward the argument that his company was entitled to claim input tax on the purchase and refurbishment of a yacht on the basis that it was wholly used for business purposes:

- he used it as an environment for creative thinking;

- he intended to promote round-Britain cruises at some time in the future;

- he also used it as an office.

The tribunal dismissed all three arguments and ruled that the expenditure was for non-business purposes.

Domestic accommodation

32.10 In general terms, no input tax can be reclaimed on expenditure relevant to domestic accommodation. For example, the managing director of a London company cannot buy a luxury apartment next to his office, and claim input tax on all of the fixtures and furnishings on the basis that it is important he lives close to his main place of business.

However, there are a few concessions where input tax can be recovered.

- *Sole proprietors and partners* – where the owner of a business clearly allocates one part of his house solely for his business, eg third bedroom used wholly as a business office for a self-employed IT consultant, then input tax on costs relevant to that room can be reclaimed. This could include the cost of decorating the room, fixtures and fittings, office furniture etc. However, it is not acceptable to claim input tax on a room only partly used for business purposes, eg a business owner who uses the dining room table to do the books once a month cannot treat this as a room for business purposes.

- *Employees* – where a business has to provide domestic accommodation to employees in order to run the business, the expenditure is classed as being wholly for a business purpose. In such cases, input tax can be reclaimed on all relevant costs (as long as the business is involved in making taxable supplies). The most common industries where this situation occurs are in the hotel and farming trades. In these industries, it important to have staff available at all times of the day – and often there are no suitable alternatives within reasonable distance of the business premises.

Repairs and renovations to farmhouses

32.11 Although this tends to be a controversial topic as far as input tax recovery is concerned, clear guidelines have been agreed between HMRC and the National Farmers Union – and often the problem occurs because farmers tend to see expenditure as being more relevant to business than is really the case. The key rules are as follows:

- for a normal working farm, 70% of VAT can be reclaimed as input tax on repair and maintenance costs to the farmhouse, eg roof repair, as long as the VAT registered person in occupation is running the farm on a full-time basis. If the farm is not a full-time occupation, then only 10% to 30% of the input tax can be reclaimed;

- if the work is classed as an alteration or improvement to the building, then 70% input tax can be reclaimed if the dominant purpose of the expenditure is business related – but if the main purpose is personal then a maximum of 40% of the VAT would be recovered.

Input tax recovery on the purchase of motor cars

32.12 In general terms, input tax cannot be reclaimed on the purchase of a motor car – even if it is purchased by a business that wholly makes taxable supplies and intends to use the vehicle for mainly business purposes. Purchase means not only outright purchase but also any purchase under a hire purchase agreement or any other agreement whereby ownership of the car eventually passes to the business acquiring the vehicle.

There are a number of exceptions to the rule regarding input tax deduction, which is allowed in the following circumstances:

- exclusive business use – see **32.13**;

- mini-cabs, self-drive hire, driving instruction;

- motor dealers and manufacturers;

- motability scheme.

Note – in the case of mini-cabs, self-drive hire or for driving instruction, the vehicle needs to be primarily for business use rather than exclusively for business use. This means a tax driver can use his car for private as well as business purposes.

A special concession applies to the leasing or hiring of a motor car, when 50% of the input tax on the monthly hire charges can be recovered as relevant to business purposes. This percentage would increase to 100% if the car was used exclusively for business – see **32.13**.

The payment to the leasing company will often include two separate elements – the hiring charge for the vehicle, and then an additional payment (usually optional) for a repair and maintenance agreement. As long as the repair/maintenance payment is shown separately on the hiring company's invoice, 100% input tax can be reclaimed on this proportion of the charge, subject to the normal rules.

Exclusive business use of a motor car

32.13   Input tax can be reclaimed on the purchase of a motor car which is used exclusively for business purposes and not available for private purposes. However, tribunal cases in recent years have highlighted that it is extremely difficult for a vehicle to be exclusively used for business.

In reality, HMRC regards a car as being used exclusively for a business purpose if it is used only for business journeys and it is not available for private use. A car is deemed to be available for private use if there is nothing to prevent the owner or employee from using the car for private use.

As a general exception, HMRC normally accepts that input tax can be recovered on a pool car purchased by a business, as long as it is kept at the principal place of business, it is not allocated to an individual and it is not kept at an employee's home.

Note – one positive point about the non-deductible input tax situation is that if a business sells a motor car, the supply becomes exempt under *VAT Act 1994, Sch 9*, Group 14 and no output tax needs to be declared. This particular group treats the supply of goods as exempt where no input tax was recovered on the initial purchase.

Apportionment of input tax for partly business and partly private expenses

32.14   When goods are acquired by a business but only partly used for business purposes (ie meaning there is partly private or non-business use), then the input tax should be apportioned so that credit is only given for the business part of the expense. This principle does not apply to motor cars, as explained at **32.13** above.

There is an alternative approach to dealing with such expenditure, which is to fully reclaim input tax on the initial expenditure, but then account for output tax on the private element over a period of time that reflects the private or non-business use. This approach is known as the *Lennartz* mechanism, named after a famous European Court case (*Lennartz v Finanzamt München III: C-97/90* [1991] ECR I-3795, [1993] 3 CMLR 689, [1995] STC 514 – see **32.17**).

Methods of apportioning expenses only partly used for business

32.15 The legislation does not specify any particular method of input tax apportionment for expenses where there is some non-business use. However, any method used must be fair and reasonable, taking into account the various activities and the purposes for which the expenditure is incurred.

In reality, there are many different methods of apportioning an expense and HMRC officers are instructed to only challenge a method that is completely unfair or unreasonable in its method and outcome. If the officer considers the non-business use to be minimal, he can decide to allow a waiver of apportionment. In such cases, it would not be cost effective for him to spend time and effort trying to calculate an assessment of tax for a small amount of money.

For example, input tax apportionment could be based on a fixed percentage between business and private use; an apportionment based on income figures; a time-based method; transaction-based method; area-based method.

Home computers made available by employers to employees

32.16 Until 13 August 2007, HMRC gave a very useful VAT concession, which meant that no output tax payment or input tax restriction was necessary in relation to computers provided by employers to their employees for home use. This concession applied even if the computer had a high percentage of private use by the individual in question.

This favourable concession was withdrawn by HMRC when it issued Revenue and Customs Brief 55/07 on 13 August 2007. The revised policy from this date is as follows.

- The business must now consider why the computer is being provided to the employee to determine the level of VAT that can be claimed.

- Businesses will only be able to claim full VAT recovery without any requirement to account for VAT on any private use where the provision of a computer is necessary for the employee to carry out the duties of his employment. In such cases, HMRC has concluded that the amount of private use will not be significant, ie no adjustment is required.

- Where a business cannot demonstrate that it is necessary to provide an employee with a computer in order to carry out the duties of his employment, then HMRC will accept any method of apportionment (to reflect the private use) as long as the end result fairly reflects the extent of business use.

The Lennartz mechanism

32.17 The key principle of the *Lennartz* mechanism is that input tax can be fully recovered on expenditure where there is part business and part non-business use, but then an output tax adjustment needs to be made at the end of each VAT period in which private or non-business use takes place. Records must be kept showing how the relevant item has been used.

The key point is that HMRC will not force a business to apply the *Lennartz* mechanism if the alternative (and probably simpler) route of input tax apportionment at the time of purchase is adopted.

See Example 5 for an indication of how the *Lennartz* basis of calculation works in practice.

Example 5

John purchases a yacht for business and private use for £500,000 plus VAT on 1 November 2008 (standard rate of VAT is 17.5%). He reclaims input tax of £87,500 on the VAT return relevant to the initial purchase, and then intends to account for output tax on a quarterly basis over a 5-year period (see 32.20 for an explanation of why a 5-year adjustment period is applicable). In the first VAT period, the yacht is used 25 days for business purposes, and 50 days for private purposes. What is the output tax adjustment in the first period?

Solution – a 5-year period comprises 20 VAT quarters, so the VAT to be adjusted on each VAT return is £4,375 (ie £87,500 divided by 20). In the first period, two thirds of usage is non-business, creating an output tax liability of £2,917 (ie £4,375 × 2/3).

Note – this calculation illustrates an important principle of *Lennartz* accounting – the private use adjustment each period is based on actual private/business use, not on expected private use when the asset was first acquired. The output tax adjustment will almost certainly produce a different figure each period in most cases. See also 32.21 regarding periods of no use, ie the 15 days in this example (90 days in quarter less 75 days when the yacht was used) when it was used for neither business nor private purposes.

Summary of key points regarding the Lennartz mechanism

32.18

● Revised guidelines concerning the operation of '*Lennartz* accounting' were introduced on 1 November 2007 – see VAT Information Sheet 14/07.

- If a business elects to apportion input tax at the time of purchasing an asset that is partly used for business and non-business purposes, then output tax is only due on the business portion if the asset is sold in the future. If the *Lennartz* mechanism is adopted (full input tax recovery and an output tax adjustment each period), then output tax us due on the full selling proceeds.

- The *Lennartz* mechanism can be adopted in relation to any asset as long as there is some business use, eg asset used for 95% private purposes can still adopt the scheme.

- However, the *Lennartz* mechanism cannot be used where the only business use of the asset relates to an exempt supply. It is the view of HMRC that there must be some entitlement to input tax deduction before an asset can come within the *Lennartz* mechanism. This requirement therefore excludes motor cars available for private use.

- When a business acquires an asset, it is at this point that a decision must be made regarding full input tax recovery (and *Lennartz* adjustment) or partial input tax recovery on the business percentage of the expense. An initial decision cannot be changed in the future if, for example, a business finds that the business percentage use has increased with time (ie initial input tax deduction too low).

- The *Lennartz* mechanism can be applied to both goods and services – see below.

Types of goods and services to which the Lennartz mechanism can be applied

32.19   The *Lennartz* mechanism can be applied to goods including computers, motor caravans, yachts, aircraft, taxable land and buildings allocated wholly to business purposes, including assets acquired from other EU countries or imported from outside the EU.

The scheme can be used for VAT on services that are used to create new goods – eg the construction of a new movable yacht, construction of new building or civil engineering works, construction of an annex or extension to an existing building.

HMRC's previous view was that the *Lennartz* approach could only be adopted in relation to property if a new asset was created. However, this approach was rejected in the case of *Whitechapel Art Gallery* (LON/07/833 20720), in relation to the VAT treatment of a £9m refurbishment project. The work related to a gallery which had some taxable activities (eg shop sales) and some non-business activities (eg art exhibitions).

In ruling for the taxpayer, the tribunal report said:

'It would be wholly unrealistic to treat the construction work otherwise than as the acquisition of capital goods. We can find no support in the case law of the Court of Justice for the proposition that the principle in *Lennartz* is confined to new acquisitions whether by purchase or construction of an entirely new asset or building. In our judgment the exclusion of the construction work in the present case would conflict with the principle of fiscal neutrality which is inherent in the common system of VAT.'

Period over which Lennartz adjustments should be made

32.20   Until 1 November 2007, there was no statutory period over which *Lennartz* adjustments needed to be made. However, the ECJ decision in *Hausgemeinschaft Jorg und Stefanie Wollny v Finansamt Landshut: C-72/05* [2006] All ER (D) 77 (Sep) confirmed that the period of adjustment should be made in accordance with the capital goods scheme – a 10-year period for land and buildings and a 5-year period for other goods.

The above periods are described as the 'economic life' of the asset. The 'economic life' commences on the day of the first use of the goods, and runs continuously until the above periods have been completed (or goods sold, whichever happens sooner).

Note – HMRC had previously indicated that all land and buildings adjustments should be made over 20 years. This is no longer relevant.

Periods of no use

32.21   Example 5 illustrated a very important point regarding periods when a *Lennartz* asset is used for neither business nor private purposes, ie periods of no use. In effect, these periods should be totally ignored when making the quarterly output tax calculations.

Example – 25 business days; 50 private days; 15 days of non-use. Private use is based on 50/75 and not 50/90.

Supply must be made to the business seeking to claim input tax

32.22   Imagine that Company A and Company B are both VAT registered and connected to each other (common ownership). Company B is partly exempt so cannot fully reclaim input tax on its VAT returns – there is no similar problem for Company A. The directors therefore decide that all expenses incurred by Company B will be invoiced to and paid for by Company A so that the latter can reclaim input tax on the expenditure. Is this allowed?

The key rule is that input tax can only be claimed if an expense (goods or services) has been supplied to the business seeking to make the claim. If this condition is not met, then it is irrelevant whether they meet the other requirements for claiming input tax, ie holding a proper tax invoice, making payment of the expense etc.

A common example and way of illustrating this principle is shown in Example 6.

Example 6

Martin is a chartered accountant and VAT registered as a sole trader. He is buying the freehold of a new office for his business and has taken out a mortgage with a bank. The bank requires a full survey to be carried out on the property as a condition of the mortgage advance. The cost of the survey is £1,000 plus VAT. What is the input tax position?

Solution – the surveyor is supplying his services and professional expertise to the bank, not to Martin. This means that he cannot reclaim input tax on the expense, despite the fact that he is fully responsible for the payment.

Input tax claims for pension funds

32.23   A funded pension scheme is usually a distinct entity, separate from the main trading business of the company, and is managed by trustees. The trustees can either be individuals or corporate members. If the fund needs to become VAT registered (see below), it will be the trustees who register because the fund has no separate legal status.

The funded pension scheme receives contributions from both employees and employers, and the trustees of the scheme have the responsibility of ensuring the fund is administered to obtain the best results for the members. This means that the funds have to be *managed* properly and *invested* with skill and knowledge in order to ensure the value of the fund grows as much as possible.

The main expenditure of a funded pension scheme falls into two distinct categories:

- management of the scheme on a day-to-day basis;
- investment activities to enhance the performance of the scheme.

The management of a pension fund for a company's employees (but not the investment activities) is deemed to be part of an employer's business, and therefore input tax can be reclaimed by the employer on the costs of setting up the fund and on its day-to-day management. This assumes that the fund has appointed independent trustees, ie the employer is not the sole trustee of a pension fund for his own employees. If the employer is the sole trustee of the fund, then the employer can reclaim input tax on all costs associated with the fund, including the investment related costs.

As a general guide, input tax cannot be reclaimed on the following costs of a funded pension scheme, even if the invoices are made out to the employer and he pays for the expenses:

- advice in connection with making investments;

- brokerage charges;

- rent and service charge collection for property holdings;

- producing records and accounts in connection with property purchases, lettings and disposals, investments etc;

- trustee services (ie services of a professional trustee in managing the assets of the fund);

- legal fees paid on behalf of representative beneficiaries in connection with changes in pension fund arrangements;

- custodian charges.

The main situation where a pension fund may need to register for VAT is if the trustees purchase commercial property as an investment, and take the decision to opt to tax the property. This means that all income connected with the property (usually rental income) will be standard-rated rather than exempt. See Example 7.

Note that the decision to opt to tax a property is very important for any business because once an election has been made (by writing to HMRC with an official notification), it cannot be revoked for 20 years. The result of making the election is that all supplies connected with the property become taxable, including the future disposal of the property. This could affect opportunities to sell the property to certain businesses unable to recover input tax, eg a business making wholly or mainly exempt supplies such as a bank or insurance company.

Example 7

The trustees of ABC Pension Fund intend to purchase a new commercial property for £800,000 plus VAT. The intention is to rent out the property to a firm of solicitors to generate rental income for the fund of £40,000 per year. The fund is not registered for VAT at the current time.

What is the best option for the trustees as far as VAT is concerned?

Solution – the only way for the fund to be able to recover the VAT on the purchase of the property (£800,000 × 17.5% = £140,000) is if the fund registers for VAT and elects to opt to tax the property.

In effect, registration for VAT will be on a voluntary basis because taxable supplies will be less than £68,000 per year (assuming the fund has no other sources of taxable income).

The solicitors renting the property are unlikely to be concerned about the VAT charge on their rental payments because they should be able to reclaim input tax in full. However, the trustees must remember that once they have opted to tax a property, the eventual sale of the property will also require output tax to be paid on the proceeds. Once made, the option to tax cannot be revoked for 20 years.

Note – even though the fund is now VAT registered, any input tax on the day-to-day management of the fund can only be reclaimed by the employer because it is the employer's responsibility to pay these costs. The only exception to this rule is if the employer has ceased to trade but the pension fund has continued to exist on its own account.

Planning points to consider

32.24   The following planning points should be given consideration.

- Input tax can be reclaimed on the costs of entertaining non-employees to attend an event or function as long as a charge is made to the non-employees and output tax is declared on this charge. The charge can be at below cost value.

- Remember that although input tax on staff entertaining costs can be reclaimed in most cases, this does not apply when the function of the staff member in question is to act as host for non-employees.

- Be aware that a potential opportunity could arise in the future to reclaim input tax on the costs of entertaining overseas customers. HMRC is currently reviewing the position following a recent ECJ case.

- Input tax can be reclaimed on staff benefits such as a staff canteen and corporate membership of a gym, as long as the facility is available to all staff, not just a select few.

- It is possible (although difficult in practice) for a business owner to justify reclaiming input tax on costs associated with a sporting or leisure activity. However, the owner (or his adviser) will need to clearly illustrate the business and commercial benefits of an arrangement. He will need to convince HMRC that he is not just trying to reclaim input tax on costs linked to a private interest.

- Review input tax recovery on motor cars to assess whether a claim could be made, for example, for a genuine pool car arrangement. There may, however, be advantages in leasing a car – 50% of the input tax on the monthly hiring charges can be reclaimed as relevant to business use.

- In the case of expenses that are only partly business, consider whether an output tax adjustment using the *Lennartz* mechanism would be a better option than apportioning input tax at the time of the initial purchase.

- If a pension fund buys a commercial property on which VAT has been charged, there may be advantages in registering the fund for VAT and making an election to tax the property in question. All input tax relevant to the property (including the input tax on the initial purchase price) can then be reclaimed on the basis that it relates to a taxable activity.

Chapter 33

Motor, Travel and Subsistence Expenses

Key topics in this chapter:

- Private motoring for business owners and employees.

- Scale charge procedures – CO_2 basis of calculation from 1 May 2007.

- Adjusting for private use by keeping detailed mileage records.

- The option to not claim input tax on any road fuel purchased by the business.

- Input tax on mileage claims.

- VAT treatment of other motoring expenses – leasing/hiring a vehicle; repair and maintenance costs; personalised number plates.

- Subsistence expenses for employees and business owners.

- Other travel costs – taxi fares, air travel, rail fares.

Private motoring adjustments

Introduction

33.1 One of the main principles of VAT is that input tax can only be reclaimed on expenses that relate to 'taxable supplies made by a business'.

In effect, this means that if a business owner or employee incurs motoring costs on a visit to a client, and the business is VAT registered and makes taxable supplies, then any VAT incurred on the journey can be recovered. If, however, the journey is to watch a football match, then this expenditure cannot be reclaimed for VAT purposes because it is now a private or non-business expense.

In reality, the reason why the VAT rules can be complicated in this area is because of the practical difficulties of making input tax claims. For example, in the situation above, if the business owner fills up his car with petrol, he does not know at this stage (unless he is a meticulous planner who knows his precise travel plans for the next 7 days!) how much of this petrol will be used for business purposes (ie input tax reclaimable) and how much will be for private purposes (ie input tax not reclaimable).

Motoring costs and adjusting for private use

33.2 Any business that pays for road fuel (either for employees or owners of the business) has three options available to it as far as VAT is concerned:

- reclaim all input tax on the road fuel and then pay the scale charge – see **33.3**;

- keep detailed mileage records to separate business mileage and private mileage for each vehicle – then calculate the amount of VAT that can be reclaimed on an apportioned basis – see **33.4**;

- it can elect to claim no VAT on the road fuel it purchases – and this will then avoid the scale charge being applied – see **33.5**.

Scale charge

33.3 The scale charge system is based on the CO_2 emissions of a vehicle. This approach was adopted with effect from 1 May 2007, the previous system having been based on the cylinder capacity (engine size) of the vehicle. To illustrate the workings of the scale charge system, consider the following example.

Example 1

Employee A drives a company car with a 180 CO_2 emissions band. In VAT period ended 30 September 2009 (standard rate of VAT is 15%), the total fuel for his vehicle (paid in full by the business) is £350. What is the VAT position?

Solution – the business can recover input tax on the fuel cost (£350 × 3/23 = £45.65). However, because some of the fuel is used for private and non-business purposes, then the scale charge must be applied, which is effectively an output tax charge on the fuel supplied to the individual. For VAT periods beginning on or after 1 May 2009, the scale charge for a 180 CO_2 emissions band vehicle is £39.39 per quarter (ie £302 x 3/23 = £39.39).

Therefore, the business will include £39.39 as output tax in Box 1 of its VAT return; the business will reclaim input tax of £45.65 in Box 4 of its VAT return; the net value of the scale charge, ie £302 – £46 = £256, will be included in Box 6 of its VAT return (outputs box).

For information purposes, the fuel scale rates for 3-month VAT periods are as follows with effect from 1 May 2009:

CO$_2$ Band	VAT inclusive 3 month charge (£) 1 Dec 2008 to 30 April 2009	VAT inclusive 3 month charge (£) From 1 May 2009
120 or less	138	126
125–135	207	189
140	221	201
145	234	214
150	248	226
155	262	239
160	276	251
165	290	264
170	303	276
175	317	289
180	331	302
185	345	314
190	359	327
195	373	339
200	386	352
205	400	365
210	414	378
215	428	390
220	442	403
225	455	416
230	469	428
235 or more	483	441

Note – the VAT amount will be accounted for in Box 1 of a business' quarterly VAT return, with the net amount included in Box 6. The figures above will obviously vary on a proportionate basis for repayment traders submitting monthly VAT returns, or taxpayers on the annual accounting scheme submitting one return each year.

For periods to 31 December 2009, the amount of VAT payable will be based on a VAT rate of 15% (ie VAT fraction of 3/23). From 1 January 2010, the calculation will be based on a VAT rate of 17.5% (ie VAT fraction of 7/47).

As a separate tip, be aware that the new rates apply for VAT periods beginning on or after 1 May 2009. So a taxpayer who adopts calendar VAT periods will use the previous scale charges rates for his June 2009 return and the new rates for his September 2009 return.

Key questions	Answers
Does it make any difference if the vehicle in question is a company car or car owned privately by the individual?	No – the scale charge applies to any vehicle where fuel is bought for private and business purposes. In effect, the scale charge deals with the situation where fuel is initially deemed to have been bought wholly for the business, but then some of this fuel is used for private purposes ie creating an output tax liability on the onward supply to the individual in question.
Is it possible for a vehicle to be wholly used for business purposes and therefore escape the scale charge?	Possible but very difficult. A detailed mileage record would need to be kept as evidence that the car is only used for business purposes. But even then, it would be difficult to prove that private use is never an issue – think of the detours to the supermarket or emergency situations that could arise where a private journey is needed, eg visiting a relative in hospital.
What if our client has a petrol account with one particular garage where all fuel is paid for through this account?	The business will have given the garage a list of vehicle registration numbers that can obtain fuel via the petrol account. All vehicles on this list will then be subject to the quarterly scale charge.
Is there any distinction between a company director, other employee of the business or sole trader or partner?	No – the key question is not the status of the driver or vehicle owner – but the principle that some of the fuel that has been bought for the vehicle will be used for private purposes.
What if the amount of the scale charge exceeds the amount of input tax that I have claimed on road fuel?	Consider the option available to a business to reclaim no input tax on road fuel – see **33.5**.

Keep detailed mileage records

33.4 The second option for dealing with the VAT implications of private motoring is for the driver(s) of the vehicle in question to keep detailed mileage records, recording every journey for both business and private purposes. Consider Example 2 below.

Example 2

Employee A has a company car and all of his petrol expenses are paid by his employer. He keeps a detailed mileage record of all journeys, and in the VAT period ended 30 September 2009, he travelled 8,000 miles of which 2,400 were private miles and 5,600 were business miles. The total petrol cost for the quarter was £900 including VAT. What is the VAT position in relation to his fuel expenses?

Solution – the total VAT on the fuel purchased by the business is £117.30 (ie £900 × 3/23 based on a VAT rate of 15%). However, the business proportion of this input tax is only £82.11 (5,600 miles business divided by 8,000 miles in total = 70% business proportion. Input tax to reclaim is therefore £117.30 × 70% = £82.11).

Therefore, include £82.11 in Box 4 of the quarterly VAT return; there is no Box 1 adjustment because the input tax apportionment above has avoided the need to apply the scale charge.

Key questions	Answers
Which is the best method to use – the mileage record apportionment or the scale charge system?	This will depend on a number of issues such as the total mileage of the car, the amount of private use, the impact of the scale charge etc. In reality, however, most businesses opt for the scale charge system because the administrative burden of an employee or business owner keeping a detailed mileage log can be very onerous.
Can the employee just record his business journeys – and then the private journeys can be assumed to be the balance?	This could be prone to challenge by a VAT officer. If a client wants to opt for the mileage route, then the records must be detailed and accurate.

Opting out of the scale charge or record-keeping system

33.5   The options at 33.3 and 33.4 could give a business two possible problems:

- in the case of the scale charge calculation at **33.3**, it is possible that output tax declared in Box 1 may exceed the total input tax recovered on fuel costs in Box 4. This situation could arise if business drivers have very little total mileage (eg localised business, users have low private usage) where the input tax is not significant;

- the mileage records system will deal with the potential problem created by the scale charge calculation, but it could be too onerous for vehicle drivers to remember to complete their mileage details after each journey.

A third option could be adopted – consider the following example.

Example 3

Mr A trades as an accountant (sole trader) with mainly local clients. He drives a 3-litre Jaguar with a high CO_2 emissions rate of 235 and his total petrol bill is always £10 per week. He is VAT registered. He has no employees so his fuel bill is wholly related to his own car. What is the best solution as far as VAT is concerned?

Solution – if Mr A opted for the scale charge route, he would be able to reclaim quarterly input tax of £16.96 (£10 × 13 weeks × 3/23) but would have an output tax liability of £441 x 3/23 = £57.52 (based on the CO_2 scale charge rate effective from 1 May 2009). His best option is to not claim input tax on any fuel costs – therefore avoiding the scale charge situation.

Key questions	Answers
Should I notify HMRC if I decide not to reclaim any input tax on fuel costs?	No – Paragraph 8.6 of Notice 700/64 (1 May 2007) makes no mention of the need to notify HMRC of a decision to not reclaim input tax on fuel costs.
Can I elect to keep some of the company vehicles in the scale charge system – and some of them out of the system by making an election?	No. Any decision to not reclaim input tax relates to all road fuel purchased by the business – not just the road fuel for certain vehicles. The decision would also apply to fuel purchased for commercial vehicles as well as motor cars – there are no exceptions to the system.
What if the circumstances of the business change so that it is now better to reclaim input tax on fuel costs and apply the scale charge?	Any change to existing procedures should be made at the beginning of a VAT period.

Mileage payments

Introduction

33.6   The VAT situation for a business that purchases road fuel was considered above – we will now look at the situation where an employee purchases the fuel himself – and then claims some recompense from his employer on a mileage basis.

Note that in reality, a business is unlikely to reimburse any mileage claims for employees making private trips – this would not be commercially realistic and would also cause benefit in kind problems. We will therefore assume in this section that mileage claims are for business journeys only.

We will split this topic into two parts:

● where the mileage payment is to cover the petrol cost only – see **33.7**;

● where the mileage payment is to cover all motoring costs, e g wear and tear on the vehicles, contribution towards insurance/repair costs – see **33.8**.

A key point to be aware of is that the rules for reclaiming input tax on mileage payments were amended with effect from 1 January 2006, so that input tax claims must now be supported by petrol receipts (tax invoices) attached to the mileage claim.

Mileage payment for petrol cost only

33.7   Consider the following example.

Example 4

Bill is sales director for ABC Ltd, and has use of a company vehicle. He is responsible for paying for all of the fuel purchased for the car – but can then reclaim 12p per mile from the company for all business trips – this reflects the cost of petrol only. In VAT period ended 30 September 2009, his total business miles were 2,500.

Solution – by concession, a company can reclaim input tax on the petrol element of any mileage costs paid to an employee, as long as the mileage in question relates to business journeys for a business making taxable supplies and tax invoices (petrol receipts) are retained as evidence to support the claim.

In this example, Bill will receive payment of £300 from the company (2,500 miles × 12p per mile) and the company will reclaim input tax of £39.13 (ie £300 × 3/23).

Key questions	Answers
Does the company need to obtain petrol receipts from the employee as evidence that he has purchased the fuel?	Yes, as explained above – but only since 1 January 2006. Up to 31 December 2005, the only evidence required by a VAT officer would be the mileage claim itself.
Is the VAT officer likely to challenge the mileage records in any way?	As long as the records look reasonable, they are unlikely to be challenged. For example, if there is a mileage claim of 2,000 miles per month for the office cleaner, then this may look a bit strange. Again, if an employee has claimed 250 miles for a trip from London to Brighton, this would also be challenged.
Is there a rule about what is an acceptable fuel allowance to pay to an employee?	HMRC publishes advisory fuel rates on a regular basis, usually twice a year, based on the engine capacity of the car and the type of fuel used. These rates are a guideline only. However, it is unlikely that HMRC would accept that a small engine car only does 10 miles to the gallon – a common sense approach is again needed.

HMRC announced new fuel advisory rates with effect from 1 July 2009. These are as follows:

Engine size	Petrol	Diesel	LPG
1400 cc or less	10p	10p	7p
1401 cc to 2000 cc	12p	10p	8p
Over 2000 cc	18p	13p	12p

The advisory rates effective from 1 January 2009 until 30 June 2009 were as follows:

Engine size	Petrol	Diesel	LPG
1400 cc or less	10p	11p	7p
1401 cc to 2000 cc	12p	11p	9p
Over 2000 cc	17p	14p	12p

The advisory rates effective from 1 July 2008 to 31 December 2008 were as follows:

Engine size	Petrol	Diesel	LPG
1400 cc or less	12p	13p	7p
1401 cc to 2000 cc	15p	13p	9p
Over 2000 cc	21p	17p	13p

Mileage payments that also include non-petrol costs

33.8 The situation where a business pays a mileage rate that is only intended to cover the petrol cost of a journey was considered at **33.7**. In reality, if an employee uses his own vehicle for a business journey carried out on behalf of his employer, then he will usually be paid a higher mileage rate – sufficient to cover the wear and tear cost to his vehicle as well as the fuel cost.

The most common mileage rates paid by a business are as follows:

- 40p per mile for first 10,000 business miles in a tax year;

- 25p per mile thereafter.

The above rates are frequently adopted because they are the rates that HMRC allows a business to adopt before any benefit in kind/income tax implications take effect.

The basic rule for reclaiming input tax on mileage rates that cover wear and tear/other costs is that the amount reclaimed should be based on the petrol element of the mileage claim only.

Consider the following example.

Example 5

John is sales manager for ABC Ltd and uses his own vehicle for company business (a 1600 cc Ford Focus with a diesel engine). ABC Ltd pays him an allowance of 40p per mile for all business journeys – and he submits a monthly mileage claim. In VAT period ended 31 March 2009, he completed 4,000 business miles.

Solution – the mileage allowance paid to John includes an allowance for wear and tear costs, repair/servicing costs – as well as the fuel costs for the journey. As far as VAT is concerned, only input tax on the diesel element of the mileage claim can be reclaimed.

The HMRC fuel advisory rate for a 1600 cc diesel vehicle is 11p per mile – input tax to reclaim on John's mileage expenses is:

4,000 miles × 11p per mile × 3/23 = £57.39.

Note – again, since 1 January 2006, the mileage claims need to be supported by proper tax invoices (petrol receipts) to support any input tax claim.

Key questions	Answers
What if my client has been adopting a mileage payment system for many years and never reclaimed any input tax on the claims paid to employees?	In effect, this situation has created a VAT overpayment on past VAT returns through underclaimed input tax. The legislation allows any past VAT errors to be adjusted for the previous 3 years only, rising to 4 years by 1 April 2010. If the amount of the adjustment is less than £10,000 or 1% of Box 6 turnover up to a ceiling of £50,000, this can be corrected on the next VAT return submitted by the business (increase Box 4 figure). If the amount of VAT exceeds these levels, it must be corrected by submitting an error notification form to HMRC.
What if my client pays a mileage rate in excess of 40p per mile?	For VAT purposes, the principle remains unchanged – namely that input tax can only be reclaimed on the petrol element of any mileage claim (and supported by petrol receipts if the claim is after 1 January 2006). However, be aware that a mileage payment in excess of 40p per mile has benefit in kind implications for the employee and employer.
What if I consider the HMRC fuel advisory rate to be too low?	A business can still assess its own petrol rates, but these must be calculated in a fair and reasonable manner.

Other motoring expenses

33.9   It should be noted that the guidance that follows assumes that the business in question does not trade in motor vehicles, for example as a car hire company, taxi business, car dealer etc.

Leasing or hiring a motor car

Lease

33.10   If a car is leased to a business, then the leasing company will charge VAT on the monthly rental payments. The car will never be the property of the business (unless it makes a payment to purchase it from the leasing company).

In such cases, input tax is reclaimable on 50% of the lease charge – this 50% restriction also applies if the monthly payment includes a charge, for example for service and repair costs. See Example 6.

Example 6

ABC Ltd has leased a BMW car for a 3-year period for use by its sales manager. The monthly charge is £300 plus VAT of £52.50 (based on 17.5% rate of VAT).

Solution – input tax of £26.25 can be reclaimed on each payment made to the leasing company (ie £52.50 × 50%).

Hiring a car

33.11   The 50% rule also applies to the short term hire of a vehicle – unless the hire period is less than 10 days, and the car is being hired specifically for business purposes. See Example 7.

Example 7

ABC Ltd has hired two vehicles for 8 days each – the first to replace the BMW of the sales director, which is being repaired following an accident; the second for use by the purchasing manager on a tour to visit suppliers.

Solution – the 50% rule will apply to the car used by the sales director – but 100% input tax can be reclaimed on the car for the purchasing manager because the hire period is less than 10 days and the car is being hired solely for a business purpose.

Repair and maintenance costs

33.12   If a vehicle is used for business purposes, VAT on repair and maintenance costs can be treated as input tax if the work done is paid for by the business.

Key questions	Answers
Can a client reclaim all of the VAT on repair and maintenance costs on a business vehicle, even though the vehicle is partly used for private purposes?	100% input tax can still be reclaimed even if the vehicle is used for some private motoring and even if no VAT is reclaimed on road fuel in order to avoid the scale charge. HMRC accepts that a vehicle needs to be in sound working order in order to carry out business journeys – and therefore allow 100% recovery of relevant costs.

Key questions	Answers
What if I agree to pay the repair and maintenance costs of an employee's vehicle which he owns privately?	If a car is never used for business purposes, then no input tax can be reclaimed on repair or service costs. However, if the employee's car is sometimes used for business purposes, and the cost of the repair is met by the employer, then input tax can be reclaimed on the cost incurred. Be aware though, that such generosity by an employer can have direct tax consequences.

Car accessories

33.13   Input tax can only be reclaimed on car accessories if it can be shown that the accessory has a business use, for example, a car phone to make business calls.

As for personalised number plates – it would need to be shown that the number plate clearly advertises and promotes the business. See Example 8.

Example 8

Jim Smith is the managing director of ABC Ltd and the company is considering buying a personalised number plate for his Mercedes car. He is undecided whether to buy the number plate 'JIM 1' after his own name, or 'ABC 1' after the company name. He is interested in the VAT issues of both choices.

Solution – there is no business advertising benefit gained from the purchase of the plate 'JIM 1' so the cost would be non-deductible as far as input tax is concerned. However, 'ABC 1' is clearly promoting the company name, so input tax could be reclaimed on this particular choice.

Subsistence costs

33.14   A lot of work performed by employees and business owners is done away from the main place of business, which inevitably involves meal and hotel expenses being incurred.

In most cases, there is no problems with these costs being reclaimed for input tax purposes – although remember that business entertaining expenses cannot be reclaimed, including the costs of employees acting as hosts.

Hotel expenses

33.15   VAT incurred on accommodation for employers and employees when away from their normal place of work on a business trip can be treated as input tax – see Example 9.

Example 9

> John works for a firm of accountants in Luton, and spends a week away from the office doing an audit in Birmingham. He stays at the Hilton Hotel in Birmingham – the hotel bill is paid for by his employer.
>
> *Solution* – input tax can be reclaimed by the employer on the invoice from the Hilton Hotel. There is no problem under current rules if the invoice from the hotel is made out in John's name, as it is common practice for hotels to invoice the guest rather than his employer. Input tax can also be reclaimed on any meal costs incurred by John on this trip – as long as a supporting tax invoice is held.

There may be occasions where an employee is required to stay at a hotel near to his place of work for business purposes. In such cases, input tax can still be claimed on the cost of the hotel – see Example 10.

Example 10

> Bill has an important job for ABC Ltd in London – he is based in Luton and commutes by train each day. There is talk of a rail strike – so ABC Ltd agree to pay for him to stay overnight at a hotel next to the office.
>
> *Solution* – the decision to pay for Bill's accommodation is made for business reasons so input tax can be reclaimed on the hotel cost. It is not a problem that the hotel is located very close to Bill's main place of work. The same rule would also apply if Bill was a sole trader or partner of the business – the key point being that the reason for the expense is for genuine business reasons.

Meal expenses

33.16   Any meal cost paid for a non-employee (eg customers or suppliers) is classed as business entertainment. Input tax cannot be reclaimed on any entertaining cost, including the costs of the employee acting as host – see Example 11.

Example 11

> ABC Ltd book a table for ten people at the local Chinese restaurant for eight customers, plus two employees who will look after the customers and keep them entertained.
>
> *Solution* – no input tax can be claimed on the charge made by the Chinese restaurant because it relates to business entertainment. This includes the cost of the employees' meals because they are acting as host for the guests.

Any meal provided for an employee (excluding directors, sole traders and partners) can be reclaimed for input tax purposes, for example, staff canteen, office Christmas party, end-of-year party to celebrate successful trading period.

In the case of a sole trader, partner or director, the only time when input tax can be reclaimed on meal costs is if they are working away from their normal location on business – these costs are then classed as subsistence expenses.

Note – how many miles would be acceptable as 'away from the normal workplace'? Five miles is a useful guide and has been accepted as reasonable by most VAT officers in the past.

In some cases, a business will pay employees a flat rate for subsistence expenses, eg £15 per day to cover meal and incidental costs if they are away from the office for more than 10 hours. There is no entitlement to input tax deduction on such flat rate payments.

Travel costs

33.17   So far in this chapter, it has been assumed that the method of transport used is by a motor vehicle – looking at the VAT implications of motoring expenses. However, now we will consider the input tax treatment of travel by other means of transport.

Air travel, rail and bus

33.18   Any form of transport that carries more than ten passengers is zero-rated for VAT purposes. Therefore, a business will never be able to reclaim any input tax on these methods of transport because they are all VAT free anyway.

Taxi fares

33.19   As a taxi holds less than ten passengers, a taxi journey is basically standard rated. However, be aware that many taxi drivers operate as self-employed persons, and because they trade below the VAT limits, are unlikely to be VAT registered.

The key point is to check if the invoice issued by the driver includes a VAT registration number. In most cases, there is unlikely to be a number.

If a taxi business is VAT registered, then input tax can be reclaimed on the cost of the journey as long as it is for business purposes.

Planning points to consider

33.20   The following planning points should be given consideration.

●   Be aware of the new scale charge rates effective for accounting periods beginning on or after 1 May 2009.

- Consider whether it would be more profitable for a business to claim no input tax on road fuel and therefore avoid the need to account for scale charges.

- For a business operating the scale charge system, consider whether it would be beneficial (and realistic) to keep mileage records to adjust for private motoring costs, which may produce a VAT saving.

- Be aware of the opportunity to reclaim input tax on the petrol element of mileage payments made to employees for business journeys, however, these must be supported by tax invoices.

- If a business has not reclaimed input tax on mileage payments in the past, then there is scope to reclaim input tax for the last 3 years (rising to 4 years by 1 April 2010) – either by making a claim in Box 4 of the next return or by submitting an error notification claim to HMRC (depending on amounts of tax involved).

- Advise clients that only 50% of input tax can be deducted on car leasing/hire charges.

Chapter 34

Supplies Involving Agents

Key topics in this chapter:

● Identifying an agency/principal arrangement.

● The main features of an agency relationship in a business arrangement, e g the agent never takes ownership of the goods or services being provided.

● Registering an agent for VAT and potential benefits of voluntary registration.

● VAT procedures to follow for an undisclosed agency arrangement.

● Input tax treatment of costs incurred by an agent and output tax liability of recharges made to the principal.

● Rules for dealing with VAT on disbursements.

● Main VAT situations affecting an employment agency – withdrawal of concessionary arrangement from 1 April 2009.

● Example of a recent case concerning supplies involving three parties (*Joppa Enterprises Ltd*).

Introduction

34.1   In many business transactions, there are three key people involved:

● the customer – the beneficiary of goods or services being provided;

● the principal – the owner of goods or provider of services;

● the agent – a third party who acts for either of the two parties above in arranging supplies of goods or services.

The key point with an agent is that he is arranging a transaction for someone else, rather than trading in goods or services on his own account. The agent never takes ownership of the goods or services being provided – the supply is always between the principal and the customer.

The most common method of payment is for the agent to receive a commission – usually according to the value of sales achieved or the number of transactions carried out on behalf of the principal or the customer.

An agent can work for either the customer or the principal. For example, a customer may ask the agent to find him a suitable car to buy, and then pay him a fee when this objective is achieved. A principal may instruct an agent to find customers for his products, and then pay the agent a fee when sales have been finalised.

Identifying an agency arrangement

34.2 A key point to remember is that the VAT liability of the services provided by an agent do not necessarily follow the liability of the goods or services being supplied between the principal and the customer. See Examples 1 and 2 for an illustration of the different VAT treatment between acting as an agent and a principal.

Example 1

John trades as an agent, trying to find customers for books produced by ABC Publishers Ltd. The latter company sells the books direct to the customer, and arranges for their delivery and invoicing. John does not take ownership of the goods at any stage, and receives £1 commission for every book that is sold – he is VAT registered.

Solution – although the books sold by ABC Publishers Ltd are zero-rated under the *VAT Act 1994, Sch 8, Group 3,* the services supplied by John are standard rated. He must charge output tax on his commission, which will be fully recovered by ABC Publishers Ltd because it relates to a taxable supply.

Example 2

John trades as a bookseller, buying books from ABC Publishers Ltd and then finding customers for the books by visiting various retailers across the UK. He applies a 50% mark-up to the price he paid for the books – he is VAT registered.

Solution – John is now buying the books as a principal and taking ownership of the goods. He is earning a profit by hopefully selling the books at a higher price than what he paid for them. John is making a zero-rated supply of books to his customers and therefore no output tax is due. He will be able to reclaim input tax on any related costs, eg motoring expenses, telephone, accountancy fees, advertising costs etc.

Note – in Example 1, John will be in a payment position for VAT purposes; in Example 2, the different arrangement means that he will be a repayment trader because all of his sales are zero-rated.

In most cases, it will be clear to identify if an arrangement between two parties is on an agency basis – and the following key points will assist the analysis of a situation.

- *Title of goods* – this is the most important point and is clearly illustrated by the different arrangement between Example 1 and Example 2 above. In Example 2, the situation gives added risk in that John could end up with unsold books that he has purchased – in Example 1, this situation would not apply because he never takes ownership of the goods.

- *Buying and selling prices* – the principal will be fully aware of the buying and selling prices of the goods in which he trades. In the case of an agency relationship, it is possible that the agent may never know the final selling price of the goods or services sold to the customer. For example, the agent's role may just be to find a customer for the principal – the value of the deal between the customer and the principal may not be disclosed to the agent.

- *Written agreements* – in most cases, there will be correspondence or a contract between the principal and the agent, clarifying the basis of trading, the method of remuneration for the agent etc. In most cases, it will be very clear from the correspondence if an agency arrangement is in place. However, any written agreement between two parties must be followed in practice as well.

The level of involvement by an agent in a deal will vary according to the arrangement agreed with the principal. In some cases, the agent may take responsibility for actually delivering the goods and dealing with most or all of the paperwork. However, even in these situations, it is still the principal who will invoice the customer for the final goods or services provided, and ownership/title would have been with the principal until the sale is made.

Case law example – agent or principal?

34.3   It can sometimes be a challenge to identify whether a customer is dealing with the principal or agent in a transaction, ie to establish the output tax position.

The case of *Joppa Enterprises Ltd* [2009] SWTI 777, [2009] STC 1279 was heard in the Scottish Court of Session and the judge upheld the decision of the VAT tribunal (case verdict delivered 6 March 2009).

The case concerned supplies involving a sauna (Joppa) and the self-employed masseuses of a venue based in Edinburgh. The customer would pay Joppa on arrival at the premises, and Joppa retained £5 of the payment for expenses, the remaining fee being split on a 50:50 basis with the masseuse. The challenge for the courts was as follows:

- Was output tax payable on the full fee paid by the customer to Joppa (the latter was obviously VAT registered)? or

- Was output tax only payable by Joppa on the £5 expense payment and its 50% share of the balance, ie the main supply was between the customer and the masseuse rather than with Joppa?

The courts considered the nature of the relationships between the three parties, and the way that the financial and administrative arrangements were managed. The court acknowledged that different structures could produce different VAT outcomes but ruled in this case that Joppa was liable to output tax on the full payment received from the customer.

- The entry fee represented a consideration to Joppa for services supplied to the customer, namely access to the premises and permission to enjoy the services therein, including the lounge, refreshments, newspapers, television, the use of a private room and services of a hostess.

- Joppa was not acting as an agent for the hostess so therefore the share of money retained by Joppa could not be classed as an agent's commission.

Registering an agent for VAT

34.4   The value of taxable supplies for an agent will be based on the fees/commission he receives from a principal and not the value of goods sold by the principal to the final customer. If an individual partly trades as an agent and partly as a principal, then the combined turnover of his activities must be taken into account.

In many cases, it will be worthwhile for an agent to register for VAT on a voluntary basis – for example, if the following situation applies:

- he is working for a principal who is registered for VAT and able to reclaim any VAT charged as input tax. This means that the agent is not losing any competitive position by adding VAT to his commission or fee; and

- the agent will then be able to recover input tax on costs relevant to his business, thereby producing a direct improvement to his bottom line profit.

Undisclosed agency arrangements

34.5   It is possible that a principal selling goods will want to keep his identity secret from the final customer and arrange for the entire deal to be handled by his agent. In such cases, it will be necessary for the agent to raise the final sales invoice to the customer in his own name, and then the principal will raise his sales invoice to the agent for the same amount. The agent will still charge his fee/commission to the principal. The HMRC approach to this situation is as follows:

- the commercial basis of the transaction remains unchanged – the main supply still being between the principal and the final customer. However, special arrangements can be applied for VAT purposes so that the agent accounts for output tax on the sales invoice raised to the customer and then reclaims the same amount of input tax on the invoice raised by the principal. The agent will then raise a separate invoice to the principal for his fees;

- the output tax and input tax in the above transactions must be accounted for and reclaimed in the same VAT period. It is not acceptable for the agent to gain a cash flow advantage by reclaiming input tax in one VAT period and delaying accounting for output tax until the next VAT period.

See Example 3 for an illustration of the above point.

Example 3

Jane is acting as an undisclosed agent and sells goods to the final customer for £1,000 plus VAT on 1 April 2009. The principal raises an invoice to her for the same amount on 31 March 2009. Jane's commission is for £200 plus VAT, ie 20% of the sales value. She raises an invoice to the principal for this amount when the sale has been made on 1 April 2009. Jane's VAT periods coincide with calendar quarters.

Solution – the first point to remember is that Jane can only reclaim input tax on the invoice raised by the principal in the same VAT period that she accounts for output tax on her invoice to the final customer, ie the June 2009 VAT period. It is not acceptable for her to reclaim input tax in the March quarter and delay accounting for output tax until the June quarter.

Jane will also account for output tax on the commission charged to the principal.

Note – the end result of this arrangement is the same as if the principal was invoicing the customer directly, ie there is no tax lost by HMRC, just a different way of collecting it.

Costs incurred by an agent

34.6 In the course of his work, an agent will incur costs trying to arrange a deal, and it is necessary for the agent to identify the cost as relevant to one of the following three categories.

(a) *Agent's own costs* – such costs are absorbed by the agent and will reduce his profit when his accounts are produced. There is no scope to recharge these costs to a client. As long as the agent's supplies are wholly taxable, he will be able to reclaim input tax on these costs subject to the normal rules.

(b) *Agent's costs that can be recharged to the client* – there may be occasions when an agent will incur a cost in the course of his business that he can recharge to the client as an additional fee. The key point to remember is that the charge to the client will still be for a supply of agency fees, it will not be acceptable to itemise some of the costs that may be zero-rated to avoid charging VAT on them. See Example 4 for an illustration of this point.

(c) *Disbursements* – it is possible that an agent will pay costs to a third party on behalf of a principal, as a practical arrangement for convenience purposes. There are special rules for disbursements – see **34.7**.

Example 4

DEF Estate Agents agree to sell a property owned by Mrs Smith on a commission basis. Mrs Smith is very keen to achieve a quick sale, so agrees to pay an additional £500 fee to DEF so they can produce special colour brochures giving details of the property. The brochure will hopefully generate increased interest among potential buyers. What is the VAT position?

Solution – the production of the brochure by a printer for the estate agent will be zero-rated for VAT purposes (*VATA 1994, Sch 8, Group 3*). However, the supply of the brochure is between the printer and the estate agent, to help them achieve a sale on Mrs Smith's property. The recharge to Mrs Smith by the estate agent is standard rated, as part of the agency fee in relation to her property.

Disbursements

34.7 The VAT rules concerning disbursements are very strict, and need to be followed in every case to avoid a potential (and often unnecessary) output tax charge.

A key point to remember is that costs incurred by an agent, e g in relation to his telephone and motoring costs cannot be recharged to his client as a non-taxable disbursement. A disbursement situation only applies when the cost properly belongs to his client, for example, a solicitor will often pay statutory fees on behalf of a client, such as court fees, stamp duty etc. These fees properly belong to the client, and are not part of the solicitor's standard rated services to the client.

It is important to remember that a profit cannot be made on recharging a disbursement to a client – the charge must be passed on at cost price, i e the amount paid by the agent. Other important rules for disbursements are as follows:

● the agent must have acted for his client when paying the third party;

● the client must have received and used the goods or services provided by the third party – or it is a cost that properly belongs to him as an individual;

- the client was responsible for paying the third party;

- the agent's outlay must be separately itemised when invoicing the client;

- as stated above, the agent must only recover the exact amount he paid to the third party.

If a payment qualifies as a disbursement, the usual method of recharging a client will be for the agent to include the amount on his invoice or statement as a VAT inclusive figure. The agent cannot reclaim input tax on the costs of the disbursement (on the basis that he is not receiving the supply) but does not need to account for output tax on the onward supply – hence the VAT inclusive figure being shown. He may need to prove to an HMRC officer that no input tax has been recovered on the disbursement and that he has correctly charged the disbursement to the client at cost price, ie without a profit element.

If the client is VAT registered and able to recover input tax, then it will be necessary for the provider of the goods or services to issue a tax invoice made out to the client, not to the agent. See Example 5 for an illustration of the treatment of two different disbursements.

Example 5

Jones Solicitors have acted for a client who has bought the freehold of a commercial property for £200,000. The client is VAT registered and the property will wholly be used in the making of taxable supplies. Jones have paid out two costs on behalf of the client, a land registry fee of £100 and the costs of a window company in repairing a broken window for £300 plus VAT. The buyers engaged the window company to carry out the work, but will reinvoice the sellers for this work as agreed when the deal was signed. The window company has issued a tax invoice for this work, correctly made out to the buyers of the property.

Solution – Jones Solicitors will charge disbursements of £352.50 (£300 plus VAT) and £100 to their client. They will have no output tax liability to declare on these amounts.

The client will be able to reclaim input tax on the cost of the window repair, but must charge output tax on the onward supply of the repair work to the seller of the property.

Employment bureau

34.8   One of the most common situations where an agent/principal relationship exists is in the case of an employment agency either hiring out its own staff to a client, or finding suitable staff that will be directly employed by the client. In the latter case, an agency will earn a commission for its services (often based on a per head basis or according to the salary paid to the individual). In the former case, the agency is paying its own staff (or self-employed staff in some cases) and then applying a mark-up to these payments when it recharges the client. The fee for the latter charge is wholly standard-rated with effect from 1 April 2009. Until this date, there was scope for the business to benefit from what was known as the 'staff hire concession'. With the staff hire concession, the employment bureau hiring out its own staff did not have to charge VAT on salary costs if the client paid the staff directly.

The abolition of the staff hire concession will mainly affect the following customers who are unable to fully recover input tax on costs they incur:

● VAT registered partly exempt businesses;

● voluntary aided schools;

● care and nursing homes.

Planning points to consider

34.9   The following planning points should be given consideration.

● The VAT liability of services provided by an agent can be different to the VAT liability of the goods being traded. For example, the services of an estate agent selling new residential properties (zero-rated) for a national housebuilder will be standard rated.

● Always review correspondence between an agent and a principal to be clear that a genuine agency arrangement is in place. The main condition is normally that the agent will never take ownership of the goods or services being provided and will receive his fee on a commission basis from the principal.

● There may be benefits in registering an agent for VAT on a voluntary basis, i e giving scope for input tax recovery on his costs.

● Be aware of the special rules that exist for transactions involving undisclosed agents – but remember that output tax and input tax on the goods or services in question must be accounted for in the same VAT period.

● Remember that zero-rated costs cannot be charged as a separate supply to a principal (e g as in the case of an estate agent paying a printer to produce colour brochures to help the sale of a property). The charge to the customer is part of the fee for his services as an agent.

● It is possible that agents will pay out costs on behalf of their clients – these costs can avoid a VAT charge if they are genuine disbursements and follow strict rules laid down by HMRC. One of the important rules is that a profit must not be made on the disbursement being recharged to the client.

● Be aware that the 'staff hire concession' was withdrawn on 1 April 2009.

This has implications for both employment agencies and any customers not able to fully reclaim input tax on their costs.

Chapter 35

Charities

Key topics in this chapter:

- Definition of a charity and charitable status.

- Identifying the business and non-business activities of a charity.

- Registering a charity for VAT – including voluntary registration.

- Allocation of input tax between business and non-business activities.

- Input tax issues for a charity with exempt supplies (partial exemption).

- VAT liability of most common sources of income for a charity.

- Issues to consider with grant income – including an important recent case.

- Potential VAT savings on the expenditure of a charity – concessions where some supplies to a charity are zero-rated or exempt.

- Possible savings with group registration if a trading subsidiary company is owned by a charity.

Introduction

35.1   In England and Wales, most charities are registered with the Charity Commission under the *Charities Act 1993*. This is important because as far as VAT is concerned, this will confirm their 'charitable status'. In Scotland and Northern Ireland, there is no requirement to register with the Charity Commission, although it is expected that most Scottish charities will register with the Scottish Charities Regulator which was formed in 2003.

The reason that 'charitable status' is important is because VAT legislation gives some concessions to charities that could produce a considerable saving of tax:

- for the income of the charity, certain sales can qualify as being zero-rated or exempt instead of standard rated. As a large percentage of charity income is generated by the general public (not able to reclaim input tax) it is important to identify potential output tax savings;

- some expenditure that would normally be standard rated can also be treated as zero-rated or exempt if supplied to a charity. Again, this concession can produce significant financial savings for the charity, allowing them to maximise the number of worthwhile causes they can fund.

An important point to note is that charities do not obtain special status as far as VAT is concerned – if they make taxable supplies exceeding £68,000 per year, they have an obligation to register in the same way as a profit-making business. The only difference is that they may benefit from certain VAT concessions as mentioned above.

Regarding the definition of 'charity', the easiest situation to confirm charitable status is if the charity in question is registered with the Charity Commission, however, this is not a requirement of the legislation. In reality, the aims of the relevant organisation are important – and the confirmation of whether a body is, or is not, a charity rests largely on the interpretation of either HMRC or, in the case of appeal, the tribunals and higher courts.

As a useful guideline, 'charitable status' can be assessed by considering the written objectives of the body in question. If these objectives are to assist 'the relief of poverty, advance education, religion and benefits to the community' then there is a strong indication that they could be classed as a charity by HMRC. For guidelines issued by HMRC to establish charitable status, see Internal Guidance V1–9, paras 5.1–5.12.

Trading subsidiary company

35.2   Charity law does not allow a charity to carry out a significant amount of 'non-primary purpose trading' as a way of raising money, eg sale of Christmas cards. In such cases, the charity usually forms a separate trading subsidiary company which, although controlled by the charity, is not an actual charity. As a result, some of the VAT reliefs available to a charity are not available to subsidiary trading companies.

Example – a subsidiary trading company can still zero-rate the sale of donated goods to the public, and income from a fundraising event is still exempt from VAT. However, the company will not benefit from zero-rating on its advertising expenditure and courses or training fee income will not be exempt as 'education' by an 'eligible' body unless the subsidiary company is a company limited by guarantee rather than a private limited company. The fact that the company donates all of its profits to the main charity is irrelevant in such cases.

Business and non-business activities

35.3   Two important questions that a charity will need to consider are as follows.

(a)   Will I need to register for VAT?

(b)   If registered, how much input tax can I reclaim?

A good starting point to both of the above questions is to be clear about the type of activities being promoted by the charity in question.

The activities of most charities can be divided into two clear divisions:

● business activities; and

● non-business activities.

The phrase 'business activity' normally indicates that the charity is performing some service or providing goods in return for a consideration – a key point to note, however, is that these goods or services do not need to be performed at a profit (or surplus). It is quite common for a charity to have a business activity that produces an overall loss – and is funded by other income or reserves of the charity.

As a general guide, the following common activities of a charity would all be classed as a business activity:

● providing facilities or advantages to a member of the organisation in return for payment of a subscription;

● the sale of donated and bought in goods to members of the public;

● the admission, in return for a payment, to any premises owned or used by the organisation, or any function it has arranged;

● the services for any other body or person provided by an office holder or committee of the organisation – in return for a payment;

● any activity that would be classed as a trade, profession or vocation, e g a charity providing counselling services for a fee.

A 'non-business activity' is an activity carried out by a charity that is not based on normal business principles, ie it may not be a regular activity, may not be carried out in return for payment by any third party etc.

See Example 1 for an illustration of a business and non-business activity of a charity.

Example 1

> Good Causes Ltd is a registered charity and its aims are to support families who are affected by divorce. The charity has two main activities – it offers a telephone helpline service so that any child affected by divorce can telephone

the helpline in confidence and talk to an adviser. The costs of the helpline are mainly funded by a grant from a local authority. It also offers a mediation service for couples who are separating – whereby the couple can speak to a mediator in private to try and find solutions to their problems. The mediation service is provided at a very low rate of £30 per hour (payable jointly by the couple), mainly because Good Causes Ltd has other sources of income from grants, donations and fundraising activities.

Solution – the telephone service for children is a non-business activity – there is no income generated by the facility, and it is funded by a grant that is outside the scope of VAT. It is not motivated by the normal principles of business – its aim is to assist the objectives of the charity.

However, the mediation service is a business activity because there is a service being provided (taxable), in return for a consideration that is based on the use of this service, being performed by people appointed by the charity (the mediators). The fact that the activity is charged at a rate that is less than the open market value for this particular type of service is irrelevant.

Registering for VAT and input tax recovery

Registering for VAT

35.4   As explained at **35.1**, there is no special exemption for charities as far as VAT registration is concerned – if they have made taxable supplies in excess of the annual registration limit or expect to make taxable supplies exceeding the registration limit in the next 30 days (£68,000 from 1 May 2009) then they have a requirement to register for VAT.

As with profit making entities, there is a potential opportunity for charities to save tax by registering for VAT on a voluntary basis. This could occur if, for example, the charity has mainly zero-rated supplies and would therefore be able to benefit from input tax recovery on its expenditure.

An important point to remember is that it is only taxable supplies that count as far as the VAT registration limits are concerned and exempt income or outside the scope income does not count. See Example 2 for an illustration of this point.

Example 2

Good Causes Ltd from Example 1 has calculated its income for the previous 12 months as follows:

Mediation services:	£50,000
Local authority grant towards costs of child helpline service:	£20,000
Donations from members:	£10,000

Does the charity need to register for VAT?

Solution – the value of taxable supplies made by the charity is £50,000 in relation to the mediation services. The income from the local authority and members' donations is outside the scope of VAT. The taxable income is therefore below the VAT registration threshold and the charity does not need to register.

The next question to consider is whether it may be worthwhile for the charity to register for VAT on a voluntary basis. The answer is probably no, because this will create an output tax liability on the mediation services, which will either create an extra VAT charge to the users of this facility – or reduce the net income of the charity if fees are kept at the same rate. The input tax benefits are unlikely to outweigh the output tax charges.

Input tax recovery

35.5   An important principle of VAT is that input tax can only be recovered to the extent that it relates to taxable supplies. If a source of input tax relates to non-business or private expenditure, or it relates to exempt supplies, then no input tax can be reclaimed.

A charity will therefore need to adopt a very logical approach to reclaiming input tax to ensure the amount claimed is accurate:

- any input tax relating directly to the non-business activities of the charity cannot be reclaimed – in effect, any expenditure on non-business activities should be entered into the accounting system on a gross basis (ie including VAT) and budgets or grant requests should also be based on VAT inclusive values;

- a proportion of input tax on general overheads should not be reclaimed to reflect usage on some of the non-business activities – this could relate to input tax on telephone costs, electricity bills, rent charges for offices etc. See **35.6** for possible methods of making this apportionment;

- having carried out the stages above, any remaining input tax will be relevant to the business activities of the charity. At this stage, a further exclusion needs to be made so that input tax is not reclaimed on any expenditure that relates to exempt activities of the charity;

- any expenditure that relates to the taxable activities of the charity can be reclaimed in full (subject to normal rules) – remember that taxable activities include zero-rated and reduced-rate supplies as well as standard-rated sales;

- a proportion of the remaining input tax on general overheads (residual input tax) will also be disallowed as relevant to exempt supplies – either through the standard method of calculation or a special method agreed with HMRC.

Note – the principles of partial exemption are covered in depth in Chapters 24 and 25 of this book. Partial exemption is a complex aspect of VAT and issues need to be considered very carefully in order to ensure input tax claims are correct.

Input tax apportionment on non-business activities

35.6   As explained at 35.5, any input tax that directly relates to a non-business activity cannot be reclaimed. In addition, any input tax that is partly used for business purposes (and partly for non-business purposes) also needs to be apportioned on a fair and reasonable basis. An alternative approach in some cases (capital expenditure) is to fully reclaim input tax and then account for output tax on non-business use over the life of the asset. This is known as the *Lennartz* mechanism – see **32.17**.

There is no specified method of apportionment in the legislation – the key point is that the final result should be fair – and reflect the usage of the expense item between business and non-business purposes.

A number of different methods could be considered:

- income-based method – apportioning input tax according to total value of business and non-business income – see Example 3;

- time-based method – e g time that staff spend on business and non-business matters;

- transaction-based method – e g number of telephone calls received for each activity of the charity;

- floor-area based method – e g apportion premises' overheads according to floor space allocated directly to business and non-business activities.

The income-based apportionment is very common, however, it would not give a fair result if there is no real link between the income received by an activity and the costs associated with the activity.

Example 3

Good Causes Ltd, from Example 2, has received its quarterly telephone bill which includes VAT of £500. The telephone in question is used for all parts of the charity's activities, i e it is not a specific line for any particular activity.

The charity's income for the period is as follows – and it has been identified that an input tax apportionment for non-business use based on income would achieve a fair result.

Mediation services:	£12,000
Local authority grant towards costs of child helpline service:	£2,000
Donations from members:	£1,000

How much input tax will be disallowed as relating to non-business use?

Solution – the percentage of business income is 80% (£12,000 divided by £15,000) so 80% input tax would be deemed as relevant to business purposes and 20% disallowed as relevant to non-business activities. Therefore, the input tax disallowed would be £100.

VAT liability of a charity's income

General principles to establish VAT liability of income

35.7   Many charities have a wide range of income sources – and each source of income needs to be considered as far as its VAT liability is concerned. Income can be generated by a charity through the supply of goods or services – or it could be income generated without a supply being provided, for example, donations from private individuals or local companies.

As a word of caution, be aware that certain sources of income could be standard-rated if supplied by a trading subsidiary of the charity – see **35.2**.

It is important to remember the logical approach to adopt as far as assessing the VAT liability of an item is concerned.

● **Is the supply specifically zero-rated under one of the 16 groups listed in *VAT Act 1994, Sch 8*?**

   The main group in the Schedule that is relevant to the income of a charity is *Group 15* – Charities etc (see **35.8–35.10**).

● **Is the supply specifically exempt from VAT under one of the 15 groups listed in *VAT Act 1994, Sch 9*?**

   The main groups that could be relevant to the income of charities are as follows:

   – *Group 7* – Health and welfare (see **35.11–35.13**);
   – *Group 12* – Fundraising events organised by charities and other qualifying bodies (see **35.11–35.13**);
   – *Group 13* – Cultural services – admission to museums, exhibitions, zoos and performances of a cultural nature supplied by public bodies and eligible bodies.

● **Is the income specifically outside the scope of VAT?**

   The main sources of income that are outside the scope of VAT are donations received from third parties and grant income received from various bodies (as long as the grant income is not based on a supply of goods or services in which case the income is likely to be taxable – see **35.15** and **35.16**).

- **Is the income subject to VAT at the reduced rate?**

    The reduced VAT rate of 5% applies to certain supplies that may be relevant to a charity, e g sale of contraceptive products.

- **If a supply is not zero-rated, exempt, outside the scope of VAT or subject to the reduced rate of VAT it will be standard rated in the normal manner.**

Charity income that is zero-rated

35.8   A number of sources of income for a charity could be zero-rated – but the two main sources are as discussed below.

Sale of donated goods

35.9   The main source of income which is zero-rated for many charities relates to the situation where they sell donated goods, for instance, through a charity shop in town centres.

Bought-in goods that are resold will follow the normal VAT rules, for example, the sale of items such as books and children's clothes will be zero-rated in accordance with normal rules; items sold that are not zero-rated (or subject to reduced rate VAT) will be charged at the standard rate.

Note – see Revenue and Customs Brief 14/08 which confirms that HMRC now accepts that the sale of abandoned cats and dogs by a charity represents a zero-rated sale of donated goods.

Zero-rating also applies to the sale of donated goods by a trading subsidiary company of a charity.

Supply of magazines/newsletters as part of a membership subscription

35.10   In normal situations, it will be necessary to consider if payment for a supply of goods and services is made in return for one main benefit or a number of different benefits subject to VAT at different rates, i e mixed supply situations. In many cases, secondary supplies will be ignored as being incidental to the main supply – the VAT liability will then be entirely based on the main supply. A detailed analysis of mixed supply situations is provided in Chapter 23.

As a special concession (ESC 3.35), HMRC has confirmed that a charity may, if it wishes, treat a membership subscription (which could be exempt or standard rated) as a multiple supply. This means that any zero-rated publication supplied as part of a membership subscription (eg magazine or newsletter) can be reflected in the cost of the membership fee, ie a percentage of the membership fee can be zero-rated.

Note – HMRC confirmed in Revenue and Customs Brief 06/09 (issued 20 February 2009) that it will not allow retrospective VAT adjustments to be made in relation to the split of subscription income where ESC 3.35 is being claimed by the taxpayer. This is because the original returns submitted by the charity would have been correct in law and therefore an adjustment cannot be made to correct returns that were accurate in the first place.

Charity income that is exempt from VAT

35.11   A number of income sources will be exempt from VAT – the most common ones are fundraising events, certain training courses and welfare services.

Fundraising events

35.12   An important concession for charities and other qualifying bodies is that they can organise certain fundraising events, the income related to this event being exempt from VAT rather than standard rated.

It should be noted that a qualifying body is generally a non-profit making body whose main aim is to provide facilities for people to take part in sport or physical recreation, for example a members' golf club.

As far as a charity (or its trading subsidiary) is concerned, the main priority is to ensure that the purpose of the event is to raise funds towards its charitable aims – and tickets sold for the event must clearly publicise the fundraising aim with wording such as 'fundraising for ...', 'in aid of ...', 'help us to build ...'.

The VAT exemption applies to all admission charges, sale of advertising space, items sold by the charity at the event (eg T-shirts) unless the item would normally be zero-rated in which case zero-rating can still be applied (eg children's T-shirts).

A fundraising event includes the following functions:

- dinner, disco, charity concert;

- fête, fair or festival;

- fireworks display;

- games of skill, contests and quizzes;

- an auction of bought-in goods (auction of donated goods is zero-rated).

The main point to remember, however, is that any input tax directly related to the event will be relevant to an exempt supply and not reclaimable unless the charity is *de minimis* as far as partial exemption is concerned (see Chapter 24 at **24.7** for an analysis of the *de minimis* rules). See Example 4 for an illustration of the VAT treatment of a fundraising event.

Example 4

Good Causes Ltd from earlier examples wishes to raise £5,000 to purchase a new computer for its child helpline facility. The chief executive of the charity decides to organise a fundraising celebrity dinner with the following budgeted income and expenditure (all figures based on 17.5% rate of VAT):

Sales of tickets – 150 at £40 each = £6,000.

Sale of advertising space to local companies = £2,000.

Cost of meals – 150 meals at £10 + VAT for each meal.

Cost of celebrity speaker – £1,000 (he is not VAT registered).

Hire of venue for dinner – £300 (no VAT charge because room hire is exempt).

Is it worthwhile to treat the dinner as a fund-raising event that is exempt from VAT?

Solution – the only disadvantage of the event being exempt is that the charity will not be able to reclaim input tax on the cost of the meals supplied by the caterer. This loss of input tax is £262.50 (ie 150 × £1.75).

However, the output tax savings are considerable (£8,000 × 7/47 = £1,191.49) even though some of the companies paying for advertising space may be in a position to reclaim input tax.

Overall, there is a significant tax saving by ensuring the dinner is a qualifying fundraising event.

As a final point, certain fund-raising events are excluded from VAT exemption:

- multiple events of the same kind at the same location – exemption does not apply to any event where in a financial year a charity or qualifying body organises more than 15 events of the same kind in the same location. There are certain concessions to assist this limit, but it is unlikely that many charities will host more than 15 events anyway, so these concessions are not analysed here;

- events where accommodation is provided;

- events that could distort competition, e g by placing a commercial enterprise at a disadvantage through the VAT savings being achieved.

Welfare services

35.13   The supply by a charity of welfare services, and of goods supplied in connection with those services, is exempt from VAT.

The exemption extends to catering supplied as part of welfare services, for example, meals for residents of care homes; supplies of food and drink (but not alcohol) from trolleys, canteens and shops to patients in hospitals or inmates in prisons.

Training courses

35.14   A charity will sometimes organise training courses, consistent with its aims and objectives, and will charge a fee to those who attend the course. In such cases, the fees will be exempt from VAT as education (*VATA 1994, Sch 9, Group 6, Item 1(a)*) as long as any profits from the courses are reinvested into future courses. The exemption only applies to registered charities or companies limited by guarantee – it would not apply to a trading subsidiary that was a private limited company.

Charity income outside the scope of VAT

Donations

35.15   The key point to remember is that a source of income will only qualify as a donation if the person making the donation does not receive any benefits in return for his donation. HMRC has confirmed that a public acknowledgement of the donation, for example, in an event programme, will not be classed as a benefit. It has also accepted that where the benefits received are disproportionate to the amount of the payment, then the payment can be treated as outside the scope of VAT. See Example 5.

Example 5

Good Causes Ltd has decided to sell Christmas Cards at £2 each (taxable activity). On the order form, it has a separate line inviting buyers to make an additional payment to support the charity as a donation.

Jill orders 15 Christmas cards and sends a cheque for £50 to the charity including a £20 donation.

Solution – Jill was only obliged to send £30 to the charity in order to buy her Christmas cards (ie 15 cards at £2 each). The additional payment of £20 has been made on a voluntary basis and she will receive no benefits in return for that money. The amount of £20 is clearly a donation that is outside the scope of VAT.

Note – if the literature circulated by Good Causes Ltd has specified that cards were available at £2 each plus a minimum donation of £10, then the £10 donation would not be outside the scope of VAT. This is because the payment is no longer optional for the donor.

Grant income

35.16   Many charities benefit from the receipt of grant income, either from local or central government, national bodies such as the lottery fund, or other organisations that are keen to support worthwhile causes.

There are three key questions to consider when deciding if grant income is a taxable source of income or outside the scope of VAT as follows.

● Does the donor receive anything in return for the funding he has given (but remember that insignificant benefits are ignored as explained at **35.15**)?

● If the donor does not benefit, does a third party benefit instead? If so, is there a direct link between the money paid by the funder and the supply received by the third party? (See Example 6 to give a practical example of when grant funding would be taxable and **35.17** for a recent court case that ruled a grant was standard-rated.)

● Are any conditions attached to the funding, which go beyond the require-ment to account for the funds? (For example, some funders like to receive a report on the benefits generated by their funding – this is not classed as a benefit to the funder that would make the grant taxable.)

Example 6

As explained in earlier examples, Good Causes Ltd is a registered charity that provides mediation services to couples who are going through a divorce.

As well as the fees charged to couples receiving mediation, Good Causes Ltd also receives a quarterly grant from a national government body, the Mediation Services Commission. The amount of the grant depends on the number of mediation hours supplied by the company during a calendar quarter.

As a separate grant, Good Causes Ltd receives £2,000 per year from the Highgrove Bank Trust, which gives grant funding to charities whose aims include the support of children.

What is the VAT position regarding these two grants?

Solution – the grant from the Mediation Services Commission is taxable and subject to standard-rated VAT. This is because there is a direct link between the services provided by the charity (to a third party) and the amount of the grant.

However, the grant from Highgrove Bank Trust is a fixed amount of money provided to the charity, irrespective of the level of services it performs or work it carries out. The grant is therefore outside the scope of VAT.

Bath Festivals Trust Ltd – taxable grant

35.17   The recent case that has strengthened the argument of grants being taxable in many cases was *Bath Festivals Trust Ltd* (11 September 2008, unreported) (LON/06/511 20840). The Trust was responsible for organising the Bath International Music Festival, an event that was very important to the local councils in Bath and North Somerset as part of their overall business strategy. The VAT Tribunal confirmed that the Trust was providing a service in return for the grants it received, an important conclusion that clarifies some of the 'grey' areas on this subject.

Charity income that is standard-rated

35.18   As explained at 35.7, all income is standard rated, unless it is specifically zero-rated, exempt, outside the scope of VAT or subject to VAT at the reduced rate.

Common sources of a charity's income that will usually be standard rated are as follows:

- admission to premises – unless the admission relates to a qualifying fundraising event (see **35.12**) or the income is covered by the special exemption for admission to museums, galleries, art exhibitions, zoos and theatrical, musical or choreographic performances;

- advertising in brochures, programmes or annual reports – again, there is an exception for advertising space sold at a qualifying fundraising event, in which case the income will be exempt;

- the resale of bought in goods which are standard rated.

VAT issues on expenditure of a charity

35.19   It is important that a charity identifies possible sources of expenditure that are either zero-rated or exempt from VAT (or subject to reduced-rate VAT) because most charities will not be in a position to reclaim all of their input tax. This is because some input tax will probably be relevant to either non-business activities or exempt supplies (or a combination of both).

In general terms, the following main categories of goods and services are specifically zero-rated if supplied to a charity – specific details (if appropriate) can be obtained by reference to relevant HMRC public notices (eg 701/7/02 – VAT reliefs for disabled people) or by contacting the National VAT Advice Helpline (0845 010 9000):

- talking books for the blind and disabled;

- wireless sets for the blind;

- aids for disabled persons;

- donation of goods for sale, export or letting by the charity;

- lifeboats;

- advertising;

- goods used by charities in connection with collecting monetary donations;

- medicinal products;

- substances for medical or veterinary research;

- major interests in land and buildings – see Chapter 27;

- construction services – see Chapter 26;

- some charity funded equipment for medical, veterinary uses etc;

- no VAT is payable on the importation of certain goods by or for charities and other philanthropic organisations.

Note – in the author's experience, many newspapers and other publications incorrectly charge VAT on advertisements for charities, which should be zero-rated. It is important that charities and their advisers are pro-active on this aspect of the legislation, taking steps to ensure the zero-rating is correctly applied. The zero-rating applies to all advertisements placed by a charity, including adverts in relation to staff recruitment and their business as well as non-business activities.

Note also that in addition to the above supplies, a charity will obviously be able to enjoy zero-rating on goods and services that are zero-rated for all businesses, eg the cost of using a printing firm to produce a charity's annual report will be zero-rated as printed matter under *VAT Act 1994, Sch 9, Group 3*.

In addition, there are two possible situations when a charity could benefit from the reduced rate of VAT (5%):

(a) Fuel and power – supplies of fuel and power can be subject to the reduced rate in certain circumstances. These include the use in a dwelling or a building used for a relevant residential purpose, eg a children's home. Also, the reduced rate applies to a charity otherwise than in the course or furtherance of a business.

(b) Energy-saving materials – the installation of certain energy saving materials in a building used solely for a relevant charitable purpose is liable to VAT at the reduced rate.

Group registration

35.20 Example 7 illustrates a useful planning point about group registration.

Example 7

Good Causes Ltd is a registered charity and owns a trading subsidiary called Good Causes Trading Ltd. Neither company is registered for VAT because their main supplies are either outside the scope of VAT or exempt from VAT. However, Good Causes Ltd incurs costs on behalf of Good Causes Trading Ltd, and wants to make a management charge of £100,000 per annum for these services.

The problem with the above situation is that Good Causes Ltd will need to charge output tax on the management services once it has exceeded the VAT registration limit (£68,000 per annum with effect from 1 May 2009) but Good Causes Trading Ltd will not be able to reclaim this VAT as input tax because it is not making any taxable supplies.

Solution – the two companies could register for VAT as a group registration, which means that supplies of goods and services between group members is ignored as far as VAT is concerned. The fact that the companies are not making any taxable supplies outside of the VAT group is not a problem – the management charges would be taxable (standard-rated) but for the group structure. The group arrangement will saved the charity a lot of tax.

Note – there is no problem with forming a VAT group because the main charity controls the trading subsidiary, ie the common control test for group registration has been met.

Planning points to consider

35.21   The following planning points should be given consideration.

• It will be clear in most cases whether an organisation is a charity and able to benefit from VAT concessions available to charities. In other cases, it will be necessary to consider the aims and objectives of the organisation and put forward a strong argument to HMRC that charitable status is appropriate.

• In some cases, it may be worthwhile for a charity to register for VAT on a voluntary basis. This would be particularly useful if the charity has a high proportion of zero-rated sales, eg sales of donated goods.

• If a charity has to register for VAT on a compulsory basis, remember that it is only the value of taxable supplies that need to be taken into account as far as the registration limit is concerned. Exempt supplies and outside the scope income are excluded from the calculations.

• An important challenge as far as VAT is concerned is to ensure that input tax is only reclaimed by a charity that relates to its taxable supplies. Effective procedures need to be in place to ensure that input tax is not reclaimed on non-business expenditure or expenditure relating to exempt supplies. This includes an apportionment of input tax on general overheads where appropriate.

- A charity can use any method to apportion input tax between business and non-business activities on general overhead items as long as the method gives a fair and reasonable result. Remember that an income-based apportionment may not be the most suitable method if the expenditure in question is not directly linked to income.

- Be aware that many sources of income for a charity can be zero-rated or exempt from VAT. For example, income from a fundraising event will be exempt in most cases – although obviously any input tax relevant to the event will not be reclaimable as it relates to an exempt supply.

- A donation can be treated as outside the scope of VAT as long as the donor does not receive any benefits for his payment. It is important to ensure that donations are freely given by the donor, for example, the request for a 'minimum donation of £x' in connection with the supply of goods or services would not be classed as a freely given donation.

- Do not assume that all grant income received by a charity is outside the scope of VAT. If grant income is linked to the performance of services by a charity, then it will be standard rated in most cases. This opinion was confirmed in the tribunal case *Bath Festivals Trust Ltd* (see **35.17**).

- There are a range of concessions available to charities as far as VAT on their expenditure is concerned. For example, a charity placing an advert in a local newspaper for a new member of staff should not pay VAT because the supply is zero-rated.

Chapter 36

VAT Rate Resumption on 1 January 2010 (15% to 17.5%)

Key topics in this chapter:

- Dealing with invoices raised in December that relate to goods or services supplied after 1 January 2010 – when will a supplementary VAT charge need to be made?

- Opportunities for advance invoicing or making payments before 31 December 2009 to benefit from the 15% rate of VAT.

- Issues to consider with the flat rate scheme and cash accounting scheme.

- Details of HMRC's anti-forestalling legislation to avoid tax point dates being manipulated.

- The right to purchase goods or services in the future – recognising situations when the supplementary VAT charge could apply.

- Practical examples of when a supplementary VAT charge will (and will not) be payable on or after 1 January 2010.

Introduction

36.1　The standard rate of VAT was reduced to 15% for the period between 1 December 2008 and 31 December 2009. The aim of the reduction was to provide a temporary fiscal stimulus to the UK economy. The rate returns to 17.5% again on 1 January 2010.

In reality, most transactions that take place either just before or just after the increase will be dealt with by normal VAT rules (tax point rules) which can be summarised as follows:

- The basic tax point for a supply of goods or services occurs when either goods are supplied or a service has been completed. This is the point when VAT needs to be declared unless an actual tax point is created in relation to the sale.

- An actual tax point occurs when either an invoice is raised or payment is received, whichever happens sooner. However, an invoice or payment must be processed within 14 days of the basic tax point, otherwise the latter date becomes the date when VAT is payable. See Example 1.

Example 1

John sells goods to Jim on 31 July 2009. He raised an invoice to Jim on 13 August 2009 and Jim makes full payment on 13 September 2009. What is the tax point as far as VAT is concerned?

Solution – the basic tax point of 31 July 2009 is superseded by the actual tax point of 13 August 2009, ie when the sales invoice is raised. The latter date is relevant because the invoice has been raised within 14 days of the goods being sold. If the invoice had been raised on 18 August 2009, then the basic tax point would have been relevant, ie 31 July 2009.

Maximise sales in December 2009

36.2 There is no doubt that the VAT increase in January 2010 should produce a boost to spending in the UK economy during December 2009. In principle, any sales made and paid for in December 2009 will be subject to the 15% rate of VAT. See Example 2.

The only potential problem with the anti-forestalling legislation is if goods or services are supplied after 1 January 2010 but were invoiced or paid for at 15% VAT before this date. However, the number of transactions where there will be a problem should be quite limited – see **36.5**.

Example 2

John sells goods to Steve on 15 December 2009 and raises an invoice on the same date, charging 15% VAT. However, John does not pay for the goods until 15 January 2010. What is the situation with regard to VAT?

Solution – both the basic tax point (supply of goods) and actual tax point (invoice being raised) have taken place in December 2009. The payment date in January 2010 is therefore irrelevant.

Cash accounting scheme and flat rate scheme

36.3 Be aware of potential pitfalls regarding both the flat rate scheme and the cash accounting scheme in relation to the change in the rate of VAT.

- The cash accounting scheme means that output tax is not included on a VAT return until payment has been received from a customer. However, if goods are sold and an invoice is raised in December 2009 (as in Example 2), followed by payment in January 2010, then the VAT declared through the cash accounting scheme is still based at 15%, even though it is being declared on the VAT return in January 2010. This is because the original sale in December was based on a 15% VAT charge.

  Note – for further details about the cash accounting scheme, see Chapter 6.

- The flat rate scheme aims to simplify VAT accounting for a small business (with annual taxable sales of £150,000 or less). The scheme means that VAT is paid according to the gross income of the business for the period and fixed percentages that depend on its trade category. The flat rate percentages will increase on 1 January 2010 when the VAT rate returns again to 17.5%. Do not assume that the same flat rates will apply as when the VAT rate was 17.5% before December 2008 – it is possible that HMRC may vary the revised flat rate percentages for other reasons. The revised rates will be published well before the VAT rate increase takes effect again.

  Note – many flat rate scheme users adopt what is known as the 'cash based turnover method', which means that VAT is only paid under the scheme when money has been received from a customer, ie giving the same outcome as with the cash accounting scheme. However, the same principle applies as explained with the cash accounting scheme, ie the lower flat rate percentages (based on 15% rate of VAT) will still apply for sales invoiced in December but paid in January.

Continuous or ongoing supplies of services – invoice at the end of December 2009

36.4   Imagine the following scenario. A business starts a job in November 2009, which is completed in January 2010. In this situation, it could be sensible for the business to raise a tax invoice at the end of December 2009, to reflect work carried out up to this point. This invoice would then be subject to VAT at 15%. In some cases, it may be possible to raise an invoice in December to cover the entire job, ie including January work as well, as long as the advance invoice does not create a problem with HMRC's anti-forestalling legislation – see **36.5**.

However, the essential point to remember is that there will be no saving in VAT if the customer is able to fully reclaim input tax on the sale in question – it is irrelevant whether he claims 15% input tax on his return or 17.5%. The only occasion when a potential benefit could occur is if the customer is not VAT registered (eg a very small business, a business that only makes exempt supplies or a member of the general public) or is VAT registered but partly exempt. The other relevant situation would be if the input tax related to a non-deductible item such as business entertainment for non-staff members.

For details of how to deal with the situation when pre-December 2009 work is being invoiced in January 2010, see **36.8.**

Anti-forestalling legislation

36.5 The purpose of HMRC's anti-forestalling legislation is to prevent the manipulation of tax points to produce a VAT charge of 15% in situations when goods or services are being supplied after 1 January 2010, ie when the VAT rate is again 17.5%.

An important point to keep in mind is that the anti-forestalling legislation will not apply if the customer is able to fully reclaim input tax on the supply in question. This is because it makes no difference whether output tax is declared and input tax reclaimed at 15% or 17.5% – the same outcome is achieved in both cases as far as the Treasury coffers are concerned.

Despite the anti-forestalling legislation announced in the 2009 Budget, there are still many opportunities to raise tax invoices in advance (before 1 January 2010) to create a tax point and therefore a 15% VAT charge rather than 17.5%. See Examples 3 and 4 to illustrate the process for deciding if the anti-forestalling legislation takes effect, and the measures that need to be considered in each case.

Note – as a starting point, there is a very high *de minimis* limit of £100,000 in relation to transactions where advance invoices are raised or prepayments are received. So having also excluded transactions where the customer can fully reclaim input tax on the charge, this has hopefully eliminated a potential problem in the majority of relevant sales.

Example 3

Bob intends to spend £100,000 plus VAT on the gardens at his mansion at the beginning of the summer in May 2010. He cannot reclaim this VAT because it is a private expense so asks his gardening contractor to raise an advance invoice on 31 December 2009 (creating an actual tax point before the VAT rate increases the next day), charging VAT of £15,000 instead of £17,500 (a saving of £2,500). Bob does not intend to pay the bill until 31 May 2010 when the work is completed and this payment date is confirmed on the sales invoice. Does this arrangement create a VAT problem?

Solution – there are four conditions to consider as far as the anti-forestalling legislation is concerned. However, the deal is compliant on all four of them:

- Bob and his gardener are not connected parties (husband, wife, common control of companies etc);

- the gardening contractor (or someone connected to him) is not funding the purchase (by lending money to his customer who then makes payment etc);

- payment is due within 6 months of the invoice date (31 May 2010 is 5 months after the invoice date);

- the pre-invoiced amount does not exceed £100,000 excluding VAT.

Note – the 15% VAT charge would have been invalid if any of the four conditions above had failed. A supplementary VAT charge of 2.5% would then have been due on 1 January 2010 when the VAT rate is back to 17.5% again.

The disadvantage is that the gardening contractor will need to include output tax on the VAT return covered by his invoice date, unless he is on the cash accounting scheme in which case he will pay output tax for the VAT period when he receives his money.

Notes on conditions relating to supplementary charge

36.6

- A connected party is based on *s 839, ICTA 1988* – it includes, for example, husbands, wives, brothers and sisters – but not uncles, aunts, nephews and nieces.

- The £100,000 limit applies to any 'related supply of goods or services' that 'spans the date of the VAT change'. So two separate sales invoices raised for £60,000 each in Example 3 would still be captured by the £100,000 limit.

- The £100,000 limit excludes VAT.

- HMRC accepts that the supplementary charge will not apply where advance invoices are raised or advance payments are raised in line with normal commercial practice. For example, this could apply in relation to many property rental arrangements where a payment might be received quarterly in advance as a matter of course. The anti-forestalling legislation attempts to prevent artificial manipulation of invoicing and payments to acquire an unfair VAT advantage.

- As explained at the beginning of this chapter, the anti-forestalling legislation will not be relevant if a customer can reclaim input tax on the supply in question.

- If a supplementary charge is payable by the supplier, it will be due on 1 January 2010, ie the date when the rate of VAT reverts to 17.5%.

Author note – a technique that will identify if an invoice is being raised or payment received within normal commercial practice is to consider whether the same invoice would have been raised or payment received if the VAT rate was remaining the same. This could perhaps be extended to consider whether similar invoices have been raised in earlier months or quarters, ie when there was no change in the rate of VAT.

Example 4

Annual membership fees for Gym Club Ltd are payable on 31 March each year – an amount of £1,000 including VAT covering the period 1 April to the following 31 March. Can the club increase its profit by raising an advance tax invoice on 31 December 2009, ie at the reduced VAT rate of 15%?

Solution – the proposed arrangement does not fail any of the anti-forestalling tests mentioned in the previous example so there is no problem with this advance invoice being raised. In this example, the VAT saving is being enjoyed by the supplier (gym club) rather than customer (gym user) because prices are charged on a VAT inclusive basis.

Author note – there were many situations when consumers paid 17.5% VAT before 1 December 2008, even though they were enjoying the goods or services in question after this date when a VAT rate of 15% was in force. It is only reasonable and fair that there will be some commercial situations when the 15% rate of VAT can be extended into 2010.

For example, season ticket holders at football clubs paid 17.5% on their 2008/09 season tickets, even though about two thirds of games were played after 1 December 2009 when the VAT rate was 15%. The opposite will apply for 2009/10 – tickets will be purchased with VAT charged at 15% (assuming they are bought before the beginning of the football season in August) even though many games will take place after 1 January 2010.

Right to receive goods or services in the future

36.7 A situation could arise where a customer purchases the right to acquire goods or services in the future, and the customer enjoys the benefits (or some of the benefits) after 1 January 2010. In such cases, a supplementary charge of 2.5% could apply to the period that relates to the post-January period if any of the following conditions apply:

- the amount of the prepayment exceeds £100,000; or

- the supplier (grantor) and customer are connected with each other (husband, wife etc); or

- the supplier (or someone connected to him) funds the payment made by the customer.

Note – HMRC accepts that one area where substantial prepayments can reflect commercial reality is in relation to property leases. Where a premium is payable, the legislation recognises this by setting the basic time of supply as the date that the lease is granted, therefore avoiding the need to apportion premium payments between the lease period occurring before the VAT rate change and that occurring after it.

HMRC also accepts that an advance invoice could also be raised in relation to the leasing of assets, which is again regarded as normal commercial procedure. The anti-forestalling legislation will therefore not apply in such circumstances as long as the period to which the invoice or payment relates does not exceed 12 months.

See Example 5 for a practical example of when a supplementary charge will apply in relation to the grant of a right to purchase services spanning the change in the rate of VAT.

Example 5

Holton Football Club is giving supporters the chance to pay £150,000 plus VAT to the club in June 2009, in return for which they will be able to purchase an executive box at the club for just £1,000 plus VAT for each of the next three seasons. What is the VAT position on this advance payment?

Solution – the benefits of the prepaid amount span the VAT rate change and exceed £100,000. A supplementary VAT charge of 2.5% will therefore be due in January 2010 – assuming that the customers cannot reclaim input tax on their own VAT returns, eg because the expense relates to business entertainment which is non-deductible unless it relates to staff.

However, the supplementary charge will only apply to the extent that the goods or services are being enjoyed after 1 January 2010. The amount of the charge should be calculated on a time-apportioned basis in a way that is fair and reasonable. As half a season out of the three seasons will take place before 1 January 2010, a fair supplementary charge basis would be:

£150,000 x 5/6 x 2.5% = £3,125

Note – the supplementary charge in this situation (and in the case of any rights to receive goods or services in the future) will apply on the first occasion after 1 January 2010 when the right to receive the goods or services is actually exercised. In the case of Holton Football Club, this will probably be the date of the first home game after 1 January 2010.

Continuous or periodic supplies of services

36.8   Imagine that a builder is carrying out repair work on a building – he started the work on 1 October 2009 and has received periodic payments (or raised periodic invoices that have led to subsequent payment) since this date. What is the VAT position if he raises an invoice on, for example, 14 January 2010 covering services (and related goods) supplied to the customer for the month of December 2009?

The normal time of supply rules for ongoing services would deem that the raising of an invoice (or receipt of payment if sooner) would create a tax point for VAT purposes – ie the builder must pay output tax based on 17.5% rate of VAT because the invoice is being raised in January 2010.

However, the legislation introduces the concept of 'listed supplies' which include:

• a supply of services where payments are received or invoices are raised on a periodic basis;

• a supply of goods together with services in connection with the construction of a building, again where invoices are raised or payments are received on a periodic basis – also including work to alter, demolish, repair or maintain a building or civil engineering work.

In the case of the VAT rules for 'listed supplies', there is an opportunity for invoices to be raised in January but only charged at 15% VAT, as long as the end of the billing period (for work carried out) is on or before 31 December 2009. In such cases, the VAT rate can be based on the billing period covered by the invoice. See Example 6.

Example 6

Jones the decorator raises an invoice on 13 January 2010, covering work carried out in December 2009 on an ongoing job at a new office building. The invoice is for £10,000 including materials. How much VAT will be charged on the invoice?

Solution – the work in question is classed as a 'listed supply' and because the billing period does not cover all work carried out to the invoice date (ie 13 January), the VAT charge can be based on the date of the end of the billing period to which the work relates. As the end of the billing period was 31 December 2009, a VAT charge of £1,500 will be made, ie at 15%. This 15% rate is also applied to the part of the invoice that relates to materials.

Credit notes

36.9 A credit note cannot refund more VAT to a customer than was charged on the original sale. So if an invoice was raised in September 2009 for £1,000 plus VAT of £150, and the goods are returned in February 2010 by the customer, then the VAT credit can only be for £150 and not £175. This assumes all other relevant rules are met in relation to credit note procedures.

Planning points to consider

36.10   The following planning points should be given consideration.

- Be aware of the opportunities to raise invoices or receive payments before 31 December 2009 that will enable some customers to benefit from a 15% rather than 17.5% charge of VAT. However, this will not be worthwhile if customers can claim input tax on the expense anyway.

- The anti-forestalling legislation is designed to prevent artificial manipulation of the tax point rules to create a 15% rather than 17.5% charge of VAT. However, it will only apply in limited circumstances – mainly if the transaction is more than £100,000 and the customer cannot reclaim all of the VAT as input tax.

- The anti-forestalling legislation should not apply if the value of a transaction exceeds £100,000 but is made within the normal commercial practices of the supplier in question. This is particularly relevant for those businesses that either rent out property or are involved with the leasing of assets.

Table of Cases

M

N

O

Q

R

Table of Statutes

Paragraph references printed in **bold** type indicate where the Statute is set out in part or in full.

Index